Modelling Biological Systems: A Computational Approach

Modelling Biological Systems: A Computational Approach

Edited by **Christina Marshall**

Syrawood
PUBLISHING HOUSE

New York

Published by Syrawood Publishing House,
750 Third Avenue, 9th Floor,
New York, NY 10017, USA
www.syrawoodpublishinghouse.com

Modelling Biological Systems: A Computational Approach
Edited by Christina Marshall

International Standard Book Number: 978-1-68286-024-3 (Hardback)

Contents

Preface

I am honored to present to you this unique book which encompasses the most up-to-date data in the field. I was extremely pleased to get this opportunity of editing the work of experts from across the globe. I have also written papers in this field and researched the various aspects revolving around the progress of the discipline. I have tried to unify my knowledge along with that of stalwarts from every corner of the world, to produce a text which not only benefits the readers but also facilitates the growth of the field.

Modelling biological systems is an applied scientific field which aims to analyze and stimulate various biological structures and functions using computational and mathematical techniques. This book elucidates the concepts and innovative methods around prospective developments with respect to modelling biological systems. The chapters included trace the progress of this field and highlight some of its key concepts such as modelling genomics and proteomics, modelling and simulation of biological networks, simulating drug interactions with biological systems, ecosystem modelling, etc. This book is an essential guide for both professionals and those who wish to pursue this discipline further.

Finally, I would like to thank all the contributing authors for their valuable time and contributions. This book would not have been possible without their efforts. I would also like to thank my friends and family for their constant support.

Editor

Modeling stochasticity and variability in gene regulatory networks

David Murrugarra[1,2*], Alan Veliz-Cuba[3], Boris Aguilar[4], Seda Arat[1,2] and Reinhard Laubenbacher[1,2]

Abstract

Modeling stochasticity in gene regulatory networks is an important and complex problem in molecular systems biology. To elucidate intrinsic noise, several modeling strategies such as the Gillespie algorithm have been used successfully. This article contributes an approach as an alternative to these classical settings. Within the discrete paradigm, where genes, proteins, and other molecular components of gene regulatory networks are modeled as discrete variables and are assigned as logical rules describing their regulation through interactions with other components. Stochasticity is modeled at the biological function level under the assumption that even if the expression levels of the input nodes of an update rule guarantee activation or degradation there is a probability that the process will not occur due to stochastic effects. This approach allows a finer analysis of discrete models and provides a natural setup for cell population simulations to study cell-to-cell variability. We applied our methods to two of the most studied regulatory networks, the outcome of lambda phage infection of bacteria and the p53-mdm2 complex.

1 Introduction

Variability at the molecular level, defined as the phenotypic differences within a genetically identical population of cells exposed to the same environmental conditions, has been observed experimentally [1-4]. Understanding mechanisms that drive variability in molecular networks is an important goal of molecular systems biology, for which mathematical modeling can be very helpful. Different modeling strategies have been used for this purpose and, depending on the level of abstraction of the mathematical models, there are several ways to introduce stochasticity. Dynamic mathematical models can be broadly divided into two classes: continuous, such as systems of differential equations (and their stochastic variants) and discrete, such as Boolean networks and their generalizations (and their stochastic variants). This article will focus on stochasticity and discrete models.

Discrete models do not require detailed information about kinetic rate constants and they tend to be more intuitive. In turn, they only provide qualitative information about the system. The most general setting is as follows. Network nodes represent genes, proteins, and other molecular components of gene regulation, while network edges describe biological interactions among network nodes that are given as logical rules representing their interactions. Time in this framework is implicit and progresses in discrete steps. More formally, let $x_1, ..., x_n$ be variables, which can take values in finite sets $X_1, ..., X_n$, respectively. Let $X = X_1 \times ... \times X_n$ be the Cartesian product. A discrete dynamical system (DDS) in the variables $x_1, ..., x_n$ is a function

$$f = (f_1, ..., f_n) : X \to X$$

where each coordinate function $f_i: X \to X_i$ is a function in a subset of $\{x_1, ..., x_n\}$. Dynamics is generated by iteration of f, and different update schemes can be used for this purpose. As an example, if $X_i = \{0, 1\}$ for all i, then each f_i is a Boolean rule and f is a Boolean network where all the variables are updated simultaneously. We will assume that each X_i comes with a natural total ordering of its elements (corresponding to the concentration levels of the associated molecular species). Examples of this type of dynamical system representation are Boolean networks, logical models and Petri nets [5-7].

To account for stochasticity in this setting several methods have been considered. Probabilistic Boolean networks (PBNs) [8,9] introduce stochasticity in the update functions, allowing a different update function to

* Correspondence: davidmur@vt.edu
[1]Department of Mathematics, Virginia Tech, Blacksburg, VA 24061-0123, USA
Full list of author information is available at the end of the article

be used at each iteration, chosen from a probability space of such functions for each network node. For other approaches, see [10-12]. These models will be discussed in more detail in the next section. In this article we present a model type related to PBNs, with additional features. We show that this model type is natural and a useful way to simulate gene regulation as a stochastic process, and is very useful to simulate experiments with cell populations.

1.1 Modeling stochasticity in gene regulatory networks

Gene regulation processes are inherently stochastic. Accurately modeling this stochasticity is a complex and important goal in molecular system biology. Depending on the level of knowledge of the biological system and the availability of data for it one could follow different approaches. For instance, viewing a gene regulatory network as a biochemical reaction network, the Gillespie algorithm can be applied to simulate each biochemical reaction separately generating a random walk corresponding to a solution of the chemical master equation of the system [13,14]. At an even more detailed level one could introduce time delays into the Gillespie simulations to account for realistic time delays in activation or degradation such as in circadian rhythms [15-17]. At a higher level of abstraction, stochastic differential equations [18] contain a deterministic approximation of the system and an additional random white noise term. However, all these schemes require that all the kinetic rate constants to be known which could represent a strong constraint due to the difficulty of measuring kinetic parameters, limiting these approaches to small systems.

As mentioned in the introduction, discrete models are an alternative to continuous models, which do not depend on rate constants. In this setting, several approaches to introduce stochasticity have been proposed. Specially for Boolean networks, stochasticity has been introduced by flipping node states from 0 to 1 or vice versa with some flip probability [12,19-21]. However, it has been argued that this way of introducing stochasticity into the system usually leads to over-representation of noise [11]. The main criticism of this approach is that it does not take into consideration the correlation between the expression values of input nodes and the probability of flipping the expression of a node due to noise. In fact, this approach models the stochasticity at a node regardless of the susceptibility to noise of the underlying biological function [11].

Probabilistic Boolean networks [8,9,22] is another stochastic method proposed within the discrete strategy. PBNs model the choice among alternate biological functions during the iteration process, rather than modeling the stochasticity of the function failure itself. We have adopted a special case of this setting, in which every

node has associated to it two functions: the function that governs its evolution over time and the identity function. If the first is chosen, then the node is updated based on its logical rule. When the identity function is chosen, then the state of the node is not updated. The key difference to a PBN is the assignment of probabilities that govern which update is chosen. In our setting, each function gets assigned two probabilities. Precisely, let x_i be a variable. We assign to it a probability $p_i^\uparrow$, which determines the likelihood that x_i will be updated based on its logical rule, if this update leads to an increase/activation of the variable. Likewise, a probability $p_i^\downarrow$ determines this probability in case the variable is decreased/inhibited. The necessity for considering two different probabilities is that activation and degradation represent different biochemical processes and even if these two are encoded by the same function, their propensities in general are different. This is very similar to what is considered in differential equations modeling, where, for instance, the kinetic rate parameters for activation and for degradation/decay are, in principle, different.

Note that all these approaches only take account of intrinsic noise which is generated from small fluctuations in concentration levels, small number of reactant molecules, and fast and slow reactions. Another source of stochasticity is related to extrinsic noise such as a noisy cellular environment and temperature. For more about intrinsic vs extrinsic noise see [3,23].

2 Method

Our aim is to model stochasticity at the biological function level under the main assumption that even if the expression levels of the input nodes of an update function guarantee activation or degradation there is a probability that the process will not occur due to stochasticity, for instance, if some of the chemical reactions encoded by the update function may fail to occur. This is similar to models based on the chemical master equation. This model type introduces activation and degradation propensities. More formally, let $x_1, ..., x_n$ be variables which can take values in finite sets $X_1, ..., X_n$, respectively. Let $X = X_1 \times ... \times X_n$ be the Cartesian product. Thus, the formal definition of a *stochastic discrete dynamical system (SDDS)* in the variables $x_1, ..., x_n$ is a collection of n triplets

$$F = \left\{ f_i, p_i^\uparrow, p_i^\downarrow \right\}_{i=1}^n$$

where

- $f_i: X \to X_i$ is the update function for x_i, for all $i = 1, ..., n$.

- $p_i^\uparrow$ is the activation propensity.
- $p_i^\downarrow$ is the degradation propensity.
- $p_i^\uparrow$, $p_i^\downarrow \in [0, 1]$.

We now proceed to study the dynamics of such systems and two specific models as illustration.

2.1 Dynamics of SDDS

Let $F = \left\{ f_i, p_i^\uparrow, p_i^\downarrow \right\}_{i=1}^n$ be a SDDS and consider $x \in X$. For all i we define $\pi_{i,\,x}(x_i \to f_i(x))$ and $\pi_{i,\,x}(x_i \to x_i)$ by

$$\pi_{i,x}(x_i \to f_i(x)) = \begin{cases} p_i^\uparrow, \text{ if } x_i < f_i(x), \\ p_i^\downarrow, \text{ if } x_i > f_i(x), \\ 1, \quad \text{ if } x_i = f_i(x). \end{cases}$$

$$\pi_{i,x}(x_i \to x_i) = \begin{cases} 1 - p_i^\uparrow, \text{ if } x_i < f_i(x), \\ 1 - p_i^\downarrow, \text{ if } x_i > f_i(x), \\ 1, \qquad \text{ if } x_i = f_i(x). \end{cases}$$

That is, if the possible future value of the i-th coordinate is larger (smaller, resp.) than the current value, then the activation (degradation) propensity determines the probability that the i-th coordinate will increase (decrease) its current value. If the i-th coordinate and its possible future value are the same, then the i-th coordinate of the system will maintain its current value with probability 1. Notice that $\pi_{i,\,x}(x_i \to y_i) = 0$ for all $y_i \notin \{x_i, f_i(x)\}$.

The dynamics of F is given by the weighted graph X which has an edge from $x \in X$ to $y \in X$ if and only if $y_i \in \{x_i, f_i(x)\}$ for all i. The weight of an edge $x \to y$ is equal to the product

$$w_{x \to y} = \prod_{i=1}^n \pi_{i,x}(x_i \to y_i)$$

By convention we omit edges with weight zero. See Additional file 1 for pseudocodes of algorithms to compute dynamics of SDDS. Software to test examples is available at http://dvd.vbi.vt.edu/adam.html[24] as a web tool (choose SDDS in the model type).

Given $F = \left\{ f_i, p_i^\uparrow, p_i^\downarrow \right\}_{i=1}^n$ a SDDS, it is straightforward to verify that F has the same steady states (fixed points) as the deterministic system $G = \{f_i\}_{i=1}^n$ (see Additional file 1). It is also important to note that the dynamics of F includes the different trajectories that can be generated from G using other common update mechanisms such as the synchronous and asynchronous schemes (see Additional file 1).

2.1.1 Example
Let $n = 2$, $X = \{0, 1\} \times \{0, 1\}$, $F = (f_1, f_2) \colon X \to X$, where Table 4 represents the regulatory rules for x1 and x2 and Table 5 represents their propensity parameters

x_1	x_2	f_1	f_2
0	0	0	0
0	1	1	0
1	0	0	1
1	1	1	0

and

	x_1	x_2
Activation	.1	.5
Degradation	.2	.9

$Pr(01 \to 10) = (.1)(.9) = .09$, $Pr(01 \to 00) = (1 - .1)(.9) = .81$
$Pr(01 \to 01) = (1 - .1)(1 - .9) = .09$, $Pr(01 \to 11) = (.1)(1 - .9) = .01$
$Pr(10 \to 10) = (1 - .2)(1 - .5) = .4$, $Pr(10 \to 01) = (.2)(.5) = .1$
$Pr(10 \to 00) = (.2)(1 - .5) = .1$, $Pr(10 \to 11) = (1 - .2)(.5) = .4$
$Pr(11 \to 11) = (1)(1 - .9) = .1$, $Pr(11 \to 10) = (1)(.9) = .9$
$Pr(00 \to 00) = (1)(1) = 1$.

Figure 1 shows that there is a 9% chance that the system will transition from 01 to 10. Similarly, there is an 81% chance that the system will transition from 01 to 00. The latter was expected because there is a high degradation propensity for f_2. Note that 00 is a fixed point, i.e., there is 100% chance of staying at this state.

3 Applications
We illustrate the advantages of this model type by applying it to two widely studied biological systems, the regulation of the p53-mdm2 network and the control of the outcome of phage lambda infection of bacteria. These regulatory networks were selected because stochasticity plays a key role in their dynamics.

3.1 Regulation in the p53-Mdm2 network
The p53-Mdm2 network is one of the most widely studied gene regulatory networks. Abou-Jaude et al. [25] proposed a logical four-variable model to describe the dynamics of the tumor suppressor protein p53 and its negative regulator Mdm2 when DNA damage occurs. The wiring diagram of this model is represented in Figure 2, where P

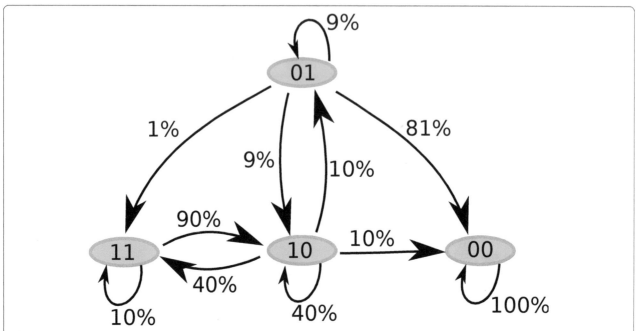

Figure 1 State Space Diagram. This diagram depicts all trajectories to follow from any given initial state of the network. The numbers next to the edges specify the transition probabilities. Note that dynamics here is not deterministic, most of the states have different trajectories to follow.

denotes cytoplasmic p53, nucleic p53, and the gene *p53*. Mc and Mn stand for cytoplasmic Mdm2 and nuclear Mdm2, respectively. DNA damage caused by ionic irradiation decreases the level of nucleic Mdm2 which enables p53 to accumulate and to remain active, playing a key role in reducing the effect of the damage. There is a negative feedback loop involving three components: p53 increases the level of cytoplasmic Mdm2 which, in turn, increases the level of nuclear Mdm2. Nucleic Mdm2 reduces p53

activity. This model also contains a positive feedback loop involving two components where p53 inhibits its negative regulator nucleic Mdm2. Note the dual role of P, as it positively regulates nucleic Mdm2 through cytoplasmic Mdm2. On the other hand, P negatively regulates nucleic Mdm2 by inhibiting Mdm2 nuclear translocation [25]. For more about the p53-Mdm2 system (see [4,25,26]).

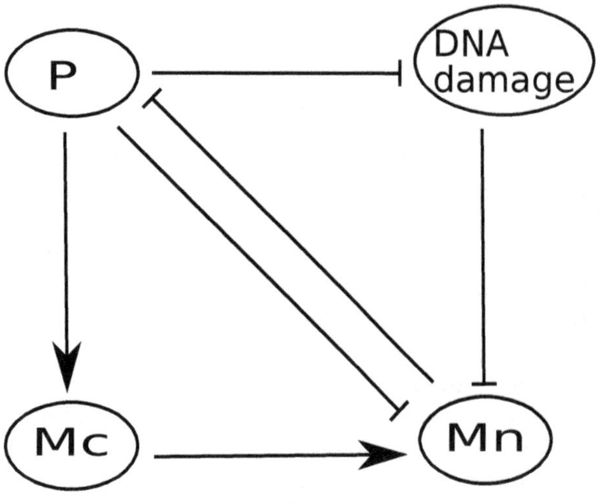

The dynamic behavior of the system is represented in a network of transitions called its state space (see Figure 3). This specifies the different paths to follow and the probabilities of following a specific trajectory from a given state. Dynamics here is not deterministic, i.e., most of the state vectors have different trajectories they can follow. The propensity parameters in Table 1 determine the likelihood of following certain paths. The state 0010 is a steady state, which is differentiated from the others by its oval shape.

The state space for this model is specified by $[0, 2] \times [0, 1] \times [0, 1] \times [0, 1]$, that is, except for the first variable P which has three levels $\{0, 1, 2\}$, all other variables are Boolean. The update functions for this model are provided in Additional file 1 and also in the model repository of our web tool at http://dvd.vbi.vt.edu/adam.html.

Individual cell simulations render plots similar to the ones shown in Figure 4. Each subfigure shows oscillations as long as the damage is present with a variability in the timing of damage repair. On the other hand, cell population simulations, Figure 5, exhibit damped

Figure 2 Four-variable model for the p53-Mdm2 regulatory network. P, Mc, and Mn stand for protein p53, cytoplasmic Mdm2, and nuclear Mdm2, respectively.

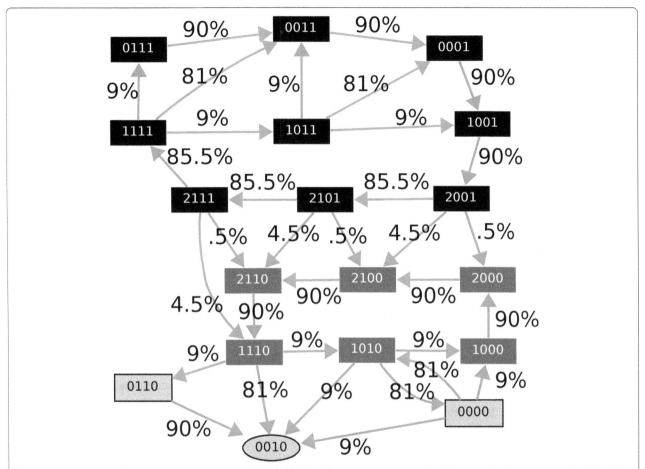

Figure 3 State space diagram for parameters described in Table 1. The numbers next to the edges encode the transition probabilities. The order of the variables in each vector state is P, Mc, Mn, DNA damage. Self-loops are not depicted. States with darker background comprise the cycle with DNA damage. A second cycle with a lighter shaded background corresponds to the cycle with no DNA damage. The oval shaped state is a steady state.

oscillations of the expression level of p53 as the degradation propensities of the damage increases. This is correlated with the fact that, if the intensity of the damage is increased, more cells exhibit oscillations in the level of p53 which was experimentally observed in [4]. The initial state for all simulations was 0011 which represents the state when DNA damage is introduced (0010 is the steady state without perturbation).

To highlight the features of our approach we compare our model with the one presented in [25] in which variability has been analyzed. The main difference between these two models is in the way the simulations are

performed. In [25], the transition from one state to the next is determined by parameters called "on" and "off" time delays. For instance, to transition from 2001 to 2101 it is required that $t_{Mc} < t_{\overline{dam}}$ which means that the "on" delay for Mc (time for activating) is less than the "off" delay (time for degrading) of the damage. Otherwise, if $t_{Mc} > t_{\overline{dam}}$ the system will transition from 2001 to 2000. In this article, transitions from one state to others are given as probabilities which are determined from the propensity probabilities. Therefore, the complexity of the model presented here is at the level of the wiring diagram (i.e. the number of variables) while the complexity of the model in [25] is at the level of the state space (i.e. number of possible states) which is exponential in the number of variables. Another key difference is the way DNA damage repair is modeled. In [25], a delay parameter $t_{\overline{dam}}$ is associated with the disappearance of the damage, and this is decreased by a certain amount τ at each iteration so that

$$t_{\overline{dam}}^{(n)} = t_{\overline{dam}}^{(0)} - n\tau \geq 0 \quad \text{where} \quad n \quad \text{is the number of}$$

Table 1 Propensity probabilities for the p53-Mdm2 regulatory network

	P	Mc	Mn	Dam
Activation	.9	.9	.9	1
Degradation	.9	.9	.9	.05

Note that there is a low degradation propensity for DNA damage.

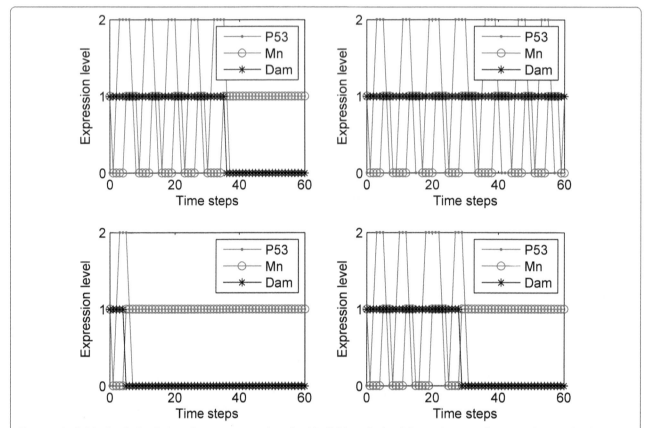

Figure 4 Individual cell simulations for parameters described in Table 1. Each subfigure shows oscillations as long as the damage is present. This figure shows variability in the timing of damage repair and in the period of the oscilations. Each frame was generated from a single simulation with sixty time steps. The x-axis represents discrete time steps and the y-axis the expression level. The initial state for all simulations is 0011.

iterations. In order to simulate DNA damage with this approach it is required to estimate τ, n, and $t\frac{(0)}{\text{dam}}$. Within our model framework a single parameter, the degradation propensity, is used to model the damage repair which is a more natural setup.

3.2 Phage lambda infection of bacteria
Control of the outcome of phage lambda infection is one of the best understood regulatory systems [3,27,28]. Figure 6 depicts its core regulatory network that was first modeled by Thieffry and Thomas [28] using a logical approach. This model encompasses the roles of the regulatory genes CI, CRO, CII, and N. From experimental reports [3,28-30] it is known that, if the gene CI is fully expressed, all other genes are off. In the absence of CRO protein, CI is fully expressed (even in the absence of N and CII). CI is fully repressed provided that CRO is active and CII is absent.

The dynamics of this network is a bistable switch between lysis and lysogeny, Figure 7. Lysis is the state where the phage will be replicated, killing the host. Otherwise, the network will transition to a state called

lysogeny where the phage will incorporate its DNA into the bacterium and become dormant. It has been suggested [28,31] that these cell fate differences are due to spontaneous changes in the timing of individual biochemical reaction events.

The state space for this model is specified by $[0, 2] \times [0, 3] \times [0, 1] \times [0, 1]$, that is, the first variable, CI, has three levels 0, 1, 2, the second variable, CRO, has four levels {0, 1, 2, 3}, and the third and fourth variables, CII and N, are Boolean. Update functions for this model are available in our supporting material, Additional file 1. This model has a steady state, 2000, and a 2-cycle involving 0200 and 0300. The steady state 2000 represents lysogeny where CI is fully expressed while the other genes are off. The cycle between 0200 and 0300 represents lysis where CRO is active and other genes are repressed.

Cell population simulations were performed to measure the cell-to-cell variability. Figure 8 was generated using the probabilities given in Tables 2 (top frame) and 3 (bottom frame). The x-axis in both subfigures represents discrete time steps while the y-axis captures the

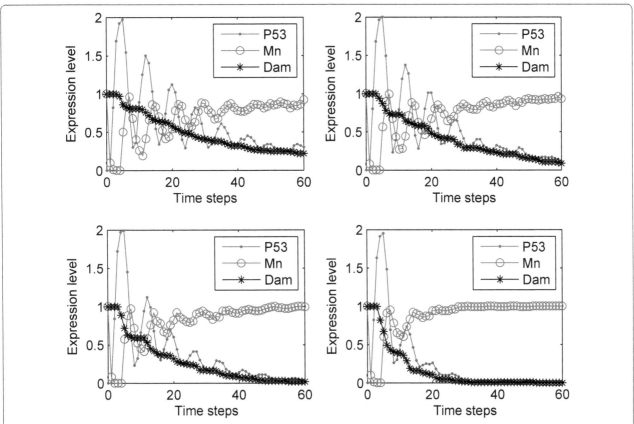

Figure 5 Cell population simulations. Each subfigure was generated from 100 simulations, each representing a single cell with sixty time steps. Starting from the top left frame to the right bottom frame the degradation propensity for DNA damage was increased by 5%, i.e. $p^{\downarrow}_{dam} = .05$ (top left), $p^{\downarrow}_{dam} = .10$ (top right), $p^{\downarrow}_{dam} = .15$ (bottom left), and $p^{\downarrow}_{dam} = .2$ (bottom right). The x-axis represents discrete time steps and the y-axis the average expression level. The initial state for all simulations was 0011. This figure shows that, if the intensity of the damage is increased more cells exhibit oscillations in the level of p53, in agreement with experimental observations [4].

average expression level. The initial state for all simulations was 0000 which represents the state of the bacterium at the moment of phage infection. Figure 8 shows variability in developmental outcome, some of the networks transition to lysis while others transition to lysogeny. To measure how sensitive the dynamics of the network is to changes in the propensity probabilities, we have plotted the outcome of lysis-lysogeny percentages for different choices of these parameters. Figure 9 shows the variation in developmental outcome as a function of the propensity parameters of *CI* and *CRO*. Star points indicate the percentage of networks that transition to lysogeny and circle shaped points indicate the percentage of networks that end up in lysis. The bottom x-axis

contains activation propensities for *CI* and degradation propensities for *CRO* while the top x-axis contains activation propensities for *CRO* and degradation propensities for *CI*. The activation and degradation propensities for *CII* and *N* were all set equal to .9. Although the probability distributions for *CI* and *CRO* are very symmetric in Figure 9, it gives a good idea of how the variability in developmental outcome will change as the propensity parameters change.

4 Conclusions

Using a discrete modeling strategy, this article introduces a framework to simulate stochasticity in gene

Table 2 Propensity parameters for Figure 7 (top frame)

	CI	CRO	CII	N
Activation	.8	.2	.9	.9
Degradation	.2	.8	.9	.9

There is a high activation propensity for *CI* while a low activation propensity for *CRO*.

Table 3 Propensity parameters for Figure 7 (bottom frame)

	CI	CRO	CII	N
Activation	.3	.7	.9	.9
Degradation	.7	.3	.9	.9

There is a high activation propensity for *CRO* while a low activation propensity for *CI*.

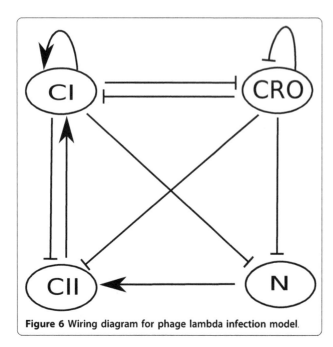

Figure 6 Wiring diagram for phage lambda infection model.

regulatory networks at the function level, based on the general concept of PBNs. It accounts for intrinsic noise due to spontaneous differences in timing, small fluctuations in concentration levels, small numbers of reactant

molecules, and fast and slow reactions. This framework was tested using two widely studied regulatory networks, the regulation of the p53-*Mdm*2 network and the control of phage lambda infection of bacteria. It is shown that in both of these examples the use of propensity probabilities for activation and degradation of network nodes provides a natural setup for cell population simulations to study cell-to-cell variability. The new features of this framework are the introduction of activation and degradation propensities that determine how fast or slow the discrete variables are being updated. This provides the ability to generate more realistic simulations of both single cell and cell population dynamics. In the example of the p53-*Mdm*2 system, one can see that individual simulations show sustained oscillations when DNA damage is present, while at the cell population level these individual oscillations average to a damped oscillation. This agrees with experimental observations [4]. In the second example, λ-phage infection of bacteria, it is observed that differences in developmental outcome due to intrinsic noise can be captured with this framework. Due to the lack of experimental data we are unable to calibrate the model so that it reproduces the correct difference in percentages due to intrinsic noise. So instead we present a plot of the difference in

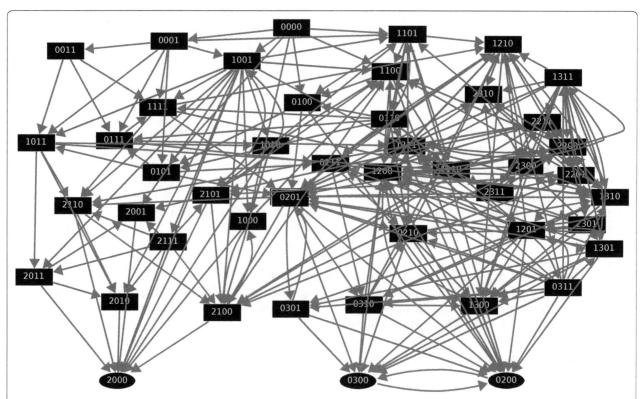

Figure 7 State space for phage lambda model. The order of variables in each vector state is *CI, CRO, CII, N*. The steady state 2000 represents lysogeny where *CI* is fully expressed while other genes are off. The cycle between 0200 and 0300 represents lysis where *CRO* is active and other genes are repressed. Self-loops are not depicted.

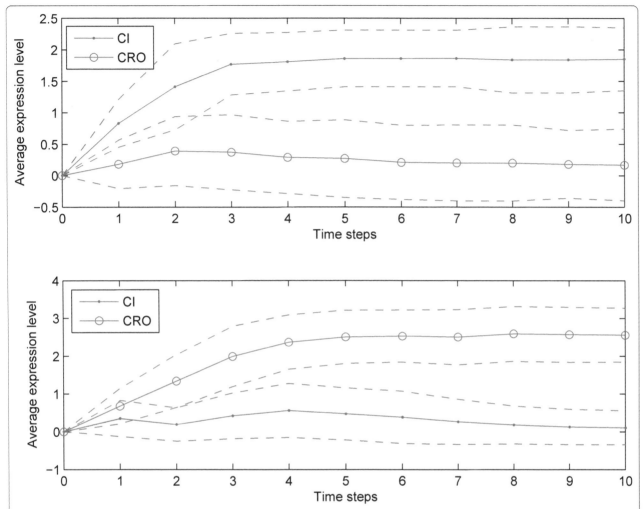

Figure 8 Cell population simulations. Both figures were generated from 100 simulations, each representing a single cell iteration of ten time steps. Top frame for parameters in Table 2 shows 93% lysis and 7% lysogeny while bottom frame for parameters in Table 3 shows 4% lysis and 96% lysogeny. The *x*-axis represents discrete time steps while the *y*-axis shows the average expression level. The initial state for all the simulations is 0000. Solid (circle) points correspond to the average of *CI* (*CRO*), and dashed lines represent standard deviations.

developmental outcome as a function of the propensity parameters.

It is worth noting that this article addresses only intrinsic noise generated from small fluctuations in concentration levels, small numbers of reactant molecules, and fast and slow reactions. Extrinsic noise is another source of stochasticity in gene regulation [3,23], and it would be interesting to see if this framework or a similar setup can be adapted to account for extrinsic stochasticity under the discrete approach. This framework also lends itself to the study of intrinsic noise and it is useful for the study of developmental robustness. For instance, one could ask what the effect of this type of noise is on the dynamics of networks controlled by biologically inspired functions.

Relating the propensity parameters to biologically meaningful information or having a systematic way for

estimating them is very important. A preliminary analysis shows that it is possible to relate the propensity parameters in this framework with the propensity functions in the Gillespie algorithm under some conditions (see Additional file 1 where for a simple degradation model, the degradation propensity is correlated by a linear equation with the decay rate of the species being degraded). More precisely, in the Gillespie algorithm [13,14], if one discretizes the number of molecules of a chemical species into discrete expression levels such that within these levels the propensity functions for this species do not change significantly, then one obtains the setup of the framework presented here as a discrete model. That is, simulation within the framework presented here can be viewed as a further discretization of the Gillespie algorithm, in a setting that does not require exact knowledge of model parameters. For a similar approach see [10].

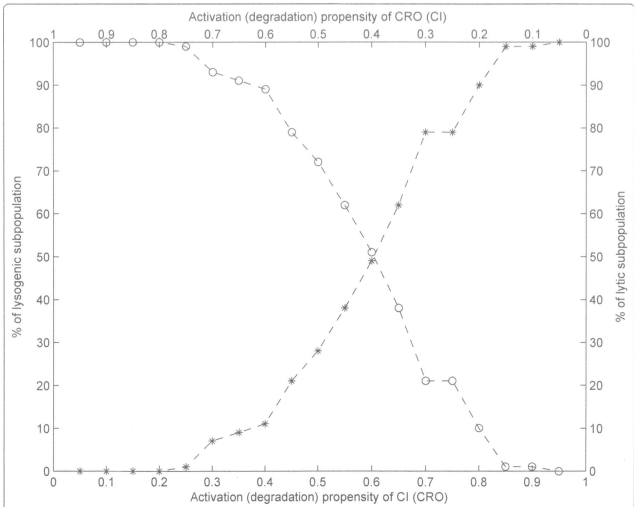

Figure 9 Variation in developmental outcome as a function of the propensity parameters. Star points indicate the percentage of networks that transition to lysogeny and circle shaped points indicate the percentage of networks that end up in lysis. Bottom axis represents the activation (and degradation) propensities for *CI* (*CRO*) in increasing order. Likewise, the top axis represents the activation (and degradation) propensities for *CRO* (*CI*) in decreasing order.

Acknowledgements

DM and RL were partially supported by NSF grant CMMI-0908201. RL and DM thank Ilya Shmulevich for helpful suggestions. The authors thank the anonymous reviewers for many suggestions that improved the article.

Additional material

Additional file 1: Additional File 1contains Supporting Material.

Author details
[1]Department of Mathematics, Virginia Tech, Blacksburg, VA 24061-0123, USA [2]Virginia Bioinformatics Institute, Virginia Tech, Blacksburg, VA 24061-0477, USA [3]Department of Mathematics, University of Nebraska-Lincoln, Lincoln, NE 68588, USA [4]Department of Computer Science, Virginia Tech, Blacksburg, VA 24061-0123, USA

Competing interests
The authors declare that they have no competing interests.

References
1. E Avigdor, M Elowitz, Functional roles for noise in genetic circuits. Nature. **467**, 167–173 (2010). doi:10.1038/nature09326
2. M Acar, J Mettetal, A van Oudenaarden, Stochastic switching as a survival strategy in fluctuating environments. Nat Gen. **40**, 471–475 (2008). doi:10.1038/ng.110
3. F St-Pierre, D Endy, Determination of cell fate selection during phage lambda infection. PNAS. **105**, 20705–20710 (2008). doi:10.1073/pnas.0808831105
4. N Geva-Zatorsky, N Rosenfeld, S Itzkovitz, R Milo, A Sigal, E Dekel, T Yarnitzky, Y Liron, P Polak, G Lahav, U Alon, Oscillations and variability in the p53 system. Mol Syst Biol. **2**. 2006.0033, (2006) doi: 10.1038/msb4100068
5. D Irons, Logical analysis of the budding yeast cell cycle. J Theor Biol. **257**, 543–559 (2009). doi:10.1016/j.jtbi.2008.12.028
6. R Thomas, R D'Ari, *Biological Feedback* (CRC Press, Boca Raton, 1990)

7. C Chaouiya, E Remy, B Mossé, D Thiery, *Qualtative Aalysisof Regulatory Graphs: A Computational Tool Based on a Discrete Formal Framework*, Lecture Notes in Control and Information Sciences, **294**, 830–832 (2003)

8. I Shmulevich, E Dougherty, S Kim, W Zhang, Probabilistic Boolean networks: a rule based uncertainty model for gene regulatory networks. Bioinformatics. **18**(2), 261–274 (2002). doi:10.1093/bioinformatics/18.2.261

9. I Shmulevich, E Dougherty, Probabilistic Boolean Networks: The Modeling and Control of Gene Regulatory Networks, (SIAM, Philadelphia, 2010)

10. S Teraguchi, Y Kumagai, A Vandenbon, S Akira, D Standley, Stochastic binary modeling of cells in continuous time as an alternative to biochemical reaction equations. Phys Rev E. **84**(4) 062903 (2011)

11. A Garg, K Mohanram, A Di Cara, G De Micheli, I Xenarios, Modeling stochasticity and robustness in gene regulatory networks. Bioinformatics. **15;25**(12), i101–i109 (2010)

12. AS Ribeiro, SA Kauffman, Noisy attractors and ergodic sets in models of gene regulatory networks. J Theor Biol. **247**, 743–755 (2007). doi:10.1016/j.jtbi.2007.04.020

13. D Gillespie, Exact stochastic simulation of coupled chemical reactions. J Phys Chem. **81**(25), 2340–2361 (1977). doi:10.1021/j100540a008

14. D Gillespie, Stochastic simulation of chemical kinetics. Annu Rev Phys Chem. **58**, 35–55 (2007). doi:10.1146/annurev.physchem.58.032806.104637

15. D Bratsun, D Volfson, LS Tsimring, J Hasty, delay-induced stochastic oscillations gene regulation. PNAS. **102**(41), 14593–14598 (2005). doi:10.1073/pnas.0503858102

16. AS Ribeiro, Stochastic and delayed stochastic models of gene expression and regulation. Math Biosci. **223**(1), 1–11 (2010). doi:10.1016/j.mbs.2009.10.007

17. AS Ribeiro, R Zhu, SA Kauffman, A general modeling strategy for gene regulatory networks with stochastic dynamics. J Comput Biol. **13**(9), 1630–1639 (2006). doi:10.1089/cmb.2006.13.1630

18. T Toulouse, P Ao, I Shmulevich, S Kauffman, Noise in a small genetic circuit that undergoes bifurcation. Complexity. **11**(1), 45–51 (2005). doi:10.1002/cplx.20099

19. ER Álvarez-Buylla, A Chaos, M Aldana, M Benítez, Y Cortes-Poza, C Espinosa-Soto, DA Hartasánchez, RB Lotto, D Malkin, GJ Escalera Santos, P Padilla-Longoria, Floral morphogenesis: stochastic explorations of a gene network epigenetic landscape. *PLoS ONE.* **3**(11), e3626 (2008). doi:10.1371/journal.pone.0003626

20. MI Davidich, S Bornholdt, Boolean network model predicts cell cycle sequence of fission yeast. PLoS ONE. **3**(2), e1672 (2008). doi:10.1371/journal.pone.0001672

21. K Willadsen, J Wiles, Robustness and state-space structure of Boolean gene regulator models. J Theor Biol. **249**(4), 749–765 (2008)

22. R Layek, A Datta, R Pal, ER Dougherty, Adaptive intervention in probabilistic Boolean networks. Bioinformatics. **25**(16), 2042–2048 (2009). doi:10.1093/bioinformatics/btp349

23. SS Peter, BE Michael, DS Eric, Intrinsic and extrinsic contributions to stochasticity in gene expression. PNAS. **99**(20), 12795–12800 (2002). doi:10.1073/pnas.162041399

24. F Hinkelmann, M Brandon, B Guang, R McNeill, G Blekherman, A Veliz-Cuba, R Laubenbacher, ADAM: analysis of the dynamics of algebraic models of biological systems using computer algebra. BMC Bioinf. **12**, 295 (2011). doi:10.1186/1471-2105-12-295

25. W Abou-Jaoudé, D Ouattara, M Kaufman, From structure to dynamics: frequency tuning in the p53-mdm2 network: I. logical approach. J Theor Biol. **258**(4), 561–577 (2009). doi:10.1016/j.jtbi.2009.02.005

26. E Batchelor, A Loewer, G Lahav, The ups and downs of p53: understanding protein dynamics in single cells. Nat Rev Cancer. **9**, 371–377 (2009). doi:10.1038/nrc2604

27. M Ptashne, A Genetic Switch: Phage λ and Higher Organisms, (Cell Press and Blackwell Scientific Publications, Cambridge, 1992)

28. D Thiery, R Thomas, Dynamical behaviour of biological regulatory networks-II. Immunity control in bacteriophage lambda. Bull Math Biol. **57**, 277–295 (1995)

29. L Reichardt, D Kaiser, Control of λ repressor synthesis. PNAS. **68**, 2185–2189 (1971). doi:10.1073/pnas.68.9.2185

30. P Kourilsky, Lysogenization by bacteriophage lambda I. Multiple infection and the lysogenic response. Mol Gen Gen. **122**, 183–195 (1973). doi:10.1007/BF00435190

31. A Arkin, J Ross, H McAdams, Stochastic kinetic analysis of developmental pathway bifurcation in Phage λ-infected *Escherichia coli* cells. Genetics. **149**, 1633–1648 (1998)

2

Model-based analysis of an adaptive evolution experiment with *Escherichia coli* in a pyruvate limited continuous culture with glycerol

Ronny Feuer[1*], Katrin Gottlieb[2], Gero Viertel[3], Johannes Klotz[3], Steffen Schober[3], Martin Bossert[3], Oliver Sawodny[1], Georg Sprenger[2] and Michael Ederer[1]

Abstract

Bacterial strains that were genetically blocked in important metabolic pathways and grown under selective conditions underwent a process of adaptive evolution: certain pathways may have been deregulated and therefore allowed for the circumvention of the given block. A block of endogenous pyruvate synthesis from glycerol was realized by a knockout of pyruvate kinase and phosphoenolpyruvate carboxylase in *E. coli*. The resulting mutant strain was able to grow on a medium containing glycerol and lactate, which served as an exogenous pyruvate source. Heterologous expression of a pyruvate carboxylase gene from *Corynebacterium glutamicum* was used for anaplerosis of the TCA cycle. Selective conditions were controlled in a continuous culture with limited lactate feed and an excess of glycerol feed. After 200–300 generations pyruvate-prototrophic mutants were isolated. The genomic analysis of an evolved strain revealed that the genotypic basis for the regained pyruvate-prototrophy was not obvious. A constraint-based model of the metabolism was employed to compute all possible detours around the given metabolic block by solving a hierarchy of linear programming problems. The regulatory network was expected to be responsible for the adaptation process. Hence, a Boolean model of the transcription factor network was connected to the metabolic model. Our model analysis only showed a marginal impact of transcriptional control on the biomass yield on substrate which is a key variable in the selection process. In our experiment, microarray analysis confirmed that transcriptional control probably played a minor role in the deregulation of the alternative pathways for the circumvention of the block.

Introduction

Since the long term evolution experiment of Lenski et al. [1], laboratory evolution has attracted much attention [2]. They demonstrated the adaptive behavior of mircoorganisms through shaking flask experiments with regular transfer in fresh culture media [1]. Already, Hoefle et al. [3] reported the presence of selective pressure in chemostat experiments. In the fermentation process, the adaptive evolution of the organisms occurs through random genetic mutation and controlled selection [4]. This process exhibits considerable potential for the design of industrial production strains [5]. Small product yields, slow growth, evolutive instability of mutated strains or toxicity of byproducts are limiting factors that are expected to be tackled with adaptive evolution [6]. Additionally, understanding of how environmental conditions shape the metabolism can be enhanced through adaptive evolution. A fine-tuning of enzyme expression levels balancing the cost and burden of protein production was demonstrated by Dekel et al. [7]. The genetic basis for such short-term evolutions has been intensely studied by using genome resequencing technology [8]. However, the genetic basis of adaptations is not always obvious. For example, a rewiring of the regulatory network is reported to be a source of adaptation [9] in the tolerance of *E. coli* to ethanol. Models for evolving regulatory networks were developed by Crombach et al. [10] and Xie et al. [11]. Constraint-based models of the metabolism are already in use for predicting maximal yields of organisms and optimal outcomes of adaptive evolution [12].

*Correspondence: ronny.feuer@isys.uni-stuttgart.de
[1] Institute for System Dynamics, University of Stuttgart, Pfaffenwaldring 9, 70569 Stuttgart, Germany
Full list of author information is available at the end of the article

Here, we present the concept of an adaptive evolution experiment in a bioreactor. In such a process, the evolutive pressure on the microorganisms for either fast growth or optimal biomass yield on a limiting substrate can be used to attain or improve the production of a desired compound. Motivated to know possible endpoints of the evolution experiment, we developed an algorithm for computing the endpoints of such an experiment. These endpoints are alternative flux distributions for the circumvention of a metabolic block. We further examined the role of a regulatory network in the usage of the alternative flux distribution and we validated the model by microarray analysis.

Adaptive Evolution Experiment

The experiment utilized a mutant of the intestinal bacterium *Escherichia coli* which lacks both the pyruvate kinases PykA/PykF and the phosphoenolpyruvate carboxylase (Ppc). The pyruvate kinases are expected to be the main source of pyruvate on a glycerol minimal medium [13]. The Ppc reaction replenishes the tricarboxylic acid cycle (TCA) with oxaloacetate derived from phosphoenolpyruvate. It can serve as an alternative endogenous pyruvate source because oxaloacetate can be converted back to pyruvate. The Ppc reaction is reported to be an essential reaction on glycerol minimal medium [14]. As replacement for the anaplerotic reaction of Ppc the pyruvate carboxylase gene (*pyc*) of *Corynebacterium glutamicum* was inserted into the chromosomal *malEG* locus under control of the *tac*-promotor. The Pyc enzyme catalyzes the carboxylation of pyruvate to form oxaloacetate [15].

Pyruvate is a precursor metabolite for several amino acids and also charges the TCA cycle. This is essential for the growth of the organism. Due to the knock outs, this strain F41*malE::pyc* is pyruvate-auxotrophic (see Figure 1). In contrast to our observation, Nakahigashi et al. [16] reported growth on glycerol of a $\Delta ppc \, \Delta pykAF$ multiple mutant in their knockout study.

In the bioreactor, F41*malE::pyc* was fed with two carbon sources: Glycerol as main carbon source and lactate, which can be converted to pyruvate by one enzymatic step (Figure 1). By limiting the supply of lactate, an evolutive pressure was applied to the population in the bioreactor. Through random mutation events (e.g., in regulatory sequences of in genes encoding regulators, or in enzymes) some mutants may modify the biomass yield. Mutants that generate more biomass from the limiting substrate tend to prevail against less efficient mutants. In the experiment, adaptive evolution proceeded until the established mutant became independent from the external pyruvate source and was again pyruvate prototrophic on glycerol. The bioreactor was being operated continuously. Both the dilution rate D [h^{-1}] and the input concentration

of lactate were controlled to facilitate the prevalence of mutants with an improved yield [17].

The evolved pyruvate-prototrophic mutants had to use alternative endogenous pathways to produce pyruvate. These alternative pathways may proceed via biotechnological interesting compounds, such as the amino acids serine, or tryptophane, or as the aromatic pathway intermediate: chorismate.

Hence, the production of pyruvate was not the goal, but a means to attain interesting byproducts of the alternative pathways (Figure 2). In the following section, we will use a metabolic network model to explore the possibilities of evolutive adaptation [12].

Model

The genome-scale metabolic reconstruction iAF1260 [18] contains 2077 reactions, 1039 metabolites, and additional thermodynamic information. Orth et al. [19] reviewed current flux balance analysis methods to give an overview of the possibilities of working with constraint based models. The following section analyzes the solution space of the network iAF1260 with respect to adaptive evolution.

Constraint based model (CBM)

The metabolic compounds $\mathbf{C}$ of the network participate as reactants and products in the reactions, described by the vector of reactions $\mathbf{J} \in \mathbb{R}^m$ in [mmol h^{-1}gDCW^{-1}] (gDCW: gram dry cell weight). The stoichiometric information for balanced compounds was described by the matrix $\mathbf{N}_0 \in \mathbb{R}^{n_0 \times m}$ and for unbalanced compounds by $\mathbf{N}_e \in \mathbb{R}^{n_e \times m}$, with n_0 and n_e as the number of balanced and unbalanced compounds, respectively. To denote the external substrate availability, the vector $\mathbf{b} \in \mathbb{R}^{n_e}$ was utilized as a boundary (e.g., if glycerol was available b_{glyc} was negative and if lactate was not available $b_{\text{lac}} = 0$). Furthermore, the growth rate was fixed to the dilution rate $J_\mu = D$ due to chemostat conditions. Since thermodynamic constraints on reactions exist, some reactions are irreversible and the direction of the flux is fixed. The following equality and inequality constraints were collected in the constraint set $\mathbb{K}_a$

$$0 = \mathbf{N}_0 \mathbf{J}; \quad \mathbf{b} \leq \mathbf{N}_e \mathbf{J}$$

$$J_\mu = D; \quad J_j \geq 0 \text{ for some } j \text{ (thermodynamic restrictions)}$$

$$(1)$$

which can be further analyzed by using objective functions for optimization.

Optimization

Properties of the constraint set $\mathbb{K}_a$ of Equation (1) can be examined by applying different objective functions. A linear objective function is given by $f = \mathbf{c}^\tau \mathbf{J}$. Minimizing f results in an optimal value f_{opt} and a particular solution

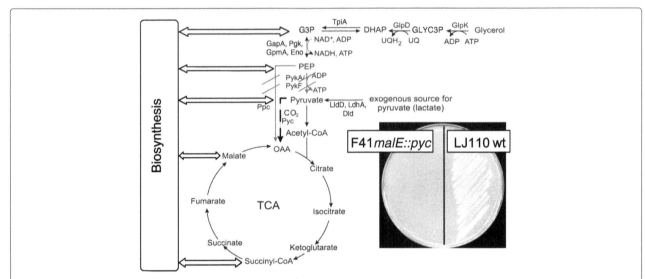

Figure 1 Strain F41*malE::pyc*. The mutant F41*malE::pyc* has a deletion of the two pyruvate kinase (Pyk) genes *pykA* and *pykF*, of the phosphoenolpyruvate carboxylase (Ppc) and an insertion of pyruvate carboxylase (Pyc). On the agar plate, F41*malE::pyc* was not able to grow on glycerol minimal media and was compared to the wild type LJ110 wt. With additional lactate, F41*malE::pyc* grew. Various endogenous pathways may lead to pyruvate prototrophy.

J_{opt}. Applying objective functions will often result in non-unique optima. Consequently, the set of optimal solutions has to be further analyzed. By extending the constraints in Equation (1) with the equation $f_{opt} = \mathbf{c}^\tau \mathbf{J}$ enforcing the optimal objective function value, a new constraint set $\mathbb{K}_b$ is obtained. The set $\mathbb{K}_b$ can be further analyzed by applying other objective functions.

Yield: The yield is defined as growth per substrate uptake $\mu J_{up,S}^{-1}$. If the biomass is in a steady state in the chemostat, the growth rate μ is determined by the dilution rate D. For optimization purposes, the yield can be maximized by minimizing the substrate uptake $J_{up,S} \rightarrow$ min.

Turnover rate: With a balanced metabolite the consumption and production rate are equal, which is a measure for the turnover. We define the turnover rate as the production rate of a compound. The objective function

$$J_i^{MTR} = 0.5 \sum_j |J_j v_{i,j}| \rightarrow \min \qquad (2)$$

results in a minimal turnover rate (MTR) of a balanced compound C_i with $v_{i,j}$ as a stoichiometric coefficient. A yield optimal minimal turnover rate (YMTR) was computed by extending the constraints with the fixed minimal substrate uptake rate $J_{up,S} = J_{up,S}^{min}$ as outlined above and then using $J_i^{MTR} \rightarrow$ min as an objective. Compounds with high turnover rates are more attractive targets for blockades in the adaptive evolution experiment, because if their main pathway is blocked the alternative pathways have to realize a high flux with potentially high formation of byproducts. The MTR were compared with YMTR in Figures 3 and 4. If the MTR is high, a blockade of these metabolites will result in a strong dependency from an external supply. If the YMTR is high compared to the MTR, the organism can improve its yield by realizing a high flux via this metabolite. Both is preferable for exerting an evolutive pressure.

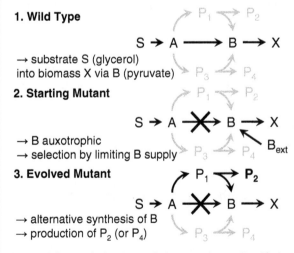

Figure 2 Scheme of adaptive evolution experiment. Simplified scheme of the strains employed and produced in the adaptive evolution experiments. Active pathways are shown in black and repressed pathways are shown in gray color.

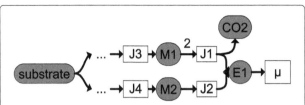

Figure 3 Minimal and yield optimal minimal turnover rates. Idea of minimal turnover rates (MTR) and yield optimal minimal turnover rates (YMTR). If $\mu > 0$, the MTR via the metabolite E1 has to be greater than zero. The MTR for M1 and M2 are zero, because the paths are alternatives. If the substrate uptake rate is minimal (yield optimal), the YMTR via M2 is greater than zero. The YMTR via M1 is zero because the path via M1 is less efficient than via M2.

Reconstruction of alternative synthesis routes of a metabolite

The adaptive evolution in the experiment was based on the circumvention of a metabolic block by mutation and selection events (see Figure 2). This section presents an approach to predict pathways for the circumvention of the block. First, a method for computing combinations of reactions which are able to produce the metabolite of interest (MOI) C_i was developed (problem illustrated in Figure 5). Second, this method was applied recursively to reconstruct alternative pathways from the external substrate to the MOI.

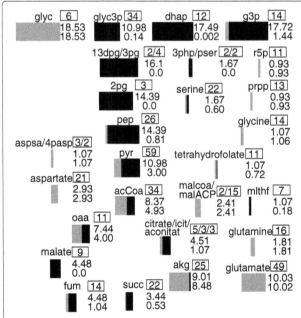

Figure 4 Turnover rates. Turnover rates of a selection of important metabolites with their number of reactions in the framed rectangle for growth on glycerol. The thickness of the black bar indicates the YMTR [mmol gDCW^{-1} h^{-1}] (upper number) and the gray bar denotes the MTR (lower number). The abbreviations of metabolites are presented in Section "Abbreviations".

1. Determine all reactions $\mathbf{J}_{C_i}$, where C_i participates as a product. Compute their minimal rate by solving the problems $|J_{C_i,j}| \to \min$ subject to $\mathbb{K}_a$ and test with a flux-variability-analysis (FVA) [20] whether the reaction rates can vary.

2. Construct a constraint set $\mathbb{K}_{C_i}$ by fixing all varying reactions of $\mathbf{J}_{C_i}$ to their minimal rate. Let l be the number of constraints in $\mathbb{K}_{C_i}$.

$$\mathbb{K}_{C_i} = \left\{ J_{C_i,1} = J_{C_i,1}^{\min}, \dots, J_{C_i,l} = J_{C_i,l}^{\min} \right\}$$

3. Starting with $k = 1$, compute the optimal yields of $\binom{l}{k}$ combinations of the joint constraints $\mathbb{K}_a \cup (\mathbb{K}_{C_i} \setminus \mathbb{K}_{r_k})$, where $\mathbb{K}_{r_k} \subseteq \mathbb{K}_{C_i}$ is a possibility to release k reactions. All $\mathbb{K}_{r_k}$ that result in a feasible solution are joint in the set $\mathbb{K}_k$.

4. If there is a feasible solution for the set restricting all previously found solutions $\mathbb{K}_a \cup \left(\bigcup_{\forall z \leq k} \mathbb{K}_z \right)$, increase k and repeat step 3.

In this manner, all minimal combinations of alternative reactions to produce C_i were obtained. To reconstruct the alternative pathways from a substrate to the MOI, this algorithm had to be used recursively. At first it was applied to the MOI, then to the reactants of the last reactions to the MOI and then to the reactants of those reactions and so on.

The computational effort is high due to the recursive usage of the algorithm. Because the point of interest was the buildup of a metabolite's carbon core, it was only necessary to track the reactants that carry parts of the carbon core for the metabolite. To decide whether or not a reactant contributes to the carbon core, we used the following equivalence relation:

Definition 1. *Given a set of cofactors Co, two metabolites C_i and C_j are equivalent up to Co ($C_i \overset{Co}{\sim} C_j$) if*

- *a reaction $C_i + Co_k \to C_j$ or $C_i \to C_j + Co_k$ exists, or*
- *a metabolite C_x exists, for that is known, that $C_i \overset{Co}{\sim} C_x \wedge C_j \overset{Co}{\sim} C_x$, or*
- *a reaction $C_i + C_x \to C_j + C_y$ with $C_x \overset{Co}{\sim} C_y$ exists.*

Those cofactors were chosen as H^+, HO_4P, NH_4, H_2O. For example, ATP, ADP, and AMP are equivalent up to these cofactors.

Furthermore, the production of many metabolites was possible via alternative end reactions but amounted to the same precursor metabolites. This fact also reduced the computational effort, because the multiple evaluation of common precursors was avoided.

The recursive application of the algorithm is an alternative approach for computing the elementary modes in this special task. Computing the elementary modes for a model like iAF1260 would be an extreme computing-intensive task, even if methods for network compression

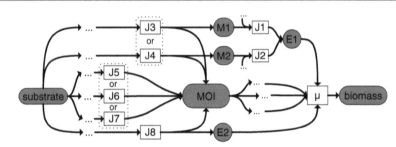

Figure 5 Alternative paths to a metabolite of interest (MOI). Illustration to identify reactions which can contribute to the production of a MOI. The metabolites E1, E2 and the MOI are essential for growth (MTR > 0). For E2 there is no alternative. Thus J8 can not vary for a fixed growth rate. The alternatives (J3,J5), (J3,J6), (J3,J7), (J4,J5), (J4,J6), and (J4,J7) have to be identified.

are used [21]. The algorithm proposed above reduces the computational effort by excluding some reactants as a source for the carbon core of a metabolite.

Evaluation for F41malE::pyc

In the experiment (see Figure 2) pyruvate was chosen as the metabolite of interest. In the model iAF1260, pyruvate appeared in 59 reactions as a reactant, it had a high MTR and YMTR (Figure 4) and several alternative synthesis routes are known. Hence a metabolic block of pyruvate formation seemed suitable to study adaptive evolution.

The above algorithm was employed to reconstruct alternative pathways from the carbon source glycerol to pyruvate. With $k = 2$, all minimal combinations of reactions to produce pyruvate were obtained (results see Figure 6). The recursive usage of the algorithm above resulted in a variety of flux distributions that represented alternative pathways

from glycerol to pyruvate, which were summarized in flux maps. Several flux distributions utilized the same precursors but differed in an alternative reaction from one precursor to another. The flux distributions were categorized using key metabolites and manual post-processing (see Figure 7 and Additional file 1: Table S1). In this manner, eight alternative pathway classes were found (see Table 1 and Figure 8).

After performing multiple independent evolution experiments with the pyruvate-auxotrophic mutant F41malE::pyc (see Figure 1), a total of five pyruvate-prototrophic strains with different characteristics were isolated after 200–300 generations each. One of the strains (K98-62) showed an increased enterobactin secretion. This property was part of the predicted shikimate pathway class (Figure 8). The strain was exposed to different media where pyruvate prototrophy had no growth benefits and the phenotype remained stable. This

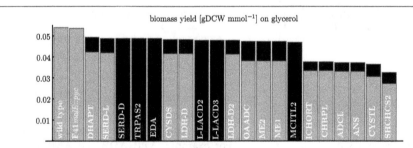

Figure 6 Yields for alternative pyruvate formation. Possible reactions to produce pyruvate (sorted by model predicted biomass yield on glycerol) computed by the proposed algorithm. The black bars show the predicted biomass yields on glycerol without regulation, gray bars with the regulatory network iMC1010v2. The bars for wild type and F41malE::pyc use combinations of reactions to pyruvate. Other bars are tagged by their final reaction to pyruvate: DHAPT - Dihydroxyacetone phosphotransferase (DhaK, DhaL, DhaM), SERD-L - L-Serine deaminase (TdcG, SdaA, SdaB, TnaA), SERD-D - D-Serine deaminase (DsdA), TRPAS2 - Tryptophanase-L-tryptophan (TnaA), EDA - 2-Dehydro-3-deoxyphosphogluconate aldolase (Eda), CYSDS - Cysteine desulfhydrase (TnaA, MetC), LDH-D - D-lactate dehydrogenase (Ldh), LACD2 - L-lactate dehydrogenase using ubiquinone (LldD), LACD3 - L-lactate dehydrogenase using menaquinone (LldD), LDH-D2 - D-lactate dehydrogenase (Dld), OAADC - Oxaloacetate decarboxylase (Eda), ME2 - Malic enzyme NADP (MaeB), ME1 - Malic enzyme NAD (MaeA), MCITL2 - Methylisocitrate lyase (PrpB), ICHORT - Isochorismatase (EntB), CHRPL - Chorismate pyruvate-lyase (UbiC), ADCL - 4-aminobenzoate synthase (PabC), ANS - Anthranilate synthase (TrpD, TrpE), CYSTL - Cystathionine-b-lyase (MalY, MetC), SHCHCS2 - 2-Succinyl-6-hydroxy-2-4-cyclohexadiene-1-carboxylate synthase (MenD). In all cases either ALATA-L - Alanine transaminase (AlaABC) (shown yields) or DXPS - Deoxy-D-xylulose-5-phosphate synthase (Dxs) contributed to pyruvate production similar to J3 and J4 in Figure 5. Other essential reactions similar to J8 in Figure 5 were: ACLS - Acetolactate synthase (IlvH or IlvB), ACHBS - 2-Aceto-2-hydroxybutanoate synthase (IlvH or IlvB) and DHDPS - Dihydrodipicolinate synthase (DapA).

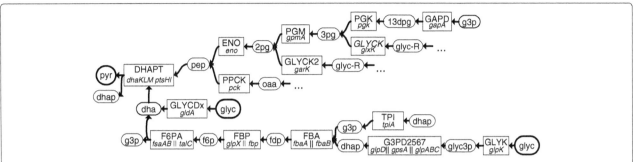

Figure 7 Alternative paths via DHAPT. Alternative paths from glycerol to pyruvate via dihydroxyacetone kinase (DHAPT). The abbreviations of metabolites are presented in Section "Abbreviations".

indicated that the pyruvate prototrophy was caused by a change of the genotype. A sequencing of the whole genome showed about 400 changes (including three deletions) compared to the wild type W3110 [22], but none of them has been yet assigned to be decisive (most mutated genes were prophage genes, operative genes with high probability of mutation were explored in detail). The genotypic alterations do not give an obvious explanation for the phenotype of the evolved strain, e.g., the enterobactin secretion. In order to clarify the relation between genotype and phenotype of the evolved strains, a transcriptional network model was studied.

Impact of transcriptional regulation

The transcriptional network of an organism can be interpreted as an information processing unit for the cell transmitting signals from the environment to enzyme availabilities via gene transcription [23]. Transcriptional regulation avoids production of enzymes which are unprofitable under certain environmental conditions. This contributes to evolutionary fitness. However, a trade-off exists between fitness advantage due to reduced protein cost and reduced response time after a change of environmental conditions [24].

After a directed genetic change of the organism (e.g., a knockout of pyruvate kinase), the regulatory network is not necessarily optimal any more. Consequently, random mutations leading to an altered regulatory network were expected by Crombach et al. [10] as a driving force for adaptive evolution.

We intended to study how transcriptional regulation affects the availability of enzymes that are essential for the predicted alternative pathways (Table 1). Therefore, the Boolean transcription factor network (TFN) iMC1010v2 [25] with 104 regulatory genes and an influence on 479 genes was adapted to the metabolic network iAF1260 (see Additional file 2: Table S2). The model provided Boolean formulas that describe how environmental conditions act on the gene expression via the transcriptional

regulatory network. The TFN had no feedback loops [26]. For this reason, variables describing environmental conditions could be used as an input of the TFN and a unique Boolean steady state was achieved. As the Boolean steady state describes on/off gene activities, these were translated via gene-protein-reaction associations of iAF1260 in reaction constraints. We assumed that a flux can not occur if genes were off that code for a respective enzyme. The proposed "off" genes extended the set of constraints for the optimization problem in Equation (1). The transcriptional constraints reduce the solution space of the metabolic model. Assuming a fixed biomass composition, the predicted biomass yield of the metabolic model without such constraints is greater than or equal to those with additional transcriptional constraints. We analyzed, as a first step, the predictive power of the combination of metabolic network (MN) and TFN.

Analysis of the metabolic and transcriptional model

We used data of the transcription factor knockout study of Haverkorn et al. [27] in order to analyze the predictive effectiveness of the metabolic model restricted by the transcriptional model. This study contains measurements of specific growth rates, specific acetate secretion rates and substrate uptake rates for glucose and galactose for 81 transcription factor and 10 σ and anti-σ factor knockouts. Only 41 of the evaluated factors are included in the iMC1010v2 model. The environmental conditions of the experiments were expressed in a constraint set such as $\mathbb{K}_a$ of Equation (1) and extended by a constraint for the measured acetate secretion rate and the measured growth rate to the constraint set of the MN $\mathbb{K}_m$. The environmental conditions of the experiment were used as an input of the TFN iMC1010v2 and resulted in the constraint set $\mathbb{K}_{tf}$. The knockouts of transcription- or σ factors changed the TFN and resulted in a changed constraint set $\mathbb{K}_{tf,-k}$, where k denoted the factor which was deleted. The objective function of minimal substrate uptake was evaluated on the constraint sets $\mathbb{K}_m$, $\mathbb{K}_m \cup \mathbb{K}_{tf}$, and $\mathbb{K}_m \cup \mathbb{K}_{tf,-k}$ yielding

Table 1 Alternative pathway classes from glycerol to pyruvate

Class	Characteristics	Max. yield	TFN prediction	Microarray	
				LJ110/ K98-62	F41 *malE::pyc*/ K98-62
dihydroxyacetone-path	dihydroxyaceton (toxic), *dhaKLM* operon is controlled by DhaR	0.0404	active (includes no DhaR)	active	active
Entner-Doudoroff-path	*eda* and *edd* controlled by GntR	0.0365	repressed	active	active
serine biosynthesis	transamination step from 3-phosphoglycerate to serine, various degenerating paths to pyruvate via L-serine, D-serine, L-cysteine and L-tryptophane	0.0384	active (via L-serine)	active	active
shikimate path	generates chorismate, pyruvate occurs as a byproduct for tryptophan-, enterobactin-, tetrahydrofolate-, ubi/menaquinone-biosynthesis; secretion of enterobactin possible	0.0214	active	active	active
methylglyoxal path	methylglyoxal (toxic) is formed from dhap and detoxified in 3 different ways to lactate	0.0365	active	active	active
acCoA synthesis	utilize deoxyribonucleotides as carbon shuttle AMP, UMP and GMP are synthesized and degraded	0.0344	repressed	active	active
murein path	via synthesis and degradation of murein	0.0297	repressed	(active)	active
CO_2 fixation	2 pyruvate are reinvested to form 2 oxaloacetate; carbon transfer between glycolysis/pentose phosphate pathway and TCA occurs only via CO_2	0.0269	active	active	active

[a] The yields [gDCW mmol^{-1}] on glycerol were calculated for the experimentally determined maximal growth rate of the evolved strain K98-62 ($\mu = 0.25$ h^{-1}). To compute the maximal yield for a single alternative pathway (AP) all other APs were restricted to their minimal value. For the prediction of the TFN, the environmental conditions of the chemostat (MM with glycerol) were used as an input. The APs have several important reactions for generating a yield. If the average expression level of genes for enzymes of those important reactions drops below a threshold of 7.0 units, we assumed that the enzymatic capacity to perform the reaction is not present.

three predictions of substrate uptake, which were then compared with the measured substrate uptake. The outcome of the comparison is shown in Figure 9. The analysis revealed that there was no improvement of the prediction of the metabolic model through the extension with the transcriptional model. However, this result should be interpreted with care. First, in case the observed uptake rate was lower than the predicted uptake rate of the MN, the model extended by the TFN had to result in an equal or even worse prediction, because the TFN additionally restricted the solution space of the MN. Second, if a transcription factor in reality has no impact on the substrate yield, the prediction of the MN should be equal to the TFN extended MN, which seemed to be the case in most predictions. Third, if the TFN is partially incomplete, the prediction tends to be conservative and does not restrict

the reaction fluxes. Under conditions of aerobic growth on glucose/galactose (conditions of the study of Haverkorn et al. [27]) the TFN had a low impact on the substrate uptake. Therefore, no real assessment of the quality of the TFN can be made. With this limitation in mind we present here the analysis of an evolutionary trajectory of F41*malE::pyc*.

Analysis for F41malE::pyc and its evolved strains

The wild type strain LJ110 (W3110) [28], the strain F41*malE::pyc* and the evolved strains showed different growth features. In fact eight alternative metabolic pathways exist to circumvent the metabolic block of regular pyruvate formation. This raised the question why F41*malE::pyc* was not able to use these eight alternative metabolic pathways on minimal media (MM) with

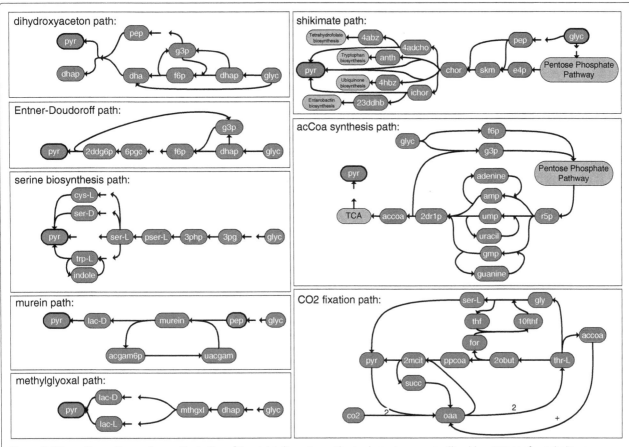

Figure 8 Alternative pathway classes. Illustration of the eight alternative pathway classes to pyruvate. The abbreviations of metabolites are presented in Section "Abbreviations".

glycerol. After a cultivation phase of F41*malE::pyc* in MM with glycerol, growth could be obtained by adding lactate. This indicated that F41*malE::pyc* was not poisoned by toxic metabolites. The useability of some of the eight alternative pathways was proven by the sheer existence of the evolved pyruvate prototrophic strains. Therefore, we examined the hypothesis if transcriptional regulation prevents the transcription of genes which are essential for the usage of the alternative pathways. We checked how the transcriptional network impacts the eight alternative pathways (Table 1) and validated the enzymatic capabilities of the strains by transcript analysis after growth in different minimal media. The alternative metabolic pathways were employed to identify important reactions for pathway functionality. The gene-protein-reaction associations were used to conclude which genes needed to be transcribed in order to ensure a reaction flux for functionality of the pathways. To decide whether the enzymatic capacity for catalyzing a reaction was available, a threshold for the average measured expression was used, neglecting regulation on a post-transcriptional level.

For the evaluation we chose a threshold of 7.0. The enzymatic capacity necessary for functionality of the eight alternative pathways as determined by mRNA measurements was summarized in Table 1 (detailed information see Additional file 1: Table S1) together with the predicted restrictions by the TFN. The wild type and K98-62 were compared on MM with glycerol; and F41*malE::pyc* and K98-62 were compared on MM with glycerol and lactate. The analysis of the differential expression values revealed no clear indication for an up/down regulation of a metabolic pathway. This statement is based on the following two findings which can be drawn from Additional file 1: Table S1. First, all the genes considered, were being transcribed under the given conditions. Thus, their gene product may contribute to pyruvate delivering pathways. Second, the absence of gross changes in transcripts did not provide hints towards regulatory changes which would explain a direct assignment to a pathway. This makes it more likely that the activity of some enzymes may be altered due to metabolic feedbacks. We looked for other systematically up/down regulated genes and found that

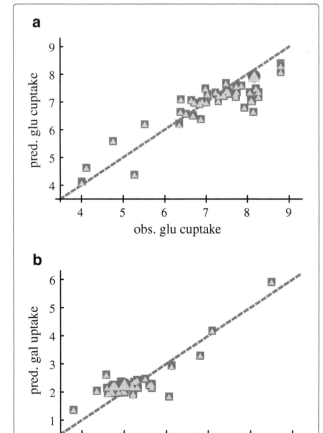

Figure 9 Predictive efficiency of metabolic network (MN) and transcriptional network (TN). Predictive efficiency of metabolic network (MN) and transcription factor network (TFN). Shown is the measured glucose **(a)**/ galactose**(b)** consumption in [mmol gDCW^{-1} h^{-1}] of the transcription factor knockout study of [27] versus the predicted consumption. The measured growth rate and acetate secretion of the study are used to predict the glucose/galactose uptake. The green triangles show predictions of the MN alone, the blue dots show predictions of the TFN combined with MN and the red squares include the knockouts of the study in the TFN combined with MN. The big green and blue dots show the values of the wild type. Statistical analysis of the model: observed uptake rate ≈ predicted uptake rate, results in an estimated error variance of 0.2811 for the MN, 0.2816 for MN with TFN and 0.2812 for MN with TFN and knockout.

genes associated with iron-sulfur cluster assembly were upregulated in the evolved strain.

The results indicated that estimating from the microarray data, the enzymatic capability of using the alternative pathways was available in all three compared strains. The TFN did not predict a transcriptional downregulation of the pathways in most cases, which was in accordance with the microarray data, except for the

Entner-Doudoroff-path and alternative acetyl-CoA synthesis path. This means that the hypothesis of restricting the alternative pathways by transcriptional regulation did not hold.

Conclusion

We have illustrated the idea of an adaptive evolution experiment in a chemostat bioreactor, where mutation and selection led to circumvention of a metabolic block. Constraint-based methods were utilized to identify targets for blocks and to predict alternative pathways for this circumvention. We performed the experiment with a pyruvate-auxotrophic strain F41*malE::pyc* on glycerol with an additional pyruvate source. The introduced algorithm for the computation of alternative pathways was employed to predict pathways from glycerol to pyruvate as possible endpoints of evolution for the strain F41*malE::pyc*. The evolution experiment with F41*malE::pyc* resulted in five evolved strains. This proved that the usage of alternative pathways was possible after adaptive evolution. However, F41*malE::pyc* was unable to grow without a pyruvate source. We assumed that transcriptional restriction of the predicted pathways hindered the growth. Therefore, a Boolean transcription factor network (TFN) was employed to further restrict the solutions of the metabolic network (MN). The prediction of the TFN together with microarray analysis revealed that in this case it is improbable that transcriptional regulation was exclusively responsible for the activation of the proposed alternative pathways during adaptation. It was shown that mRNA of genes which are important for the functionality of the predicted pathways were present in all compared strains.

However, a clear elucidation of the course of genetic events during adaptation was not yet possible. Metabolic feedbacks and non-regulatory effects may play an important role. We believe that the TFN will help to support further analysis by giving the possibility to determine the regulatory effects of metabolic and environmental signals and to distinguish between cause and effect of the up/down regulation of a gene. This will warrant further study in the field of transcription factor networks and their input in order to understand the whole sequence of events during adaptive evolution.

Materials and methods
Strains, medium, and growth conditions

The strains used in the experiments are listed in Table 2. The minimal medium (MM) (modified after [29]) used for all experiments consisted of 4.7 g NaH$_2$PO$_4$·2 H$_2$O, 11.5 g K$_2$PO$_4$, 2.64 g (NH$_4$)$_2$SO$_4$, 0.74 g MgSO$_4$·7H$_2$O, 14.7 mg CaCl$_2$·2H$_2$O, 13.5 mg ZnCl$_2$, 2.8 mg FeSO$_4$·7H$_2$O, 10μl 1N HCl, 20 mg Thiamine, 0.2 mM IPTG per liter. In shaking flask experiments 0.5% (w/v) glycerol was used as

Table 2 Strains

Strain	Genetic properties
W3110 (LJ110)	F⁻ λ⁻ rpoS(Am) rph-1 Inv (rrnD-rrnE) ([30]; [22])
F41malE::pyc	LJ110 ΔppcΔpykAΔpykFΔmalE − G::P_{tac} − pyc⁺ [17]
K98-62	Evolved from F41malE::pyc during longterm cultivation in a chemostat on minimal medium with glycerol as carbon source; pyruvate-prototrophic (this study)

carbon source. When a mixture of glycerol and D,L-lactate was used the concentrations were 0.4% glycerol and 0.1% D,L-lactate in order to have constant carbon availability in all experiments. Cells were cultivated in 250 ml shaking flasks filled with 25 ml growth medium. Prior to use, the cells were streaked onto LB-agar plates freshly from −80°C frozen stocks and incubated overnight at 37°C. Single colonies from LB-agarplates were then adapted to growth on minimal medium on MM agar plates for three days. Cultures were initiated directly from MM agar plates at OD600 = 0.1. After overnight incubation at 37°C without shaking the cells were grown at 37°C and 70 rpm.

Bioreactor

Chemostat fermentations were performed in a Bioengineering fermentor KLF at 37°C, with stirring rate of 500−1000 rpm, an input air of 1 L/min, controlled pH at 7 and pO₂ was kept above 50%. The feeding contained MM with 5 g/L glycerol and lactate concentrations in the range from 0.125 g/L down to 0 g/L of 95% L-lactate. The last 100 fermentation hours the feeding contained no lactate. The glycerol concentration measured in the fermentation broth was close to zero.

Genome resequencing

For genome resequencing the cells were grown to stationary phase. Chromosomal DNA was isolated via Phenol/Chloroform precipitation [31]. The resequencing was performed by LGC Genomics (Berlin, Germany) using 454 FLX Titanium Sequencing. The sequence of K98-62 was mapped to the online available sequence of E. coli W3110 (AP009048.1).

Transcriptome analysis

For transcriptome analysis strains K98-62 and LJ110 were compared after growth on minimal medium containing glycerol as carbon source and K98-62 and F41malE::pyc were compared after growth on minimal medium containing glycerol and D,L-lactate as carbon source. Cells were harvested after reaching OD600 = 0.8. The DNA chips were custom-synthesized by Agilent company and processed according to the manufacture's instruction. A complete description of transcript data will be published elsewhere, but can be obtained from the authors directly.

The average expression is the mean value of all normalized Log₂ spot intensities over all biological replicates and colors. If the average expression value of a mRNA was measured below 6 units, it is uncertain that the mRNA was present in the probe. If the fold change value was not significantly different from zero and the average expression value was above 7.0, we assumed that mRNA of a gene was present in both compared strains. Observing significant fold change values, we studied the strain specific average expression to assess whether mRNA was present or not. The mean average expression value over all spots was 6.93 in the comparison K98-62 versus wild type and 7.37 for K98-62 versus F41malE::pyc. Data to estimate the enzymatic capability of the predicted pathways was included in Additional file 1: Table S1.

Constraint based model analysis

In Equation (1), we regarded also ATP requirements for the maintenance metabolism J_{ATPm} in $\mathbb{K}_a$. Although the maintenance metabolism may vary on different substrates and in the evolved strains, we decided to fix the rate of this flux for the computations and therefore the value for an aerobic culture on glucose J_{ATPm} = 8.39 [mmol h⁻¹gDCW⁻¹] from Feist et al. [18], which is a theoretical calculation. This value, however, does not influence the structure of the identified pathways, but it has an impact on the yield numbers in Figures 4 and 6.

Combination of iAF1260 and iMC1010v2: The computation of a regulatory model combined with metabolic model was outlined by Covert et al. [32]. The network iMC1010v2 was originally designed for the metabolic network iJR904 [33]. The model extension iAF1260 has a much more detailed reaction of biomass formation. Hence, some reactions became essential due to model extension, but were downregulated by the iMC10010v2. We identified these reactions and made these independent from the Boolean regulatory model. Details are shown in Additional file 2: Table S2.

Abbreviations

accoa: Acetyl-CoA; prpp: 5-Phospho-α-D-ribose-1-diphosphate; acgam6p: N-Acetyl-Dglucosamine6phosphate; pser: Phospho-L-serine; akg: Oxoglutarate; pyr: Pyruvate; anth: Anthranilate; r5p: α-D-Ribose-5-phosphate; aspsa: L-Aspartate-4-semialdehyde; ser-D/L: D/L-Serine; chor: Chorismate; skm: Shikimate; cys-L: L-Cysteine; succ: Succinate; dha: Dihydroxyacetone; thf: Tetrahydrofolate; dhap: Dihydroxyacetone-phosphate; thr-L: L-Threonine; e4p: D-Erythrose-4-phosphate; trp-L: L-Tryptophan; fdp: D-Fructose-1-6-bisphosphate; uacgam: UDP-N-Acetyl-D-glucosamine; for:

Formate; 10fthf: 10-Formyltetrahydrofolate; fum: Fumarate; 13dpg: 3-Phospho-D-glyceroyl-phosphate; f6p: D-Fructose-6-phosphate; 2ddg6p: 2-Dehydro3deoxy-D-gluconate6phosphate; glyc: Glycerol; 2dr1p: 2-Deoxy-D-ribose-1-phosphate; glyc-R: R-Glycerate; 2mcit: 2-Methylcitrate; glyc3p: Glycerol-3-phosphate; 2obut: 2-Oxobutanoate; g3p: Glyceraldehyde-3-phosphate; 2pg: D-Glycerate-2-phosphate; ichor: Isochorismate; 23ddhb: 2-3-Dihydro-2-3-dihydroxybenzoate; lac-D/L: D/L-Lactate; 3pg: 3-Phospho-D-glycerate; malACP: Malonyl-acyl-carrier-protein; 3php: 3-Phosphohydroxypyruvate; malcoa: Malonyl-CoA; 4abz: 4-Aminobenzoate; mlthf: 5-10-Methylenetetrahydrofolate; 4adcho: 4-Amino-4-deoxychorismate; mthgxl: Methylglyoxal; 4hbz: 4-Hydroxybenzoate; oaa: Oxaloacetate; 4pasp: 4-Phospho-L-aspartate; pep: Phosphoenolpyruvate; 6pgc: 6-Phospho-D-gluconate; ppcoa: Propanoyl-CoA. The abbreviations of iAF1260 [18] for reaction and metabolite names are used.

Additional files

Additional file 1: Alternative pathway classes. Additional file 1 contains detailed information about the alternative pathway classes from Section "Abbreviations".

Additional file 2: Modifications of iMC1010v2, input signals and predicted inactive genes. Additional file 2 describes how iMC1010v2 can be adapted to the metabolic model iAF1260. It contains input signals for three environmental conditions and the according outputs.

Competing interests

The authors declare that they have no competing interests.

Authors' contributions

RF has written the manuscript, has done modeling and experimental study and did conceptual study. KG has done experimental study including transcript analysis. GV has done the computations for the model analysis of transcription factor knockout study. JK and SS have supervised the study of GV and did theoretical studies with the transcriptional network. MB and OS contributed to the design of the project. GS contributed to the design of the project and to the interpretation of data. ME contributed to the design of the project, has developed a preliminary version of the computational algorithm, has done conceptual study on the article and helped to interpret the data. All authors read and approved the final manuscript.

Acknowledgements

This study was funded by the German Research Foundation (DFG) priority program SPP 1395 InkoMBio (SA 847/11-2) and supported by the DFG funding program Open Access Publishing. We thank Karin Lemuth for her support with the microarray analysis, Natalie Trachtmann for the construction of strain F41*malE::pyc* and Silvia Lorenz for the labor-intensive analysis of the evolved strains in her diploma thesis.

Author details

[1]Institute for System Dynamics, University of Stuttgart, Pfaffenwaldring 9, 70569 Stuttgart, Germany. [2]Institute of Microbiology, University of Stuttgart, Stuttgart, Germany. [3]Institute of Communications Engineering, University of Ulm, Ulm, Germany.

References

1. SF Elena, RE Lenski, Evolution experiments with microorganisms: the dynamics and genetic bases of adaptation. Nat. Rev. Genet. **4**(6), 457–469 (2003)
2. TM Conrad, NE Lewis, BØ Palsson, Microbial laboratory evolution in the era of genome-scale science. Mol. Syst. Biol. **7**, 509 (2011)
3. MG Höfle, Long-term changes in chemostat cultures of Cytophaga johnsonae. Appl. Environ. Microbiol. **46**(5), 1045–1053 (1983)
4. RU Ibarra, JS Edwards, BO Palsson, Escherichia coli K-12 undergoes adaptive evolution to achieve in silico predicted optimal growth. Nature. **420**(6912), 186–189 (2002)
5. SS Fong, AP Burgard, CD Herring, EM Knight, FR Blattner, CD Maranas, BO Palsson, In silico design and adaptive evolution of Escherichia coli for production of lactic acid. Biotechnol. Bioeng. **91**(5), 643–648 (2005)
6. VA Portnoy, D Bezdan, K Zengler, Adaptive laboratory evolution–harnessing the power of biology for metabolic engineering. Curr. Opinion Biotechnol. **22**(4), 590–594 (2011)
7. E Dekel, U Alon, Optimality and evolutionary tuning of the expression level of a protein. Nature. **436**(7050), 588–592 (2005)
8. TM Conrad, AR Joyce, MK Applebee, CL Barrett, B Xie, Y Gao, BØ Palsson, Whole-genome resequencing of Escherichia coli K-12 MG1655 undergoing short-term laboratory evolution in lactate minimal media reveals flexible selection of adaptive mutations. Genome Biol. **10**(10), R118 (2009)
9. H Goodarzi, BD Bennett, S Amini, ML Reaves, AK Hottes, JD Rabinowitz, S Tavazoie, Regulatory and metabolic rewiring during laboratory evolution of ethanol tolerance in E. coli. Mol. Syst. Biol. **6**, 378 (2010)
10. A Crombach, P Hogeweg, Evolution of evolvability in gene regulatory networks. PloS Comput. Biol. **4**(7), e1000112 (2008)
11. D Xie, CC Chen, X He, X Cao, S Zhong, Towards an evolutionary model of transcription networks. PloS Comput. Biol. **7**(6), e1002064 (2011)
12. NE Lewis, KK Hixson, TM Conrad, JA Lerman, P Charusanti, AD Polpitiya, JN Adkins, G Schramm, SO Purvine, D Lopez-Ferrer, KK Weitz, R Eils, R König, RD Smith, BØ Palsson, Omic data from evolved E.coli are consistent with computed optimal growth from genome-scale models. Mol. Syst. Biol. **6**, 390 (2010)
13. E Ponce, N Flores, A Martinez, F Valle, F Bolívar, Cloning of the two pyruvate kinase isoenzyme structural genes from Escherichia coli: the relative roles of these enzymes in pyruvate biosynthesis. J. Bacteriol. **177**(19), 5719–5722 (1995)
14. AR Joyce, JL Reed, A White, R Edwards, A Osterman, T Baba, H Mori, SA Lesely, BØ Palsson, S Agarwalla, Experimental and computational assessment of conditionally essential genes in Escherichia coli. J. Bacteriol. **188**(23), 8259–8271 (2006)
15. PG Peters-Wendisch, C Kreutzer, J Kalinowski, M Pátek, H Sahm, BJ Eikmanns, Pyruvate carboxylase from Corynebacterium glutamicum: characterization, expression, and inactivation of the pyc gene. Microbiology (Reading, England). **144**(Pt 4), 915–927 (1998)
16. K Nakahigashi, Y Toya, N Ishii, T Soga, M Hasegawa, H Watanabe, Y Takai, M Honma, H Mori, M Tomita, Systematic phenome analysis of Escherichia coli multiple-knockout mutants reveals hidden reactions in central carbon metabolism. Mol. Syst. Biol. **5**, 306 (2009)
17. R Feuer, M Ederer, ED Gilles, GA Sprenger, O Sawodny, T Sauter, Analyse der evolutiven adaptation am beispiel einer pyruvat-auxotrophen Escherichia coli-mutante (analysis of the evolutive adaptation of a pyruvate-auxotrophic Escherichia coli. mutant). at - Automatisierungstechnik. **56**(5), 257–268 (2008)
18. AM Feist, CS Henry, JL Reed, M Krummenacker, AR Joyce, PD Karp, LJ Broadbelt, V Hatzimanikatis, BØ Palsson, A genome-scale metabolic reconstruction for Escherichia coli K-12 MG1655 that accounts for 1260 ORFs and thermodynamic information. Mol. Systs. Biol. **3**, 121 (2007)
19. JD Orth, I Thiele, BØ Palsson, What is flux balance analysis. Nat. Biotechnol. **28**(3), 245–248 (2010)
20. R Mahadevan, CH Schilling, The effects of alternate optimal solutions in constraint-based genome-scale metabolic models. Metabolic Eng. **5**(4), 264–276 (2003)
21. J Gagneur, S Klamt, Computation of elementary modes: a unifying framework an dthe new binary approach. BMC Bioinf. **5**, 175 (2004)
22. K Hayashi, N Morooka, Y Yamamoto, K Fujita, K Isono, S Choi, E Ohtsubo, T Baba, BL Wanner, H Mori, T Horiuchi, Highly accurate genome sequences of Escherichia coli K-12 strains MG1655 and W3110. Mol. Systs. Biol. **2**, 2006.0007 (2006)
23. U Alon, *An Introduction to Systems Biology: Design Principles of Biological Circuits Chapman & Hall/CRC mathematical and computational biology series*: (Chapman &amp Hall/CRC, Boca Raton Fla. u.a, 2007)
24. F Wessely, M Bartl, R Guthke, P Li, S Schuster, C Kaleta, Optimal regulatory strategies for metabolic pathways in Escherichia coli depending on protein costs. Mol. Systs. Biol. **7**, 515 (2011)
25. MW Covert, EM Knight, JL Reed, MJ Herrgard, BO Palsson, Integrating high-throughput and computational data elucidates bacterial networks. Nature. **429**(6987), 92–96 (2004)

26. JG Klotz, R Feuer, K Gottlieb, O Sawodny, GA Sprenger, M Bossert, M Ederer, S Schober, Properties of a Boolean network model of Escherichia coli. in *Proc. of the 8th International Workshop on Computational Systems Biology (WCSB) 2011*. Zuerich: TICSP series 57, 97-100, 2011)

27. BRB Haverkorn van Rijsewijk, A Nanchen, S Nallet, RJ Kleijn, U Sauer, Large-scale 13C-flux analysis reveals distinct transcriptional control of respiratory and fermentative metabolism in Escherichia coli. Mol. Systs. Biol. **7**, 477 (2011)

28. T Zeppenfeld, C Larisch, JW Lengeler, K Jahreis, Glucose transporter mutants of Escherichia coli K-12 with changes in substrate recognition of IICB(Glc) and induction behavior of the *ptsG* gene. J. Bacteriol. **182**(16), 4443–4452 (2000)

29. S Tanaka, SA Lerner, ECC Lin, Replacement of a Phosphoenolpyruvate-dependent Phosphotransferase by a Nicotinamide Adenine Dinucleotide-linked Dehydrogenase for the Utilization of Mannitol. J. Bacteriol. **93**(2), 642–648 (1967)

30. BJ Bachmann, Pedigrees of some mutant strains of Escherichia coli K-12. Bacteriol. Rev. **36**(4), 525–557 (1972)

31. FM Ausubel, R Brent, RE Kingston, DD Moore, JG Seidman, JA Smith, K Struhl, *Current Protocols in Molecular Biology*, Vol. 1. (New York: John Wiley & Sons, 1995)

32. MW Covert, BØ Palsson, Transcriptional regulation in constraints-based metabolic models of Escherichia coli. J. Biol. Chem. **277**(31), 28058–28064 (2002)

33. JL Reed, TD Vo, CH Schilling, BO Palsson, An expanded genome-scale model of Escherichia coli (iJR904 GSM/GPR). Genome Biol. **4**(9), R54 (2003)

3

Dynamical modeling of drug effect using hybrid systems

Xiangfang Li[1][*], Lijun Qian[2] and Edward R Dougherty[1,3,4]

Abstract

Drug discovery today is a complex, expensive, and time-consuming process with high attrition rate. A more systematic approach is needed to combine innovative approaches in order to lead to more effective and efficient drug development. This article provides systematic mathematical analysis and dynamical modeling of drug effect under gene regulatory network contexts. A hybrid systems model, which merges together discrete and continuous dynamics into a single dynamical model, is proposed to study dynamics of the underlying regulatory network under drug perturbations. The major goal is to understand how the system changes when perturbed by drugs and give suggestions for better therapeutic interventions. A realistic periodic drug intake scenario is considered, drug pharmacokinetics and pharmacodynamics information being taken into account in the proposed hybrid systems model. Simulations are performed using MATLAB/SIMULINK to corroborate the analytical results.

Keywords: Drug effect, Hybrid systems, PK/PD, Gene regulatory network (GRN), Dosing regimens

Introduction

The ultimate goal of drug therapy is to modulate the phenotypic behavior of cells by altering the behavior of the gene and protein components of the cell [1]. This approach is possible because the phenotypic behavior of the cell reflects the dynamics of the gene and protein-based regulatory network. When it comes to drug therapeutics and disease modeling, the major goal is to understand how the system changes when perturbed and how to modify the system to achieve a desired outcome. To understand and exploit the complicated mapping between genome and phenome, especially in the context of drug discovery, it is critical to evaluate the regulatory interactions between the genes and proteins that form the gene regulatory network (GRN). To date, the hope of the rapid translation of "genes to drugs" has foundered on the reality that disease biology is complex and drug development must be driven by insights into biological responses [2]. A systems approach is crucial for moving biology from a descriptive to a predictive science [3,4]. This calls for appropriate modeling to establish a functional understanding of disease–drug interaction, in order to better predict drug effects and make drug discovery a faster and more systematic process.

Pharmacokinetics (PK) is the study of *what the body does to the drug*, i.e., the absorption, distribution, metabolism, and excretion of the drug, and pharmacodynamics (PD) seeks to study *what the drug does to the body*. A salient challenge is to link a drug's PK information with PD characteristics to provide a better understanding of the time course of drug effect (PK/PD) after drug administration [5]. Modeling and simulation tools are required to integrate PK and PD data and optimize drug regimens.

A salient problem is finding a dosing regimen of a drug candidate that is both efficacious and safe [6]. Traditionally, drugs have been administered on an experimental basis, but it is virtually impossible to optimize dosing regimens using strictly empirical methods, especially since different patients may respond differently to the same drug dosage [7]. Moreover, traditionally designing the dosing regimen to achieve some desired target goal such as relatively constant serum concentration may not be optimal because of underlying dynamic biological networks. For example, Shah et al. [8] demonstrate that BCR–ABL inhibitor dasatinib, which has greater potency and a short half-life, can achieve deep clinical remission in CML patients by achieving transient potent BCR–ABL inhibition, while traditionally approved tyrosine kinase

*Correspondence: xiangfangli@ieee.org
[1]Department of Electrical and Computer Engineering, Texas A&M University, College Station, TX 77843, USA
Full list of author information is available at the end of the article

inhibitors usually have prolonged half-lives that result in continuous target inhibition. A similar study of whether short pulses of higher dose or persistent dosing with lower doses has the most favorable outcomes has been carried out by Amin et al. [9] in the setup of inactivation of HER2–HER3 signaling. Finding an optimal dosing regimen based on the dynamics of biological systems and relevant PK/PD information is critically important.

System modeling is emerging as a valuable tool in therapeutics to address these challenges [3,10-12]. The process begins with building a quantitative model of a biological system. Consequences of particular perturbations, such as optimal dosing regimens, optimal drug targets, or combinational therapy, can be simulated in time courses using such models. In this study, we propose a hybrid systems model for GRNs and incorporate a drug's PK and PD information by using a state-space approach. We first study drug effect assuming the drug target to be a gene or protein in the proposed drug perturbation model using dynamical system theory, considering the case of periodic drug intake and analytically deriving the conditions for the drug to be effective. We extend the analysis to the 2-gene case and then to the case of a network with multiple coupled genes and positive feedback loops. Simulations are performed using MATLAB/SIMULINK to supplement our analytical results.

Model formulation

While discrete modeling leaves out many details, continuous modeling includes so many details that computational demands preclude their applications to many larger systems. Hybrid systems, which aim to merge ideas from both continuous and discrete modeling into one paradigm, are appealing for GRN modeling under drug perturbations because biological systems are naturally nonlinear, have highly varied regulatory requirements, and possess a wide range of control strategies for meeting their needs. While some simple, local, feedback control methods can provide sufficient regulation of many more-or-less continuous cellular processes, the regulation of discontinuous processes possessing the character of computational decision making requires more elaborate regulatory methods [13]. In particular, some genes display regulation in a thresholded switch-like manner [14].

Hybrid systems include a broad space of models and systems. Several hybrid systems models have been developed for biological networks. Some of these have been used to perform reachability analysis to elucidate biologically meaningful properties. For example, the Lac operon system has been well studied both experimentally and using continuous models [15,16]. A hybrid model and use of a reachability algorithm were validated by comparison with experimental data and continuous models [17]. Other biological hybrid systems analyzed in similar ways include

the Delta-Notch decision process [18,19], GRNs of carbon starvation [20], and nutritional stress response [21] in *Escherichia coli*. As far as we know, the only hybrid systems modeling concerning treatment or drug effects is contained in our earlier work [22].

Gene regulation can be modeled by rate equations expressing the difference between rate of production and rate of degradation [23,24]. We adopt the general model

$$\dot{x}_i = f_i(x) - \gamma_i x_i, \tag{1}$$

where $x_i \geq 0$ corresponds to the concentrations of proteins encoded by genes in the network and can be interpreted as the gene expression level. $f_i(.)$ is a general nonlinear function and represents the rate of synthesis. It can be approximated by a sigmoidal function or a unit step function, and unit step function is used in this article. $\gamma_i x_i$ is the rate of degradation. To use hybrid systems and incorporate drug effect, we propose the following model for a GRN of N genes under drug perturbation:

$$
\dot{x}_i = \sum_{k=1}^{K_i} \left\{ \beta_i^k \left(\prod_{j \in \Psi_i} \Omega_i^j \right) \left[1 - \left(\prod_{j \in \Phi_i} \Xi_i^j \right) \right] \right\} \\
- \gamma_i x_i + \beta_i^u \Omega_i^u - \gamma_i^u \Xi_i^u x_i, \quad \forall i = 1, 2, \ldots, N, \tag{2}
$$

where the last two terms on the right-hand side of Equation (2) correspond to drug perturbation u. $\beta > 0$ and $\gamma > 0$ are synthesis and degradation rates, respectively. $K_i \geq 1$ is an integer representing the number of activation/synthesis terms. Ω_i^j and Ξ_i^j describe how other genes affect gene i. They are the functions of $s^+(x_j, \theta_j^{t+i})$ and $s^-(x_j, \theta_j^{t-i})$, where $s^+(.)$ is the unit step function, $s^-(.) = 1 - s^+(.)$, and the θ terms are the corresponding threshold values. For each gene j, the set of threshold values related to gene i is denoted by $\mathbb{T}_j^i$, where $t+i$ and $t-i$ are indices of the threshold values, $0 \leq \theta_j^{t+i} \in \mathbb{T}_j^i$, and $0 \leq \theta_j^{t-i} \in \mathbb{T}_j^i$. Ψ_i and Φ_i represent the two sets of genes that affect the expression of gene i in different manners. Specifically, in this article, we consider

$$\Omega_i^j = s^+(x_j, \theta_j^{t+i}) s^-(x_j, \theta_j^{t-i}), \tag{3}$$

with Ξ_i^j defined similarly. Ω_i^j and Ξ_i^j may be set to 0 or 1, or different forms when appropriate threshold values are chosen. For example, $\Omega_1^1 = s^+(x_1, 0^-) s^-(x_1, \infty) = 1$ and $\Omega_1^2 = s^+(x_2, 0^-) s^-(x_2, \theta_1^2) = s^-(x_2, \theta_2^2)$. Ω_i^u and Ξ_i^u describe how the drug u affect gene i. $\beta_i^u \geq 0$ and $\gamma_i^u \geq 0$ are the synthesis and degradation factors of the drug on gene i. $\beta_i^u \Omega_i^u$ and $-\gamma_i^u \Xi_i^u x_i$ are used when the drug is activating or repressing certain genes, respectively. Since most drugs are used to repress genes, only $-\gamma_i^u \Xi_i^u x_i$ is considered in the examples of this article. Note that γ^u is defined as a drug-effect factor, which is closely related to the drug pharmacology model discussed in the following section.

It should be kept in mind that the focus of this article is studying the effect of dosing, in particular, dosing regimens, on the expression of genes involved in a pathology by using hybrid systems theory. Whereas the simpler Equation (1) is widely accepted, it does not contain drug-effect terms. Equation (2) extends Equation (1) by including such terms. While the structure is intuitively reasonable and somewhat general, the actual details of the drug-effect terms are unknown. Finding the specific form of Equation (2) for a specific disease is a system identification problem, which is quite distinct from the analysis problem addressed in this article. We are addressing optimization of treatment intervention, given the system. The details of our analysis might change when the details of Equation (2) are clarified, but we expect that the hybrid systems approach taken in the article will go through with appropriate modifications in the mathematical details.

We consider a 2-gene example to illustrate the feasibility of using hybrid systems for modeling drug effect. Specifically, we assume that there are two interactive genes x_1, x_2 that repress each other, and x_1 is a disease gene which loses its self-regulation. We also assume that a drug targets x_1 by reducing its expression level and providing a negative feedback term $-\gamma_1^u x_1$. The resulting 2-gene network is given by

$$\dot{x}_1 = \beta_1 s^-(x_2, \theta_2^1) - \gamma_1^u x_1 \qquad (4)$$
$$\dot{x}_2 = \beta_2 s^-(x_1, \theta_1^2) - \gamma_2 x_2 \qquad (5)$$

where β_1, β_2 are synthesis factors, γ_2 is a degradation factor, and θ_1^2, θ_2^1 are threshold values. γ_1^u is a drug-effect factor. Using dynamical systems theory, the state-trajectory schematic diagrams of this 2-gene network without and with drug input are obtained and plotted in Figures 1 and 2, respectively. It is observed that without drug input, the gene expression level of x_1 increases unbounded, while

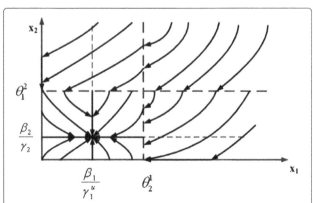

Figure 2 State trajectory schematic of 2-gene example *with* drug intake.

with proper drug input, $\beta_1/\gamma_1^u < \theta_1^2$, the system converges to a new steady state, $(\beta_1/\gamma_1^u, \beta_2/\gamma_2)$.

We assume periodic drug intake and the drug concentration level in the effect-site follows exponential decay during each period τ_i, i.e., $u_i(t) = \zeta_i e^{-\lambda_d(t-k\tau_i)}$, where $k\tau_i \leq t \leq (k+1)\tau_i$ and λ_d is the degradation factor. The response of gene expression levels of the two genes under periodic drug intake is shown in Figure 3. The state-space trajectory of gene expression level of x_1 vs. the drug concentration level u is given in Figure 4. A comparison of trajectory of the gene expression level x_1 vs. x_2 with and without drug are provided in Figures 5 and 6, respectively. It is observed that the drug is quite effective in bringing down the expression level of x_1. The simulation study matches the theoretical analysis, as in Figures 1 and 2, that with proper drug intervention the system will converge to a new steady state, $x_1 = \beta_1/\gamma_1^u$ and $x_2 = \beta_2/\gamma_2 = 1$, while $x_2 \to 0$ and $x_1 \to \infty$ without drug input.

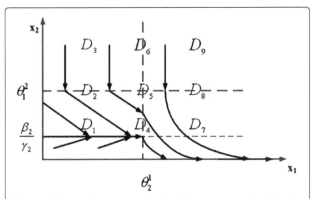

Figure 1 State trajectory schematic of 2-gene example *without* drug intake.

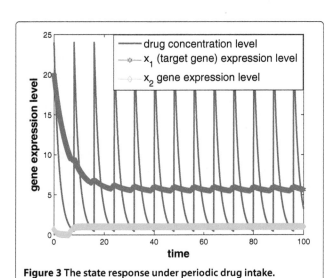

Figure 3 The state response under periodic drug intake.

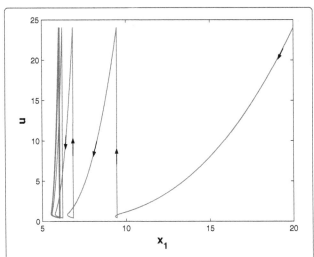

Figure 4 The state-space trajectory under periodic drug intake.
Parameter setting of Figures 3 and 4: $x_1(0) = 20$, $x_2(0) = 0.7$, $\tau = 8$, $u(k\tau) = 24$, $q_1^u = 0.21$, $\beta_1 = \beta_2 = 1$, $\gamma_2 = 1$, $\theta_1^2 = 10$, $\theta_2^1 = 2$, $\lambda_d = 0.5$.

Pharmacology model

The basis of clinical pharmacology is the fact that the intensities of many pharmacological effects are functions of the amount of drug in the body and, more specifically, the concentration of drug at the effect-site [5]. Historically, PK and PD were considered as separate disciplines; however, the information provided by these disciplines is limited if regarded in isolation [25]. A drug-effect factor γ^u is included in our proposed model (Equation 2), which is related to drug's PD characteristic (concentration–response) and its PK information (dose–concentration). In order to describe the time course of drug effect in response to different dosing regimens, the

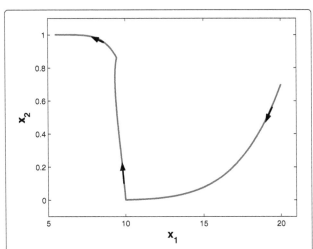

Figure 5 The state-space trajectory *with* drug: $\tau = 8$, $u(k\tau) = 24$, $q_1^u = 0.21$, $\lambda_d = 0.5$. The rest parameter settings are the same with Figures 3 and 4.

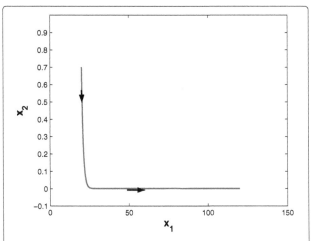

Figure 6 The state-space trajectory *without* drug intake. The rest parameter settings are the same with Figures 3 and 4.

integrated PK/PD model is indispensable because it builds the bridge between these two classical disciplines of pharmacology [25]. Following each dosing regimen, instead of a two-dimensional PK and PD relationship, the proposed approach enables a description of a three-dimensional dose–concentration–effect relationship. Specifically, PK and PD are linked through γ^u by a state-space approach to facilitate the description and prediction of the time course of drug effects resulting from different drug administration regimens.

Drug concentration–response curve: PD model

In general, the magnitude of a pharmacological effect increases monotonically with increased dose, eventually reaching a plateau level where further increase in dose has little additional effect [6]. The classic and most commonly used concentration–response model is the Hill equation [26], also known as the sigmoidal $E_{\max}$ model [27] or logistic model [28]. The relationship between the concentration of the drug and its effect is most often nonlinear. In this study, we use hybrid systems to approximate PD curves. A common method is to replace certain slowly changing variables by their piecewise linear approximations (see Figure 7). For example, the PD model used in our study can approximate the popular sigmoidal $E_{\max}$ model (see Figure 8). The $E_{\max}$ model has the general form $E = \frac{E_{\max}C^m}{EC_{50}^m + C^m}$, where $E_{\max}$ is the maximum effect, C is the concentration, EC_{50} is the concentration necessary to produce 50% of $E_{\max}$, and m represents a sigmoidity factor or steepness of the curve.

We assume a threshold of concentration below which the drug candidate is ineffective, the minimum effective dose (MinED), and another threshold value, called maximum effective dose (MaxED), above which there is no clinically significant increase in pharmacological effect in

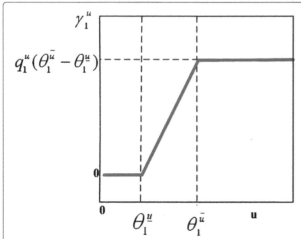

Figure 7 The PD model: concentration-response curve used in this study.

this study. As an example, we use a linear curve to approximate the concentration–response curve between MinED and MaxED. It is assumed that the drug-effect coefficient γ_1^u (the drug target is x_1) is related to the concentration u through a sigmoid function and can be approximated by the curve shown in Figure 7. The corresponding relationship can be expressed as

$$\gamma_1^u = \begin{cases} 0 & u < \theta_1^{\underline{u}} \\ q_1^u(u - \theta_1^{\underline{u}}) & \theta_1^{\underline{u}} \le u \le \theta_1^{\overline{u}} \\ q_1^u(\theta_1^{\overline{u}} - \theta_1^{\underline{u}}) & u > \theta_1^{\overline{u}} \end{cases}, \tag{6}$$

where q_1^u is the ratio between the drug-effect factor γ_1^u and the effective drug concentration $u - \theta_1^{\underline{u}}$ in the linear range. This reflects the fact that the drug only starts to take effect when its concentration level is above a lower threshold $\theta_1^{\underline{u}}$ and its effect saturates when its concentration level

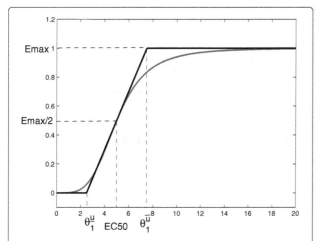

Figure 8 Sigmoidal E_{max} model ($m = 4$), and approximation by our PD model.

exceeds an upper threshold $\theta_1^{\overline{u}}$. Note that the sigmoidal E_{max} model can be well approximated by the proposed PD model. By taking the derivative of E with respect to C and evaluating it at EC_{50}, we obtain the slope as $q_1^u = \frac{mE_{\text{max}}}{4EC_{50}}$. The upper and lower bounds should satisfy $q_1^u(\theta_1^{\overline{u}} - \theta_1^{\underline{u}}) = E_{\text{max}}$. An example of the sigmoidal E_{max} model when $m = 4$ and our proposed PD model are plotted together in Figure 8, where the proposed model closely resembles the sigmoidal E_{max} model.

Periodic drug intake: PK model

Drug concentration at the effect-site is critical for its pharmacological effect. Currently, plasma drug concentrations are markers that serve as surrogates for drug concentration at the effect-site for beneficial and adverse effects; however, markers not grounded on a sound theoretical foundation and therapeutic mechanism-based intervention can limit the usefulness of PK/PD modeling to drug development. For example, it has been demonstrated that the intracellular PK of a drug is quite different from plasma drug concentration [29,30]. As observed in the study by Kuh et al. [29], the intracellular concentration of a drug will exponentially increase as the drug is absorbed after each drug intake. The drug concentration may change very slowly (in our model, we approximate that as a flat curve) when the intracellular and extracellular drug concentration approach equilibrium. In time, drug concentration will exponentially decrease as the rate at which it is eliminated is more than the rate at which it enters the effect-site and, as a result, effects diminish.

Based on the study by Kuh et al. [29], a general model for drug concentration-time profile is given in Figure 9. Drug concentration is plotted on a logarithmic scale against time following each periodic drug intake. λ_a denotes the exponential increase quotient; λ_d is the exponential decrease quotient; τ is the interval between each drug intake; and p_1, p_2, and p_3 denote the time stayed in the increase, equilibrium, and decrease stage, respectively. Different drugs work in different ways and the proposed model is general enough to cover various cases. Drug concentration may increase very quickly and, as a result, the increase stage may be neglected, or the equilibrium stage may be very short and can be ignored for simplicity. By adjusting the parameters in the proposed model, specific drug characteristics can be represented. In the case when the proposed model cannot approximate a drug's PK profile, extensive simulations can be performed based on the drug's actual PK profile. In this article, we consider a periodic drug intake scenario. Specifically, we are interested in investigating and comparing the following two potential scenarios: large dose with a longer interval versus small dose with a shorter interval.

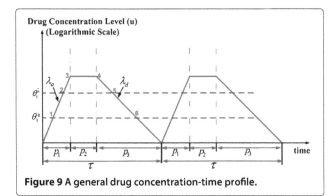

Figure 9 A general drug concentration-time profile.

Mathematical analysis of drug effect

In this section, we study the time course of drug effect for different dosage and schedule arrangements where the drug is designed to repress a "target gene". The case with a special PK profile (drug concentration only has exponential decay) was analytically studied in our previous work [22]. In this study, we extend the analysis considering a general PK profile given in Figure 9 and PD model given in Figure 8. Closed-form analytical solution is provided and simulations are performed to validate theoretical analysis. In later sections, we show that the same methodology can be applied to interactive genes, where not only will the drug affect the gene expression level, but the target gene is also coupled with other genes.

It is assumed that the disease gene has lost part of its self-regulation capacity and the dynamical equation of the expression level x_1 is given by

$$\dot{x}_1 = \beta_1 - \gamma_1 x_1. \tag{7}$$

There is a steady state $x_1 = \beta_1/\gamma_1$ in such a system, however, if the synthesis rate is much bigger than the self-degradation rate, $\beta_1 \gg \gamma_1$, then the gene expression level will be too high. A drug is used as a control input to repress the target gene expression level. The corresponding dynamical equation after drug intake is changed to

$$\dot{x}_1 = \beta_1 - \gamma_1 x_1 - \gamma_1^u x_1, \tag{8}$$

where γ_1^u is the drug-effect factor defined in the previous section. After incorporating a drug's PK/PD (Figures 7 and 9) into our proposed hybrid system model Equation (8), considering the scenario that the patient is taking the drug periodically, the resulting model is given by

$$\dot{x}_1 = \beta_1 - \gamma_1 x_1 - q_1^{u_i}(u_i - \theta_1^{u_i})s^+(u_i, \theta_1^{u_i})s^-(u_i, \theta_1^{\overline{u}_i})x_1$$
$$\quad - q_1^{u_i}(\theta_1^{\overline{u}_i} - \theta_1^{u_i})s^+(u_i, \theta_1^{\overline{u}_i})x_1,$$
$$u_i(t) = (e^{\lambda_a(t-k\tau_i)} - 1)s^-(t, k\tau_i + p_1)$$
$$\quad + \zeta_i s^-(t, k\tau_i + p_1 + p_2)s^+(t, k\tau_i + p_1)$$
$$\quad + \zeta_i e^{-\lambda_d(t-k\tau_i-p_1-p_2)}s^+(t, k\tau_i + p_1 + p_2)s^-(t, (k+1)\tau_i),$$
$$\tag{9}$$

where for $k\tau_i \leq t \leq (k+1)\tau_i$ and $i = 1, 2, \ldots$ denoting the index of different dosing regimens, $q_1^{u_i} = q_1^u, \theta_1^{u_i} = \theta_1^u$, $\theta_1^{\overline{u}_i} = \theta_1^{\overline{u}}$, for any i, since we assume that the same drug is taken in different dosage and schedule settings. ζ_i is the highest concentration level reached after taking the drug.

State-space analysis

The state-space and a sample trajectory schematic of the state (target gene expression and drug concentration level) under periodic drug intake are shown in Figure 10. As is common in hybrid systems, there are both continuous quantitative changes and discrete transitions in our proposed model. The entire state space may be divided into different domains according to the value of discrete state. As shown in Figure 10, there are five domains in the state space, with D_1, D_3, D_5 not being transient domains. The figure shows the case when the drug is effective and the drug dosage is large enough that ζ_i is higher than the upper threshold $\theta_1^{\overline{u}}$. The sample trajectory of the state corresponds to two periods of drug intake (numbers 1–6 corresponding to the junctions of the drug concentration and the boundaries of the domains, also marked in Figure 9). Another possible scenario is that the drug dosage is not large enough that ζ_i is between the upper threshold $\theta_1^{\overline{u}}$ and the lower threshold θ_1^{u}. The third scenario is the case that $\zeta_i < \theta_1^{u}$ and the drug is not effective.

When the state transits in each period under periodic drug intake, it may pass through different domains (depending on the changes of drug concentration along time). During the transit time through domains D_5 and D_3, the gene expression level is pushed lower (to the left), while the driving strength will depend on the drug's PD characteristic. During the transit time through D_1, the expression level will rise (to the right), since the drug concentration is lower than θ_1^{u}. For the drug to be effective, the reduction of the expression level in D_5 and D_3 has to be larger than the increase of the expression level in D_1. In summary, we should have $x_1((k+1)\tau) < x_1(k\tau)$,

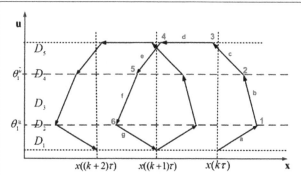

Figure 10 The state trajectory schematic (target gene expression versus drug concentration) under PK profile (Figure 9) assuming dose $> \theta_1^{\overline{u}}$.

so that after each treatment the expression level x_1 will decrease.

State trajectory analysis

We analyze the drug effect considering the scenario shown in Figure 10, where $\zeta_i > \theta_1^{\overline{u}}$. The same methodology can be applied to a simpler scenario where $\theta_1^{u} < \zeta_i < \theta_1^{\overline{u}}$. We divide the state trajectory in a period $k\tau_i \leq t \leq (k+1)\tau_i$ into stages a, b, c, d, e, f, and g as marked in Figure 10 and examine the drug effect stage-by-stage. The time notations used in the derivation are given by

- t_1: the traveling time from the initial state to the boundary between D_3 and D_1.
- t_2: from initial state to boundary between D_5 and D_3.
- t_3: from initial state to the end of stage c, $t_3 = k\tau_i + p_1$.
- t_4: time at which the drug concentration starts to decrease, $t_4 = k\tau_i + p_1 + p_2$.
- t_5: from the initial state to the end of stage e.
- t_6: from the initial state to the end of stage f.

For $k\tau_i \leq t \leq (k+1)\tau_i$, where i is the index for different dosing regimens, the corresponding equations and solutions for each stage are given by:

- **Stage (a)** - D_1 ($k\tau_i \leq t \leq t_1$):

$$\dot{x}_1 = \beta_1 - \gamma_1 x_1, \implies$$
$$x_1(t) = \frac{\beta_1}{\gamma_1} + \left[x_1(k\tau_i) - \frac{\beta_1}{\gamma_1} \right] e^{-\gamma_1(t-k\tau_i)},$$
$$u_i(t) = e^{\lambda_a(t-k\tau_i)} - 1. \tag{10}$$

- **Stage (b)** - D_3 ($t_1 \leq t \leq t_2$):

$$\dot{x}_1 = \beta_1 - [\gamma_1 + q_1^u(u - \theta_1^u)] x_1 \implies$$
$$x_1(t) = \frac{x_1(t_1)A(t_1)}{A(t)}$$
$$+ \frac{1}{A(t)} \int_{t_1}^{t} \beta_1 e^{-[(q_1^u(1+\theta_1^u)-\gamma_1)\sigma - \frac{q_1^u}{\lambda_a}e^{\lambda_a(\sigma-k\tau_i)}]} d\sigma,$$
$$A(t) = e^{-[(q_1^u(1+\theta_1^u)-\gamma_1)t - \frac{q_1^u}{\lambda_a}e^{\lambda_a(t-k\tau_i)}]},$$
$$u_i(t) = e^{\lambda_a(t-k\tau_i)} - 1. \tag{11}$$

- **Stage (c)** - D_5 ($t_2 \leq t \leq t_3 = k\tau_i + p_1$):

$$\dot{x}_1 = \beta_1 - [\gamma_1 + q_1^u(\theta_1^{\overline{u}} - \theta_1^u)] x_1 \implies$$
$$x_1(t) = \frac{\beta_1}{\gamma_1 + q_1^u(\theta_1^{\overline{u}} - \theta_1^u - \theta_1^u)}$$
$$+ \left[x_1(t_2) - \frac{\beta_1}{\gamma_1 + q_1^u(\theta_1^u)} \right] \tag{12}$$
$$\times e^{-[\gamma_1 + q_1^u(\theta_1^{\overline{u}} - \theta_1^u)](t-t_2)},$$
$$u_i(t) = e^{\lambda_a(t-k\tau_i)} - 1$$

- **Stage (d)** - D_5 ($t_3 \leq t \leq t_4 = k\tau_i + p_1 + p_2$):

$$\dot{x}_1 = \beta_1 - [\gamma_1 + q_1^u(\theta_1^{\overline{u}} - \theta_1^u)] x_1 \implies$$
$$x_1(t) = \frac{\beta_1}{\gamma_1 + q_1^u(\theta_1^{\overline{u}} - \theta_1^u)}$$
$$+ \left[x_1(t_3) - \frac{\beta_1}{\gamma_1 + q_1^u(\theta_1^{\overline{u}} - \theta_1^u)} \right] \tag{13}$$
$$\times e^{-[\gamma_1 + q_1^u(\theta_1^{\overline{u}} - \theta_1^u)](t-t_3)},$$
$$u_i(t) = u_i^{\max} = \zeta_i$$

- **Stage (e)** - D_5 ($t_4 \leq t \leq t_5$):

$$\dot{x}_1 = \beta_1 - [\gamma_1 + q_1^u(\theta_1^{\overline{u}} - \theta_1^u)] x_1 \implies$$
$$x_1(t) = \frac{\beta_1}{\gamma_1 + q_1^u(\theta_1^{\overline{u}} - \theta_1^u)}$$
$$+ \left[x_1(t_4) - \frac{\beta_1}{\gamma_1 + q_1^u(\theta_1^{\overline{u}} - \theta_1^u)} \right] \tag{14}$$
$$\times e^{-[\gamma_1 + q_1^u(\theta_1^{\overline{u}} - \theta_1^u)](t-t_4)},$$
$$u_i(t) = \zeta_i e^{-\lambda_d(t-t_4)}.$$

- **Stage (f)** - D_3 ($t_5 \leq t \leq t_6$):

$$\dot{x}_1 = \beta_1 - [\gamma_1 + q_1^u(u - \theta_1^u)] x_1 \implies$$
$$x_1(t) = \left[x_1(t_5)e^{-[\frac{q_1^u}{\lambda_d}\theta_1^{\overline{u}} + (q_1^u\theta_1^u - \gamma_1)t_5]} \right.$$
$$\left. + \int_{t_5}^{t} \beta_1 e^{-[\frac{q_1^u}{\lambda_d}\theta_1^{\overline{u}}e^{-\lambda_d(\sigma-t_5)} + (q_1^u\theta_1^u - \gamma_1)\sigma]} d\sigma \right]$$
$$\times e^{[\frac{q_1^u}{\lambda_d}\theta_1^{\overline{u}}e^{-\lambda_d(t-t_5)} + (q_1^u\theta_1^u - \gamma_1)t]},$$
$$u_i(t) = \theta_1^{\overline{u}} e^{-\lambda_d(t-t_5)}. \tag{15}$$

- **Stage (g)** - D_1 ($t_6 \leq t \leq (k+1)\tau_i$):

$$\dot{x}_1 = \beta_1 - \gamma_1 x_1 \implies$$
$$x_1(t) = \frac{\beta_1}{\gamma_1} + \left[x_1(t_6) - \frac{\beta_1}{\gamma_1} \right] e^{-\gamma_1(t-t_6)},$$
$$u_i(t) = \theta_1^{u} e^{-\lambda_d(t-t_6)}. \tag{16}$$

We can deduce the necessary and sufficient condition for the effectiveness of the drug by expressing the inequality $x_1((k+1)\tau) < x_1(k\tau)$ in terms of dosing period τ and unit dose, assuming the dosage is proportional to the maximum drug concentration ζ_i reached after taking the drug. When the initial conditions are $x_1 = x_1(k\tau_i)$, the equations governing the state trajectory from time $k\tau_i$ to time $(k+1)\tau_i$ are given by

$$x_1(t_1) = \frac{\beta_1}{\gamma_1} + \left[x_1(k\tau_i) - \frac{\beta_1}{\gamma_1}\right]e^{-\gamma_1(t_1-k\tau_i)}, \qquad (17)$$

$$x_1(t_2) = \frac{x_1(t_1)A(t_1)}{A(t_2)} + \frac{1}{A(t_2)}$$
$$\times \int_{t_1}^{t_2} \beta_1 e^{-[(q_1^u(1+\theta_1^u)-\gamma_1)\sigma - \frac{q_1^u}{\lambda_a}e^{\lambda_a(\sigma - k\tau_i)}]}d\sigma, \qquad (18)$$

$$A(t_2) = e^{-[(q_1^u(1+\theta_1^u)-\gamma_1)t_2 - \frac{q_1^u}{\lambda_a}e^{\lambda_a(t_2-c)}]},$$

$$x_1(t_5) = \frac{\beta_1}{\gamma_1 + q_1^u(\theta_1^{\overline{u}} - \theta_1^u)}$$
$$+ \left[x_1(t_2) - \frac{\beta_1}{\gamma_1 + q_1^u(\theta_1^{\overline{u}} - \theta_1^u)}\right] \qquad (19)$$
$$e^{-[\gamma_1 + q_1^u(\theta_1^{\overline{u}} - \theta_1^u)](t_5-t_2)},$$

$$x_1(t_6) = \left[x_1(t_5)e^{-[\frac{q_1^u}{\lambda_d}\theta_1^{\overline{u}} + (q_1^u\theta_1^u - \gamma_1)t_5]}\right.$$
$$\left. + \int_{t_5}^{t_6} \beta_1 e^{-[\frac{q_1^u}{\lambda_d}\theta_1^{\overline{u}}e^{-\lambda_d(\sigma-t_5)} + (q_1^u\theta_1^u - \gamma_1)\sigma]}d\sigma\right]$$
$$e^{[\frac{q_1^u}{\lambda_d}\theta_1^{\overline{u}}e^{-\lambda_d(t_6-t_5)} + (q_1^u\theta_1^u - \gamma_1)t_6]}, \qquad (20)$$

$$x_1((k+1)\tau_i) = \frac{\beta_1}{\gamma_1} + \left[x_1(t_6) - \frac{\beta_1}{\gamma_1}\right]e^{-\gamma_1((k+1)\tau_i - t_6)}, \quad (21)$$

$$t_1 = k\tau_i + \frac{1}{\lambda_a}\ln(1 + \theta_1^u), \qquad (22)$$

$$t_2 = k\tau_i + \frac{1}{\lambda_a}\ln(1 + \theta_1^{\overline{u}}), \qquad (23)$$

$$p_1 = \frac{1}{\lambda_a}ln(1 + \zeta_i), \qquad (24)$$

$$t_5 = k\tau_i + p_1 + p_2 + \frac{1}{\lambda_d}\ln\left(\frac{\zeta_i}{\theta_1^{\overline{u}}}\right), \qquad (25)$$

$$t_6 = t_5 - \frac{1}{\lambda_d}\ln\left(\frac{\theta_1^u}{\theta_1^{\overline{u}}}\right), \qquad (26)$$

For the drug to be effective, we need the disease gene expression level to decrease following each period of drug intake. Hence, we can express $x_1((k+1)\tau) < x_1(k\tau)$ in terms of dosage and frequency schedule and derive the region where the drug is effective using the above listed equations.

Results and analysis

Based on the theoretical analysis in previous two sections, we demonstrate that the drug efficacy depends on total drug intake, different dosages, and frequencies. The density of drug intake is defined as $\alpha = \frac{Dose1}{\tau_1} = \frac{Dose2}{\tau_2}$. It is proportional to the total drug intake, and hence, related to the drug toxicity level in practice. First, we demonstrate the effect of total drug intake (equivalently, α) towards drug efficacy. For each fixed total drug intake, we plot the target gene expression reduction based on Equations 17 to 26 for different dosing period τ as a curve in Figure 11. It is observed that the curve is "U" shaped and there exist "sweet spot" for certain dosages and schedules given a fixed α. If we define *drug efficacy region* (DER) as the drug drives down the target gene expression by more than a desired percentage (say 60% in this case), it is demonstrated that the DER is related to the total drug intake, dosing period τ and dosage. DER is marked by the shaded area in Figure 11 for the case that $\alpha \leq 0.5$. It is also observed that when α gets bigger, which indicating more toxicity, DER is getting bigger accordingly. We would like to emphasize that toxicity is one of the primary causes for drug attrition and long development cycle times [31]. If a drug's toxicity profile is available, for example, the maximum dosage and maximum exposure (α), we can find a good compromise between toxicity and drug efficacy based on such study, and determine the "sweet spot" (a good dosage and schedule balance) given the obtained α, and hence provide valuable suggestions of the dosing regimens to the clinical study.

Second, we test the analytical results via numerical simulation using MATLAB/SIMULINK. Given a fixed total drug intake, or equivalently, a fixed density of drug intake ($\alpha = 0.4$), three typical scenarios are studied by simulation: small frequent drug intake with $\tau = 7$ and $dose = 2.8$; big infrequent drug intake with $\tau = 22$ and $dose = 8.8$; and intermediate dosage and frequency with $\tau = 12$ and $dose = 4.8$. The results are shown in Figure 12a–f, with the first row corresponding to the state responses and the second row corresponding to the state space trajectory. Although the three cases have the same total drug intake and initial condition (initial gene expression level $x(0) = 20$), the drug efficacy is different. In the small frequent intake case, the dosage is small and the drug concentration is mostly changing between domains D_3 and D_1. Figure 12d shows that the state-space trajectory settles in a small limit cycle and disease gene expression level settles at 11.5 at the end of each period of treatment. On the other hand, the big infrequent drug intake case results in a big limit cycle as in Figure 12f. Although the dosage is high, the long period between dosages means that the period stayed in D_1 is getting longer (where drug concentration is below θ_1^u, hence not effective), and disease gene expression level settles at 12.1 at the end of each

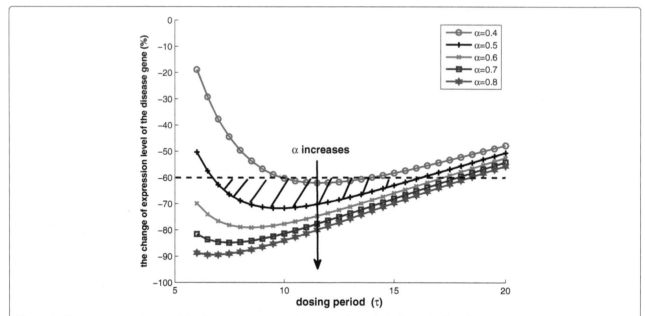

Figure 11 The percentage change of the disease gene expression versus the period of drug intake τ for $\alpha = 0.4, 0.5, 0.6, 0.7, 0.8$, respectively. The change must be significant (say at least 60%) and α must be smaller than the acceptable toxic level. Parameters used: $q_1^u = 0.1$, $\beta_1 = 1$, $\gamma_1 = 0.04$, $\theta_1^{\overline{u}} = 10$, $\theta_1^u = 2$, $x(0) = 20$; $p_1 = 1$; $p_2 = 5$; $\lambda_d = 0.3$.

period of treatment. As a comparison, the drug effect for the case with intermediate dosage and frequency shown in Figure 12b,e is superior to the other two cases. Disease gene expression level settles at 8.8 at the end of each treatment period. If we check the curve in Figure 11 with $\alpha = 0.4$, the intermediate dosage case with $\tau = 12$ is located near the bottom of the "U" shape. Lastly, we observe that all state-space trajectories follow the state trajectory schematic in Figure 10, as predicted by the analytical results.

Analysis of 2-gene networks

We extend the theoretical analysis to 2-gene networks and show that the same framework applies to the modeling and analysis of drug effect in more complex gene networks. We assume that x_1 is the target gene, there exists a positive feedback loop between x_1 and another gene x_2, and that a drug targets x_1 by reducing its expression level and providing a negative feedback term $-\gamma_1^u x_1$. The resulting 2-gene network is shown in Figure 13 and is given by

$$\dot{x}_1 = \beta_1 + \eta_1 x_2 - \gamma_1 x_1 - \gamma_1^u x_1$$
$$\dot{x}_2 = \beta_2 + \eta_2 x_1 - \gamma_2 x_2 \qquad (27)$$

where β_1, β_2 are synthesis factors, γ_1 and γ_2 are degradation factors, and γ_1^u is a drug-effect factor. $\eta_1 > 0$ and $\eta_2 > 0$ are the parameters of the positive feedback loop between the two genes. The 2-gene network under

drug perturbation model, Equation (27), can be rewritten as a second-order ODE:

$$\ddot{x}_1 + (\gamma_1 + \gamma_1^u + \gamma_2)\dot{x}_1 + ((\gamma_1 + \gamma_1^u)\gamma_2 - \eta_1\eta_2)x_1 = \beta_1\gamma_2 + \beta_2\eta_1 \qquad (28)$$

The solution of this equation is given by

$$x_1(t) = \begin{cases} k_1 e^{\lambda_1 t} + k_2 e^{\lambda_2 t} & \lambda_1 \neq \lambda_2 \\ k_1 e^{\lambda_1 t} + k_2 t e^{\lambda_1 t} & \lambda_1 = \lambda_2 \end{cases}, \qquad (29)$$

where λ_1 and λ_2 are the two eigenvalues of Equation 28 and k_1 and k_2 are parameters depending on the initial conditions. Letting $a = \gamma_1 + \gamma_1^u + \gamma_2$, $b = (\gamma_1 + \gamma_1^u)\gamma_2 - \eta_1\eta_2$ and $d = \beta_1\gamma_2 + \beta_2\eta_1$, the two eigenvalues are given by $\lambda_{1,2} = \frac{-a \pm \sqrt{a^2 - 4b}}{2}$. It is easy to verify that $a^2 - 4b = (\gamma_1 + \gamma_1^u - \gamma_2)^2 + 4\eta_1\eta_2 > 0$. Since $a^2 - 4b > 0$, we conclude that $\lambda_1 \neq \lambda_2$ and both eigenvalues are real. Furthermore, one of the eigenvalues, λ_2, is always negative since $\lambda_2 = \frac{-a - \sqrt{a^2 - 4b}}{2} < 0$. The sign of λ_1 will be determined by the sign of b:

$$\begin{array}{l} \lambda_1 < 0, \text{ if } b > 0 \\ \lambda_1 = 0, \text{ if } b = 0 \\ \lambda_1 > 0, \text{ if } b < 0 \end{array} \qquad (30)$$

In other words,

$$\begin{array}{l} \lambda_1 < 0, \ \lambda_2 < 0 \text{ if } (\gamma_1 + \gamma_1^u)\gamma_2 > \eta_1\eta_2 \\ \lambda_1 = 0, \ \lambda_2 < 0 \text{ if } (\gamma_1 + \gamma_1^u)\gamma_2 = \eta_1\eta_2 \\ \lambda_1 > 0, \ \lambda_2 < 0 \text{ if } (\gamma_1 + \gamma_1^u)\gamma_2 < \eta_1\eta_2 \end{array} \qquad (31)$$

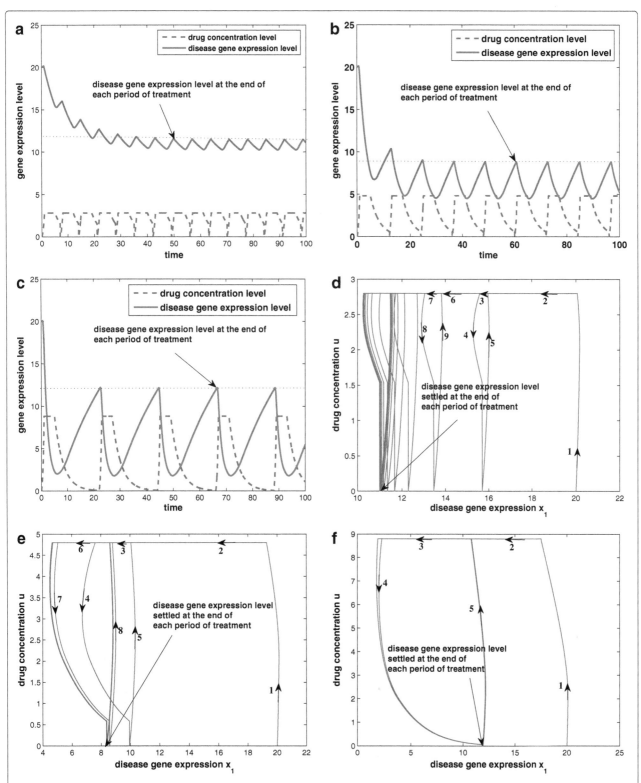

Figure 12 Drug response at three different schedules but same drug intake: (a–c) the state response at $\tau = 7, 12, 22$, respectively; (d–f) the state space trajectory at $\tau = 7, 12, 22$, respectively. Other parameters are $q_1^u = 0.1$, $\beta_1 = 1$, $\gamma_1 = 0.04$, $\theta_1^{\bar{u}} = 10$, $\theta_1^u = 2$, $x(0) = 20$; $p_1 = 1$; $p_2 = 5$; $\lambda_d = 0.3$.

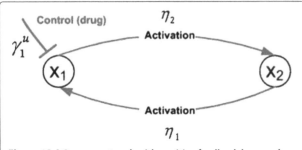

Figure 13 A 2-gene network with positive feedback loop and drug input.

The above equation has an important biological interpretation: when the degradation of x_1 due to the strength of the drug is faster than the increase of x_1 due to the positive feedback loop, both eigenvalues are negative, the system is stable and x_1 will experience exponential decay; on the other hand, if the effect of the positive feedback loop is dominant, then one of the eigenvalues will be positive and x_1 will increase exponentially.

Given initial condition $x_1(t_0)$ and $\dot{x}_1(t_0)$, then for the case $\lambda_1 \neq \lambda_2$, we have

$$k_1 = \frac{e^{-\lambda_1 t_0}}{\lambda_1 - \lambda_2}(d\lambda_2/b + \dot{x}_1(t_0) - \lambda_2 x_1(t_0)) \quad (32)$$

$$k_2 = \frac{e^{-\lambda_2 t_0}}{\lambda_2 - \lambda_1}(d\lambda_1/b + \dot{x}_1(t_0) - \lambda_1 x_1(t_0)) \quad (33)$$

Now with the baseline analysis of the second-order system, we provide detailed state trajectory analysis by taking into account the practical form of PK/PD (γ_1^u) when the drug is taken periodically.

State trajectory analysis
We analyze the drug-effect following the same framework given in the subsection "State trajectory analysis" under the main section "Mathematical analysis of drug effect". For $k\tau_i \leq t \leq (k+1)\tau_i$, $i = 1, 2, \ldots$, the corresponding equations and solutions for each stages are given as follows:

- **Stage (a)** - D_1 $(k\tau_i \leq t \leq t_1)$:

$$\dot{x}_1 = \beta_1 + \eta_1 x_2 - \gamma_1 x_1$$
$$\dot{x}_2 = \beta_2 + \eta_2 x_1 - \gamma_2 x_2$$
$$u_i(t) = e^{\lambda_a(t - k\tau_i)} - 1. \quad (34)$$

The solution of $x_1(t)$ is given by Equation (29), with k_1 and k_2 given by Equations (32) and (33), and $t_0 = k\tau_i$.

- **Stage (b)** - $D_3(t_1 \leq t \leq t_2)$:

$$\dot{x}_1 = \beta_1 + \eta_1 x_2 - \gamma_1 x_1 - \gamma_1^u x_1$$
$$\dot{x}_2 = \beta_2 + \eta_2 x_1 - \gamma_2 x_2$$
$$\Longrightarrow$$
$$\ddot{x}_1 + a\dot{x}_1 + bx_1 = d$$
$$u_i(t) = e^{\lambda_a(t - k\tau_i)} - 1 \quad (35)$$

where a, b, d are defined as before. When incorporating the practical form of $\gamma_1^u = q_1^u(u - \theta_1^u)$ and $u = e^{\lambda_a(t - k\tau_i)} - 1$, the above second-order ODE has no closed-form solution. In this case, the solution can be obtained numerically.

- **Stage (c)** - D_5 $(t_2 \leq t \leq t_3 = k\tau_i + p_1)$: The set of equations are the same as in Stage (b) except that $\gamma_1^u = q_1^u(\theta^{\bar{u}} - \theta_1^u)$. Since γ_1^u does *not* depend on $u = e^{\lambda_a(t - k\tau_i)} - 1$ explicitly, x_1 has a closed-form solution given by Equation (29).

- **Stage (d)** - D_5 $(t_3 \leq t \leq t_4 = k\tau_i + p_1 + p_2)$: The solution of x_1 is the same as that in Stage (c) except the start and end times, and the equation of u, which is $u_i(t) = u_i^{max} = \zeta_i$ in this stage.

- **Stage (e)** - D_5 $(t_4 \leq t \leq t_5)$: The solution of x_1 is the same as in Stage (c) except the start and end times, and the equation of u, which now is $u_i(t) = \zeta_i e^{-\lambda_d(t - t_4)}$.

- **Stage (f)** - D_3 $(t_5 \leq t \leq t_6)$: The solution of x_1 is the same as in Stage (b) except the start and end times, and the equation of u, which now is $u_i(t) = \theta_1^{\bar{u}} e^{-\lambda_d(t - t_5)}$.

- **Stage (g)** - D_1 $(t_6 \leq t \leq (k+1)\tau_i)$: The solution of x_1 is the same as in Stage (a) except the start and end times, and the equation of u, which now is $u_i(t) = \theta_1^u e^{-\lambda_d(t - t_6)}$.

We can deduce the necessary and sufficient condition for the effectiveness of the drug by expressing the inequality $x_1((k+1)\tau) < x_1(k\tau)$ in terms of dosing period τ and unit dose. In the 2-gene case, no explicit closed-form expression can be deduced for the solutions in stages (b) and (f) and numerical methods have to be applied. However, through such analysis, it is observed that the same methodology for analyzing drug effect can be extended to GRNs with multiple interactive genes, although the mathematics involved will become more complicated and sometimes numerical methods must be applied when there is no closed-form solution.

Simulation results and analysis
When drug input is not present, the disease gene expression will grow unbounded owing to the positive feedback loop between the two genes. Here, we study response of the disease gene expression to drug input and compare two different schedules for $\tau = 20$ and $\tau = 30$, keeping

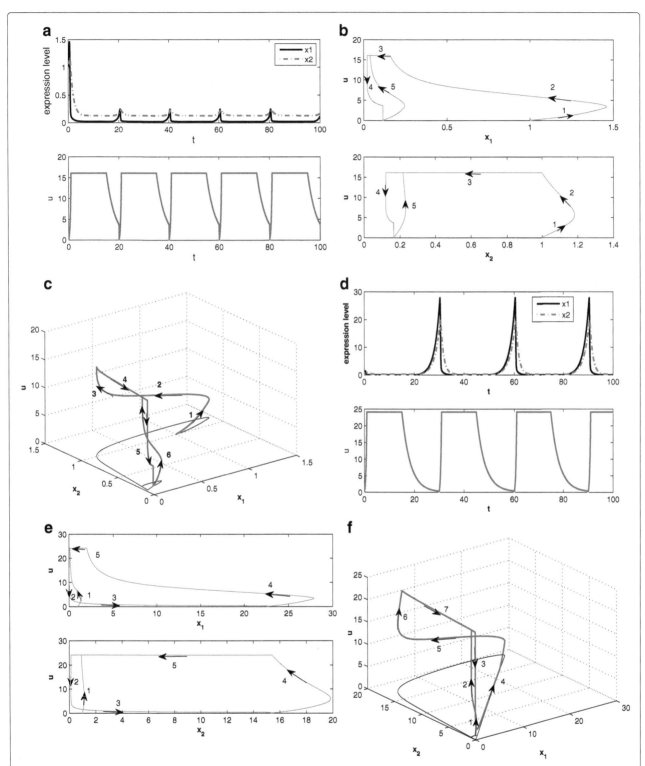

Figure 14 Drug response follows two different schedules but same drug intake ($\alpha = 0.8$): (a–c) the state response, state space trajectory, and 3D state-space trajectory at $\tau = 20$, respectively; (d–f) the state response, state space trajectory, and 3D state space trajectory at $\tau = 30$, respectively. Other parameters are $q_1^u = 2, \beta_1 = 0.1, \beta_2 = 0.1, \eta_1 = 1, \eta_2 = 1, \gamma_1 = 0.2, \gamma_2 = 1, \theta_1^{\overline{U}} = 8, \theta_1^u = 3, x_1(0) = 1, x_2(0) = 1, p_1 = 1, p_2 = 15, \lambda_d = 0.3$.

$\alpha = 0.8$ fixed. The response and state trajectories in 2D and 3D are given in Figure 14a–f, with the first and second rows corresponding to $\tau = 20$ and $\tau = 30$, respectively. We observe that both cases have periodic responses, but the disease gene expression is much better controlled when $\tau = 20$. This is because the drug concentration is high enough in both cases compared to the threshold ($\theta_1^{\overline{u}}$), while the decay of the drug concentration is shorter in the case when $\tau = 20$. In Figure 14c,f, the 3D state (disease gene expression) trajectories show that the trajectory settles to an inner circle when $\tau = 20$, whereas the trajectory settles to an outer circle when $\tau = 30$. Similar observations apply to Figure 14b,e. Note the scale of x-axis of Figure 14e is 20 times bigger than that of Figure 14b.

Extension and discussion

In previous sections, we have considered the drug-effect on one-gene and a 2-gene case. In this section, we will consider the drug-effect on a target gene in a more sophisticated GRN context.

3-gene network with multiple feedback loops

Suppose a 3-gene network is given by

$$\dot{x}_1 = \beta_1 s^-(x_2, \theta_2^1) - \gamma_1^u x_1 + \eta_1 x_3 \tag{36}$$

$$\dot{x}_2 = \beta_2 s^-(x_1, \theta_1^2) - \gamma_2 x_2 \tag{37}$$

$$\dot{x}_3 = \beta_3 s^-(x_2, \theta_2^3) - \gamma_3 s^-(x_1, \theta_1^3) x_3, \tag{38}$$

where η_1 is a perturbation parameter (from x_3 to x_1), β_1, β_2, β_3 are activation factors, γ_2, γ_3 are degradation factors, and θ_1^2, θ_2^1, θ_1^3, θ_2^3 are threshold values. γ_1^u is a drug-effect factor. We assume periodic drug intake and drug concentration level follows exponential decay during each period, i.e., $u_i(t) = \zeta_i e^{-\lambda_d(t-k\tau_i)}$, where $k\tau_i \leq t \leq (k+1)\tau_i$. A graphical model of the 3-gene network is given in Figure 15. There exist two positive feedback loops between x_1 and x_3.

When the target gene is in GRN context, not only its expression level is related to drug perturbation, but also depends on network contexts. Several interesting phenomena are observed through our simulations study:

1. Drug response is related to disease stage. Simulations are performed with different initial target gene expression level ($x_1(0)$). Figure 16a–c shows the system responses with $x_1(0) = 20$, which is not too high (corresponding to early disease state). As shown in Figure 16a, x_1 expression level reduces to the range $[7.7, 8.4]$ under periodic drug intake, while x_2 and x_3, the two other interactive genes settle at 1.0 and 4.0, respectively. The system reaches a new steady state (a semi-stable limit cycle, to be exact), with $x_1^s = \frac{\beta_1 + \eta_1 x_3^s}{\gamma_1^u} = \frac{\beta_1 + \eta_1 \beta_3 / \gamma_3}{\gamma_1^u}$, $x_2^s = \frac{\beta_2}{\gamma_2}$, and

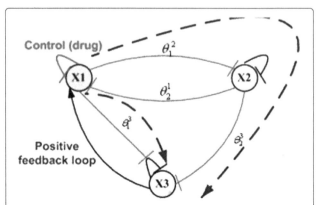

Figure 15 The 3-gene GRN model. The solid line is the real interaction between genes. The dashed line is derived to show the positive feedback loop for certain conditions.

$x_3^s = \frac{\beta_3}{\gamma_3}$, where x_1 is well controlled. The trajectories of x_1 vs. u and x_1 versus x_3 are given in Figure 16b,c, respectively. The semi-stable limit cycle is shown in Figure 16b.

System responses with $x_1(0) = 40$ (corresponding to late disease state) are shown in Figure 16d–f for comparison. Although the other parameter settings are exactly the same, the drug will not repress the disease gene x_1 (Figure 16d) owing to the interaction between the disease gene x_1 and gene x_3. When $x_1(0) = 20 < \theta_1^3 = 21$, Equation (36) becomes $\dot{x}_3 = \beta_3 s^-(x_2, \theta_2^3) - \gamma_3 x_3$, and thus x_3 is negative regulated by x_1 and converge to $x_3^s = \frac{\beta_3}{\gamma_3}$. However, when initial condition $x_1(0) = 40 > \theta_1^3 = 21$, Equation (36) becomes $\dot{x}_3 = \beta_3 s^-(x_2, \theta_2^3)$, and thus x_3 is positively regulated by x_2 and its expression level will keep increasing. As a result, x_1 will keep increasing as well, and a positive feedback loop is formed between x_1 and x_3. This is confirmed by the trajectories of x_1 versus u and x_1 versus x_3 given in Figure 16e,f, respectively.

2. Under certain conditions, single drug perturbation may not be enough. A drug is usually designed to a specific target. In this example, the drug tries to provide negative feedback to the regulation of x_1 (tries to repress x_1); however, since the target gene is interactive (or, in a more general setting, pathways have crosstalk), only repressing the target gene (or blocking the signal of one pathway) may not prevent the target gene from expressing itself through interactions with other genes (or through inter-connected pathways). In our case, x_1 is interactive with x_3. To continue with previous simulation (results shown in Figure 16d–f, we try to increase the drug dosage tenfold from $u(k\tau) = 24$ to $u(k\tau) = 240$ with the same dosing period $\tau = 8$

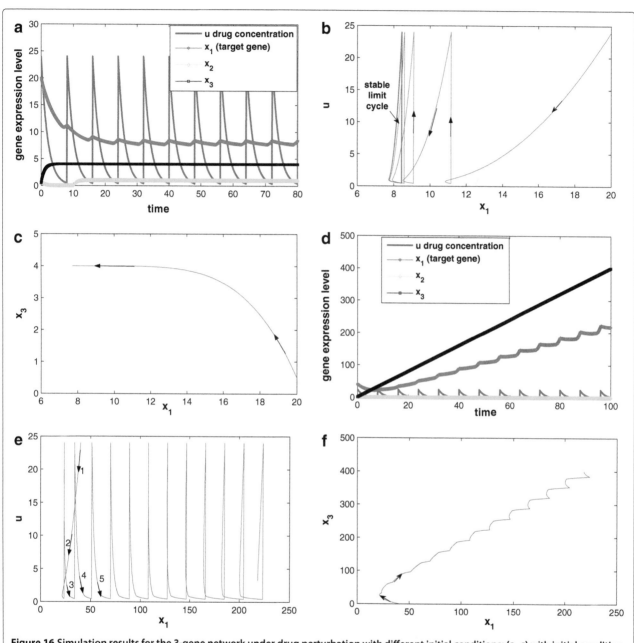

Figure 16 Simulation results for the 3-gene network under drug perturbation with different initial conditions: **(a–c)** with initial condition $(x_1(0) = 20)$, **(d–f)** with initial condition $(x_1(0) = 40)$. Other parameter settings are: $x_2(0) = 0.7$, $x_3(0) = 0.5$, $\tau = 8$, $u(k\tau) = 24$, $q_1^u = 0.21$, $\beta_1 = \beta_2 = 1$, $\beta_3 = 4$, $\gamma_2 = 1$, $\gamma_3 = 1$, $\theta_1^2 = 10$, $\theta_2^1 = 2$, $\theta_1^3 = 21$, $\theta_2^3 = 10$, $\eta_1 = 0.1$, $\lambda_d = 0.5$.

trying to bring down the expression level of x_1. However, from system responses shown in Figure 17a–c, it is observed that the drug is not effective although the dosage is increased tenfold. One step further, not only we increase dosage to $u(k\tau) = 240$, but also to increase the dosing frequency (dosing period is decreased from $\tau = 8$ to $\tau = 2$), systems responses are shown in Figure 18a–d, where Figure 18c shows the left part of the trajectory shown in Figure 18b. It can be

observed that although the drug perturbation is very strong, and the drug concentration is always staying in domain D_5, drug is still not effective.

From the nonlinear dynamical system perspective, the equation $x_1^s = \frac{\beta_1 + \eta_1 x_3^s}{\gamma_1^u} = \frac{\beta_1 + \eta_1 \beta_3 / \gamma_3}{\gamma_1^u}$ represents a semi-stable limit cycle. If the initial condition is from the inside of the limit cycle, then the system will converge to the limit cycle; however, if the initial condition is from the outside of the limit cycle, then the system will diverge from the

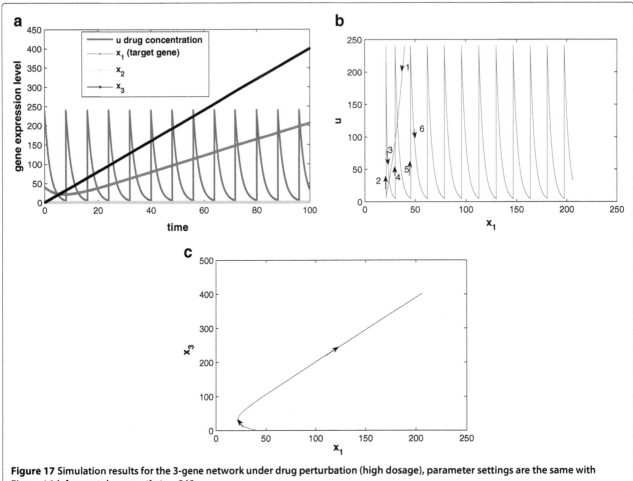

Figure 17 Simulation results for the 3-gene network under drug perturbation (high dosage), parameter settings are the same with Figure 16d–f except dosage $u(k\tau) = 240$.

limit cycle. Such simulation results demonstrate the heterogeneity of the drug's responses due to the nonlinearities in complex systems, where multiple inputs affect each output and the underpinning structure may include parallel, redundant, and feedback loop processes, it is likely that some cases will not respond to a single drug perturbation no matter how strong it is. As a result, innovative perturbation methods, such as finding a better target or combinatorial therapy, are necessary.

Simulation of effects of different drugs and a drug combination on $NF - \kappa B$ pathway

In this article, the models and examples are selected such that they are mathematically tractable and important insights can be obtained, and we can verify the theoretical results with simulation results. For large-scale networks and multiple drugs/drug targets, the proposed model is still applicable; however, analytical results may not be attainable even for this simplistic model. In that case, simulations can be carried out case-by-case. To illustrate this point of view, we carried out a simulation study of the

$NF - \kappa B$ pathway under two different drugs and each drug with different drug targets.

$NF - \kappa B$ signaling regulates inflammation, cell proliferation, and apoptosis by increasing the expression of specific cellular genes in response to a variety of extracellular ligands. How to explore therapeutic strategies to prevent the prolonged activation of the $NF - \kappa B$ pathway attracts lots of attention [32,33]. An ODE model of the $NF - \kappa B$ pathway [34] is adopted and the two drugs under consideration are drug X (drug A in [35]) and FDA approved drug proteasome inhibitor Bortezomib (Velcade) [36]. The detailed simulation setup is available in the Appendix and the SIMULINK model is given in Figure 19. The specificity of some drugs to inhibit several of these components of the $NF - \kappa B$ pathway is one of the concerns. For example, the proteasome which is responsible for the $I\kappa B\alpha$ degradation has many other important functions. Thus, Bortezomib modulates a variety of cellular processes that may contribute to toxicity if the dosage is too high [36]. Hence, we design combination therapy to induce a better effect and at the same time to contain toxicity to a certain threshold.

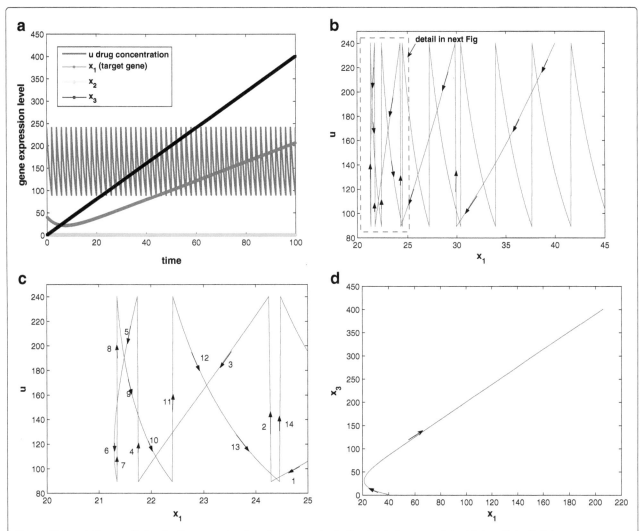

Figure 18 Simulation results for the 3-gene network under drug perturbation (high dosage and short interval): **(a-d)** state response, trajectory of x_1 versus u, detailed initial trajectory of x_1 versus u, and trajectory of x_1 versus x_3, **respectively.** Parameter settings are the same with Figure 16 except $u(k\tau) = 240$ and $\tau = 2$.

To achieve this, drug X is a protein kinase inhibitor, which competitively inhibit IKK with the binding kinetics the same as that of the natural reaction involving $NF - \kappa B : I\kappa B\alpha$ and IKK [35]. While Bortezomib is a proteasome inhibitor that will inhibit $I\kappa B\alpha$ degradation, its effect is adjusted through the parameter setting related to individual terms for $I\kappa B\alpha$ and $NF - \kappa B : I\kappa B\alpha$ molecules rescued from inhibition of $I\kappa B\alpha$ degradation [35]. We first validate the results in [34,35]. In Figure 20a, we show that oscillatory behaviors occur for $NF - \kappa B$ pathway with constant stimulus. Under this constant stimulus, it is observed in Figure 20b,c that only very high dose of drug X can effectively block $NF - \kappa B$ nuclear translocation. Similar observation is obtained for Bortezomib from Figure 20d,e, where low drug dosage (65% inhibition) is not effective, while the side effects

are unacceptable when the drug is effective (95% inhibition). All the above simulation results are consistent with those in [34,35]. In this article, we go a step further and consider the combination of these two drugs. It is interesting to see in Figure 20f that some combinations of the drugs with non-overlapping toxicities, e.g., combined Bortezomib (65% inhibition) and drug X (0.2 μM), might provide enormous benefit by keeping the level of nuclear $NF - \kappa B$ low while having tolerable toxicities.

Conclusions and future work

This article provides systematic mathematical analysis and dynamical modeling of drug effect in the GRN context, where a drug functions as a control input to reduce the elevated target gene expression level. A hybrid systems

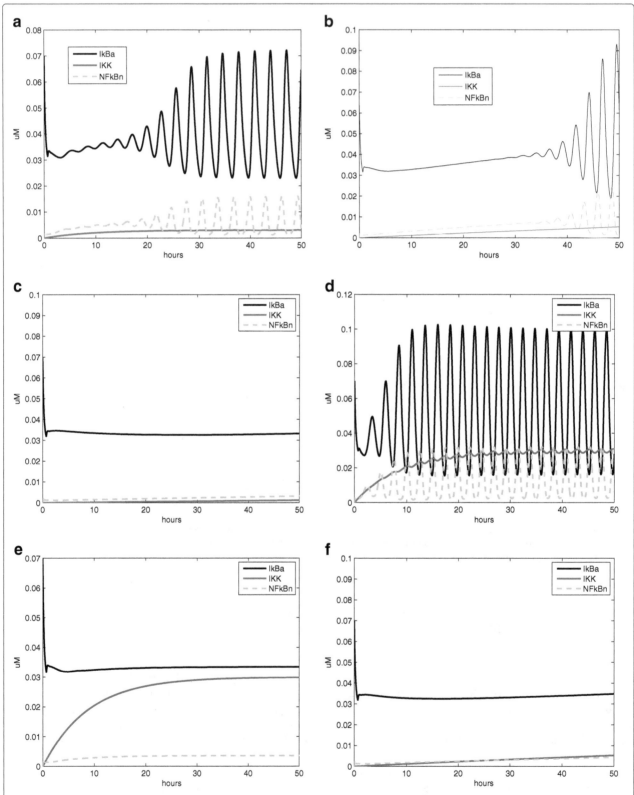

Figure 19 Simulation results for the $NF - \kappa B$ pathway under various drug perturbations with different drug administration. (a) Effect of continuous stimulus, no drug input. **(b)** Effect of drug X (0.2 μM). **(c)** Effect of drug X (1.0 μM). **(d)** Effect of Bortezomib (65% inhibition). **(e)** Effect of Bortezomib (95% inhibition). **(f)** Effect of combined Bortezomib (65% inhibition) and drug X (0.2 μM). The detailed parameters are available in the Appendix.

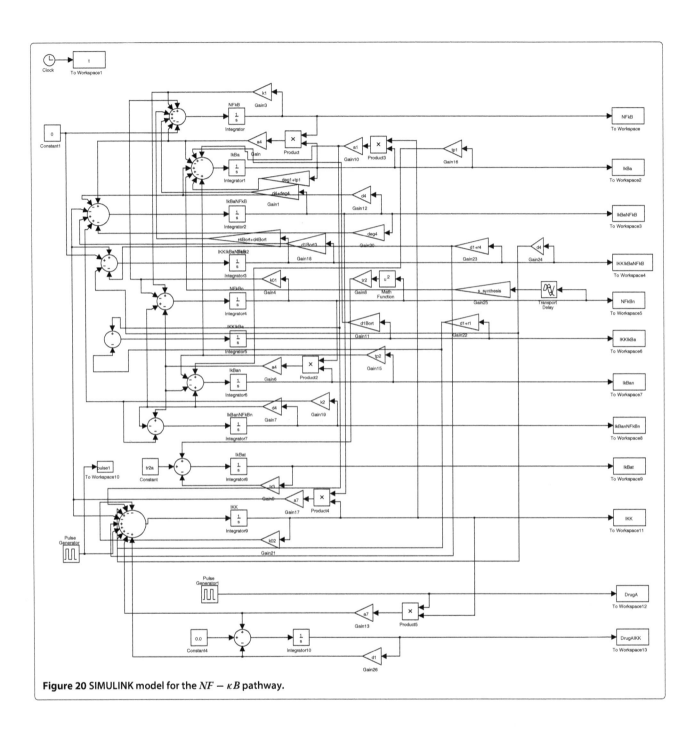

Figure 20 SIMULINK model for the $NF - \kappa B$ pathway.

model is proposed to study the dynamics of the underlying regulatory network under drug perturbation. Drug pharmacology information is incorporated into drug therapeutic response modeling to demonstrate the significant difference in drug effect for different dosing regimens. Considering the complicated nature of gene regulation, this study is a small step towards quantitative modeling of therapeutic effect. We have kept the examples mathematically tractable so that valuable insights and reasonable predictions can be obtained from theoretical analysis.

Compared to our previous work [22], where drug effect was only studied for a specific PK profile (drug concentration only has exponential decay stage) when the drug is targeted to a single gene, three major extensions are provided in this article: (i) we provide analytical results of drug effect under a very general PK profile, where three stages of drug concentration change (increase, equilibrium, and decrease) are considered; (ii) the proposed methodology is applied to interactive genes in a GRN context, with detailed analytical derivations

Table 1 Definition of variables

x_1	$NF - \kappa B$
x_2	$I\kappa B\alpha$
x_3	$I\kappa B\alpha : NF - \kappa B$
x_4	$NF - \kappa B_n$
x_5	$I\kappa B\alpha_n$
x_6	$I\kappa B\alpha_n : NF - \kappa B_n$
x_7	IKK
x_8	$IKK : I\kappa B\alpha$
x_9	$IKK : I\kappa B\alpha : NF - \kappa B$

for both one-gene and two-gene cases; and (iii) we perform extensive simulations for a more complicated GRN setting and explain several interesting observations due to multiple feedback loops and the existence of limit cycles.

It is expected that the theoretical framework proposed in this article, when correlated to real biological networks, can help improve drug development productivity and make drug discovery more systematic. During such process, cross disciplinary effort is indispensable. For example, application of such a framework will require experiments designed to elucidate model parameters, such as protein concentration levels and synthesis and degradation speeds. While some parameters may be relatively easy to obtain, others may be difficult to get based on current

techniques and model simplification may be necessary; nonetheless, the basic hybrid systems model and the conclusions drawn from it, such as the nature of DERs and the role of limit cycles, will remain valid, only their particular forms being changed to represent experimental instantiation of the model.

Appendix
See Tables 1 and 2.

ODE model of the $NF - \kappa B$ pathway
The ODE model of the $NF - \kappa B$ pathway is adopted from [34,35].

$$\frac{dx_1}{dt} = -a_4x_1x_2 + d_4x_3 - a_4x_1x_8 + (r_4 + d_4)x_9 \tag{39}$$
$$+ deg_4x_3 - k_1x_1 + k_{01}x_4$$

$$\frac{dx_2}{dt} = -a_1x_2x_7 + d_1x_8 - a_4x_1x_2 + d_4x_3 - deg_1x_2$$
$$- tp_1x_2 + tp_2x_5 + s_{\text{synthesis}}x_4(t - \tau) \tag{40}$$

$$\frac{dx_3}{dt} = a_4x_1x_2 - d_4x_3 - a_7x_3x_7 + d_1x_9 \tag{41}$$
$$+ k_2x_6 - deg_4x_3$$

$$\frac{dx_4}{dt} = k_1x_1 - a_4x_4x_5 + d_4x_6 - k_{01}x_4 \tag{42}$$

Table 2 Parameter values

Parameter	Reaction type	Biochemical reaction	Value	Unit
a_4	Complex formation	$NF - \kappa B + I\kappa B\alpha \rightarrow NF - \kappa B : I\kappa B\alpha$	30	$\mu M^{-1} min^{-1}$
a_7	Complex formation	$NF - \kappa B : I\kappa B\alpha + IKK \rightarrow NF - \kappa B : I\kappa B\alpha : IKK$	11.1	$\mu M^{-1} min^{-1}$
a_1	Complex formation	$I\kappa B\alpha + IKK \rightarrow I\kappa B\alpha : IKK$	1.38	$\mu M^{-1} min^{-1}$
d_4	Dissociation	$NF - \kappa B + I\kappa B\alpha \leftarrow NF - \kappa B : I\kappa B\alpha$	0.03	min^{-1}
d_1	Dissociation	$NF - \kappa B : I\kappa B\alpha + IKK \leftarrow NF - \kappa B : I\kappa B\alpha : IKK$	0.075	min^{-1}
d_1	Dissociation	$I\kappa B\alpha + IKK \leftarrow I\kappa B\alpha : IKK$	0.075	min^{-1}
deg_1	Degradation	$I\kappa B\alpha \rightarrow 0$	0.006	min^{-1}
deg_4	Degradation	$NF - \kappa B : I\kappa B\alpha \rightarrow NF - \kappa B$	0.0013	min^{-1}
k_{01}	Transport	$NF - \kappa Bn \rightarrow NF - \kappa B$	0.0048	min^{-1}
tp_2	Transport	$I\kappa B\alpha n \rightarrow I\kappa B\alpha$	0.025	min^{-1}
k_2	Transport	$NF - \kappa Bn : I\kappa B\alpha n \rightarrow NF - \kappa B : I\kappa B\alpha$	0.84	min^{-1}
k_1	Transport	$NF - \kappa B \rightarrow NF - \kappa Bn$	5.4	min^{-1}
tp_1	Transport	$I\kappa B\alpha \rightarrow I\kappa B\alpha n$	0.05	min^{-1}
τ	Synthesis (delay)	$NF - \kappa Bn \rightarrow NF - \kappa Bn + I\kappa B\alpha$	40	min
k_{02}	Inactivation	$IKK \rightarrow 0$	0.002	min^{-1}
$r_4 + d_4$	Catalyzed degradation	$NF - \kappa B : I\kappa B\alpha : IKK \rightarrow NF - \kappa B + IKK$	11.1	min^{-1}
r_1	Catalyzed degradation	$I\kappa B\alpha : IKK \rightarrow IKK$	2.22	min^{-1}
$s_{\text{synthesis}}$	Synthesis	$NF - \kappa Bn \rightarrow NF - \kappa Bn + I\kappa B\alpha$	0.24	min^{-1}

$$\frac{dx_5}{dt} = tp_1x_2 - tp_2x_5 - a_4x_4x_5 + d_4x_6 \tag{43}$$

$$\frac{dx_6}{dt} = a_4x_4x_5 - d_4x_6 - k_2x_6 \tag{44}$$

$$\frac{dx_7}{dt} = k(t) - k_{02}x_7 - a_1x_2x_7 + (d_1 + r_1)x_8 \\ - a_7x_3x_7 + (d_1 + r_4)x_9 \tag{45}$$

$$\frac{dx_8}{dt} = a_1x_2x_7 - (d_1 + r_1)x_8 \tag{46}$$

$$\frac{dx_9}{dt} = a_7x_3x_7 - (d_1 + r_4)x_9 \tag{47}$$

Competing interests
The authors declare that they have no competing interests.

Acknowledgements
This study was supported in part by the National Cancer Institute (2 R25CA090301-06) and the National Science Foundation (NSF-1238918).

Author details
[1]Department of Electrical and Computer Engineering, Texas A&M University, College Station, TX 77843, USA. [2]Department of Electrical and Computer Engineering, Prairie View A&M University, Prairie View, TX 77446, USA. [3]Computational Biology Division, Translational Genomics Research Institution, Phoenix, AZ 85004, USA. [4]Department of Bioinformatics and Computational Biology, University of Texas M.D. Anderson Cancer Center, Houston, TX 77030, USA.

References
1. S Huang, Rational drug discovery: what can we learn from regulatory networks. Drug Discov. Today. **7**, 163–169 (2002)
2. E Butcher, E Berg, E Kunkel, System biology in drug discovery. Nat. Biotechnol. **22**, 1253–1259 (2004)
3. N Kumar, B Hendriks, K Janes, D Graaf, D Lauffenburger, Applying computational modeling to drug discovery and development. Drug Discov. Today. **11**, 806–811 (2006)
4. J Chen, E Dougherty, S Demir, C Friedman, C Li, S Wong, Grand challenges for multimodal bio-medical systems. IEEE Circuits Syst. Mag. **5**(2), 46–52 (2005)
5. H Derendorf, B Meibohm, Modeling of pharmacokinetic/pharmacodynamic (PK/PD) relationships: concepts and perspectives. Pharm. Res. **16**(2), 176–185 (1999)
6. N Ting, in *Dose Finding in Drug Development*, ed. by N Ting. Introduction and new drug development process (Springer, New York, 2006)
7. S Undevia, G Gomez-Abuin, M Ratain, Pharmacokinetic variability of anticancer agents. Nat. Rev. Cancer. **5**, 447–458 (2005)
8. N Shah, C Kasap, C Weier, M Balbas, J Nicoll, E Bleickardt, C Nicaise, C Sawyers, Transient potent BCR-ABL inhibition is sufficient to commit chronic myeloid leukemia cells irreversibly to apoptosis. Cancer cell. **14**(6), 485–493 (2008)
9. D Amin, N Sergina, D Ahuja, M McMahon, J Blair, D Wang, B Hann, K Koch, K Shokat, M Moasser, Resiliency and vulnerability in the HER2-HER3 tumorigenic driver. Sci. Transl. Med. **2**(16), 1–9 (2010)
10. P Rajasethupathy, S Vayttaden, U Bhalla, Systems modeling: a pathway to drug discovery. Curr. Opin. Chem. Biol. **9**, 400–406 (2005)
11. E Butcher, Can cell systems biology rescue drug discovery? Nat. Rev. Drug Discov. **4**, 461–467 (2005)
12. X Li, L Qian, J Hua, M Bittner, E Dougherty, Assessing the efficacy of molecularly targeted agents on cell line-based platforms by using system identification. BMC Genomics. **13**(6), S11 (2012)
13. E Dougherty, M Brun, J Trent, M Bittner, Conditioning-based modeling of contextual genomic regulation. IEEE/ACM Trans. Comput. Biol. Bioinf. **6**, 310–320 (2009)
14. A Kringstein, F Rossi, A Hofmann, H Blau, Graded transcriptional response to different concentrations of a single transactivator. Proc. Natl Acad. Sci. USA. **95**, 13670–13675 (1998)
15. M Santillan, M Mackey, Quantitative approaches to the study of bistability in the lac operon of *Escherichia coli*. J. R. Soc. Interface. **5**(Suppl 1), S29–S39 (2008)
16. B Muller-Hill, *The Lac Operon: A Short History of a Genetic Paradigm* (Walter de Gruyter, New York, 1996)
17. A Halasz, V Kumar, M Imielinski, C Belta, O Sokolsky, S Pathak, H Rubin, Analysis of lactose metabolism in *E. coli* using reachability analysis of hybrid systems. IET Syst. Biol. **1**, 120–148 (2007)
18. R Ghosh, A Tiwari, C Tomlin, Automated symtolic reachability analysis; with application to delta-notch signaling automata. Hybrid Syst.: Comput. Control. **LNCS 2623**, 233–248 (2003)
19. R Ghosh, C Tomlin, Symbolic reachable set computation of piecewise affine hybrid automata and its application to biological modelling: delta-notch protein signalling. IET Syst. Biol. **1**, 170–183 (2004)
20. S Drulhe, G Ferrari-Trecate, H de Jone, A Viari, Reconstruction of switching thresholds in piecewise-affine models of genetic regulatory networks. Hybrid Syst.: Comput. Control. **LNCS 3927**, 184–199 (2006)
21. G Batt, D Ropers, H de Jone, J Geiselmann, M Page, D Schneider, Qualitative analysis and verification of hybrid models of genetic regulatory networks: nutritional stress response in *Escherichia coli*. Hybrid Syst.: Comput. Control. **LNCS 3414**, 134–150 (2005)
22. X Li, L Qian, M Bittner, E Dougherty, Characterization of drug efficacy regions based on dosage and frequency schedules. IEEE Trans. Biomed. Eng. **58**(3), 488–498 (2011)
23. H de Jong, Modeling and simulation of genetic regulatory systems: a literature review. J. Comput. Biol. **9**, 67–103 (2002)
24. L Glass, S Kauffman, The logical analysis of continuous non-linear biochemical control networks. J. Theor. Biol. **39**, 103–129 (1973)
25. J Prez-Urizar, V Granados-Soto, FJ Flores-Murrieta, G Castada-Hernndez, Pharmacokinetic–pharmacodynamic modeling: why? Arch. Med. Res. **31**(6), 539–545 (2000)
26. AV Hill, The possible effects of the aggregation of the molecules of haemoglobin on its dissociation curves. J. Physiol. **40**, iv–vii (1910)
27. NH Holford, LB Sheiner, Understanding the dose–effect relationship: clinical application of pharmacokinetic–pharmacodynamic models. Clin. Pharmacokinet. **6**(6), 429–453 (1981)
28. DR Waud, RB Parker, Pharmacological estimation of drug–receptor dissociation constants. Statistical evaluation. II. Competitive antagonists. J. Pharmacol. Exp. Ther. **177**, 13–24 (1971)
29. H Kuh, S Jang, M Wientjes, J Au, Computational model of intracellular pharmacokinetics of paclitaxel. J. Pharmacol. Exp. Ther. **293**(3), 761–770 (2000)
30. AR Tzafriri, ER Edelman, Endosomal receptor kinetics determine the stability of intracellular growth factor signalling complexes. Biochem. J. **402**, 537–549 (2007)
31. J Kramer, J Sagartz, D Morris, The application of discovery toxicology and pathology towards the design of safer pharmaceutical lead candidates. Nat. Rev. Drug Discov. **6**, 636–649 (2007)
32. Y Yamamoto, R Gaynor, Therapeutic potential of inhibition of the NF-κB pathway in the treatment of inflammation and cancer. J. Clin. Invest. **107**(2), 135–142 (2001)
33. V Baud, M Karin, Is NF-κB a good target for cancer therapy? Hopes and pitfalls. Nat. Rev. Drug Discov. **8**, 33–40 (2009)
34. A Hoffmann, A Levchenko, ML Scott, D Baltimore, The IkBNF-kB signaling module: temporal control and selective gene activation. Science. **298**(8), 1241–1245 (2002)
35. M Sung, R Simon, *In silico* simulation of inhibitor drug effects on nuclear factor-kB pathway dynamics. Mol. Pharmacol. **66**, 70–75 (2004)
36. R Orlowski, D Kuhn, Proteasome inhibitors in cancer therapy: lessons from the first decade. Clin. Cancer Res. **14**(6), 1649–1657 (2008)

4

Statistical discovery of site inter-dependencies in sub-molecular hierarchical protein structuring

Kirk K Durston[1*], David KY Chiu[1], Andrew KC Wong[2] and Gary CL Li[2]

Abstract

Background: Much progress has been made in understanding the 3D structure of proteins using methods such as NMR and X-ray crystallography. The resulting 3D structures are extremely informative, but do not always reveal which sites and residues within the structure are of special importance. Recently, there are indications that multiple-residue, sub-domain structural relationships within the larger 3D consensus structure of a protein can be inferred from the analysis of the multiple sequence alignment data of a protein family. These intra-dependent clusters of associated sites are used to indicate hierarchical inter-residue relationships within the 3D structure. To reveal the patterns of associations among individual amino acids or sub-domain components within the structure, we apply a k-modes attribute (aligned site) clustering algorithm to the ubiquitin and transthyretin families in order to discover associations among groups of sites within the multiple sequence alignment. We then observe what these associations imply within the 3D structure of these two protein families.

Results: The k-modes site clustering algorithm we developed maximizes the intra-group interdependencies based on a normalized mutual information measure. The clusters formed correspond to sub-structural components or binding and interface locations. Applying this data-directed method to the ubiquitin and transthyretin protein family multiple sequence alignments as a test bed, we located numerous interesting associations of interdependent sites. These clusters were then arranged into cluster tree diagrams which revealed four structural sub-domains within the single domain structure of ubiquitin and a single large sub-domain within transthyretin associated with the interface among transthyretin monomers. In addition, several clusters of mutually interdependent sites were discovered for each protein family, each of which appear to play an important role in the molecular structure and/or function.

Conclusions: Our results demonstrate that the method we present here using a k-modes site clustering algorithm based on interdependency evaluation among sites obtained from a sequence alignment of homologous proteins can provide significant insights into the complex, hierarchical inter-residue structural relationships within the 3D structure of a protein family.

Keywords: k-modes algorithm, Site cluster, Associations, Ubiquitin, Transthyretin, Pattern discovery, Cluster tree, Attribute clustering, Protein structural sub-domains

Introduction

The determination of protein 3D structure using methods such as NMR and X-ray crystallography has made tremendous progress. Although the 3D structure of many proteins has been solved, there still remains the problem of understanding the internal relationships within the structure. Certain residues may require specific associations with other residues within the structure that are not necessarily spatially proximal. Certain pairwise, third-order, fourth-order, and higher-order associations may be essential for obtaining a stable structure, while other parts of the structure have a less important role. The challenge is to be able to identify key structural associations within the larger structure, with the objective of understanding what role they play within the larger structure or global function of the protein.

Granular computing is emerging as a computing paradigm of information processing based on the abstraction of information entities called information granules [1-3], which we define here as related entities

* Correspondence: kdurston@uoguelph.ca
[1]School of Computer Science, University of Guelph, 50 Stone Road East, Guelph, ON N1G 2W1, Canada
Full list of author information is available at the end of the article

that are abstracted from the protein family multiple sequence alignment data based on a possible shared function. Functional bioinformatics is a sub-discipline of bioinformatics that incorporates functionality into the analysis of biopolymers [4-6]. Within a multiple sequence alignment, each column represents an aligned site, where a *site* refers to a location within an amino acid sequence. For example, a set of aligned sequences for a protein family that, on average, consists of 150 amino acid positions (with inserted gaps), would have 150 sites in its sequence. It is useful for estimating the functionality characteristics of sequence segments and/or functional sites, which can add enormous insights into understanding the characteristics of biopolymers.

The importance of patterns of associated sites within protein sequences has long been recognized. Structural and functional characteristics of a protein family may often be dependent upon two or more sites that maintain the stability of the molecule [7,8], such as in the situation of compensatory substitutions. In the late 1970s, based on statistics and information theory, Wong et al. [9] proposed a statistical analysis of site variability and interdependence in a protein family relating to the structural and functional relationships of sites in cytochrome c. Smith and Smith [10] developed a computer algorithm for detecting relationships among different sites in an amino acid sequence. Lichtarge et al. [11,12] have developed an evolutionary trace method (ETM) to identify clusters of sites associated with function, by mapping sites with a high degree of conservation onto the surface of the solved structure. Liu and Califano [13] have suggested a method for the functional classification of proteins through pattern discovery. Further work extended to data from aligned sequences has been conducted by Wong et al. [9,14,15] and Chiu et al. [16-18] in the developing of pattern discovery and analysis. An important goal of our proposed work is to extend our understanding of sub-molecular, internal relationships within the 3D structure of proteins by analyzing their multiple sequence alignments. In this article, we introduce a powerful new form of analysis based on the concept of granular computing and the *k*-modes attribute clustering algorithm (*k*-modes algorithm for abbreviation) to reveal statistical associations among multiple amino acids, using the aligned sequence data of both the ubiquitin and transthyretin protein families as the test bed. We make several discoveries, including three types of multiple amino acid associations as well as the observation that some of them form nested hierarchical branches and modules within the larger structure, indicating that our proposed granular computing method is conceptually sound and renders new understanding of internal relationships within the 3D structure of globular proteins.

Application of the *k*-modes algorithm to multiple sequence alignments

Consider a given alignment of multiple sequences, possibly representing the different members of a protein or gene family. A multiple sequence alignment is defined formally as follows.

Definition 1: (Multiple sequence alignment)

Consider that a family of molecular sequences is properly aligned. Let the aligned sites be represented as $X = (X_1, X_2, \ldots, X_N)$ where N is the number of columns (aligned sites) in the multiple sequence alignment. Each aligned site is considered as an *attribute*. A realization of X is a particular sequence within the alignment and can be denoted as $x_i = (x_{i1}, x_{i2}, \ldots, x_{iN})$ where i is the row number within the alignment and x_{ij} may assume any value in its alphabet set G. For proteins, G consists of the 20 amino acids and for DNA or RNA, G consists of the 4 nucleotides. We refer to an ensemble of outcomes of X as a *Multiple Sequence Alignment*

To clarify, a multiple sequence alignment consisting of M sequences and N columns (aligned sites or attributes) is shown below.

$$X_1, X_2, X_3, \ldots, X_N$$
$$x_{11}, x_{12}, x_{13}, \ldots x_{1N}$$
$$x_{21}, x_{22}, x_{23}, \ldots x_{2N}$$
.
.
.
$$x_{M1}, x_{M2}, x_{M3}, \ldots x_{MN}$$

where Xn represents the column/aligned site/attribute number and x_{ij} represents the particular amino acid or nucleotide found in row i and column j. For a protein family, the data for the two-dimensional array is the multiple sequence alignment for the family contained in databases such as Pfam [19,20].

Evaluating interdependency between attributes

For aligned protein sequences, an aligned site is considered as an attribute. To evaluate the interdependency between two aligned sites, we use the method proposed by Wong et al. [9,21] where the interdependency redundancy measure between two attributes X_i and $X_{i'}$ is given by the normalized mutual information

$$R_{ii'} = \frac{I(X_i, X_{i'})}{H(X_i, X_{i'})} \tag{1}$$

where

$$I(X_i, X_{i'}) = \sum_{x \in X_i} \sum_{y \in X_{i'}} p(x, y) log\left(\frac{p(x, y)}{p(x)p(y)}\right) \tag{2}$$

is the mutual information between X_i and $X_{i'}$ (a measure of the average decrease in uncertainty about X_i that results from learning the value of $X_{i'}$) and

$$H(X_i, X_{i'}) = -\sum_{x \in X_i} \sum_{y \in X_{i'}} p(x,y) \log p(x,y) \qquad (3)$$

is the joint entropy between X_i and $X_{i'}$. Since $I(X_i, X_{i'})$ increases with the number of possible attribute values, $R_{ii'}$ must be normalized. This avoids biasing the search for associations among sites toward larger clusters, which may actually have a low level of internal interdependency. The function p refers to the estimated probability from the sample data.

One should note that the stronger the interdependency between X_i and $X_{i'}$, the higher the $I(X_i, X_{i'})$ value. As indicated by Equation (2), from the statistics standpoint, the normalized $R_{ii'}$ also accounts for the amount of deviation from the independence hypothesis between X_i and $X_{i'}$. $R_{ii'} = 1$ if X_i and $X_{i'}$ are perfectly dependent and $R_{ii'} = 0$ if they are completely independent. Since $R_{ii'}$ is a normalized interdependency measure, the interdependence relationship is not affected by the number of attribute values. If there is an interdependency between two attributes, there is a greater degree of correlation between them than when compared to two attributes that are less interdependent or independent. For this reason, $R_{ii'}$ is able to measure the interdependence or correlation between attributes [9,15]. If $R_{ii'} > R_{ih}$, $h \in \{1,\ldots,N\}$, $h \neq i \neq i'$, the dependency between X_i and $X_{i'}$ is greater than that between X_i and X_h. In searching for higher-order relations between attributes in a sequence alignment, we use $R_{ii'}$ to measure the interdependence between attributes X_i and $X_{i'}$. On the basis of $R_{ii'}$, a statistical test is introduced to test whether or not two attributes are interdependent (or are deviating from independence) [22]. Recall that $0 \leq R_{ii'} \leq 1$, and $R_{ii'} = 0$ if X_i and $X_{i'}$ are totally independent, and $R_{ii'} = 1$ if totally dependent. The test, in terms of $R_{ii'}$, then becomes as follows.

Two attributes X_i and $X_{i'}$ are dependent if $R_{ii'} \geq c^2_{(Gi-1)(Gi'-1)}/2n\ H(X_i, X_{i'})$ and false otherwise, where $c^2_{(Gi-1)(Gi'-1)}$ represents a chi-square distribution with $(Gi-1)(Gi'-1)$ degrees of freedom (recall that for proteins G represents the alphabet set of 20 amino acids) and n represents the number of specimens in the cluster.

For sequences that presume to encode embedded functionality such as DNA, RNA, or proteins, $I(X_i, X_{i'})$ can be considered to reflect the mutual *functional* information governed by known (or predicted) functionality of a pair of sites. A measure of functional complexity (FC) was proposed by Durston et al. [6] for the case where the sequences are specified by a defined input class. Here, however, we are measuring the FC of the relationships *between* aligned sites, as specified by the attribute cluster.

To estimate the overall significant dependence of an attribute X_i with other attributes in a cluster of sites, the sum of normalized interdependency redundancy $SR(i)$ of X_i with other attributes in the data array is calculated, where

$$SR(i) = \sum_{(i,i') \in N^*} R_{i,i'} \qquad (4)$$

and N^* is the set of (i,i') attribute pairs [9,15,17,21].

Definition 2: (Mode of a set of attributes)
Within a cluster of attributes, we define the *mode* as the attribute with the highest normalized interdependency redundancy (SR) value. Formally, X_i is the mode of cluster X if $SR(i) \geq SR(i')$ for all attributes $X_{i'}$ in X.

For the purpose of this article, and to compare clusters of different numbers of attributes, the highest normalized interdependency redundancy ($SR(i)$) divided by the number of attribute pairs N^* in the cluster (i.e., $SR(i)/N^*$) will be designated as $SR(mode)$. The $SR(mode)$, therefore, in quantifying the interdependency between the mode and the other attributes within the cluster, provides one method to quantify the average degree of interdependency within the cluster, as well as an objective method to rank different attribute clusters in terms of their internal interdependency.

Often, within a sequence alignment, it may be that two or more sites are closely associated by their amino acid composition, possibly due to residue–residue contacts [7]. It has been found that such amino acid associations could form compensatory relationships in certain mutational events [7]. As a result, amino acids at one site could have a functional relationship with particular amino acids at the other sites within the associated sites. We define these amino acid associations as *patterns* if the association is statistically significant.

Definition 3: (pattern)
An *event* is an observation of an instance in a given data ensemble, either involving a single value or multiple jointly observed values. A *single-valued event* is referred to as a *primary event* and is a realization of X_i that takes on a value from α_i, where α represents a symbol from the alphabet set G. For a primary event, only one outcome of a variable in X is involved. A multiple valued event is referred to as a *compound event*. A pattern is a compound event (an observation from a subset of n different variables of the N-tuple X) which is statistically significant as reflected by its frequency of occurrences [23,24]. A pattern is denoted as $\lambda = (\alpha^p_i, \alpha^q_{i'}, \ldots, \alpha^r_n)$ where $(i, i', i'', \ldots, n)$ is a set of aligned site indices (e.g.,

sites 2, 15, and 19), within the multiple sequence alignment. It represents the joint outcomes of $X_i = \alpha_i^p$, $X_{i'} = \alpha_{i'}^q$, ..., $X_n = \alpha_n^r$ and that such association is statistically significant in the sense that the frequency of their occurrences deviate significantly from the default expected frequency if they are just a random occurrence or if they are a completely independent set.

For example, cluster (11) in Table 1 has two third-order patterns (sites 60, 63–64), where $\lambda_1 = $ amino acid pattern NKE, and $\lambda_2 = $ amino acid pattern GDG, in the corresponding sites in the alignment. Here, both patterns on these three sites are statistically significant according to their frequency of occurrences as observed in the sub-array of the aligned protein data.

Attribute clustering

In traditional pattern recognition, clustering is a process that groups similar samples together, maximizing the intra-group similarity and inter-group dissimilarity based on certain similarity or distance measures. An example is the method proposed by Li and Scheraga [25] for grouping similar sequences on the basis of their *information distance*, the length of the smallest binary computer program that will convert two sequences to each other. Clustering algorithms that group according to similarity between attributes are not appropriate for clustering in terms of interdependency, since dissimilar attributes may be interdependent. (For example, two aligned sites may be composed of dissimilar amino acids, yet be interdependent.)

If we analyze the relationship among attributes with the objective of clustering them into groups, we consider their interdependence instead. Using a sample clustering analogy in clustering attributes, we should maximize the intra-group interdependence (correlation) and inter-group independence. Hence, the attribute clusters within the sequence alignment could be obtained by using attribute interdependence values for associations.

There is a subtle difference between attribute interdependence and statistically significant patterns. The former describes dependence between attributes such as sites within an amino acid sequence, while the latter relates an associated set of amino acids at a respective set of sites in a sequence as joint events based on their statistically significant association. (To clarify, taking the same example 11 in Table 1, we observe that three attributes are mutually dependent. Yet, within these three sites we observe two third-order events $\lambda_1 = $ NKE and

$\lambda_2 = $ GDG which are statistically interdependent.) Hence, one third-order cluster of aligned sites can contain two or more third-order patterns of amino acids within those sites. We could anticipate that attribute clusters usually contain statistically significant patterns among the amino acids in the clusters. Before we define attribute clusters, we first introduce the algorithm by which attribute clusters could be found.

Attribute clustering algorithm

For sample clustering, a well-known process is the *k-medoids* algorithm [26]. To cluster samples into k groups, it first selects a random sample to represent each group and considers it as the center or *medoid* for that group. Thus, it selects k samples around which to build k groups. That is why the algorithm is referred to as the *k-medoids* algorithm. Using a distance measure, it clusters each of the remaining samples into the group for which the sample is closest to the medoid. After the first round, it updates a sample as the medoid of a group if the sum of distances of that sample to all other samples in that group is minimal. Based on their closest distance to these new medoids, all samples are then regrouped. The process is repeated until there is no more shift of samples between clusters. This method can work well for similarity-based clustering, but as pointed out earlier, interdependency might not be a function of similarity; two very dissimilar attributes may actually be interdependent. That is, different amino acids at distant sites could still be inter-associated if their occurrences are observed together.

The ETM, mentioned earlier, forms clusters of highly conserved sites that, when mapped to a 3D model, are correlated with a function such as binding. In this approach, an interdependency measure is not used. Instead, interdependency is inferred. Also, the interdependency that is inferred is between the function and the cluster of highly conserved sites. The sites (or attributes) may not necessarily all be interdependent between themselves. Furthermore, the ETM can be used only in proteins that have a known structure and are relatively free of noise.

A concept similar to the *k-medoids* algorithm was developed by Wong and Wang [27] and adopted to cluster genes from micro-array gene expression data [15]. It is known as a *k*-modes attribute clustering algorithm. In the *k*-modes algorithm, we replace the medoid, representing the center of a cluster of samples in the *k*-medoids algorithm, with the

Table 1 Attribute clusters with two high residual patterns

Cluster	Sites	k	λ_1 amino acids	λ_1-adjusted residual	λ_2 amino acids	λ_2-adjusted residual
10	54–59	6	RTLSDY	31.0	RTLADY	30.5
11	60,63–64	3	NKE	29.9	GDG	14.3
3	18–19,21	3	ESD	13.4	EPD	9.6

'mode' which is the attribute that has the highest $SR(i)$ within that attribute cluster. The k-modes algorithm uses the interdependency redundancy measure $R_{ii'}$ between attributes for attribute clustering instead of the similarity measure used in sample clustering. The k-modes algorithm, shown in Figure 1, then proceeds as follows.

The first step is initialization where k, the prescribed number of clusters, is inputted and an attribute is randomly selected for each cluster, representing a candidate for the mode of that cluster. Step 2 is to calculate the interdependency redundancy measure $R_{ii'}$ between each cluster mode and each of the remaining attributes. Each of these remaining attributes is then assigned to the cluster for which it has the highest $R_{ii'}$ value. Step 3 is to compute the updated mode for each of the k clusters (recalling that the initial mode was only a candidate used to start the process). In the subsequent iterative step, once the new mode of each of the k clusters has been calculated, steps 2 and 3 are repeated until the calculated mode for each of the k clusters does not change, that is, there is no exchange of attributes between attribute clusters. The algorithm is terminated at that point or, alternatively, at a pre-specified number of iterations.

For protein family multiple sequence alignments, all unassociated insertions and gaps are computationally removed from the previous procedure. Because it is

generally recognized that sequence determines structure [28], and structure is important for function, it is assumed that each of the remaining sites within the sequence is either directly or indirectly interdependent with every other site in the sequence. To clarify, one pairwise interdependency may not be directly related to another attribute cluster consisting of three interdependent sites, but both clusters may be nested within larger clusters that are directly related to form a still larger cluster. An exception might be a cluster of sites that are interdependent only due to an external function, such as a highly conserved binding site. Thus, in order to discover the full range of the nested clusters, the k-modes algorithm is run for all values of k from $k = N - 1$ down to $k = 2$. For example, a multiple sequence alignment with 100 aligned sites would first be run with k set to $N - 1 = 99$. This would result in 1 pairwise cluster and 98 single attribute clusters to account for all 100 aligned sites. The value for k would be reduced by 1 each time all the way down to 2, which would yield 2 large attribute clusters comprising all 100 aligned sites. It is possible that the structure of a protein may not actually fit into two high-order attribute clusters. For example, a protein family that has a 3D structure composed of three structural domains may yield valid results for a k as small as 3 but not for a k as small as 2. If this is the case, it will become evident when the cluster tree of nested hierarchical attribute clusters is built, which will be explained shortly. Because the k-modes algorithm clustering method is data driven, it should yield the same results for multiple runs of the same k, even though a random attribute is chosen at the initial step. This was found to be the case for both protein families analyzed.

Regarding the complexity of the algorithm, the k-modes algorithm for N attributes and n samples requires $O(nN)$ operations to assign each attribute to a cluster (step 2) and $O(nN^2)$ operations to compute the mode X_m for each cluster. If t represents the number of iterations, then the computational complexity of the k-modes algorithm is

$$O\left[k\left(nN + nN^2\right)t\right] \tag{5}$$

or

$$O\left(knN^2t\right) \tag{6}$$

This order of computational complexity is manageable within a reasonable space and time on any recent laptop computer.

An attribute cluster is formally defined as follows.

Definition 4: (attribute cluster)

For an ensemble of data $X = (X_1, X_2, \ldots, X_N)$ with N attributes, if X is partitioned vertically into k sub-arrays by

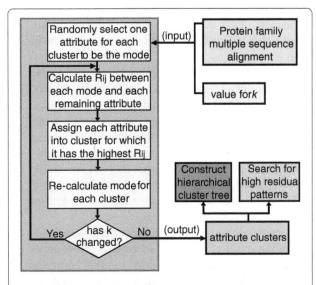

Figure 1 Overview of algorithm for attribute clustering and pattern discovery. The k-modes algorithm is summarized in the green portion of the flowchart. The algorithm can be run for a particular value for k or for multiple values. In order to build a hierarchical cluster tree for a protein family, represented by a multiple sequence alignment with N aligned sites, the value of k is increased each time from a starting value of $N - 1$ down to 2. The entire set of attribute clusters can then be arranged into a cluster tree for that protein family, or individual clusters can be computationally analyzed for patterns.

the *k*-modes attribute clustering algorithm, then each sub-array is defined as an attribute cluster in the *k*-cluster configuration of *X*.

Applying this definition to a protein sequence alignment, an attribute cluster is simply a cluster of sites that are mutually interdependent. For example, several attribute clusters for the ubiquitin family are shown in Table 2. One such attribute cluster is 11, consisting of sites 60, 63, and 64 in the aligned sequences.

In this study, we consider only those patterns observed within an attribute cluster even though some might span across attribute clusters with weak interdependence. The set of attributes (as random variables) within an attribute cluster is then defined as a new pattern subspace as below.

Definition 5: (A significant pattern subspace)

Consider a subset Y of N^* $(N \geq N^* > 1)$ attributes of X such that at least one pattern is spanning that subset. Let $G_y = \{\lambda^1, \lambda^2, \ldots \lambda^m\}$ denote the set of m patterns contained in the subset Y. We refer the vector subspace Y as a significant pattern subspace containing the m patterns which span that subspace.

For example, in Table 2, cluster 11 forms a transformed attribute, consisting of the attribute set of aligned sites 60, 63, and 64. The attribute cluster 11 is not the pattern, rather, it is a result contributed by two amino acid patterns $\lambda_1 = NKE$ and $\lambda_2 = GDG$ at two different subsequent instances in the significant pattern subspace (second row in Table 1). Note that the variables in a subset of X forming a subset Y in the new significant pattern subspace will not be overlapped, as our attribute clustering algorithm will ensure that they are disjoint. Later, we will discuss how a hierarchical structure can be constructed in the form of a cluster tree.

Attribute clusters and information granules

The concept of granular computing allows analysis of granular units, in terms of modularity and hierarchy as a web structure of relationships [29-36]. Applying this concept to proteins entails analyzing them in terms of a hierarchical assembly of modules, each of which is associated with an attribute cluster.

Within a group composed of different types, a granule was originally conceptualized and served as a focal point of similar types within the group to study their collective properties [2]. For our problem of understanding the internal association relationships of a protein, the clusters of sites in the alignment can be considered as a set of granular units (which we called *information granules*) such that their information reflects the inferred associative properties of the protein family under study. A low-order attribute cluster may represent two or three residues that are in contact through H-bonds or in van der Waals interaction distances. The two or three residues can also be more distant from each other, yet be mutually associated, possibly through the effects the members of the cluster have on torsion angles and free

Table 2 Representative clusters from each primary branch in ubiquitin

Cluster	Sites	Highest pattern residual	k	Structural relationship	Functional factors
1	7,9–11	25.9	4	Double bond between 7 and the other sites	11 is a binding site
2	12,14–17,20	57.6	6		12 is adjacent to binding site 11
3	18–19,21	13.4	3	Double bond between 18 and 21	
4	23,25–27	6.7	4	Double bond between 23 and other sites	27 is a binding site
5	29–31,41	22.6	4	30 in Van der Waals contact with 41	29 is a binding site
6	34–36,38	27.9	4	Van der Waals contact 34 & 36	34 is adjacent to binding site 33
7	37,39–40,43	20.8	4	37 bonds to 40	43 is adjacent to possible external recognition site 42 and external contact site 44
8	44–47	646.1	4	Van der Waals contact 44 & 47	sites 44 and 47 are external contact points, 47 is adjacent to major binding site 48
9	49–50,52	7.5	3		site 49 is an external contact point
10	54–59	31.0	6	8 internal H-bonds	
11	60,63–64	29.9	3		63 is a major binding site
12	66,68–70	27.8	4		site 70 is an external contact point
13	43,69,74	13.0	3	43 in tight Van der Waals contact with 69	74 is a possible external recognition site
14	70,72–73	22.6	3		70 is an external contact point, 73 is an external recognition site

energy during folding. Low-order clusters may be nested within higher-order clusters, which represent important sub-domain structural components.

To analyze the nested hierarchical relationships between the clusters, a cluster tree can be built, as illustrated in Figure 2. The cluster tree will also clearly distinguish between valid and invalid clusters that were forced by using a k value (the number of clusters) that was too small. The cluster tree can either be built computationally or manually. The first step is to arrange all the second order (pairwise, involving two attributes) clusters from left to right, according to approximately where the pairwise clusters appear in the sequence. (For example, a pairwise cluster composed of sites 1 and 3 would be on the left and the highest site number pairwise cluster would be on the right, with all others arranged in between.) Not all aligned sites will necessarily form pairwise clusters. The next step continues with all the third-order clusters (or clusters composed of three interdependent sites) and so on. If a second-order cluster is nested within a third-order cluster, then the third-order cluster should be placed directly beneath the second-order cluster to form the beginnings of one branch of the cluster tree. Most clusters will likely be nested within larger order clusters, so the lower-to-higher order nested clusters will form the branches of the cluster tree. Since some sites may be associated with more than one cluster, they may switch branches as the order of the clusters is increased. A *node* occurs when two or more branches converge to form a large cluster. Some nodes may be nested within even larger clusters forming a larger branch representing a larger portion of the protein. In this case, the entire section of branches that converges into a larger node comprising a significant portion of the protein is called a *module*. If a branch reaches a point where the cluster is not nested in a higher-order cluster, then that branch should be left unattached to the cluster tree; it may have functional or structural significance on a local scale and should be retained in the cluster tree diagram.

As already mentioned, each higher-order cluster should contain most of the sites included in the lower-order cluster(s) that are nested within it by choosing a reasonable number of clusters, or a k value that is not too small. The completed tree should be a valuable tool in identifying and understanding sub-molecular relationships, both functional and structural, within the generalized 3D structure of the protein family being investigated.

Each information granule is defined as an attribute cluster and allows for local analysis, as well as a global analysis under this framework. The hierarchical levels of analyses then provide multiple views into the protein structure including key residue–residue contacts, pairwise, third- and fourth-order relationships with multiple sites on up to larger sub-domains.

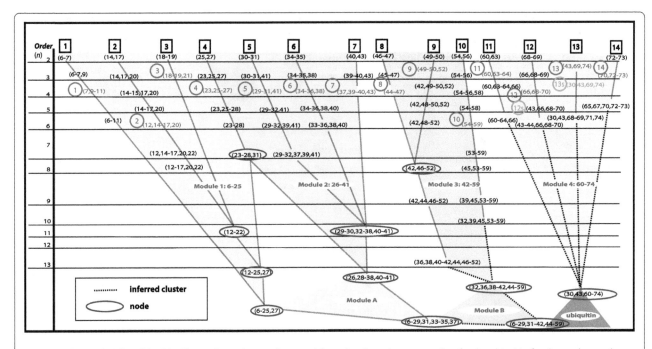

Figure 2 Cluster tree for ubiquitin. The attribute clusters discovered from the aligned sequence data for the ubiquitin family are shown above and organized vertically according to their order (the number of interdependent sites they contain). The organized clusters form primary branches, numbered 1 to 14 across the top of the figure. In each branch, the attribute cluster with the highest internal interdependency (highest *SR(mode)* value) was chosen as the representative cluster for that branch and is labeled according to its branch number. Two secondary clusters, discussed in the text, are labeled 12 s and 13 s. From this cluster tree, new insights can be gained into details of folding and structure.

Table 2 lists 14 attribute clusters within the aligned sequences of the ubiquitin family. Each of these reflects complex variability and association information that can be analyzed and compared to the functional and structural characteristics necessary for the ubiquitin family. By studying these generated granules, detailed insights can be gained on the sub-molecular characteristics of the ubiquitin family.

To summarize our approach, Figure 1 shows a flow chart diagram for the attribute cluster analysis of protein families. The analysis begins with the downloading of a sequence alignment of all sequences predicted for a protein family. Redundant sequences are then removed so that the resulting alignment consists only of unique sequences for that family. The resulting alignment is then analyzed using our method to detect attribute clusters. The attribute clusters are then grouped into hierarchical families of clusters forming branches, some of which may form a hierarchical cluster tree, an example of which can be seen in Figure 2. The clusters are then analyzed for structural and functional contributions with the objective of better understanding the key internal hierarchical structural sub-domain relationships and at various levels.

Statistical significance of results

Our approach is to locate statistically significant associations among sites in a multiple sequence alignment, as well as statistically significant patterns of amino acids within those associations. For locating associations between sites, the normalized mutual information $R_{ii'}$ (Equation 1) between attributes X_i and $X_{i'}$, known as redundancy, is used.

To ensure that patterns are statistically significant, the adjusted residual of each possible pattern within cluster is calculated [23]. The *residual* of a pattern λ is defined as the difference between the actual occurrence of λ and its expected occurrence, or

$$\delta\lambda = o\lambda - e\lambda \tag{7}$$

where $e\lambda$ is the expected occurrence of the pattern which, in this case, is that there are no patterns. The *adjusted residual* of the pattern λ is defined as

$$\gamma\lambda = \frac{\delta\lambda}{\sqrt{\nu\lambda}} \tag{8}$$

where $\nu\lambda$ is the variance of $\delta\lambda$. To find an amino acid pattern within a given cluster, a lower cutoff value for the adjusted residual is chosen. The adjusted residuals are calculated based on the amino acids observed within the multiple sequence alignment within the particular cluster being examined (i.e., only one cluster is analyzed at a time, which reduces the computational search to just the

aligned sites in the cluster). An adjusted residual that is less than the cutoff value is rejected and an adjusted residual higher than the cutoff value is retained as significant to a certain confidence level. (For example, an adjusted residual of 2.58 means that an amino acid pattern is statistically significant to a confidence level of 99%, and an adjusted residual of 3.29 is statistically significant to a confidence level of 99.9%.)

In this way, only statistically significant results are obtained and spurious results preempted. Thus, statistical significance is the operative criterion throughout the search process, ensuring statistically significant results. For a multiple sequence alignment, the minimum number of non-redundant aligned sequences required for statistically significant results is five [23]. However, only very strong associations and patterns will be revealed with such a small sample size. Adding additional non-redundant sequences to the alignment will increase the likelihood of finding additional patterns within the same association of sites, and of locating the smaller associations among sites that may be nested within the stronger, larger associations. Thus, the larger the non-redundant multiple sequence alignment, the more attribute clustering detail can be resolved.

Computational results for ubiquitin and transthyretin

Several dozen attribute clusters were generated by the program from the sequence alignment for both the ubiquitin and transthyretin (TTR) families, ranging from simple, pair-wise clusters up to one 58th-order cluster in the case of TTR. For clarity and logical flow, we shall discuss the results in the step-wise order as they emerged in the process of our analysis, dealing first with ubiquitin, then with TTR. To assist in clarity, a summary of the most significant results and predictions is shown in Table 3.

Ubiquitin
The cluster tree

A cluster tree was assembled as described in the Section "Attribute clusters and information granules", and is shown in Figure 2. Two types of branches can be observed. A Type I branch is made up of aligned site clusters which exhibit little or no interlacing with clusters residing in other branches (for example, primary branch (1) in Figure 2). The lack of interlacing between a Type 1 branch and other branches may indicate that the residues within a Type I branch are assembled completely prior to folding into the larger structure. The Type II branch, as illustrated by branches (5), (6), and (7), is made up of attribute clusters containing sites that interlace with sites in other branches. The overlapping/interlacing sites in the attribute clusters among Type

Table 3 Overview of experimental results and predictions

	Results	Predictions for further research
1.	Attribute clusters can be grouped into a hierarchical cluster tree composed of branches, nodes, and modules	Cluster trees may reveal details of folding constraints and other functionality relationships
2.	Within modules, two types of branches were found: (i) Type I; independent/non-interlacing with other branches and (ii) Type II; interlacing with other branches	The relationship between Types I and II branches may indicate constraints in the folding, tertiary structure and functionality of protein molecules
3.	Attribute clusters with highest $SR(mode)$ values were most commonly third- and fourth-order (3 to 4 associated sites)	Support for the next largest building block in proteins above single amino acids is typically a 3 to 4 amino acid structural unit
4.	Three types of attribute clusters were found: (i) H-bonded clusters, (ii) Van der Waals clusters, and (iii) extended clusters	Identifying attribute clusters may support possibility of predicting protein tertiary structural relationships involving H-bonds, van der Waals interactions, or multiple site effects
5.	Representative clusters found in ubiquitin confirm that the statistical criterion used can identify structural constraints such as bonding, binding and recognition sites (Table 2)	Can be used to locate key sub-molecular components of a protein, as well as components critical for the function of that protein
6.	Ubiquitin molecule found to be composed of four major modules	Consistent with the four major areas of chemical shift perturbations between Ub_1 and Ub_2

II branches suggest that there is a strong structural relationship among those branches, giving robust structural stability in the region containing them. A prediction that arises out of the observation of two neighboring, strongly interlaced Type II branches, is that during translation, the two branches may fold into each other before folding as a cohesive unit back onto the part of the protein that has already been formed by earlier branches.

Figure 2 reveals that the 14 primary branches converged into 4 primary modules (labeled in Figure 2 as modules 1–4). Modules formed as the result of merging two or more primary modules are labeled as modules A and B (Figure 2). For example, modules 1 and 2 converged to form module A. Since branches 8, 9, and 10 were strongly interlaced, and showed no signs of converging with branches 11–14, branches 8–10 were grouped to form their own module 3. The strong interlacing of branches 11–14 resulted in the formation of module 4. Once the cluster tree was completed, the next steps were to analyze a representative cluster from each branch, and then analyze the four modules. The next three sections contain the results of these steps.

Representative clusters

For the next step, we chose a set of representative clusters for detailed examination. Any cluster can be chosen to represent a primary branch, but for ubiquitin, the cluster with the highest $SR(mode)$ value was chosen to be the representative cluster. The representative cluster for each branch is shown highlighted in red in Figure 2 and labeled 1 to 14, where the numeral denotes the primary branch number. Table 2 contains a list of the representative clusters for the primary branches 1–14 together with the highest adjusted residue value of the strongest pattern within each representative cluster.

Using the secondary structure revealed in the X-ray diffraction 1.8 angstrom solved structure 1UBQ [37,38]

available from the Protein Data Bank, of the representative attribute clusters in each branch, we observe that (a) 11 out of 14 clusters included loops or turns; (b) 9 out of 14 included beta strands; and (c) 5 out of 14 included helices. We also note that three of the clusters occurred entirely within loops or turns, with only one cluster occurring entirely within a helix and only one entirely within a beta strand. Since loops and turns can be highly constrained structurally, it may explain why a higher occurrence of clusters included loops and turns.

Another observation from the representative clusters (highlighted in red in Figure 2) is the percentage of fourth-order (involving four sites) clusters. Of the set of clusters, one from each primary branch, that had the highest $SR(mode)$ value (i.e., the strongest average interdependency between sites), 7 were fourth-order (50%), 5 were third-order (36%), sixth-order clusters comprised only 14%, and there were no fifth-order high $SR(mode)$ value clusters in the individual branches. This suggests that the most common structural units within proteins may involve 3 to 4 amino acids. The node for Module 1 composed of the 21st-order cluster (6–25, 27) had a high $SR(mode)$ value of 0.202. This high internal interdependency may be a strong predictor of a structural sub-domain . A high $SR(mode)$ value at the node of a module indicates the level of internal interdependency and stability once the folding is complete for that module.

The k-modes algorithm found one or more patterns for each of the representative clusters. Recall that a pattern consists of an association of specific amino acids among the sites in the cluster. For statistical significance, an adjusted residual value was calculated for each pattern in a cluster. The residual value for each of the representative clusters shown in Table 2 is only for the pattern with the highest residual found within each representative cluster. Many of the clusters had other patterns as well. For example, two patterns for each of three different representative clusters are shown in Table 1. The fact that patterns were discovered for each of the representative clusters is verification that the attributes clusters discovered by this method contain high residual associations of amino acids.

Classifying the clusters

The third step was to examine and classify the clusters to see what significance they had within the 3D structure. We note that the representative clusters chosen for their high $SR(mode)$ values within each branch can be interpreted as functionally significant either for structure or external binding and interaction. The 3D structure of ubiquitin is shown in Figure 3A, using the solved structure 1UBQ. In Table 2, comparisons between the clusters and model 1UBQ were made. For functional significance, known and suspected sites that are involved in external binding or recognition are as follows:

(a) Sites 6, 11, 27, 29, 33, 48, and 63 are thought to be possible binding sites in the formation of poly-ubiquitin, with sites 48 and 63 thought to be the most common [39,40].

(b) Sites 8, 44, and 70 form hydrophobic patches that appear to contact the corresponding sites in Ub$_2$, stabilizing the dimer in its closed conformation [41].

(c) Sites 47, 49, and 71 form hydrogen bonds with corresponding sites in the other moiety in Lys-48 linked Ub$_2$ [42].

(d) Sites 42, 72, and 74 are located at the interface between the two ubiquitin domains, which may represent possible interaction sites that distinguish multi-ubiquitin chains from a single ubiquitin molecule, providing a means of external recognition [42].

Using these comparisons, the representative clusters (1–14) in each branch were then examined. All of the major clusters were found to be either functionally or structurally significant (Table 2). Some clusters in particular were found to have an important internal structural relationship and are discussed in detail below. Even though the *k-modes* algorithm is blind to the position of a site in the sequence, most of the discovered clusters contain sites that are either consecutive, or very close in sequence proximity, which one could expect to be structurally associated.

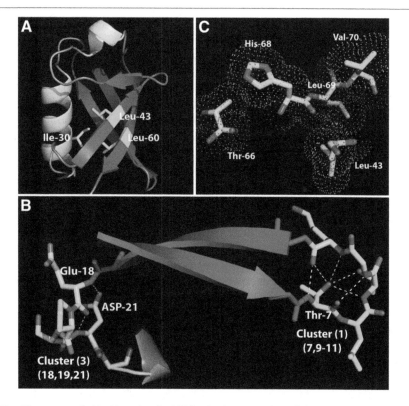

Figure 3 Ubiquitin. (A) The 3D structure of ubiquitin, using the 1UBQ solved structure. Part of cluster 13 s is also shown within the ubiquitin molecule. The three sites are all within van der Waals interaction distance of each other and may have an important role in the stability of the overall structure. **(B)** Module 1. This module contains two H-bonded clusters, which may play a role both in folding and then maintaining structural stability once folding is complete, especially cluster 1 with six H-bonds anchoring the loop. **(C)** Cluster 12 s, a strong example of a van der Waals cluster discovered by the *k*-modes algorithm.

This result suggests that the method presented here is able to pick up local structural associations remarkably well. Furthermore, there are some cases where the associated sites of the clusters are located at a distance (e.g., sites 30, 43, 68, and 69) with binding site relationships, or other structural or functional relationships (Table 2).

In addition to the Types I and II branches describing how the sites are interlaced, at least three types of attribute clusters were also observed which we designate: H-bonded clusters, van der Waals clusters, and extended clusters. *H-bonded clusters* contain residues that are in mutual H-bond contact. An example of this type of cluster is (1) shown in Figure 3B, forming a loop stabilized by no less than six predicted (PyMol) internal H-bonds. The second type of cluster, the *van der Waals cluster*, has sites that are not bonded but are in van der Waals contact. An example of this type is cluster (12 s), modeled in Figure 3C. The 1UBQ model reveals that the last cluster in the primary branch (12) (although quite dispersed along the primary sequence) contains van der Waals interactions, as well as predicted H-bonds, with sites 43 and 44 in van der Waals contact with sites 68 and 69, and two additional hydrogen bonds predicted by PyMol between site 44 and site 68. Hence, the clusters help to identify sites that are closely related in the tertiary structure, and often in actual contact, though widely separated in the primary sequence.

These first two types of clusters predicted by the pattern recognition software used in this research can readily be corroborated by mapping the attribute clusters to a solved 3D structure for the protein. The third type, however, designated as the *extended cluster*, is composed of sites that are distant both in the primary sequence, as well as the final 3D structure, yet they have a very high $SR(mode)$ value, indicating strong association. When mapped onto the solved 3D structure of the protein, it is less obvious why the constituent sites form an attribute cluster. There are two possible reasons why some clusters may consist of sites that are not within van der Waals interaction distance from each other in the 3D structure, yet demonstrate a strong interdependency. First, it is possible that for extended clusters, the interdependence is due to the net effect of the conformation angles ψ and ϕ and the conformations of the side chains for the amino acids within the cluster [43] upon the short and medium range structure and free energy state of the protein in the area containing the extended attribute cluster. This net effect may be required to minimize free energy and directly maintain the stable tertiary structure. Second, the association of sites that are not structurally proximate to each other may be due to external functional constraints such as external binding as first conjectured by Wong et al. [9]. From Table 2, it can be observed that some clusters with no obvious internal

structural relationship, such as 9, 11, 12, and 14, all contain external binding sites or, where the interaction is not yet known, external contact points with the external molecule it binds to [39]. Thus, the mutual interdependency of the sites in an extended cluster may be due to external binding requirements of functional controls where a number of sites are involved.

The success of this method in identifying important structural associations within ubiquitin does not mean that it will identify all such bonds, especially when the association among sites is weak. It does, however, demonstrate the ability to identify some key residue–residue contacts from the alignment data. This relationship among statistical association, molecular structure, and functionality is also consistent with earlier findings that identified the relationship among statistical patterns and 3D bonding structure [18] and functionality such as heredity factors in cancer suppressor genes [16,17]. The current results bring to light further details of statistical patterns that are strongly indicative of molecular structure and functionality in an alignment of proteins. Further work needs to be done to enable distinctions among clusters that predict residue-residue contacts, extended clusters that are keys in achieving structural stability, and those associated with external binding sites. One possible approach which has not been explored is to compare the FC of each site, which may be more heavily influenced by external binding, with the site clusters [6]. Another approach would be to compare the results of steered molecular dynamic computational modeling [44,45] on the more interesting parts of the cluster tree to see how those results would correlate with the cluster tree.

The modules

The final step was to examine the modules predicted by the cluster tree. For better visualization of the module locations and the major branch node-forming clusters on the sequence, Figure 4 shows the modules as boxes superimposed over the sequence with its color-coded secondary structure (taken from the 1UBQ model). Major clusters (color coded boxes) are also included. To avoid a confusing number of modules and clusters superimposed on just one sequence, two identical sequences are used for clarity, with two modules shown on each one.

To evaluate the validity of this modular view of ubiquitin, it has already been observed that at pH values of 6.8 to 7.5, the chemical shift perturbations are modular between the single ubiquitin molecule and the Lys-48 linked dimer form of ubiquitin (Ub_2), with four areas of perturbations [41]. The same four areas of perturbations have also been observed for Lys-63 linked Ub_2 [40]. The remarkable correspondence among the four modules

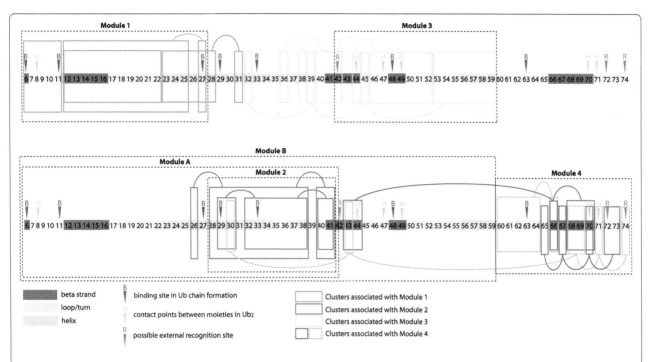

Figure 4 Secondary structure of ubiquitin with locations of modules and major clusters. The location of the major clusters associated with the four major modules is shown, for clarity, on two identical secondary structure ribbons, taken from model 1UBQ. An example of smaller clusters nested within larger clusters can be seen in the clusters associated with Module 2. The attribute (site) clusters associated with Modules 1 and 2 were found to be compact, with only a small region of interlacing involving sites 26, 28, and 31. Of particular interest are the two clusters associated with Module 4 that contain some sites that are quite distant in the primary structure. The key sites in these very extended clusters are sites 30, 43, and 69 which, although widely separated in the primary sequence, are actually in Van der Waals contact, as shown in Figure 3.

obtained by our method and the four areas of chemical shift perturbations is summarized in Table 4, providing validation that these four modules actually represent structural units within ubiquitin.

Module 1

The tertiary structure of Module 1 is shown in Figure 3B. The cluster with the highest $SR(mode)$ value, discovered in our experiment, was cluster (1), with a $SR(mode)$ value of .26. Cluster (1) is also labeled in Figure 2 and consists of sites (7, 9–11). The high $SR(mode)$ value shows that the sites are highly associated. From the 1UBQ model in Figure 3B, no less than six H-bonds are predicted by the MacPyMol model between Thr-7 and the other members of the cluster, sites 9–11. The number of internal H-bonds not only explains why it has such a high $SR(mode)$ value,

but it also indicates that site 7 is especially important within the cluster. Furthermore, the presence of the six predicted bonds in the cluster is an indication that cluster (1) provides structural stability to the loop and as a result, may have an important role in folding the two beta strands into a beta sheet. Site 11 within cluster (1) is also a known binding site [39] (Table 2).

Cluster (3) also has one of the higher $SR(mode)$ values in the alignment, with a value of 0.19. From Figure 3B, it can be observed that this cluster, containing sites (18–19, 21) is part of the next loop after the beta sheet. In this particular cluster, there are two predicted bonds between Asp 21 and Glu 18, providing verification for the significance of the computationally discovered association. The double bond has the effect of providing structural rigidity to the loop.

Table 4 Module and perturbation area comparison

Module number	Sites spanned in module	Sites spanned in perturbation areas of Ub_2
1	6–25	6–20
2	26–41	20–39
3	42–59	40–60
4	60–74	61–76

Module 2

From Figure 2, the core of Module 2 is composed of three interlacing Type II branches 5 to 7, made up of attribute clusters from sites 29 to 43. An examination of the clusters for each branch reveals that the sites in each of the three clusters straddle sites in the other two. For this reason, these three branches appear to form a very stable, interlocking structural unit. The high internal structural stability predicted by the Type II branches may explain why, in earlier work by Varadan et al. [40,41], the area spanned by module 2 was observed to demonstrate significantly lower chemical shift perturbations than those observed in the areas spanned by the other three modules. It is often the case that sites within a cluster, though separated in the primary structure of sequence, may have members that are close once folding has occurred and may actually be bonded to each other. Sites 37 and 40 in cluster (7) are an example of this common occurrence. The 1UBQ model also provides a clear interpretation for cluster (5), by revealing the van der Waals relationship within the cluster between sites 30 and 41.

Module 3

The unique feature of this module stands out in the cluster tree (Figure 2) as it reveals its relative independence from the other modules. This leads to a prediction that the branches in module 3 may fold into a stable sub-domain first, and then the entire sub-domain folds into the already folded module A to form module B. It is also notable that module 3 has a very close correspondence to the previously discovered third perturbation area shown in Table 4 [40,41].

Module 4

Recent work involving ubiquitin unfolding kinetics using hydrogen/deuterium exchange methods correlates with the results found here [46,47]. For example, the B5 strand, represented by module 4, appears to unfold before the loop and helix represented by primary branch 10 in module 3. This echoes what the cluster tree reveals regarding the independence of module 4. The cluster tree method demonstrated here may work very well in conjunction with unfolding studies in revealing details of protein folding.

Transthyretin results

Transthyretin (TTR) is a homotetramer composed of a dimer of dimers. The tetramer contains a solvent channel within which is a binding pocket for two thyroxine molecules. Each dimer interface includes sites 114 to 120, forming an 8-strand, anti-parallel β-sheet, which constitutes the wall of the solvent channel. TTR is often found in complex with Retinol Binding Protein (RBP). At the center of this interface for human TTR are sites 20, 81, and 84 [48]. There are some TTR variants that

result in amyloid formation. Two of the most common forms are Val30Met and Leu55Pro variants, both of which produce amyloidosis [49].

A multiple sequence alignment consisting of a total of 465 non-redundant sequences for the TTR family [50] was downloaded from Pfam and computationally analyzed using the k-modes algorithm. A large number of associated sites within the TTR alignment were discovered. The clusters were then arranged into a cluster tree as shown in Figure 5. The cluster tree for TTR shown in Figure 5 is remarkably different from the cluster tree for ubiquitin shown in Figure 2. Only three major branches, labeled as 5, 6, and 7 in Figure 5, converge into nodes forming a sub-domain module. This sub-domain module forms the TTR dimer interface and is shown in Figure 6B. Of the remaining, non-converging branches, there are six short branches that only achieve a fifth- or sixth-order cluster before terminating. These branches are labeled in Figure 5. Each of these branches are composed of hierarchically nested clusters, but only up to the fifth- or sixth-order. At that point, they abruptly end, rather than being absorbed into a higher order cluster or node. This suggests that the clusters in these branches play an important, but localized role in the structure or function of TTR. As mentioned earlier, each cluster within a nested hierarchical set is interesting to examine. To gain some understanding into these short branches, sample third-order clusters from branches A to F were examined individually within the context of the solved transthyretin structures available in the Protein Data Bank, pdb 2F7I, and pdb 1OO2 [51-54]. The importance of cluster A3 is revealed by its location, squarely at the TTR/RBP interface. This suggests that the clusters forming branch A may be critical to successful TTR/RBP binding. Cluster B3 straddles site 30, a site previously known to be highly sensitive to the proper folding of TTR, as mentioned above. Cluster B3 and site 30 are shown in Figure 6B. This suggests that cluster B3 is critical to the proper folding of TTR. The Val30Met variant may result in a failure in the formation of the β-sheet between sites 29 and 44 which, in turn, results in a misfolded structure prone to the formation of amyloids. Clusters D3 and E3, shown in Figure 6C, appear to be closely related in structure and function. Both trios consist of one site at either end of the channel β-sheet and one site at the centre, in close proximity to the thyroxin molecule. It appears that the two clusters play an important role in stabilizing that region of the β-sheet for the purpose of providing the proper structure for the thyroxin pocket. Cluster F4 is positioned at the dimer interface between the two TTR monomers. Cluster C3 is at the tetramer interface between the two dimers. All six clusters appear to be situated at key locations within the homotetramer that are either structurally important, or important for binding, or both.

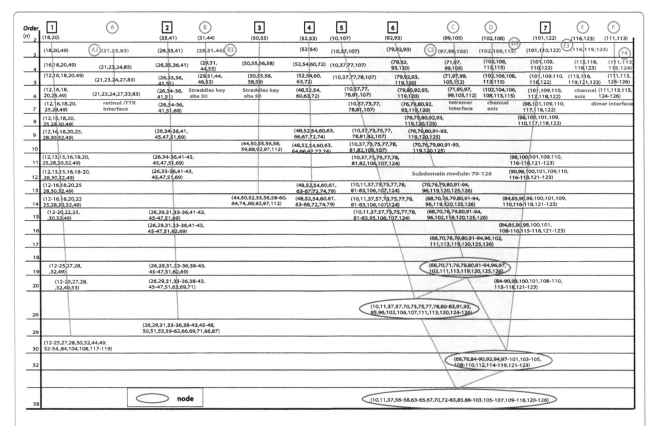

Figure 5 TTR cluster tree. The above diagram shows clusters of mutually associated sites found within a multiple sequence alignment for transthyretin, composed of 465 non-redundant sequences. It is remarkable that although some of the branches converge to a large node forming a major module, many of the branches do not converge to large nodes. This suggests that much of Transthyretin lacks the structural stability that comes with large nodes composed of many interdependent branches. This may provide insight as to why Transthyretin is susceptible to misfolding.

The overall cluster tree for TTR is remarkably different from the ubiquitin cluster tree in that there are large branches in TTR that do not converge into the rest of the tree. This may suggest that TTR does not have the internal stability that ubiquitin has, and may be more prone to misfolding. Further work on other proteins that are prone to misfolding would be warranted here, to see if non-converging cluster trees are characteristic of potential instability. Those results would need to be compared with the cluster trees for strongly stable proteins. An overview of our results and predictions is provided in Table 3.

Conclusions

We have introduced here a powerful new approach for analyzing the multiple sequence alignment data of protein families and discovering key associations among aligned sites and their importance within the 3D structure. Using two proteins of known structure and function as a test bench, our method revealed key associations among residues and sites that appear to have important structural and functional significance. It can, therefore, be applied to protein families of unknown structure and function. From our work, statistically analyzing the multiple aligned sequences for a protein family through the pattern discovery method presented in this paper revealed many key residue–residue contacts, as well as the sub-domain structure of ubiquitin and TTR. When the discovered attribute clusters were arranged according to their order, cluster trees were constructed which rendered further insights (dependent upon the hierarchy) into how the protein may fold. With our site clustering results, the secondary structure of ubiquitin forms four modules, which are closely associated with the four regions of perturbation in Lys-48 and Lys-63 linked Ub_2 previously reported. Two categories of cluster branches, Types I and Type II, as we proposed, were discovered that may render a more a detailed understanding of how the protein folds. Furthermore, we observe that

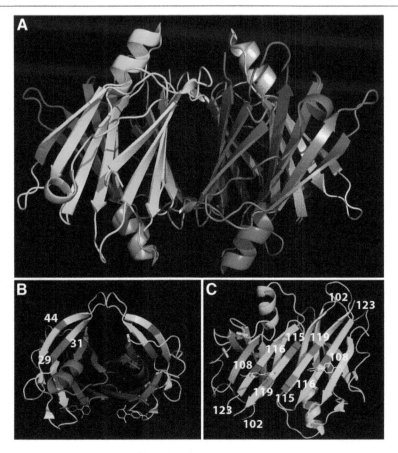

Figure 6 Transthyretin subdomain module and clusters. (A) The structure for the complete tetramer (pdb 1002), composed of four transthyretin monomers. **(B)** The sub-domain module, formed by three converging branches in the cluster tree (shown in light green in Figure 5) is shown in red. This module forms the dimer interface. Cluster B3 is shown in magenta in **(B)**. Its importance is indicated by the fact that it straddles site 30, for which there is a well known val30met mutation that leads to misfolding and amyloidosis. This suggests that cluster B3, consisting of sites 29, 30 and 44 **(B)**, has a critical roll in achieving a stable folded 3D structure. **(C)** Clusters D3 (labeled in yellow) and E3 (labeled in white) appear to be closely related. Each trio of mutually associated sites has remarkable symmetry, with one site at each end of the homotetramer channel, and one site in the center of the thyroxin binding site. The two residues at each end of both trios is likely important for the stabilization of the thyroxin pockets.

three types of attribute clusters were identified by our method, H-bonded, van der Waals, and extended clusters associated with binding sites. Such observations give additional insights into which associations of aligned sites make key contributions to a protein's structural stability. Using the binding sites in the 1UBQ model and previous discoveries in the literature, we validate that the discovered clusters have both structural and functional significance. The TTR cluster diagram revealed further secrets of its 3D structure. Six short, non-converging branches were found, all of which contain clusters that have important structural or functional significance. Only one multi-branch sub-domain module was found for TTR, associated with the interface between the two monomers. The number of non-converging branches into large modules, however, suggests that TTR may be prone to instability when folding.

The method presented here, backed by previous work with ubiquitin and TTR, suggests that granular computing as a concept can make an important new framework for revealing the relationship between low-order (three or four residues) residue–residue contacts and the demarcation of higher-order sub-domains, using a cluster tree. This sub-molecular hierarchical view also identifies sites within a protein that may be of particular structural or functional importance in the design of new drugs, for example. The ability to discover key residue–residue contacts, branches, and larger structural sub-domains within a protein through the k-modes analysis of the multiple sequence alignment will be a significant asset in understanding the details in the sequence of protein folding, structure, and functionality among different residue locations within a hierarchical global protein framework. Furthermore, by discovering the important attribute clusters within a protein, predictions can also be made as to which mutations could be more harmful or more stable than others. All these play an important role in furthering our understanding of the information processing capability of genes and proteins, in terms of the specific use of functional units at specific locations on the sequence to create the 3D structure as well as the internal and external functionality of the molecules.

Methods

The ubiquitin protein family was chosen as a suitable workbench to test our method for three reasons. First, the number of samples is reasonably large, numbering a few thousand, permitting a meaningful statistical analysis. Second, the structure of ubiquitin is well known and a 3D model is available from the Protein Database [38]. The available 1UBQ 3D model permitted us to compare the results and analyze their implication in terms of their structure and folding. Finally, there is considerable knowledge of the functions of ubiquitin, the most well known of which is the labeling of proteins for destruction within the cells of eukaryotic life [39,55].

In our experiment, an aligned set of 2,442 sequences for ubiquitin was downloaded from the Pfam database [56]. The data were then computationally post processed to retain columns less than 20% gapped. After the insertions and duplicate sequences were removed, the number of unique sequences remaining was 1,066 and the number of aligned sites remaining was 69. The alignment did not include the first 5 sites that were missing from the Pfam alignment at the time we performed our analyses. These 69 sites represented sites 6–74 of the ubiquitin primary structure using the 1UBQ 3Dmodel from the protein data base [38].

At the onset of our experiment, the pre-processed data, consisting of 1,066 aligned, unique sequences was then analyzed using the k-modes algorithm for discovering clusters of attributes (sites) within the primary structure of ubiquitin. The data were also analyzed to compute the $SR(mode)$ value for each cluster.

The first step in analyzing the results was to manually arrange the clusters into a cluster tree as described earlier in the Section "Attribute clusters and information granules". Branches containing the lowest-order clusters are denoted as *primary branches* and are numbered from 1 to 14 across the top of Figure 2. Within a nested hierarchical set of clusters, each cluster will be informative to examine; there is no official representative cluster. One way of choosing a representative cluster is to pick out clusters that have higher mutual interdependency than others, indicated by a high $SR(mode)$ for the cluster. For the ubiquitin family only, this method was chosen, although any other cluster could have been picked as a representative cluster for a particular branch. The first step was to compute the $SR(mode)$ value

for each cluster in the primary branch. The cluster in each branch with the highest $SR(mode)$ value was chosen as the representative cluster, since it had the highest mutual interdependency. If two clusters in the same branch had similar values for $SR(mode)$ the cluster with the higher order was selected, since the higher-order cluster would contain more sites and, thus, be more informative and interesting. For the same reason, if a higher-order cluster in the branch had a $SR(mode)$ value that was only slightly lower than the highest $SR(mode)$ value of another, lower-order cluster, the higher-order cluster instead was chosen as the representative cluster for that primary branch. For consistency, a certain percentage difference can be chosen as the cutoff. These representative clusters, each composed of two or more sites with a high interdependence as indicated by the $SR(mode)$ value, were then computationally analyzed to determine what patterns (associations of specific amino acids within the sites spanned by the attribute cluster) were contained within each representative cluster. The residual of each of the patterns was also computed. The discovered attribute clusters of ubiquitin were examined in terms of their relevance to the 3D structure using the 1UBQ model. They were also analyzed for function as described in the literature. Statistically significant patterns were computationally discovered by searching for amino acid combinations that had an adjusted residual value greater than 3.29, which corresponds to a confidence level greater than 99.9%. A multiple sequence alignment for TTR, downloaded from Pfam [50], was also analyzed using the same procedure outlined above for ubiquitin with the exception as to how the representative clusters were chosen. Since all clusters are statistically significant, any cluster can be chosen as a sample cluster. For TTR, we chose the third-order clusters as the sample clusters. Since the criterion was different for TTR, they were referred to as sample clusters rather than representative clusters. Ideally, if time and resources permit, all clusters should be examined to more fully understand their significance.

Abbreviations

3D: Three-dimensional; DNA: Deoxyribonucleic acid; ETM: Evolutionary trace method; FC: Functional complexity; G: The set of 20 normally occurring amino acids; K: Number of clusters to be output by the k-modes algorithm; M: Number of sequences in a multiple sequence alignment; N: Number of sites in an individual protein or multiple sequence alignment; NMR: Nuclear magnetic resonance; RBP: Retinol binding protein; Rii': Normalized redundancy measure; RNA: Ribonucleic acid; $SR(i)$: Normalized interdependency redundancy; TTR: Transthyretin; Ub_2: Ubiquitin dimer; X: A N-tuple; Y: Represents a cluster of mutually associated sites; α: Represents a particular amino acid; λ: Represents a pattern of amino acids.

Competing interests

The authors declare that they have no competing interests.

Acknowledgments

The authors are grateful to the Natural Science and Engineering Research Council of Canada (NSERC) Discovery Grants; the Advanced Food and Materials Network (AFMnet), the National Centre of Excellence of Canada; and the National Natural Science Foundation Grant of China.

Author details
[1]School of Computer Science, University of Guelph, 50 Stone Road East, Guelph, ON N1G 2W1, Canada. [2]Department of System Design Engineering, University of Waterloo, 200 University Ave. W, Waterloo, ON N2L 3G1, Canada.

References
1. Y Yao, International Conference on rough Sets and Emerging Intelligent Systems Paradigms, Warsaw, Poland 2007. Lecture Notes in Computer Science, in *Rough Sets and Intelligent Systems Paradigms: International Conference, RSEISP 2007, Warsaw, Poland, 28–30 June 2007: Proceedings*, ed. by M Kryszkiewicz (Springer, 2007), pp. 101–112. vol. 4585/2007
2. Y Yao, IEEE International Conference on Granular Computing, in *Granular Computing. IEEE International Conference. 2008*, ed. by TY Lin, X Hu, Q Liu, X Shen, J Xia, J Wang, T He, N Cercone (Institute of Electrical and Electronics Engineers, Hangzhou, China, 2008), pp. 80–85
3. W Pedrycz, A Skowron, V Kreinovich, *Handbook of Granular Computing* (Wiley, West Sussex, 2008)
4. J Sorace, K Canfield, S Russell, Functional bioinformatics: the cellular response database. Front Biosci **2**, a31–a36 (1997)
5. SE Ilyin, A Bernal, D Horowitz, CK Derian, H Xin, Functional informatics: convergence and integration of automation and bioinformatics. Pharmacogenomics **5**, 721–730 (2004)
6. KK Durston, DK Chiu, DL Abel, JT Trevors, Measuring the functional sequence complexity of proteins. Theor Biol Med Model **4**, 1–14 (2007)
7. TWH Lui, DKY Chiu, Associative classification using patterns from nested granules. Int. J. Granular Comput. Rough Sets Intell. Syst. **1**, 393–406 (2010)
8. TWH Lui, DKY Chiu, in *Foundations of Compuational Intelligence*, ed. by A Abraham, AE Hassanien, AP de Carvalho, V Snael (Springer-Verlag, 2009)
9. AK Wong, TS Liu, CC Wang, Statistical analysis of residue variability in cytochrome. c. J. Mol. Biol. **102**, 287–295 (1976)
10. RF Smith, TF Smith, Automatic generation of primary sequence patterns from sets of related protein sequences. Proc. Natl Acad. Sci. USA **87**, 118–122 (1990)
11. O Lichtarge, HR Bourne, FE Cohen, An evolutionary trace method defines binding surfaces common to protein families. J Mol Biol **257**, 342–358 (1996)
12. S Erdin, RM Ward, E. Venner, O Lichtarge, Evolutionary trace annotation of protein function in the structural proteome. J Mol Biol **396**, 1451–1473 (2010)
13. AH Liu, A Califano, Functional classification of proteins by pattern discvoery and top-down clustering of primary sequences. IBM Syst J **40**, 379–393 (2001)
14. AKC Wong, DKY Chiu, W Huang, A discrete-valued clustering algorithm with applications to biomolecular data. Inf Sci **139**, 97–112 (2001)
15. WH Au, KC Chan, AK Wong, Y Wang, Attribute clustering for grouping, selection, and classification of gene expression data. IEEE/ACM Trans. Comput. Biol. Bioinf **2**, 83–101 (2005)
16. DK Chiu, Y Wang, Multipattern consensus regions in multiple aligned protein sequences and their segmentation. EURASIP J. Bioinf. Syst. Biol. 2006, 2006 **35809**, 1–8 (2006). doi:10.1155/BSB/2006/35809
17. DKY Chiu, TWH Lui, Integrated use of multiple interdependent patterns for biomolecular sequence analysis. Int. J. Fuzzy Syst **4**, 766–775 (2002)
18. DKY Chiu, T Kolodziejczak, Inferencing consensus structure from nucleic acid sequences. Comput. Appl. Biosci. (currently Bioinformatics) **7**, 347–352 (1991)
19. RD Finn, J Tate, J Mistry, PC Coggill, SJ Sammut, HR Hotz, G Ceric, K Forslund, SR Eddy, EL Sonnhammer, A Bateman, The Pfam protein families database. Nucleic Acids Res **36**, D281–D288 (2008)
20. SJ Sammut, RD Finn, A Bateman, Pfam 10 years on: 10,000 families and still growing. Brief Bioinf. **9**, 210–219 (2008)
21. AKC Wong, GCL Li, Simutaneous pattern and data clustering for pattern cluster analysis. IEEE Trans. Knowl. Data Eng. **20**, 911–923 (2008)
22. AKC Wong, TS Liu, Typicality, diversity, and feature pattern of an ensemble. IEEE Trans Comput **c-24**, 158–181 (1975)
23. AKC Wong, Y Wang, High-Order Pattern Discovery from Discrete-Valued Data. IEEE Trans. Knowl. Syst **9**, 877–893 (1997)
24. AKC Wong, Y Wang, GCL Li, in *Encyclopedia of Data Warehousing and Mining*, ed. by J. Wang, 2nd edn. (IGI Global, 2008), pp. 1497–1504
25. Z Li, HA Scheraga, Monte Carlo-minimization approach to the multiple-minima problem in protein folding. Proc. Natl Acad. Sci. USA **84**, 6611–6615 (1987)
26. S Theodoridis, K Koutroumbas, *Pattern Recognition*, 3rd edn. (Academic Press, San Diego, CA, 2006)
27. AKC Wong, Y Wang, *Data Mining and Discover*e, a White Paper on PDS Data Mining Technologies* (Pattern Discovery Software Systems Ltd, 2002). http://www.google.ca/url?sa=t&rct=j&q=v0009869_003.doc&source=web&cd=1&ved=0CCcQFjAA&url=http%3A%2F%2Fwww2.technologyevaluation.com%2Fcommon%2Fuploads%2FV0009869_003.doc&ei=Xa3OT4v_J6Ti0QHtwMCNBw&usg=AFQjCNGJBK0sJ60HUc09W02nqilyNVxdYw
28. CB Anfinsen, Points of current interest in protein chemistry. Lab Invest **10**, 987–991 (1961)
29. W Zhu, in *IEEE International Conference on Granular Computing*, ed. by TY Lln, X Hu, Q Liu, X Shen, J Xia, J Wang, T He, N Cercone (Institute of Electrical and Electronics Engineers, Hangzhou, China, 2008), p. 94
30. A Bargiela, W Pedrycz, *Granular Computing: An Introduction* (Kluwer, Netherlands, 2002)
31. A Bargiela, W Pedrycz, Toward a theory of granular computing for human-centered information processing. IEEE Trans Fuzzy Syst **16**, 320–330 (2008)
32. W Pedrycz, A Bargiela, Granular clustering: a granular signature of data. IEEE Trans Syst Man Cybern B **32**, 212–224 (2002)
33. TY Lin, IEEE International Conference on Granular Computing, in *Granular Computing. IEEE International Conference. 2008*, ed. by TY Lln, X Hu, Q Liu, X Shen, J Xia, J Wang, T He, N Cercone (Institute of Electrical and Electronics Engineers, Hangzhou, China, 2008), pp. 5–10
34. TY Lin, IEEE International Conference on Granular Computing, in *Granular Computing. IEEE International Conference. 2008*, ed. by TY Lln, X Hu, Q Liu, X Shen, J Xia, J Wang, T He, N Cercone (Institute of Electrical and Electronics Engineers, Hangzhou, China, 2008), pp. 48–53
35. G Wang, J Hu, Q Zhang, X Liu, J Zhou, IEEE International Conference on Granular Computing, in *Granular Computing. IEEE International Conference. 2008*, ed. by TY Lln, X Hu, Q Liu, X Shen, J Xia, J Wang, T He, N Cercone (Institute of Electrical and Electronics Engineers, Hangzhou, China, 2008), p. 67
36. J Yao, IEEE International Conference on Granular Computing, in *Granular Computing. IEEE International Conference. 2008*, ed. by TY Lln, X Hu, Q Liu, X Shen, J Xia, J Wang, T He, N Cercone (Institute of Electrical and Electronics Engineers, Hangzhou, China, 2008), pp. 74–79
37. S Vijay Kumar, CE Bugg, WJ Cook, Structure of ubiquitin refined at 1.8 A resolution. J Mol Biol **194**, 531–544 (1987)
38. S Vijay Kumar, CE Bugg, WJ Cook, *1UBQ Structure of ubiquitin refined at 1.8 angstroms resolution*, http://www.rcsb.org/pdb/explore/explore.do?structureId=1ubq
39. L Hicke, HL Schubert, CP Hill, Ubiquitin-binding domains. Nat Rev Mol Cell Biol **6**, 610–621 (2005)
40. R Varadan, M Assfalg, A Haririnia, S Raasi, C Pickart, D Fushman, Solution conformation of Lys63-linked di-ubiquitin chain provides clues to functional diversity of polyubiquitin signaling. J Biol Chem **279**, 7055–7063 (2004)
41. R Varadan, O Walker, C Pickart, D Fushman, Structural properties of polyubiquitin chains in solution. J Mol Biol **324**, 637–647 (2002)
42. WJ Cook, LC Jeffrey, M Carson, Z Chen, CM Pickart, Structure of a diubiquitin conjugate and a model for interaction with ubiquitin conjugating enzyme (E2). J Biol Chem **267**, 16467–16471 (1992)
43. C Branden, J Tooze, *Introduction to Protein Structure* (Garland Publishing Inc., New York, NY, 1999), pp. 9–10
44. CL McClendon, G Friedland, DL Mobley, H Amirkhani, MP Jacobson, Quantifying Correlations Between Allosteric Sites in Thermodynamic Ensembles. J Chem. Theory Comput **5**, 2486–2502 (2009)
45. B Isralewitz, M Gao, K Schulten, Steered molecular dynamics and mechanical functions of proteins. Curr Opin Struct Biol **11**, 224–230 (2001)
46. Z Zheng, TR Sosnick, Protein vivisection reveals elusive intermediates in folding. J Mol Biol **397**, 777–788 (2010)
47. P Schanda, V Forge, B Brutscher, Protein folding and unfolding studied at atomic resolution by fast two-dimensional NMR spectroscopy. Proc. Natl Acad. Sci. USA **104**, 11257–11262 (2007)
48. HM Naylor, ME Newcomer, The structure of human retinol-binding protein (RBP) with its carrier protein transthyretin reveals an interaction with the carboxy terminus of RBP. Biochemistry **38**, 2647–2653 (1999)
49. SE Kolstoe, PP Mangione, V Bellotti, GW Taylor, GA Tennent, S Deroo, AJ Morrison, AJ Cobb, A Coyne, MG McCammon, TD Warner, J Mitchell, R Gill, MD Smith, SV Ley, CV Robinson, SP Wood, MB Pepys, Trapping of palindromic ligands within native transthyretin prevents amyloid formation. Proc. Natl Acad. Sci. USA **107**, 20483–20488 (2010)

50. Pfam (Wellcome Trust Sanger Institute), http://pfam.sanger.ac.uk/family/PF00576. Accessed June 2011

51. SL Adamski-Werner, SK Palaninathan, JC Sacchettini, JW Kelly, Diflunisal analogues stabilize the native state of transthyretin. Potent inhibition of amyloidogenesis. J Med Chem **47**, 355–374 (2004)

52. SL Adamski-Werner, SK Palaninathan, JC Sacchettini, JA Kelly, *2F7I structure for human transthyretin*, http://www.rcsb.org/pdb/explore/explore.do?structureId=2F7I

53. C Folli, N Pasquato, I Ramazzina, R Battistutta, G Zanotti, R Berni, Distinctive binding and structural properties of piscine transthyretin. FEBS Lett **555**, 279–284 (2003)

54. C Folli, N Pasquato, I Ramazzina, R Battistutta, G Zannotti, R Berni, *1OO2 Structure of piscine transthyretin*, http://www.rcsb.org/pdb/explore/explore.do?structureId=1oo2

55. M French, K Swanson, SC Shih, I Radhakrishnan, L Hicke, Identification and characterization of modular domains that bind ubiquitin. Methods Enzymol **399**, 135–157 (2005)

56. Pfam (Wellcome Trust Sanger Institute), http://pfam.sanger.ac.uk/family/PF00240. Accessed October 2010

5

Inference of dynamic biological networks based on responses to drug perturbations

Noah Berlow[1], Lara Davis[2], Charles Keller[2] and Ranadip Pal[1]*

Abstract

Drugs that target specific proteins are a major paradigm in cancer research. In this article, we extend a modeling framework for drug sensitivity prediction and combination therapy design based on drug perturbation experiments. The recently proposed target inhibition map approach can infer stationary pathway models from drug perturbation experiments, but the method is limited to a steady-state snapshot of the underlying dynamical model. We consider the inverse problem of possible dynamic models that can generate the static target inhibition map model. From a deterministic viewpoint, we analyze the inference of Boolean networks that can generate the observed binarized sensitivities under different target inhibition scenarios. From a stochastic perspective, we investigate the generation of Markov chain models that satisfy the observed target inhibition sensitivities.

Keywords: Drug perturbation experiments; Network inference; Pathway design

1 Introduction

Personalized medicine based on individual genetic circuit is a primary goal of Systems Medicine research. The application of a population-averaged pathway for an individual cancer patient limits the success of targeted therapies since there can be huge variations in the regulatory pathways of distinct cancer patients [1-5]. Generating a detailed model of the specific regulatory pathway of the patient is extremely difficult due to the enormous experimental data requirements on model parameter estimation. Often, only a specific aspect of the regulatory system is considered based on the final objective of modeling. For instance, the goal of individual tumor sensitivity to targeted drugs is frequently based on genetic mutations [6], gene expression measurements [7], or a combination of genetic and epigenetic information [8,9]. The approach of using genetic mutations for predicting the sensitivity is restricted by the presence of non-functional mutations and other latent variables. Statistical tests have been used to show that genetic mutations can be predictive of the drug sensitivity in non-small cell lung cancers [6], but the classification rates for the aberrant samples are still low. In [7], gene expression profiles are used to predict the binarized efficacy of a drug over a cell line with the accuracy of the designed classifiers ranging from 64% to 92%. In [10], a co-expression extrapolation (COXEN) approach was used to predict the drug sensitivity for samples outside the training set with an accuracy of around 80%. [8] uses Elastic Net modeling over multiple genetic characterizations to achieve Pearson correlation coefficients in the range of 0.1 to 0.8 between experimental and predicted drug sensitivities. [11] has used Random Forests over the NCI 60 cancer cell lines for drugs sensitivity prediction. Tumor sensitivity prediction has also been considered as (a) a drug-induced topology alteration [12] using phospho-proteomic signals and prior biological knowledge of generic pathway and (b) a molecular tumor profile-based prediction [6,13].

We have considered a functional approach based on tumor cell viability to multiple kinase inhibitor drugs [14,15]. The experimental data is generated using a drug screen consisting of D multi-target kinase inhibitor compounds and subjecting tumor cells to this array. Sensitivity for the individual drugs is measured after 72 h. The model developed from this approach is able to predict the steady state behavior of target inhibitor combinations but does not provide us with the dynamics of the model or the directionality (upstream or downstream) of the inferred target blocks.

*Correspondence: ranadip.pal@ttu.edu
[1] Department of Electrical and Computer Engineering, Texas Tech University, Lubbock, TX 79409, USA
Full list of author information is available at the end of the article

In this article, we analyze the generation of possible dynamic models satisfying the steady state model representation. We first show that the Target Inhibition Map (TIM) [14,15] approach can generate blocks of targets that are connected in series to form a pathway but the directionality of the blocks are unknown. Subsequently, we establish that a directional pathway can be converted to a deterministic Boolean network (BN) [16] model. The discrete representation of the TIM as a directional pathway allows us to select a minimal number of sequential inhibition experiments for inferring the actual dynamic model. To incorporate the continuous sensitivity behavior following drug inhibition, we consider the inverse problem of generation of Markov chains that satisfies for every target inhibition condition: the steady-state probability of non-tumorous state is equal to the normalized sensitivity. The set of dynamic models producing the static TIM can be utilized for robustness analysis of the combination therapy design and design of time-dependent combination therapies. The approach presented in this paper extends the static design to incorporate possible dynamics.

The paper is organized as follows. Section 2 provides a brief description of the TIM approach; Section 3 describes inference of deterministic BNs from TIM. The generation of stochastic Markov chains based on the TIM is presented in Section 4, and the conclusions are included in Section 5.

2 Target inhibition map model

In a recently proposed approach (details available in [14,15]), we considered experimental data on tumor sensitivity for various target inhibition combinations (corresponding to different multi-target inhibitory drugs) and generated a TIM model. The TIM predicts the steady-state tumor phenotypes for binary combinations of inhibition of functionally relevant targets (i.e. for n targets, there will be 2^n possible inhibition combinations). An example TIM for three targets K_1, K_2, K_3 is shown in Figure 1. The map in Figure 1 shows that inhibition of K_3 alone can inhibit the tumor or inhibition of both K_1 and K_2 can inhibit the tumor. The current setting of the TIM approach will consider only those targets that are functionally relevant in cell death in a new cancer

sample. These targets are often up-regulated in cancer either due to their own mutations or activations by some other enzymes (from now onwards, we will call such activations by enzyme(s) not considered in the final TIM as *latent activations*). The TIM approach has also been extended to model continuous scaled sensitivity predictions, i.e., the steady state predictions for various binary target inhibition combinations will be in the range $[0, 1]$.

We should note that the TIM only provides a steady state snapshot of the regulatory behavior occurring in a cancer pathway following application of various target inhibitors. The TIM can be used to arrive at possible infinite horizon simultaneous combination therapies with fixed intervention at all-time steps. The next step in the framework is exploring the possible dynamical models producing the steady state TIM. The advantages of exploring the dynamics of the TIM include (a) *model-based experimentation,* having a constrained set of dynamical models that can produce the TIM will allow us to algorithmically generate the optimal set of target expression measurements required to decipher the actual unique dynamical model, and (b) *sequential drug delivery,* the dynamical models can be used to analyze the behavior of sequential combination drug application.

3 Discrete deterministic dynamic model inference
The primary contribution of the paper lies in the generation of stochastic Boolean network models satisfying the given normalized sensitivities for different inhibition combinations. We consider the generation of the Markov models based on altering the deterministic dynamical models. In this section, a review of the work generating discrete deterministic dynamical models reported in [14] is presented to enhance the readability of the subsequent section on inference of stochastic dynamical models.

To arrive at potential discrete deterministic dynamical models, we consider the likely directional pathways that can generate the inferred TIM and map the directional pathways to deterministic BN models. The TIM can be used to locate the feasible mutation patterns and constrain the search space of the dynamic models generating the TIM. For instance, mutation or external activation of K_2 or

$k_1 k_2$ / k_3	0 0	0 1	1 1	1 0
0	0	0	1	0
1	1	1	1	1

Figure 1 TIM for mutations in K_1 and K_2.

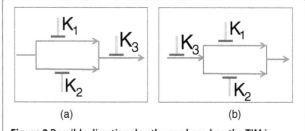

Figure 2 Possible directional pathways based on the TIM in Figure 1 (a, b).

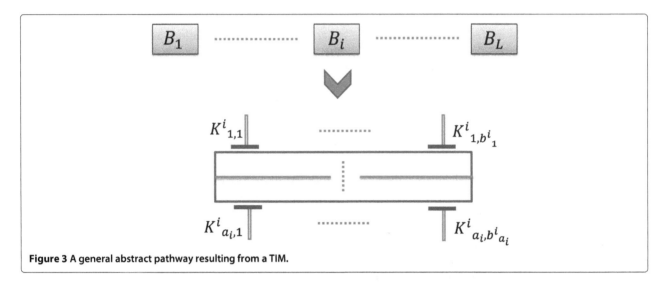

Figure 3 A general abstract pathway resulting from a TIM.

K_1 alone cannot result in the TIM of Figure 1; otherwise, the inhibition of K_2 or K_1 should have been able to block the tumor. Thus, feasible mutations or latent activation patterns are reduced to the following five sets of combinations, $\{K_1, K_2\}, \{K_1, K_3\}, \{K_2, K_3\}, \{K_3\}, \{K_1, K_2, K_3\}$, out of possible eight combinations. For each mutation or latent activation pattern, we can arrive at possible directional pathways producing the required steady state TIM output. For instance, Figure 2 shows two directional pathway possibilities for mutation or activation patterns $\{K_1, K_2\}$ and $\{K_3\}$, respectively. The pathways in Figure 2 show possible tumor survival circuits. In this model, if a left-to-right tumor survival pathway exists, the cancer survives. If the path is stopped, the tumor cells stop growing or involute.

3.1 Optimal set of experiments to infer the directional pathway structure

In this subsection, we analyze the minimum number of expression measurement experiments required to decipher the pathway directionality once the steady state structure (TIM) has been inferred. Knowledge of target expressions can be used to narrow down the possible

directional pathways. For instance, expressed K_1 following inhibition of K_3 for our earlier example will denote the feasibility of directional pathway of Figure 2a and removing the possibility of the directional pathway shown in Figure 2b. Note that latent activations and functionally irrelevant mutations may restrict the usefulness of mutation status in restricting the pathway search space. In the following paragraphs, we will consider a general pathway obtained from a TIM having the structure shown in Figure 3 but with unknown directionalities of the blocks and target positions. We will consider that the pathway has L blocks in series $(B_1, B_2, \cdots, B_L)$ and each block B_i has a_i parallel path segments with each segment j containing b_j^i targets $\left(K_{1,1}^i, K_{1,2}^i \cdots, K_{1,b_j^i}^i \right)$. The total number of targets in the general map is $N_K = \sum_{i=1}^{L} \sum_{j=1}^{a_i} b_j^i$.

Assuming that the N_K targets are distinct, the maximum number of distinct discrete dynamic models satisfying the structure is $L! \prod_{i=1}^{L} \prod_{j=1}^{a_i} (b_j^i)!$. If Figure 3 represents a possible directional orientation, the only targets that will have initial activations for the target inhibition combination $K_{1,1}^1, K_{2,1}^1 \cdots K_{a_1,1}^1$ to be effective is $K_{1,1}^1, K_{2,1}^1 \cdots K_{a_1,1}^1$. For our analysis, we are assuming that we can inhibit specific

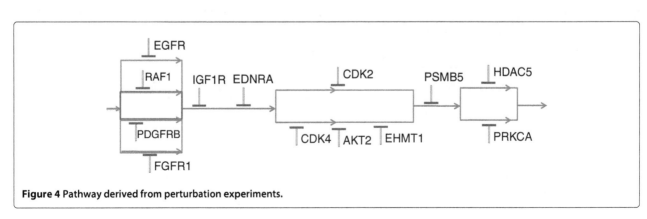

Figure 4 Pathway derived from perturbation experiments.

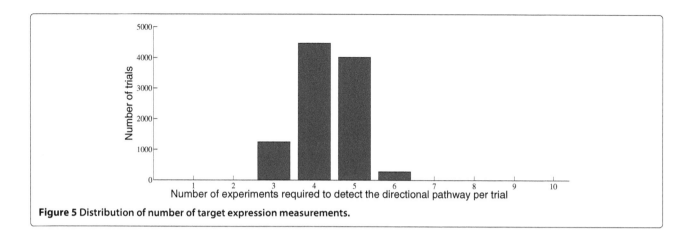

Figure 5 Distribution of number of target expression measurements.

targets of our choice and we can measure the steady state target expression following application of the target inhibitions. We can locate the directionality of the blocks B_1 to B_L with respect to each other (downstream or upstream) with the worst-case scenario of $L - 1$ steady state measurements. The expected number of experiments required to detect the directionality of L serial blocks is $\frac{2L-1}{3}$ for $L \geq 2$. To infer the directionality of targets in each parallel line of the block, one target from each line up to a maximum of $a_i - 1$ lines will be inhibited for each block B_i. If we consider a single block B_i, each experiment can detect the location of $a_i - 1$ targets; thus, the total number of experiments required to decipher the possible directionalities (upstream or downstream) of the targets in the block B_i is $\leq \max\left(\max_{j \in S_i} b_j^i - 2, \lceil \frac{\sum_{j \in S_i} b_j^i - a_i}{a_i - 1} \rceil - 1\right)$ where $S_i = \{1, \cdots, a_i\}$. Thus for the overall map, the worst case number of experiments N_E^w required to decipher the directionalities of all the targets is upper-bounded by [17]

$$N_E^w \leq \max_{i \in S}\left\{\max\left(\max_{j \in S_i} b_j^i - 2, \lceil \frac{\sum_{j \in S_i} b_j^i - a_i}{a_i - 1} \rceil - -1\right)\right\} + L - 1 \tag{1}$$

where $S = \{1, \cdots, L\}$. The expected number of experiments N_E^a required to decipher the directionalities of all the targets is upper-bounded by

$$N_E^a \leq \max_{i \in S}\left\{\max\left(\max_{j \in S_i} \frac{2b_j^i - 4}{3}, \lceil \frac{\sum_{j \in S_i} 2b_j^i - a_i}{3(a_i - 1)} \rceil - -1\right)\right\} + \frac{2L-1}{3} \tag{2}$$

3.1.1 Simulation results on optimal experimental steps

For our simulation results, we consider a pathway derived from targeted drug perturbation experiments carried out at Keller Laboratory at Oregon Health and Science University on canine osteosarcoma cell cultures. Sixty targeted cancer drugs were tested on cell cultures, and a TIM was generated based on the viability data using the approach provided in [14,15]. For our simulation results, we will consider one of the plausible directional pathways derived from the TIM to be the actual pathway and estimate the number of target expression measurements required to arrive at it if the directional information is not known. The directional pathway assumed to be the actual pathway is shown in Figure 4 consisting of 13 targets. If we compare Figure 4 with the general pathway in Figure 3,

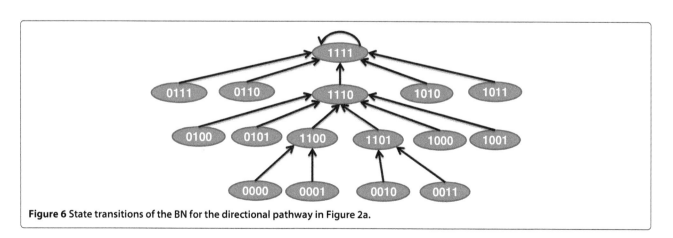

Figure 6 State transitions of the BN for the directional pathway in Figure 2a.

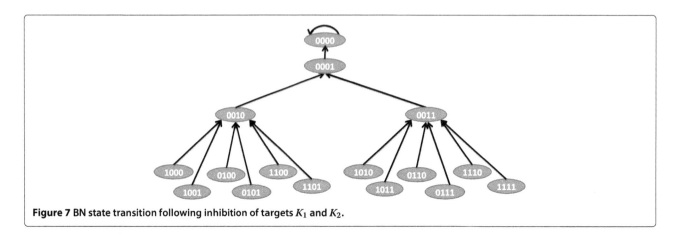

Figure 7 BN state transition following inhibition of targets K_1 and K_2.

the number of serial blocks $L = 6$. Similarly, $a_1 = 4, a_2 = 1, a_3 = 1, a_4 = 2, a_5 = 1, a_6 = 2$, and $b_j^i = 1$ for all i and j except $b_2^4 = 3$. Since there is only one serial block with $b_j^i > 2$, we can reduce Equation 1 to $N_E^w \leq \max_{i \in S, j \in S_i} b_j^i - 2 + L - 1 = 6$ and Equation 2 to $N_E^a \leq \max_{i \in S, j \in S_i} \frac{2b_j^i - 4}{3} + \frac{2L-1}{3} = 4.33$. To compare these numbers with simulation results, we conducted 10,000 simulation runs to detect the pathway shown in Figure 4 starting from random inhibition of serial blocks. The distribution of the number of steady state experiments required to detect the directional pathway is shown in Figure 5. We note that the maximum number of experiments required was 6 as given by N_E^w in Equation 1, and the expectation of the distribution is 4.33 which is the same as the bound on N_E^a given by Equation 2.

3.2 Deterministic dynamical model from directional pathway

To generate a BN model of a directional pathway, we will first consider the starting mutations or latent activations. The number of states in the BN will be 2^{n+1} for n targets. Each state will have $n + 1$ bits with first n bits referring to the discrete state of the n targets and the least significant bit (LSB) will correspond to the binarized phenotype, i.e., tumor (1) or normal (0).

The rules of state transition for this special class of BNs are as follows [17]:

Rule a. A target state at time $t + 1$ becomes 1 if any immediate upstream neighbor has state 1 at time t for OR relationships or all immediate upstream neighbors have state 1 at time t for AND relationships. Note that the

Table 1 Inhibition matrix T_c for inhibition of K_1 and K_2

	0000	0001	0010	0011	0100	0101	0110	0111	1000	1001	1010	1011	1100	1101	1110	1111
0000	1	0	0	0	0	0	0	0	0	0	0	0	0	0	0	0
0001	0	1	0	0	0	0	0	0	0	0	0	0	0	0	0	0
0010	0	0	1	0	0	0	0	0	0	0	0	0	0	0	0	0
0011	0	0	0	1	0	0	0	0	0	0	0	0	0	0	0	0
0100	1	0	0	0	0	0	0	0	0	0	0	0	0	0	0	0
0101	0	1	0	0	0	0	0	0	0	0	0	0	0	0	0	0
0110	0	0	1	0	0	0	0	0	0	0	0	0	0	0	0	0
0111	0	0	0	1	0	0	0	0	0	0	0	0	0	0	0	0
1000	1	0	0	0	0	0	0	0	0	0	0	0	0	0	0	0
1001	0	1	0	0	0	0	0	0	0	0	0	0	0	0	0	0
1010	0	0	1	0	0	0	0	0	0	0	0	0	0	0	0	0
1011	0	0	0	1	0	0	0	0	0	0	0	0	0	0	0	0
1100	1	0	0	0	0	0	0	0	0	0	0	0	0	0	0	0
1101	0	1	0	0	0	0	0	0	0	0	0	0	0	0	0	0
1110	0	0	1	0	0	0	0	0	0	0	0	0	0	0	0	0
1111	0	0	0	1	0	0	0	0	0	0	0	0	0	0	0	0

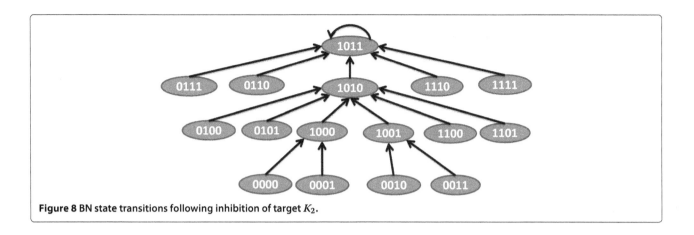

Figure 8 BN state transitions following inhibition of target K_2.

examples have OR type of relations as they are the most commonly found relations in biological pathways (based on illustrated pathways in KEGG).

Rule b. For the BN without any drug, the targets that are mutated or have latent activations will transition to state 1 within one-time step.

Rule c. For a target with no inherent mutation or latent activation, the state will become 0 at time $t + 1$ if the immediate upstream activators of the target has state 0 at time t.

The BN construction from directional pathways mentioned above is described for targets acting as oncogenes (activation causing cancers), but it can also be extended to tumor suppressors (inhibition causing cancers) by considering the inverse state of the tumor suppressor in the above framework.

We illustrate the BN construction algorithm using the example of the pathway shown in Figure 2a. The downstream target K_3 can be activated by either of the upstream activated targets K_1 or K_2. The corresponding BN transition diagram for this pathway is shown in Figure 6. For instance, if we consider the state 1001 at time t, it denotes K_2, K_3 being inactive and K_1 being active and the phenotype being tumorous. Based on the directional pathway in Figure 2a, tumor proliferation is caused by activated K_3 and thus the phenotype will change to non-tumorous (i.e., 0) at $t + 1$. The activated K_1 will activate K_3 at time $t+1$ and K_2 will also be activated in the absence of continued inhibition as we assumed that mutation or latent activations activate both K_1 and K_2. Thus, the next state at time $t + 1$ will be 1110. Note that we are considering that the effect of one application of the drug remains for one-time step and thus the targets K_1 and K_2 revert back to 1 if the drug is not continued in the next time step. If the drug effect continues for multi-time steps, then 1001 will transition to 1010. Note that some transitions may appear like the tumor state is oscillating in the transient phase such as the path $0010 \rightarrow 1101 \rightarrow 1110 \rightarrow 1111$. The reason is that the network can only be in the starting state 0010 where K_1 and K_2 is inactivated through application of some external intervention and not through normal transitions as the network has K_1 and K_2 mutated. Scenarios following application of drugs can produce alternating tumor proliferation and inactivation states in the transient phase.

3.3 Altered BN following target inhibition

The BN in Figure 6 can also be represented by a 16×16 transition matrix P representing the state transitions. To generate the dynamic model after inhibition of s specific targets $I = \{K_1, K_2, \cdots, K_s\}$ (by application of targeted drugs), the transition $i \rightarrow j$ in the untreated system will be converted to $i \rightarrow z$ in the treated system where z is j with targets I set to 0. Each target inhibition combination can be considered as multiplying the initial transition matrix P by an intervention matrix T_c. Each row of T_c contains only one non-zero element of 1 based on how the inhibition alters the state. If we consider n targets, n T_c's in combination can produce a total of 2^n possible transformation

k_3 \ $k_1 k_2$	0 0	0 1	1 1	1 0
0	p_0	p_2	p_6	p_4
1	p_1	p_3	p_7	P_5

Figure 9 A probabilistic TIM.

Table 2 Example PTIM

	0 0	0 1	1 1	1 0
0	0	0	0.8	0
1	0.55	0.65	0.9	0.7

Table 3 Example of Markov chain transition probability matrix

	0000	0001	0010	0011	0100	0101	0110	0111	1000	1001	1010	1011	1100	1101	1110	1111
0000	0	0.1	0.12	0	0	0	0	0	0	0	0	0	0.78	0	0	0
0001	0	0.1	0	0	0	0	0	0	0	0	0	0	0.9	0	0	0
0010	0	0	0	0.2	0	0	0	0	0	0	0	0	0	0.8	0	0
0011	0	0	0	0.2	0	0	0	0	0	0	0	0	0.8	0	0	0
0100	0	0	0	0	0	0.3	0	0	0	0	0	0	0	0.7	0	0
0101	0	0	0	0	0	0.3	0	0	0	0	0	0	0	0.7	0	0
0110	0	0	0	0	0	0	0	0	0	0	0	0	0	0	0	1
0111	0	0	0	0	0	0	0	0	0	0	0	0	0	0	0	1
1000	0	0	0	0	0	0	0	0	0	0.35	0	0	0	0	0.65	0
1001	0	0	0	0	0	0	0	0	0	0.35	0	0	0	0	0.65	0
1010	0	0	0	0	0	0	0	0	0	0	0	0	0	0	0	1
1011	0	0	0	0	0	0	0	0	0	0	0	0	0	0	0	1
1100	0	0	0	0	0	0	0	0	0	0	0	0	0	0.45	0.55	0
1101	0	0	0	0	0	0	0	0	0	0	0	0	0	0.45	0.55	0
1110	0	0	0	0	0	0	0	0	0	0	0	0	0	0	0	1
1111	0	0	0	0	0	0	0	0	0	0	0	0	0	0	0	1

matrices $T_1, T_2, \cdots, T_{2^n}$. The TIM denotes the state of the LSB of the attractor for the 2^n transition matrices $PT_1, PT_2, \cdots, PT_{2^n}$ starting from initial state $11 \cdots 1$ (i.e., all targets considered in the TIM and tumor are activated). For instance, if we consider that our drug inhibits the targets K_1 and K_2 (i.e., set $S_1 = \{K_1, K_2\}$), the discrete dynamic model following application of the drug is shown in Figure 7. The intervention matrix corresponding to the inhibition of K_3 is shown in Table 1. The transition $i \to j$ is 1 only when inhibition of the first and second bits of i results in j.

We should note that the equilibrium state of the network 0000 has 0 for the tumor state. This is because the tumor is activated by K_3 and inhibition of K_1 and K_2 blocks activation of K_3 and thus should eradicate the tumor. On the other hand, since both K_1 and K_2 can cause tumor through activation of intermediate K_3, inhibition of only one of K_1 and K_2 will not block the tumor. The BN following inhibition of K_2 is shown in Figure 8 where the attractor 1011 denotes a tumorous phenotype.

4 Discrete stochastic dynamic model inference

The analysis so far has considered deterministic discrete binary states for the targets and tumor phenotype. A stochastic modeling approach will be preferred when we want to take into consideration that tumor phenotype (measured in terms of tumor size reduction, IC_{50} or cell cycle arrest) is a continuous variable. We have extended our TIM approach to probabilistic target inhibition map (PTIM) where the PTIM provides continuous sensitivity prediction values between 0 to 1 for all possible kinase inhibition combinations [14,15]. From a stochastic dynamical model perspective, we can consider the sensitivity prediction value provided by the PTIM as the steady state probability of the tumor phenotype being 0 (a similar approach with deterministic differential equation models for modeling the tumor sensitivity was considered in [18] and experimental data was assumed to reflect the steady state values). For instance, if we consider that a Markov chain of 16 states explain our dynamical model for the pathway shown in Figure 9, the entry PTIM (i, j) will reflect the steady state probability for the LSB = 0 for the model with target inhibitions i, j. For instance, p_5 reflects the sensitivity with target inhibition K_1 and K_3.

In this article, the discrete stochastic dynamic behavior will be modeled by a Markov chain where the states of the Markov chain contain information on the protein

Table 4 Simulated PTIM from Markov chain

	0 0	0 1	1 1	1 0
0	0.002003	0.002994	0.800463	0.002995
1	0.549716	0.649251	0.89785	0.698992

Table 5 Example PTIM 2

	0 0	0 1	1 1	1 0
0	0.02	0.01	0.98	0.03
1	0.65	0.89	1	0.9

Table 6 TIMs for the BN$_1$, BN$_2$, and BN$_3$, respectively

	0 0	0 1	1 1	1 0
BN$_1$	0	0	1	0
	1	1	1	1
BN$_2$	0	0	1	0
	0	1	1	1
BN$_3$	0	0	1	0
	0	0	1	0

expressions of the targets and the tumor status. Note that a detailed stochastic master equation model is a continuous time Markov chain and can be approximated by a discrete time Markov chain based on a suitable time step [19]. Also, Boolean networks can be incorporated as Markov chains where each row of the transition probability matrix contains a single 1 with remaining all entries being 0.

For the subsequent analysis, we will consider that we have n binarized targets in our model and the states of the Markov chain will be $0 \cdots 0$ to $1 \cdots 1$ where the LSB will denote the state of the tumor (1 denoting tumor proliferation and 0 denoting tumor reduction) and the remaining n bits denote the state of the n targets. The set of states of the Markov chain, denoted by the set $\mathcal{I}$, is of size $N = 2^{n+1}$. Let P denote the $N \times N$ transition probability matrix. Let $f_c(j)$ denote the value of the state j following Boolean intervention equal to the inverse binary value of decimal c, i.e., under intervention $f_3(x) = x$ AND (0011) denoting intervention of first and second targets and $f_5(x) = x$ AND (0101) denoting intervention of first and third targets. Let $\mathcal{I}_c$ denote the possible set of states following application of intervention c, i.e., $\mathcal{I}_c$ contains only the states i s.t. $f_c(i) = i$. For the above example, $\mathcal{I}_3 = \{0000, 0001, 0010, 0011\}$. Let $S_{c,i}$ denote the set of states j for which $i = f_c(j)$. Here, $S_{3,0} = \{0000, 1000, 0100, 1100\}$,

the set of states which, under inhibition $f_3(\cdot)$, transition into state i.

The targeted drugs usually inhibit a set of target proteins and modeling such a behavior can be approached in one of the two following ways:

(A_i) If the targeted drugs inhibit the set of proteins I, the dynamics of the system under drug delivery can be considered as a new Markov chain with transition probability matrix P_2 where the jth row of P_2 is same as the ith row of P, where j is i with targets I set to 0. For instance, in a four-target system where I is targets 1 and 2, rows 0000, 1000, 0100, and 1100 of P_2 will be the same as row 0000 of P. This approach refers to resetting the system to the state obtained by applying the drug and let it evolve from there. Note that the above described system will still show non-zero transition probabilities to states where the target set I may have non-zero values.

(A_{ii}) If we have transition probability $P(i, j)$ of moving from state i to state j in the uncontrolled system, for the new system with transition probability matrix P_3, we will add the transition probability $P(i, j)$ to $P(i, z)$ where z is j with targets I set to 0. This encompasses the behavior that if the system transitions from i to j, j has been turned to z by the intervention.

The following theorem proves that the aggregated steady state probability distribution for both the approaches are equal.

Theorem 4.1. Let π_2 and π_3 denote the stationary probability distributions of P_2 and P_3. If π_2^* denotes the aggregration of states after intervention C, i.e., $\pi_2^*(i) = \sum_{i_1 \in S_{i,c}} \pi_2(i_1)$ for $i \in \mathcal{I}_C$ and $\pi_2^*(i) = 0$ for $i \notin \mathcal{I}_C$, then π_2^* also satisfies the stationary probability distribution equations for P_3, i.e., $\pi_2^* = \pi_2^* P_3$. If P is ergodic, then $\pi_2^* = \pi_3$.

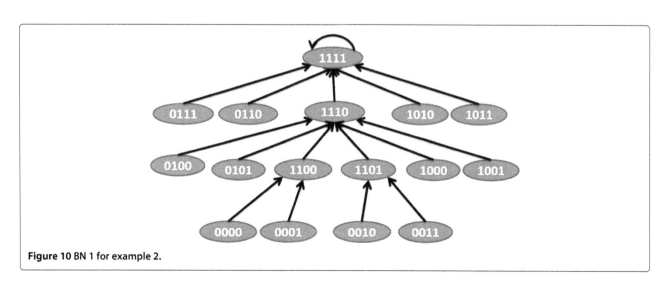

Figure 10 BN 1 for example 2.

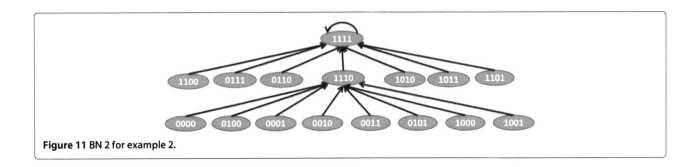

Figure 11 BN 2 for example 2.

Proof. Let $f_c(\cdot)$ be a Boolean intervention function. We have $\forall\, i, j \in \mathcal{I}$

$$P_2(i,j) = P(f_c(i),j) \tag{3}$$

and $P_3(i,j) = \sum_{k \in S_{c,j}} P(i,k)$. The stationary distribution for P_2 will satisfy

$$
\begin{aligned}
\pi_2(i) &= \sum_{j \in \mathcal{I}} \pi_2(j) P_2(j,i) \\
&= \sum_{z \in \mathcal{I}_C} P(z,i) \sum_{k \in S_{c,z}} \pi_2(k) \tag{4}
\end{aligned}
$$

Similarly, the stationary distribution for P_3 will satisfy $\pi_3(i) = 0$ for $i \notin \mathcal{I}_C$ and for $i \in \mathcal{I}_C$:

$$
\begin{aligned}
\pi_3(i) &= \sum_{j \in \mathcal{I}} \pi_3(j) P_3(j,i) \\
&= \sum_{z \in \mathcal{I}_C} \pi_3(z) P_3(z,i) \\
&= \sum_{z \in \mathcal{I}_C} \pi_3(z) \sum_{k \in S_i} P(z,k) \tag{5}
\end{aligned}
$$

If π_2^* denotes the aggregation of states, i.e., $\pi_2^*(i) = \sum_{i_1 \in S_{c,i}} \pi_2(i_1)$ for $i \in \mathcal{I}_C$, then we have for $i \in \mathcal{I}_C$:

$$
\begin{aligned}
\pi_2^*(i) &= \sum_{k \in S_{c,i}} \pi_2(k) = \sum_{k \in S_{c,i}} \sum_{z \in \mathcal{I}_C} P(z,k) \sum_{j \in S_z} \pi_2(j) \\
&= \sum_{z \in \mathcal{I}_C} \sum_{k \in S_{c,i}} P(z,k) \sum_{j \in S_{c,z}} \pi_2(j) \\
&= \sum_{z \in \mathcal{I}_C} \pi_2^*(z) \sum_{k \in S_{c,i}} P(z,k) \tag{6}
\end{aligned}
$$

Comparing Equations 5 and 6, we note that π_2^* also satisfies the stationary probability distribution equation for P_3, i.e., $\pi_2^* P_3 = \pi_2^*$. $\square$

We will model the target intervention based on perspective A_i. We next analyze whether every PTIM can be represented by a Markov chain. Theorem 4.2 shows that there always exists a Markov chain construction that can satisfy the PTIM steady state sensitivities.

Theorem 4.2. *For any given PTIM, $\exists$ at least one Markov chain satisfying the PTIM.*

Proof. Consider a PTIM with n targets $K_1, K_2, \cdots, K_n$ and thus 2^n PTIM entries $p_0, p_1, \cdots p_{2^n - 1}$, where p_i

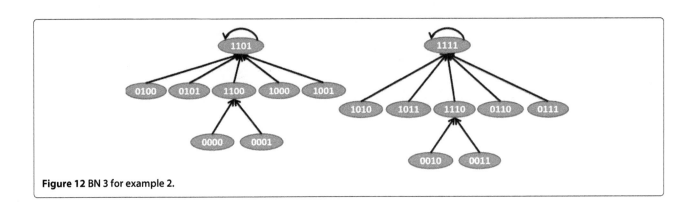

Figure 12 BN 3 for example 2.

denotes the PTIM-predicted steady state probability of tumor reduction when the active targets in the binary representation of i are inhibited. Denote the treatments corresponding to each p_i as g_i. A trivial Markov chain satisfying the PTIM can be generated as follows: $\forall i \in [0, \cdots, 2^n - 1]$, we can generate a unique pair of $n + 1$ dimensional states $D_1 = 2(2^n - i - 1)$ and $D_2 = 2(2^n - i - 1) + 1$. D_1 and D_2 differ only in the last bit indicating tumor proliferation status. Here, LSB of $D_1 = 0$ and LSB of $D_2 = 1$. The first n bits of the binary representation of D_1 and D_2 are 0 where the representation of i has value 1. Consider a $2^{n+1} \times 2^{n+1}$ Markov chain with transition probability matrix P. $\forall i \in [0, \cdots, 2^n - 1]$, let us assign probabilities as $P(D_1, D_1) = p_i$, $P(D_1, D_2) = 1 - p_i$, $P(D_2, D_1) = p_i$, and $P(D_2, D_2) = 1 - p_i$. This particular Markov chain will satisfy our given PTIM. Since, there are 2^n closed classes of 2 states each, the stationary probability for inhibiting i can be calculated from considering the steady state probabilities of the Markov chain

$$\begin{vmatrix} p_i & 1 - p_i \\ p_i & 1 - p_i \end{vmatrix}$$

which is p_i for the state with tumor = 0 and $1 - p_i$ for the state with tumor = 1.   □

4.1 Generation of Markov chains based on pathway constraints

In this section, we will discuss two algorithms to generate Markov chains satisfying the PTIM steady state sensitivities while incorporating the directional pathway structures as emphasized in Section 3.

Each target inhibition combination can be considered as multiplying a matrix T_c to the initial Markov chain P. Each row of T_c contains only one non-zero element of 1 based on how the inhibition alters the state. If we consider n targets, n T_c's in combination can produce a total of 2^n possible transformation matrices $T_1, T_2, \cdots, T_{2^n}$. The PTIM denotes the stationary state probability of the LSB = 0 for the 2^n Markov chains $PT_1, PT_2, \cdots, PT_{2^n}$ starting from initial state $11 \cdots 1$ (i.e., all kinases considered in the PTIM and tumor are activated). The transition probability matrix has $2^{n+1} \times 2^{n+1}$ variables to be inferred and the number of equations available is 2^n. To narrow down the constraints, we will consider the possible BNs that can be generated for each set of possible mutations or outside activations of the thresholded PTIM. Each BN corresponding to a different mutation or initial activation pattern can provide information on possible alterations producing the required PTIM.

4.1.1 Algorithm 1
The first algorithm to generate Markov chains satisfying the PTIM sensitivities is presented in Algorithm 1.

Algorithm 1 Algorithm to generate a Markov chain P from PTIM Ψ

Step 1. Convert the PTIM Ψ to a TIM ψ using a threshold of α.

Step 2. Based on the genetic mutation information or sequential protein expression measurements, generate the BN Ω corresponding to the TIM ψ using approach of Section 3.

Step 3. If we have n targets, the TIM has n levels 0 to n representing the number of target inhibitions. Consider each level, starting from level n. For the inhibition $B_{n,1} = [1\ 1 \cdots 1]$, if PTIM $\Psi(B_{n,1}) < 1$, then we should consider a latent variable that may be responsible for tumor growth. Thus, the dynamic model should allow a transition from $0\ 0 \cdots 0\ 0$ to $0\ 0 \cdots 0\ 1$ and $0\ 0 \cdots 0\ 1$ to $0\ 0 \cdots 0\ 1$. The probabilities of this transition should be equal to $1 - \Psi(B_{n,1})$.

Step 4. Consider level $n - 1$. There are n possibilities of inhibition at this level $011111..1, 10111..1,...,11....10$ denoted by $B_{n-1,1}, B_{n-1,2}, \cdots B_{n-1,n}$, respectively. For the invition $B_{n-1,i}$, removing inhibition of target i has opened up another tumor proliferation pathway with a steady state mass of $1 - \Psi(B_{n-1,i})$. To capture this behavior, we will assign the following transition probability $0\ 0 \cdots 0\ 1\ 0 \cdots 0 \rightarrow 0\ 0 \cdots 0\ 1\ 0 \cdots 1 = 1 - \Psi(B_{n-1,i})$ and $0\ 0 \cdots 0\ 1\ 0 \cdots 1 \rightarrow 0\ 0 \cdots 0\ 1\ 0 \cdots 1 = 1 - \Psi(B_{n-1,i})$. The 1 is in position i.

Step 5. The next step is to consider level $n - 2$. There are $n(n - 1)/2$ possibilities of inhibition at this level $001111..1, 01011..1,...,11....00$ denoted by $B_{n-2,[1,1]}, B_{n-2,[1,2]}, \cdots B_{n-2,[n-1,n]}$, respectively. For inhibition $B_{n-2,[i,j]}$ in this level, it means that removing inhibition of the targets i and j has opened up another tumor proliferation pathway with a steady state mass of $1 - \Psi(B_{n-2,[i,j]})$. To capture this constraint, we will assign the following transition probability $00..10..1..00 \rightarrow 00..10..1..01 = 1 - \Psi(B_{n-2,[i,j]})$ and $00..10..1..01 \rightarrow 00..10..1..01 = 1 - \Psi(B_{n-2,[i,j]})$. Note that any of these transitions will not affect the inhibitions of its supersets in levels $n - 1$ and n. This is because state $B_{n-2,[i,j]}$ will not be reached if one of its supersets in levels $n - 1$ or n is inhibited.

Steps 6 to $n + 3$. Repeat the above process till level 0.

Step $n + 4$. Finally, we have to consider the cases where activation cannot be sustained based on our initial mutation assumptions. As an example, let us consider that $p_1, p_3, p_7, p_5, p_6 \geq 0.5$ and $p_0, p_2, p_4 = 0$ for the PTIM in Figure 9. Using a threshold of 0.5, we will arrive at the TIM of Figure 1 that has Figure 6 as the deterministic dynamic model assuming K_1 and K_2 as initial mutations. Thus, for the case of inhibition of K_1 and K_2, the system may not return to 0010 and 0011 once it leaves the states. An approach to tackle this is to allow transition back from 0000 to 0010 and the transition probability is based on the value of p_6 and p_7.

A simulation example for the application of Algorithm 1 is shown next based on the PTIM in Table 2. If we consider a threshold of $\alpha = 0.5$ and assuming K_1 and K_2 as initial mutations, the inferred deterministic BN is as shown in Figure 6. Note that the threshold α is selected based

Table 7 Simulated PTIM based on Algorithm 2 with $p = 0.001$ and $q = 0.001$

	0 0	0 1	1 1	1 0
0	0.0017	0.0029	0.9964	0.0029
1	0.6495	0.8982	0.9981	0.8982

on the minimum sensitivity considered significant from the perspective of intervention. Since a drug is often considered effective if the concentration to reduce the tumor volume by 50% is within approved dosage, we considered a threshold of 0.5 for normalized sensitivity to denote effectiveness. The threshold should be decreased if we want to incorporate low sensitivity inhibitions in our modeling. To achieve the probabilities shown in Table 2, we apply steps 3 to 7 of Algorithm 1 to generate the Markov chain shown in Table 3. Note that the Markov chain shown in Table 3 is not ergodic and thus the stationary distribution may depend on the starting state. To make the Markov chain ergodic, we can add a small perturbation probability to the Markov chain [20]. The corresponding steady state sensitivities generated by the Markov chain for a perturbation probability $p = 0.001$ is shown in Table 4 which closely reflects the PTIM steady state sensitivities shown in Table 2.

4.1.2 Algorithm 2

Another perspective on this issue is based on considering that the tumor is heterogeneous and the observed PTIM response is the aggregate effect of inhibition on multiple clones. The dynamics of each clone can be represented by a BN and there is a small probability q of one clone converting to another clone. Thus, the overall system can be represented by a context-sensitive probabilistic Boolean network with perturbation probability p and network transition probability q [21]. The algorithm to generate a context-sensitive PBN satisfying the observed PTIM behavior is presented as Algorithm 2.

Note that based on collapsed steady state probabilities of context-sensitive PBNs [21], Algorithm 2 will always achieve the desired PTIM response within an error of ϵ when p and q are selected to be small.

Algorithm 2 Algorithm to generate a Markov chain P from PTIM Ψ based on context-sensitive PBN approach

---

Let ϵ denote the minimum change in PTIM values that needs to be differentiated.
Initialize $L_{\max} = \epsilon$, $L_{\text{last}} = 0$, count = 0
while $L_{\max} < 1$ **do**
    Let $L_{\min}$ = minimum among the PTIM values $> L_{\max}$
    if $L_{\min} \neq \emptyset$ **then**
        Let $L_{\max} = \min(1, L_{\min} + \epsilon)$
        Binarize the PTIM using $L_{\min}$ as the threshold.
        count = count + 1
        This provides BN count with selection probability $L_{\max} - L_{\text{last}}$.
        $L_{\text{last}} = L_{\max}$
    else
        increase selection probability of BN count by $1 - L_{\max}$
        $L_{\max} = 1$
    end if
end while

As an example of application of Algorithm 2, let us consider the PTIM shown in Table 5. Based on Algorithm 2 with $\epsilon = 0.05$, we will have three individual BNs BN_1, BN_2, BN_3 with selection probabilities of 0.65, 0.25, and 0.1 respectively. The TIMs corresponding to the BNs are shown in Table 6. The BNs satisfying the TIMs in Table 6 are shown in Figures 10, 11 and 12. Using a $p = 0.001$ and $q = 0.001$, we arrive at the simulated PTIM shown in Table 7 which closely reflects the starting PTIM shown in Table 5.

Note that the dynamical models allow us to generate further insights on possible outcomes with sequential application of drugs. For instance, if we consider the previous example with the inferred context-sensitive PBN

Table 8 PTIM generated from a 60 drug screen data for canine tumor sample Sy [14]

					IGF1R PSMB5 TGFBR2	PSMB5 TGFBR2	PSMB5	IGF1R PSMB5	IGF1R PSMB5 TGFBR2	IGF1R TGFBR2	IGF1R
				0.11	0.38	1	1	1	1	0.68	0.60
			HDAC1	0.55	0.64	1	1	1	1	0.76	0.68
		EGFR	HDAC1	0.64	0.64	1	1	1	1	0.76	0.76
		EGFR		0.17	0.52	1	1	1	1	0.68	0.68
	AKT2	EGFR		0.58	0.64	1	1	1	1	0.76	0.76
	AKT2	EGFR	HDAC1	0.73	0.76	1	1	1	1	0.88	0.84
	AKT2		HDAC1	0.64	0.73	1	1	1	1	0.84	0.76
	AKT2			0.47	0.57	1	1	1	1	0.76	0.68

Table 9 TIM generated from the PTIM in Table 8 using a threshold of 0.3

							IGF1R	IGF1R	IGF1R	IGF1R
					PSMB5	PSMB5	PSMB5	PSMB5		
				TGFBR2	TGFBR2			TGFBR2	TGFBR2	
			0	1	1	1	1	1	1	1
		HDAC1	1	1	1	1	1	1	1	1
	EGFR	HDAC1	1	1	1	1	1	1	1	1
	EGFR		0	1	1	1	1	1	1	1
AKT2	EGFR		1	1	1	1	1	1	1	1
AKT2	EGFR	HDAC1	1	1	1	1	1	1	1	1
AKT2		HDAC1	1	1	1	1	1	1	1	1
AKT2			1	1	1	1	1	1	1	1

generating the PTIM shown in Table 5 and continuously apply a drug D_1 that inhibits K_2 and K_3, we achieve a sensitivity of 0.9. Similarly, continuous application of a drug D_2 that inhibits K_1 and K_3 will generate a sensitivity of 0.9. However, if we alternate the application of D_1 and D_2, we achieve a sensitivity 0f 0.94. It shows that alternate inhibition of these pathways allows us to lower the steady state mass of tumorous states. On the other hand, different sequence of inhibitions can negatively affect the final sensitivity. For instance, if a drug D_3 that inhibits K_1 and K_2 and another drug D_4 that inhibits K_3 is applied alternatively, we achieve a sensitivity of 0.50. Note that D_3 alone produces a sensitivity of 0.99 and D_4 produces a sensitivity of 0.65. This shows that stopping the inhibition of D_3 or D_4 at every alternate step causes the tumor to grow back again. For instance, if no inhibition is applied at every alternate time step, we achieve a sensitivity of 0.49 for D_3 and 0.01 for D_4.

In this section, we presented two algorithms for generation of Markovian models that have inhibition profiles (termed model generated PTIM) similar to our starting PTIM. The motivation behind the two algorithms is based on two widely accepted evolution models of cancer (cancer stem cell model and clonal evolution model [22]) since the primary application of this study is in the context of modeling tumor proliferation pathways. A cancer stem cell model assumes that observed heterogeneity in cancer is due to tumorigenic cancer cells that can differentiate into diverse progeny of cells forming the bulk of tumor [22]. Thus, Algorithm 1 tries to capture this idea of starting with a single network model and altering parts of the model to generate the observed inhibition response. The clonal evolution of cancer model assumes that tumor can consist of multiple clones without hierarchical organization [22]. Thus, Algorithm 2 considers the inhibition response to be based on diverse multiple clones (modeled as separate Boolean networks) with different responses to target inhibitions. The PTIM sensitivity values are used to estimate the network selection probabilities that are similar to proportions of each clone in the heterogeneous tumor. Similar to clonal evolution of cancer model, no single starting network model and its alterations is assumed in Algorithm 2 to generate the stochastic model.

4.2 Biological example

In this example, we consider a PTIM generated from actual biological data and infer a stochastic dynamic network model that produces inhibition responses similar to the experimental PTIM. We consider a canine osteosarcoma tumor sample perturbed with 60 targeted drugs with unique target inhibition profiles to generate steady state cell viability values [14]. Note that available time series data for perturbation studies are mostly for single gene knockouts/knockdowns [23] which are unable to provide the sufficient information to estimate the cell viability response for all possible target inhibition combinations. Thus, due to the absence of time series data and ground truth dynamic networks for drug inhibition studies, our model design criteria is to generate dynamic models that can create the experimentally inferred

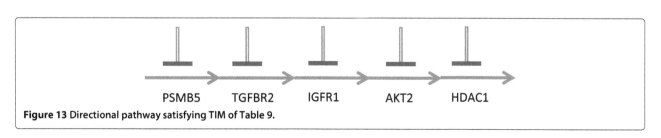

Figure 13 Directional pathway satisfying TIM of Table 9.

Table 10 TIM generated from the PTIM in Table 8 using a threshold of 0.55

							IGF1R	IGF1R	IGF1R	IGF1R
				PSMB5	PSMB5	PSMB5	PSMB5			
			TGFBR2	TGFBR2			TGFBR2	TGFBR2		
			0	0	1	1	1	1	1	1
		HDAC1	1	1	1	1	1	1	1	1
	EGFR	HDAC1	1	1	1	1	1	1	1	1
	EGFR		0	0	1	1	1	1	1	1
AKT2	EGFR		1	1	1	1	1	1	1	1
AKT2	EGFR	HDAC1	1	1	1	1	1	1	1	1
AKT2		HDAC1	1	1	1	1	1	1	1	1
AKT2			0	1	1	1	1	1	1	1

PTIM while satisfying structural constraints of cancer pathways.

The PTIM generated from experimental 60 drug screen data and satisfying biological constraints [14] for canine tumor sample Sy is shown in Table 8. There are 6 target kinases (IGF1R, PSMB5, TGFBR2, AKT2, EGFR, HDAC1) in this model and the 64 entries in Table 8 refers to the $2^6 = 64$ possible target inhibitions of the kinases. For instance, second row and seventh column entry of 0.76 refers to sensitivity of 0.76 when the tumor culture is inhibited by IGFR1, TGFBR2, and HDAC1.

Considering the overall idea of generation of context-sensitive PBNs, we arrive at the TIM shown in Table 9 using a threshold of 0.3. One of the possible directional pathways that will produce the TIM of Table 9 is shown in Figure 13. Note that there can be multiple other possible directional pathway combinations that can produce the above TIM and we are selecting only one of them with assumed mutation in PSMB5. Further biological data such as gene mutation and expression data and analysis presented in Section 3.1 can be used to narrow down the possible combinations.

Subsequently, to select the next level of differences in sensitivities, we considered a threshold of 0.55 which introduces three more possible combinations that fail to stop proliferation (i.e., binarized sensitivity of 0). The TIM is shown in Table 10 and a corresponding directional pathway that produces the TIM is shown in Figure 14. Note that the pathway in Figure 14 requires inhibition of multiple targets as compared to the previous pathway in Figure 13 for stopping tumor proliferation. The first three kinases are the same for the two pathways but the next possibilities are combinations of two kinases rather than single kinase inhibitions.

We next consider a threshold of 0.8 that differentiates the cluster of sensitivity values {0.84, 0.84, 0.88} from the remaining values. The TIM for this threshold is shown in Table 11, and a corresponding directional pathway that produces the TIM is shown in Figure 15. The directional pathway is more constrained than the previous pathways in having blocks of targets that require more number of inhibitions to stop tumor proliferation.

Note that the thresholds can be selected in various ways. For instance, we considered equal intervals of 0.25 following the starting threshold of 0.3 resulting in thresholds of 0.3, 0.55, and 0.8. Another approach can be using unequal increment thresholds to maintain sensitivity clusters. Since the experiments conducted to generate the sensitivity information can contain noise, it is preferable to ignore small sensitivity differences.

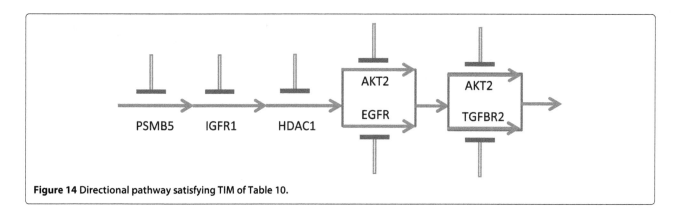

Figure 14 Directional pathway satisfying TIM of Table 10.

Table 11 TIM generated from the PTIM in Table 8 using a threshold of 0.8

								IGF1R	IGF1R	IGF1R	IGF1R
					PSMB5	PSMB5	PSMB5	PSMB5			
				TGFBR2	TGFBR2			TGFBR2	TGFBR2		
			0	0	1	1	1	1	0	0	
		HDAC1	0	0	1	1	1	1	0	0	
	EGFR	HDAC1	0	0	1	1	1	1	0	0	
	EGFR		0	0	1	1	1	1	0	0	
AKT2	EGFR		0	0	1	1	1	1	0	0	
AKT2	EGFR	HDAC1	0	0	1	1	1	1	1	1	
AKT2		HDAC1	0	0	1	1	1	1	1	0	
AKT2			0	0	1	1	1	1	0	0	

Once we have the three directional pathways, we used the directional pathway to BN approach of Section 3.2 to generate the Boolean networks $BN_1, BN_2,$ and BN_3 corresponding to the directional pathways of Figures 13, 14, 15, respectively. Based on the limits of the thresholds, we assigned a selection probability of 0.5 for BN_1 ($0.25 < 0.5 < 0.55$), 0.25 for BN_2 ($0.55 < 0.5 + 0.25 < 0.8$), and remaining 0.25 for BN_3. Using a value of $p = 0.001$ and $q = 0.001$, we generated a context-sensitive PBN and calculated the PTIM for the model by generating the steady state probabilities of tumor state = 0 for each target inhibition combination. The generated PTIM for the designed model is shown in Table 12 (up to two decimal digits). The model generated PTIM is similar to our initial experimental PTIM shown in Table 8. The mean and maximum absolute errors of the entries between the experimental and model generated PTIM are 0.043 and 0.2, respectively, which is low considering that only three BNs were used

to generate the context-sensitive PBN. Further reduction in the differences between the experimental and model-generated PTIM can possibly be achieved by increasing the number of BNs and optimizing the thresholds and network selection probabilities to reduce the mean error.

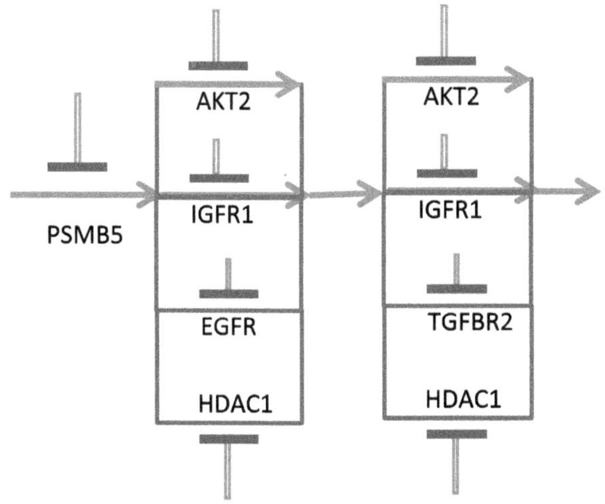

5 Conclusions

In this article, we analyzed the inference of dynamical models from static target inhibition map models. We showed that the inferred blocks from the TIM approach could be converted to directional pathways based on different mutation scenarios and subsequently converted to dynamic BN models. In terms of stochastic model inference, we presented two algorithms where (i) the first technique was based on altering the BN generated from binarizing the PTIM based on a single threshold and (ii) the second approach considered as generation of multiple BNs based on different thresholds and integrating them in the form of a context-sensitive PBN. We provided examples to show the application of the algorithms to generate Markovian models whose steady state inhibition profiles are close to the experimental PTIMs.

Note that the inference algorithms designed in this article are primarily focused on dynamic models of tumor proliferation. The number of targets considered is small as they are a subset of the targets of targeted drugs (usually tyrosine kinase inhibitors) that are required to faithfully capture the tumor proliferation of a particular system without overfitting. Consequently, any properties of large-scale genetic regulatory networks [23,24] such as adherence to power law [25] were not incorporated in these studies. Future studies will try to explore the incorporation of characteristics of large-scale networks in inference of dynamic models from PTIMs. The PTIM can be considered as a model expressing the relative sensitivity of the tumor proliferation following inhibition. If we consider

Figure 15 Directional pathway satisfying TIM of Table 11.

Table 12 PTIM generated from context-senstive probabilistic Boolean network model based on Algorithm 2

								IGF1R	IGF1R	IGF1R	IGF1R
					PSMB5	PSMB5	PSMB5	PSMB5			
				TGFBR2	TGFBR2				TGFBR2	TGFBR2	
			0.00	0.50	0.99	0.99	0.99	1.00	0.75	0.75	
		HDAC1	0.75	0.75	1.00	0.99	0.99	1.00	0.75	0.75	
	EGFR	HDAC1	0.75	0.75	1.00	0.99	0.99	1.00	0.75	0.75	
	EGFR		0.00	0.50	0.99	0.99	0.99	1.00	0.75	0.75	
AKT2	EGFR		0.75	0.75	1.00	0.99	0.99	1.00	0.75	0.75	
AKT2	EGFR	HDAC1	0.75	0.75	1.00	1.00	1.00	1.00	1.00	1.00	
AKT2		HDAC1	0.75	0.75	1.00	0.99	0.99	1.00	1.00	0.75	
AKT2			0.50	0.75	1.00	0.99	0.99	1.00	0.75	0.75	

the definition of relative expression level variation (RELV) [26] as $\frac{\eta_{ij}}{x_i^{wt}}$ where η_{ij} is the steady state expression level variation of gene i after the knockout/knockdown of gene j and x_i^{wt} is the expression level of gene i in wild type, a corresponding analogous sensitivity mapping can be derived by replacing x_i^{wt} by cell viability without any inhibition and η_{ij} being replaced by change in cell viability following inhibition j. Here, j consists of 2^T combinations for T targets as compared to $T + 1$ knockouts usually considered in RELV analysis. For individual protein targets in the binary deterministic BN models, the RELVs can be mapped to the relative change in the attractor states of P and PT_j where P denotes the transition matrix for the BN without inhibition and PT_j denotes the transition matrix following inhibition j. The binarization of the different proteins will be based on different thresholds based on their relative behavior. Similarly, for the Markov chain model, the relative change in the steady state probabilities of expressed protein i in P and PT_j will be analogous to RELV. Note that the binary deterministic and stochastic formulation employed in our analysis incorporates the relative sensitivity behavior that has been earlier observed to be more appropriate for regulatory network inference [26].

Future research will involve analyzing mutation data to restrict the possible directional pathways along with time series experimentation for inference of the unique dynamic model.

Competing interests

The authors declare that they have no competing interests.

Authors' contributions

NB and RP designed the algorithmic framework. NB and RP implemented the algorithms. LD and CK participated in the collection of biological experimental data. NB and RP analyzed the results. All authors read and approved the final manuscript.

Acknowledgements

This research was supported by NSF grant CCF 0953366.

Author details

[1] Department of Electrical and Computer Engineering, Texas Tech University, Lubbock, TX 79409, USA. [2] Department of Pediatrics, Oregon Health & Science University, Portland, OR 97239, USA.

References

1. C Sawyers, Targeted cancer therapy. Nature. **432**, 294–297 (2004)
2. MR Green, Targeting targeted therapy. N. Engl. J. Med. **350**:21, 2191–2193 (2004)
3. BJ Druker, Molecularly targeted therapy: have the floodgates opened? Oncologist. **9**(1), 357–360 (2004)
4. A Hopkins, J Mason, J Overington, Can we rationally design promiscuous drugs? Curr. Opin. Struct. Biol. **16**(1), 127–136 (2006)
5. ZA Knight, KM Shokat, Features of selective kinase inhibitors. Chem. Biol. **12**(6), 621–637 (2005)
6. ML Sos, K Michel, T Zander, J Weiss, P Frommolt, M Peifer, D Li, R Ullrich, M Koker, F Fischer, T Shimamura, D Rauh, C Mermel, S Fischer, I Stückrath, S Heynck, R Beroukhim, W Lin, W Winckler, K Shah, T LaFramboise, WF Moriarty, M Hanna, L Tolosi, J Rahnenführer, R Verhaak, D Chiang, G Getz, M Hellmich, J Wolf et al, Predicting drug susceptibility of non-small cell lung cancers based on genetic lesions. J. Clin. Investig. **119**(6), 1727–1740 (2009)
7. JE Staunton, DK Slonim, HA Coller, P Tamayo, MJ Angelo, J Park, U Scherf, JK Lee, WO Reinhold, JN Weinstein, JP Mesirov, ES Lander, TR Golub, Chemosensitivity prediction by transcriptional profiling. Proc. Nat. Acad. Sci. **98**, 10787–10792 (2001). doi:10.1073/pnas.191368598
8. J Barretina, J Barretina, G Caponigro, N Stransky, K Venkatesan, AA Margolin, S Kim, CJ Wilson, J Lehár, GV Kryukov, D Sonkin, A Reddy, M Liu, L Murray, MF Berger, JE Monahan, P Morais, J Meltzer, A Korejwa, J Jané-Valbuena, FA Mapa, J Thibault, E Bric-Furlong, P Raman, A Shipway, IH Engels, J Cheng, GK Yu, J Yu, P Aspesi, et al, The Cancer Cell Line Encyclopedia enables predictive modelling of anticancer drug sensitivity. Nature. **483**(7391), 603–607 (2012)
9. MJ Arnett, EJ Edelman, SJ Heidorn, CD Greenman, A Dastur, KW Lau, P Greninger, IR Thompson, X Luo, J Soares, Q Liu, F Iorio, D Surdez, L Chen, RJ Milano, GR Bignell, AT Tam, H Davies, JA Stevenson, S Barthorpe, SR Lutz, F Kogera, K Lawrence, A McLaren-Douglas, X Mitropoulos, T Mironenko, H Thi, L Richardson, W Zhou, F Jewitt, et al, Systematic identification of genomic markers of drug sensitivity in cancer cells. Nature. **483**(7391), 570–575 (2012)
10. JK Lee, DM Havaleshko, H Cho, JN Weinstein, EP Kaldjian, J Karpovich, A Grimshaw, D Theodorescu, A strategy for predicting the chemosensitivity of human cancers and its application to drug discovery. Proc. Nat. Acad. Sci. **104**(32), 13086–13091 (2007)

11. G Riddick, H Song, S Ahn, J Walling, D Borges-Rivera, W Zhang, HA Fine, Predicting in vitro drug sensitivity using Random Forests. Bioinformatics. **27**(2), 220–224 (2011)

12. A Mitsos, IN Melas, P Siminelakis, AD Chairakaki, J Saez-Rodriguez, LG Alexopoulos, Identifying drug effects via pathway alterations using an integer linear programming optimization formulation on phosphoproteomic data. PLoS Comput. Biol. **5**(12), 1000591 (2009). doi:10.1371/journal.pcbi.1000591

13. Z Walther, J Sklar, Molecular tumor profiling for prediction of response to anticancer therapies. Cancer J. **17**(2), 71–79 (2011)

14. N Berlow, LE Davis, EL Cantor, B Seguin, C Keller, R Pal, A new approach for prediction of tumor sensitivity to targeted drugs based on functional data. BMC Bioinformatics. **14**, 239 (2013)

15. R Pal, N Berlow, A kinase inhibition map approach for tumor sensitivity prediction and combination therapy design for targeted drugs, in *Pacific Symposium on Biocomputing*, (2012), pp. 351–362. http://psb.stanford. edu/psb-online/proceedings/psb12/pal.pdf PMID: 22174290

16. SA Kauffman, *The Origins of Order: Self-Organization and Selection in Evolution.* (Oxford Univ. Press, New York, 1993)

17. N Berlow, R Pal, L Davis, C Keller, Analyzing pathway design from drug perturbation experiments, in *Statistical Signal Processing Workshop (SSP) 2012 IEEE*, (2012), pp. 552–555. doi:10.1109/SSP.2012.6319757

18. S Nelander, W Wang, B Nilsson, Q-B She, C Pratilas, N Rosen, P Gennemark, C Sander, Models from experiments: combinatorial drug perturbations of cancer cells. Mol. Syst. Biol. **4**(1) (2008). doi:10.1038/msb.2008.53

19. R Pal, S Bhattacharya, Characterizing the effect of coarse-scale PBN modeling on dynamics and intervention performance of genetic regulatory networks represented by stochastic master equation models. IEEE Trans. Signal Process. **58**, 3341–3351 (2010)

20. R Pal, A Datta, ML Bittner, ER Dougherty, Intervention in context-sensitive probabilistic Boolean networks. Bioinformatics. **21**, 1211–1218 (2005)

21. R Pal, Context-sensitive probabilistic boolean networks: steady state properties, reduction and steady state approximation. IEEE Trans. Signal Proces. **58**, 879–890 (2010)

22. M Shackleton, E Quintana, ER Fearon, SJ Morrison, Heterogeneity in cancer: cancer stem cells versus clonal evolution. Cell. **138**(5), 822–829 (2009)

23. RJ Prill, D DM, S-J Rodriguez, PK Sorger, D Marbach, J Saez-Rodriguez, PK Sorger, LG Alexopoulos, X Xue, ND Clarke, G Altan-Bonnet, G Stolovitzky, Towards a rigorous assessment of systems biology models: the DREAM3 challenges. PLoS ONE. **5**(2), 9202 (2010)

24. H De Jong, Modeling and simulation of genetic regulatory systems: a literature review. J. Comput. Biol. **9**, 67–103 (2001)

25. T Zhou, Y-L Wang, Causal relationship inference for a large-scale cellular network. Bioinformatics. **26**(16), 2020–2028 (2010)

26. IY Wang, T Zhou, A relative variation-based method to unraveling gene regulatory networks. PLoS One. **7**(2), 31194 (2012)

6

Hierarchical Dirichlet process model for gene expression clustering

Liming Wang[1] and Xiaodong Wang[2]*

Abstract

Clustering is an important data processing tool for interpreting microarray data and genomic network inference. In this article, we propose a clustering algorithm based on the hierarchical Dirichlet processes (HDP). The HDP clustering introduces a hierarchical structure in the statistical model which captures the hierarchical features prevalent in biological data such as the gene express data. We develop a Gibbs sampling algorithm based on the Chinese restaurant metaphor for the HDP clustering. We apply the proposed HDP algorithm to both regulatory network segmentation and gene expression clustering. The HDP algorithm is shown to outperform several popular clustering algorithms by revealing the underlying hierarchical structure of the data. For the yeast cell cycle data, we compare the HDP result to the standard result and show that the HDP algorithm provides more information and reduces the unnecessary clustering fragments.

1 Introduction

The microarray technology has enabled the possibility to monitor the expression levels of thousands of genes in parallel under various conditions [1]. Due to the high-volume nature of the microarray data, one often needs certain algorithms to investigate the gene functions, regulation relations, etc. Clustering is considered to be an important tool for analyzing the biological data [2-4]. The aim of clustering is to group the data into disjoint subsets, where in each subset the data show certain similarities to each other. In particular, for microarray data, genes in each clustered group exhibit correlated expression patterns under various experiments.

Several clustering methods have been proposed, most of which are distance-based algorithms. That is, a distance is first defined for clustering purpose and then the clusters are formed based on the distances of the data. Typical algorithms in this category include the K-means algorithm [5] and the self-organizing map (SOM) algorithm [6]. These algorithms are based on simple rules, and they often suffer from robustness issue, i.e., they are sensitive to noise which is extensive in biological data [7]. For example, the SOM algorithm requires user to provide number of clusters in advance. Hence, incorrect estimation of the parameter may provide wrong result.

Another important category of clustering methods is the model-based algorithms. These algorithms employ a statistical approach to model the structure of clusters. Specifically, data are assumed to be generated by some mixture distribution. Each component of the mixture corresponds to a cluster. Usually, the parameters of the mixture distribution are estimated by the EM algorithm [8]. The finite-mixture model [9-11] assumes that the number of mixture components is finite and the number can be estimated using the Bayesian information criterion [12] or the Akaike information criterion [13]. However, since the estimation of the number of clusters and the estimation of the mixture parameters are performed separately, the finite-mixture model may be sensitive to the different choices of the number of clusters [14].

The infinite-mixture model has been proposed to cope with the above sensitivity problem of the finite-mixture model. This model does not assume a specific number of components and is primarily based on the Dirichlet processes [15,16]. The clustering process can equivalently be viewed as a Chinese restaurant process [17], where the data are considered as customers entering a restaurant. Each component corresponds to a table with infinite capacity. A new customer joins a table according to the current assignment of seats.

*Correspondence: wangx@ee.columbia.edu
[2]Department of Electrical Engineering, Columbia University, New York, NY 10027, USA
Full list of author information is available at the end of the article

Hierarchical clustering (HC) is yet another more advanced approach especially for biological data [18], which groups together the data with similar features based on the underlying hierarchical structure. The biological data often exhibit hierarchical structure, e.g., one cluster may highly be overlapped or could be embedded into another cluster [19]. If such hierarchical structure is ignored, the clustering result may contain many fragmental clusters which could have been combined together. Hence, for biological data, such HC has its advantages to many traditional clustering algorithms. The performances of such HC algorithms depend highly on the quality of the data and the specific agglomerative or divisive ways the algorithms use for combining clusters.

Traditional clustering algorithms for microarray data usually assign each gene with a feature vector formed by the expressions in different experiments. The clustering is carried out for these vectors. It is well known that many genes share different levels of functionalities [20]. The resemblances of different genes are commonly represented at different levels of perspectives, e.g., at the cluster level instead of individual gene level. In other words, The relationships among different genes may vary during different experiments. In Figure 1, we illustrate the gene hierarchical structures for microarray data. Genes group A and B may show close relationship to genes group C in some experiments. While the genes group D shows correlations to groups A, B, and C in other experiments. The group D obviously has a hierarchical relationships to other gene groups. In this case, we desire to have a HC algorithm recognizing the gene resemblances not at the single gene level but at the higher cluster level, to avoid unnecessary fragmental clusters that impede the proper interpretation

of the biological information. Such a HC algorithm may also provide new information by taking the hierarchical similarities into account.

In this article, we propose a model-based clustering algorithm for gene expression data based on the hierarchical Dirichlet process (HDP) [21]. The HDP model incorporates the merits of both the infinite-mixture model and the HC. The hierarchical structure is introduced to allow sharing data among related clusters. On the other hand, the model uses the Dirichlet processes as the nonparametric Bayesian prior, which do not assume a fixed number of clusters *a priori*.

The remainder of the article is organized as follows. In Section 2, we introduce some necessary mathematical background and formulate the HC problem as a statistical inference problem. In Section 3, we derive a Gibbs sampler-based inference algorithm based on the Chinese restaurant metaphor of the HDP model. In Section 4, we provide experimental results of the proposed HDP algorithm for two applications, regulatory network segmentation and gene expression clustering. Finally, Section 5 concludes the article.

2 System model and problem formulation

As in any model-based clustering method, it is assumed that the gene expression data are random samples from some underlying distributions. All data in one cluster are generated by the same distribution. For most existing clustering algorithms, each gene is associated with a vector containing the expressions in all experiments. The clustering of the genes is based on their vectors. However, such approach ignores the fact that genes may show different functionalities under various experiment conditions, i.e., different clusters may be formed under different experiments. In order to cope with this phenomenon, we treat each expression separately. More specifically, we allow different expressions of the same individual gene to be generated by different statistical models.

Suppose that for the mircoarray data, there are N genes in total. For each gene, we conduct M experiments. Let g_{ji} denote the expression of the ith gene in the jth experiment, $1 \leq i \leq N$, and $1 \leq j \leq M$. For each g_{ji}, we associate a latent membership variable z_{ji}, which indicates the cluster membership of g_{ji}. That is, if genes i and i' are in the same cluster under the conditions of experiments j and j', we have $z_{ji} = z_{j'i'}$. Note that z_{ji} is supported on a countable set such as $\mathbb{N}$ or $\mathbb{Z}$. For each g_{ji}, we associate a coefficient $\theta_{z_{ji}}$, whose index is determined by its membership variable z_{ji}. In order to have a Bayesian approach, we also assume that each coefficient θ_k is drawn independently from a prior distribution G_0

$$\theta_k \sim G_0, \qquad (1)$$

where k is determined by z_{ji}.

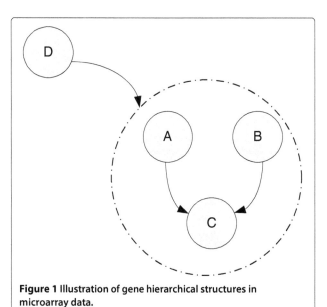

Figure 1 Illustration of gene hierarchical structures in microarray data.

The membership variable $\mathbf{z} = \{z_{ji}\}_{j,i}$ has a discrete joint distribution

$$\mathbf{z} \sim \pi. \tag{2}$$

Note that in this article, the bold-face letter always refers to a set formed by the elements with specified indices.

We assume that each g_{ji} is drawn independently from a distribution $F(\theta_{z_{ji}})$

$$g_{ji} \sim F\left(\theta_{z_{ji}}\right), \tag{3}$$

where $\theta_{z_{ji}}$ is a coefficient associated with g_{ji} and F is a distribution family such as the Gaussian distribution family. In summary, we have the following model for the expression data

$$\begin{aligned} \theta_k &\sim G_0 \\ \mathbf{z} &\sim \pi \\ g_{ji}|z_{ji}, \theta_k &\sim F\left(\theta_{z_{ji}}\right). \end{aligned} \tag{4}$$

The above model is a relatively general one which can induce many previous models. For example, in all Bayesian approaches, all variables are assigned with proper priors. It is very popular to use the mixture model as the prior, which models the data generated by a mixture of distributions, e.g., a linear combination of a family of distributions such as Gaussian distributions. Each cluster is generated by one component in the mixture distribution given the membership variable [14]. The above approach corresponds to our model if we assume that π is finitely supported and F is Gaussian.

The aim for clustering is to determine the posterior probability of the latent membership variables given the observed gene expressions

$$P(\mathbf{z}|\mathbf{g}), \tag{5}$$

where $\mathbf{g} = \{g_{ji}\}_{j,i}$.

As a clustering algorithm, the final result is given in the forms of clusters. Each gene has to be assigned to one and only one cluster. Once we have the inference result in (5), we can apply the maximum *a posterior* criterion to obtain an estimate of membership variable $\hat{z}_{\cdot i}$ for the ith gene as

$$\hat{z}_{\cdot i} = \arg_a \max \sum_j P(z_{ji} = a|\mathbf{g}). \tag{6}$$

We note that in case one is interested in finding other related clusters for one gene, we can simply use the inferred distribution to membership variable to obtain this information.

2.1 Dirichlet processes and infinite mixture model

Instead of assuming a fixed number of clusters *a priori*, one can assume infinite number of clusters to avoid the estimation accuracy problem on the number of clusters as we mentioned earlier. Correspondingly in (4), the prior π is an infinite discrete distribution. Again as in the Bayesian

fashion, we will introduce priors for all parameters. The Dirichlet process is one such prior. It can be viewed as a random measure [15], i.e., the domain of this process (viewed as a measure) is a collection of probability measures. In this section, we will give a brief introduction to the Dirichlet process which serves as the vital prior part in our HDP model.

Recall that the Dirichlet distribution $\mathcal{D}(u_1, \ldots, u_K)$ of order K on a $(K-1)$-simplex in $\mathbb{R}^{K-1}$ with parameter $u_1, \ldots, u_K$ is given by the following probability density function

$$\mathcal{D}(x_1, \ldots, x_{K-1}; u_1, \ldots, u_K) = \frac{\Gamma\left(\sum_{i=1}^{K} u_i\right)}{\prod_{i=1}^{K} \Gamma(u_i)} \prod_{i=1}^{K} x_i^{u_i - 1} \tag{7}$$

where $\sum_{i=1}^{K} x_i = 1, u_i > 0, i = 1, \ldots, K$, and $\Gamma(\cdot)$ is the Gamma function. Since every point in the domain is a discrete probability measure, the Dirichlet distribution is a random measure in the finite discrete probability space.

The Dirichlet processes are the generalization of the Dirichlet distribution into the continuous space. There are various constructive or non-constructive definitions of Dirichlet processes. For simplicity, we use the following non-constructive definition.

Let (X, σ, μ_0) be a probability space. A Dirichlet process $D(\alpha_0, \mu_0)$ with parameter $\alpha_0 > 0$ is defined as a random measure: for any non-trivial finite partition $(\chi_1, \ldots, \chi_r)$ of X with $\chi_i \in \sigma$, we have the random variable

$$(\mathcal{G}(\chi_1), \ldots, \mathcal{G}(\chi_r)) \sim \mathcal{D}(\alpha_0 \mu_0(\chi_1), \ldots, \alpha_0 \mu_0(\chi_r)), \tag{8}$$

where $\mathcal{G}$ is drawn from $D(\alpha_0, \mu_0)$.

The Dirichlet processes can be characterized in various ways [15] such as the stick-breaking construction [22] and the Chinese restaurant process [23]. The Chinese restaurant process serves as a visualized characterization of the Dirichlet process.

Let $x_1, x_2, \ldots$ be a sequence of random variables drawn from the Dirichlet process $D(\alpha_0, \mu_0)$. Although we do not have the explicit formula for D, we would like to know the conditional probability of x_i given $x_1, \ldots, x_{i-1}$. In the Chinese restaurant model, the data can be viewed as customers sequentially entering a restaurant with infinite number of tables. Each table corresponds to a cluster with unlimited capacity. Each customer x_i entering the restaurant will join in the table already taken with equal probability. In addition, the new customer may sit in a new table with probability proportional to α_0. Tables that have already been occupied by customers tend to gain more and more customers.

One remarkable property of the Dirichlet process is that although it is generated by a continuous process, it is discrete (countably many) almost surely [15]. In other words, almost every sample distribution drawn from the Dirichlet process is a discrete distribution. As a consequence, the Dirichlet process is suitable to serve as a non-parametric prior of the infinite mixture model.

The Dirichlet mixture model uses the Dirichlet process as a prior. The model in (4) can then be represented as follows:

$$g_{ji}|z_{ji}, \theta_k \sim F(\theta_{z_{ji}}); \qquad (9)$$

θ_k is generated by the measure μ_0

$$\theta_k \sim \mu_0; \qquad (10)$$

$\{z_{ji}\}$ is generated by a Dirichlet process $D(\alpha_0, \mu_0)$

$$\{z_{ji}\} \sim D(\alpha_0, \mu_0). \qquad (11)$$

Recall that $D(\alpha_0, \mu_0)$ is discrete almost everywhere, which corresponds to the indices of the clusters.

2.2 HDP model

Biological data such as the expression data often exhibit hierarchical structures. For example, although clusters can be formed based on similarities, some clusters may still share certain similarities among themselves at different levels of perspectives. Within one cluster, the genes may share similar features. But on the level of clusters, one cluster may share some similar feature with some other clusters. Many traditional clustering algorithms typically fail to recognize such hierarchical information and are not able to group these similar clusters into a new cluster, producing many fragments in the final clustering result. As a consequence, it is difficult to interpret the functionalities and meanings of these fragments. Therefore, it is desirable to have an algorithm that is able to cluster among clusters. In other words, the algorithm should be able to cluster based on multiple features at different levels. In order to capture the hierarchical structure feature of the gene expressions, we now introduce the hierarchical model to allow clustering at different levels. The clustering algorithm based on the hierarchical model not only reduces the number of cluster fragments, but also may reveal more details about the unknown functionalities of certain genes as the clusters sharing multiple features.

Recall that in the statistical model (11), the clustering effect is induced by the Dirichlet process $D(\alpha_0, \mu_0)$. If we need to take into account different level of clusters, it is natural to introduce a prior with clustering effect to the base measure μ_0. Again in this case, the Dirichlet process can serve as such prior. The intuition is that given the base measure, the clustering effect is represented through a Dirichlet process on the single gene level. By the Dirichlet process assumption on the base measure, the base measure also exhibits the clustering effect, which leads to

clustering at cluster level. We simply set the prior to the base measure μ_0 as

$$\mu_0 \sim D_1(\alpha_1, \mu_1), \qquad (12)$$

where $D_1(\alpha_1, \mu_1)$ is another Dirichlet process. In this article, we use the same letter for the measure, the distribution it induces, and the corresponding density function as long as it is clear from the context. Moreover, we could extend the hierarchies to as many levels as we wish at the expense of complexity of the inference algorithm. The desired number of hierarchies can be determined by the prior biological knowledge. In this article, we focus on a two-level hierarchy.

As a remark, we would like to point out the connection and difference on the "hierarchy" in the proposed HDP method and traditional HC [4]. Both the HDP and HC algorithms can provide HC results. The hierarchy in the HDP method is manifested by the Chinese restaurant process which will be introduced later, where the data sit in the same table can be viewed as the first level and all tables sharing the same dish can be viewed as the second level. While the hierarchy in the HC is obtained by merging existing clusters based on their distances. However, its specific merging strategy is heuristic and is irreversible for those merged clusters. Hierarchy formed in this fashion often may not reflect the true structure in the data since various hierarchical structures can be formed by choosing different distance metrics. However, the HDP algorithm captures the hierarchical structure at the model level. The merging is carried out automatically during the inference. Therefore, it naturally takes the hierarchy into consideration.

In summary, we have the following HDP model for the data:

$$\mu_0 \sim D_1(\alpha_1, \mu_1)$$
$$\{z_{ji}\}|\mu_o, \alpha_0 \sim D(\alpha_0, \mu_0)$$
$$\alpha_0, \alpha_1 \sim \Gamma(a, b)$$
$$\theta_k \sim \mu_1$$
$$g_{ji}|z_{ji}, \theta_k \sim F(\theta_{z_{ji}}), \qquad (13)$$

where a and b are some fixed constants. We assume that F and μ_1 are conjugate priors. In this article, F is assumed to be the Gaussian distribution and μ_1 is the inverse Gamma distribution.

3 Inference algorithm

It is intractable to get the closed-form solution to the inference problem (5). In this section, we develop a Gibbs sampling algorithm for estimating the posterior distribution in (5). At each iteration l, we draw a sample $z_{ji}^{(l)}$ sequentially from the distribution:

$$P\left(z_{ji}^{(l)}|z_{11}^{(l)}, z_{12}^{(l)}, \ldots, z_{j(i-1)}^{(l)}, z_{j(i+1)}^{(l-1)}, \ldots, z_{MN}^{(l-1)}, \mathbf{g}\right). \qquad (14)$$

Under regularity conditions, the distribution of $\{z_{ji}^{(l)}\}_{j,i}$ will converge to the true posterior distribution in (5) [24]. The proposed Gibbs sampling algorithm is similar to the HDP inference algorithm proposed in [21], since both the Gibbs algorithms use the Chinese restaurant metaphor which we will elaborate later. However, because of the differences in modeling, we still need to provide details for the inference algorithm based on our model.

3.1 Chinese restaurant metaphor

The Chinese restaurant model [23] is a visualized characterization for interpreting the Dirichlet process. Because there is no explicit formula to describe the Dirichlet process, we will employ the Chinese restaurant model for HDP inference instead of directly computing the posterior distribution in (5). We refer to [23,25] for the proof and other details of the equivalence between the Chinese restaurant metaphor and the Dirichlet processes.

In the Chinese restaurant metaphor for the HDP model (13), we view $\{z_{ji}\}$ as customers entering a restaurant sequentially. The restaurant has infinite number of rows and columns of tables which are labeled by t_{ji}. Each z_{ji} will associate to one and only one table in the jth row. We use $\phi(z_{ji})$ to denote the column index of the table in the jth row taken by z_{ji}, i.e., z_{ji} will sit at table $t_{j\phi(z_{ji})}$. If it is clear from the context, we will use ϕ_{ji} in short for $\phi(z_{ji})$. The index of the random variable θ_k in (13) is characterized by a menu containing various dishes. Each table picks one and only one dish from the menus $\{m_k\}_{k=1,2,\ldots}$, which are drawn independently from the base

measure μ_1. g_{ji} is drawn independently according to the dish it chooses through the distribution $F(\cdot)$ as in (13). We denote $\lambda(t_{ji})$ as the index of the dish taken by table t_{ji}, i.e., table t_{ji} chooses dish $m_{\lambda(t_{ji})}$. As before, we may write λ_{ji} in short of $\lambda(t_{ji})$. In summary, customer z_{ji} will sit at table $t_{j\phi_{ji}}$ and enjoy dish $m_{\lambda_{j\phi_{ji}}}$. The HDP is reflected in this metaphor such that the customers choose the tables as well as the dishes in a Dirichlet process fashion. The customers sitting at the same table are classified into one cluster. Moreover, the customers sitting at different tables but ordering the same dish will also be clustered into the same group. Hence, the clustering effect is performed at the cluster level, i.e., we allow "clustering among clusters". In Figure 2, we show an illustration of the Chinese restaurant metaphor. The different patterns of shades represent different clusters. We also introduce two useful counter variables: c_{ji} denotes the number of customers sitting at table t_{ji}; d_{jk} counts the number of tables in row j serving dish m_k.

Using the Chinese restaurant metaphor, instead of inferring z_{ji}, we can directly infer ϕ_{ji} and λ_{ji}. The membership variable z_{ji} is completely determined by $\lambda(t_{j\phi(z_{ji})})$. That is, $z_{ji} = z_{j'i'}$ if and only if $\lambda(t_{j\phi(z_{ji})}) = \lambda(t_{j\phi(z_{j'i'})})$. As we pointed out before, the specific values of the membership variable z_{ji} are not relevant to the clustering as long as z_{ji} is supported on a countable set. Hence, we could simply let

$$z_{ji} = \lambda\left(t_{j\phi(z_{ji})}\right). \tag{15}$$

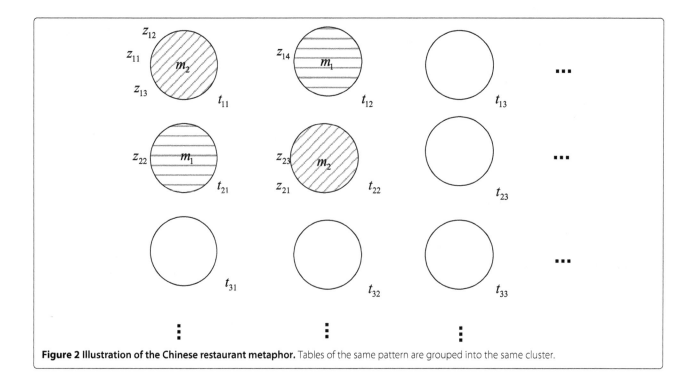

Figure 2 Illustration of the Chinese restaurant metaphor. Tables of the same pattern are grouped into the same cluster.

According to [25], we have the following conditional probabilities for the HDP model

$$\phi_{ji}|\phi_{j1},\dots,\phi_{ji-1},\alpha_0,\mu_0 \sim \sum_{m=1}^{\sum_k d_{jk}} \frac{c_{jm}}{i-1+\alpha_0}\delta_{t_{j\phi_{ji}}} \quad (16)$$
$$+ \frac{\alpha_0}{i-1+\alpha_0}\mu_0,$$

where $\sum_k d_{jk}$ calculates the number of tables taken in the rth row and $\delta_{(\cdot)}$ is the Kronecker delta function. The interpretation of (16) is that customer z_{ji} chooses a table already taken with equal probability. In addition, z_{ji} may choose a new table with probability proportional to α_0.

By the hierarchical assumption, the distribution of the dish chosen at an occupied table is another Dirichlet process. We have the following conditional distribution of the dishes

$$\lambda_{j\phi_{ji}}|\lambda_{1\phi_{11}},\dots,\lambda_{j\phi_{j(i-1)}},\alpha_1,\mu_1 \sim \sum_{k=1}^{K_{ji}} \frac{\sum_j d_{jk}}{\sum_{jk} d_{jk}+\alpha_1}\delta_{m_k}$$
$$+ \frac{\alpha_1}{\sum_{jk} d_{jk}+\alpha_1}\mu_1,$$
$$(17)$$

where $\sum_j d_{jk}$ counts the number of tables serving dish m_k; $\sum_{jk} d_{jk}$ counts the number of tables serving dishes; K_{ji} denotes the net number of dishes served till λ_{ji}'s coming by counting only once each dish that has been served multiple times.

3.2 A Gibbs sampler for HDP inference
Instead of sampling the posterior probability in (5), we will sample $\phi = \{\phi_{11},\phi_{12},\dots\}$ and $\lambda = \{\lambda_{11},\lambda_{12},\dots\}$ from the following posterior distribution

$$P(\phi,\lambda|\mathbf{g}). \quad (18)$$

We can calculate the related conditional probabilities as follows.

If a is a value that has been taken before, the conditional probability of $\phi_{ji} = a$ is given by

$$P\left(\phi_{ji} = a|\phi_{ji}^c,\lambda,\theta,\alpha_1,\alpha_0,\mu_1,\mathbf{g}\right) \propto c_{ja}f_{\lambda_{ja}}(g_{ji}|\mathbf{g}_{ji}^c), \quad (19)$$

where $\theta = \{\theta_{ji}\}_{j,i}$ and $\lambda = \{\lambda_{ji}\}_{j,i}$. The superscript c denotes the complement of the variables in its category, i.e., $\mathbf{g}_{ji}^c = \{g_{j'i'}\}_{(j',i')\neq(j,i)}$ and $\phi_{ji}^c = \{\phi_{j'i'}\}_{(j',i')\neq(j,i)}$. $f_{\lambda_{ja}}\left(g_{ji}|\mathbf{g}_{ji}^c\right)$ denotes the conditional density of g_{ji} given all other data generated according to menu $m_{\lambda_{ja}}$, which can be calculated as

$$f_{\lambda_{ja}}\left(g_{ji}|\mathbf{g}_{ji}^c\right) = \frac{\int \prod_{\lambda_{j'\phi_{j'i'}}=\lambda_{ja}} F(g_{j'i'}|\theta)\mu_1(\theta)d\theta}{\int \prod_{j'i'\neq ji,\lambda_{j'\phi_{j'i'}}=\lambda_{ja}} F(g_{j'i'}|\theta)\mu_1(\theta)d\theta}.$$
$$(20)$$

The numerator of (20) is the joint density of the data which are generated by the same dish. By the assumption that $g_{j'i'}$ are conditionally independent given the chosen dish, we have the conditional density of the data in the product form. The denominator is the joint density excluding the specific g_{ji} term. The integrals in (20) can either be calculated using the numerical method or using the Monte Carlo integration. For example, in order to calculate the following integral $\int_a^b f(x)p(x)dx$, where $p(x)$ is a density function, we can draw samples $x_1, x_2, \dots, x_n$ from $p(x)$ and approximate the integral by $\int_a^b f(x)p(x)dx = E_{p(x)}[f(x)] \approx \frac{1}{n}\sum_{i=1}^n f(x_i)$. To calculate (20), we view $\mu_1(\cdot)$ as $p(\cdot)$ and $F(g_{j'i'}|\cdot)$ as $f(\cdot)$.

On the other hand, if a is a new value then we have

$$P\left(\phi_{ji} = a|\phi_{ji}^c,\lambda,\theta,\alpha_1,\alpha_0,\mathbf{g}\right) \propto \alpha_0$$
$$\left[\sum_{k=1}^{K_{ja}} \frac{\sum_j d_{jk}}{\sum_{jk} d_{jk}+\alpha_1}f_k\left(g_{ji}|\mathbf{g}_{ji}^c\right)\right.$$
$$\left. + \frac{\alpha_1}{\sum_{jk} d_{jk}+\alpha_1}\int F(g_{ji}|\theta)\mu_1(\theta)d\theta\right]. \quad (21)$$

We also have the following conditional probabilities for λ_{ji}. If a is used before, we have

$$P\left(\lambda_{j\phi_{ji}} = a|\phi,\lambda_{j\phi_{ji}}^c,\theta,\alpha_1,\alpha_0,\mathbf{g}\right) \propto \left(\sum_j d_{ja}\right)f_a\left(g_{ji}|\mathbf{g}_{ji}^c\right);$$
$$(22)$$

otherwise we have

$$P\left(\lambda_{j\phi_{ji}} = a|\phi,\lambda_{j\phi_{ji}}^c,\theta,\alpha_1,\alpha_0,\mathbf{g}\right) \propto \alpha_1 \int F(g_{ji}|\theta)\mu_1(\theta)d\theta.$$
$$(23)$$

The derivations of (19), (21), (22), and (23) are given in Appendix.

Before we present the Gibbs sampling algorithm, we recall the Metropolis–Hastings (M–H) algorithm [26] for drawing samples from a target distribution whose density function $f(x)$ is only known up to a scaling factor, i.e., $f(x) \propto p(x)$. To draw samples from $f(x)$, we make use of some fixed conditional distribution $q(x_2|x_1)$ that satisfies $q(x_2|x_1) = q(x_1|x_2)$, $\forall x_1, x_2$. The M–H algorithm proceeds as follows.

- Start with an arbitrary value x_0 with $p(x_0) > 0$.
- For $l = 1, 2, \dots$

    - Given the previous sample x_{l-1}, draw a candidate sample $x^\star$ from $q(x^\star|x_{l-1})$.
    - Calculate $\beta = \frac{p(x^\star)}{p(x_{l-1})}$. If $\beta \geq 1$ then accept the candidate and let $x_l = x^\star$. Otherwise accept it

with probability β, or reject it and accept the previous sample with probability $1 - \beta$.

After a "burn-in" period, say l_0, the samples $\{x_l\}_{l>l_0}$ follow the distribution $f(x)$.

We now summarize the Gibbs sampling algorithm for the HDP inference as follows.

- Initialization: randomly assign the indices
  $$\boldsymbol{\phi}^{(0)} = \left\{ \phi_{11}^{(0)}, \phi_{12}^{(0)}, \ldots \right\} \text{ and } \boldsymbol{\lambda}^{(0)} = \left\{ \lambda_{11}^{(0)}, \lambda_{12}^{(0)}, \ldots \right\}.$$
  Note that once we have all the indices, the counters $\{c_{ji}\}$ and $\{d_{jk}\}$ are also determined.
- For $l = 1, 2, \ldots, l_0 + L$,

  – Draw samples of $\left\{ \phi_{ji}^{(l)} \right\}$ from their posteriors

  $$P\left(\phi_{ji}^{(l)} = a | \boldsymbol{\phi}_{ji}^{(l-1)c}, \boldsymbol{\lambda}^{(l-1)}, \alpha_1^{(l-1)}, \alpha_0^{(l-1)}, \mathbf{g} \right) \tag{24}$$

  given by (19) and (21) using the M–H algorithm. We view the probability in (24) as the target density and choose $q(\cdot|\cdot)$ to be a distribution supported on $\mathbb{N}$. For example, we can use $q(i|j) = \frac{j}{(j+1)^i}$, $i, j \in \mathbb{N}$.

  – Draw samples of $\left\{ \lambda_{j\phi_{ji}^{(l)}}^{(l)} \right\}$ from their posteriors

  $$P\left(\lambda_{j\phi_{ji}^{(l)}}^{(l)} = a | \boldsymbol{\phi}^{(l)}, \boldsymbol{\lambda}_{j\phi_{ji}^{(l)}}^{(l-1)c}, \alpha_1^{(l-1)}, \alpha_0^{(l-1)}, \mathbf{g} \right) \tag{25}$$

  given by (22) and (23) using M–H algorithm. We view the probability in (25) as the target density and use $q(\cdot|\cdot)$ as specified in the previous step.

  – Since $P(\alpha_0 | \boldsymbol{\phi}, \boldsymbol{\lambda}, \alpha_1, \mathbf{g}) = P(\alpha_0)$ and $P(\alpha_1 | \boldsymbol{\phi}, \boldsymbol{\lambda}, \alpha_0, \mathbf{g}) = P(\alpha_1)$, simply draw samples of $\alpha_0^{(l)}$ and $\alpha_1^{(l)}$ from their prior Gamma distributions.

- Using the samples after the "burn-in" period $\left\{ \boldsymbol{\phi}^{(l)}, \boldsymbol{\lambda}^{(l)} \right\}_{l=l_0+1}^{l_0+L}$ to calculate $\hat{P}(\boldsymbol{\phi}, \boldsymbol{\lambda}|\mathbf{g})$, which is given by

$$\hat{P}\left(\phi_{ji} = a, \lambda_{j\phi_{ji}} = b \right) = \frac{\sum_{l=l_0+1}^{l_0+L} \mathbf{1}\left\{ \phi_{ji}^{(l)} = a, \lambda_{j\phi_{ji}^{(l)}}^{(l)} = b \right\}}{L}, \tag{26}$$

where $\mathbf{1}(\cdot)$ is the indicator function. Determine the membership distribution $P(\mathbf{z}|\mathbf{g})$ from the inferred joint distribution $\hat{P}(\boldsymbol{\phi}, \boldsymbol{\lambda}|\mathbf{g})$ by
$P(z_{ji} = a|\mathbf{g}) = \sum_b \hat{P}(\lambda_{jb} = a|\mathbf{g}, \phi_{ji} = b)\hat{P}(\phi_{ji} = b|\mathbf{g})$.

- Calculate the estimation of clustering index $\hat{z}_{\cdot i}$ for the ith gene by $\hat{z}_{\cdot i} = \arg_a \max \sum_j P(z_{ji} = a|\mathbf{g})$.

3.3 A numerical example

In this section, we provide a simple numerical example to illustrate the proposed Gibbs sampler. Let us consider the case $N = M = 2$, i.e., there are 2 genes and 2 experiments. Assume that the expressions are as $g_{11} = 0, g_{12} = 1, g_{21} = -1$, and $g_{22} = 2$. We assume $\mu_1(\theta) \sim \mathcal{N}(0, 1)$ and $F(g_{ji}|\theta) \sim \mathcal{N}(\theta, 1)$. For initialization, we set $\phi_{11}^{(0)} = 1, \phi_{12}^{(0)} = 2, \phi_{21}^{(0)} = 3, \phi_{22}^{(0)} = 4$; $\lambda_{1\phi_{11}^{(0)}}^{(0)} = 1, \lambda_{1\phi_{12}^{(0)}}^{(0)} = 1, \lambda_{2\phi_{21}^{(0)}}^{(0)} = 2, \lambda_{2\phi_{22}^{(0)}}^{(0)} = 2$, and $\alpha_0^{(0)} = \alpha_1^{(0)} = 1$.

We first show how to draw sample from $P\left(\phi_{11}^{(1)} | \boldsymbol{\phi}_{11}^{(0)c}, \boldsymbol{\lambda}^{(0)}, \alpha_1^{(0)}, \alpha_0^{(0)}, \mathbf{g} \right)$ by the M–H algorithm. Given the initial value, assume that $q(\cdot|\cdot)$ returns $\phi_{11} = 3$ as a candidate sample. By (19), we have $P\left(\phi_{11}^{(1)} = 1 | \boldsymbol{\phi}_{11}^{(0)c}, \boldsymbol{\lambda}^{(0)}, \alpha_1^{(0)}, \alpha_0^{(0)}, \mathbf{g} \right) \propto c_{11} f_{\lambda_{11}}\left(g_{11} | \mathbf{g}_{11}^c \right)$, where $c_{11} = 1$ and $\lambda_{11} = 1$. We also have

$$f_1\left(g_{11} | \mathbf{g}_{11}^c \right) = \frac{\int \prod_{\lambda_{j'\phi_{j'i'}} = 1} F(g_{j'i'}|\theta)\mu_1(\theta)d\theta}{\int \prod_{(j',i') \neq (1,1), \lambda_{j'\phi_{j'i'}} = 1} F(g_{j'i'}|\theta)\mu_1(\theta)d\theta}$$
$$= \frac{\int F(g_{11}|\theta)F(g_{12}|\theta)\mu_1(\theta)d\theta}{\int F(g_{12}|\theta)\mu_1(\theta)d\theta} \approx 0.22971. \tag{27}$$

Note that the above integral can be calculated either numerically or by using the Monte Carlo integration method.

By (21) and using the specific values of the variables, we obtain

$$P\left(\phi_{11}^{(1)} = 3 | \boldsymbol{\phi}_{11}^{(0)c}, \boldsymbol{\lambda}^{(0)}, \alpha_1^{(0)}, \alpha_0^{(0)}, \mathbf{g} \right)$$
$$\propto \alpha_0 \left[\sum_{k=1}^{K_{11}} \frac{\sum_j d_{jk}}{\sum_{jk} d_{jk} + \alpha_1} f_k\left(g_{11} | \mathbf{g}_{11}^c \right) \right.$$
$$\left. + \frac{\alpha_1}{\sum_{jk} d_{jk} + \alpha_1} \int F(g_{11}|\theta)\mu_1(\theta)d\theta \right] \tag{28}$$

with $K_{11} = 1, \sum_j d_{j1} = 2, \sum_{jk} d_{jk} = 4, \alpha_0 = \alpha_1 = 1$. Plugging in these values, we have

$$P\left(\phi_{11}^{(1)} = 3 | \boldsymbol{\phi}_{11}^{(0)c}, \boldsymbol{\lambda}^{(0)}, \alpha_1^{(0)}, \alpha_0^{(0)}, \mathbf{g} \right)$$
$$\propto \frac{2}{5} f_1\left(g_{11} | \mathbf{g}_{11}^c \right) + \frac{1}{5} \int F(g_{11}|\theta)\mu_1(\theta)d\theta \approx 0.1483. \tag{29}$$

Since $\beta = \frac{0.1483}{0.22971} \approx 0.6456 < 1$, we should accept this candidate sample $\phi_{11} = 3$ with a probability of 0.6456. After the burn-in period, say the sample returned by the M–H algorithm is $\phi_{11} = 4$, then we update $\phi_{11}^{(1)} = 4$ and move on to draw samples of the remaining variables ϕ_{12}, ϕ_{21}, and ϕ_{22}.

Assuming that we obtain samples of $\boldsymbol{\phi}^{(1)}$ as $\phi_{11}^{(1)} = 4, \phi_{12}^{(1)} = 1, \phi_{21}^{(1)} = 1, \phi_{22}^{(1)} = 2$. We next draw the sample $\boldsymbol{\lambda}^{(1)}$. Given the initial value $\lambda_{1\phi_{11}^{(1)}} = 1$ and $q(\cdot|\cdot)$ returns $\lambda_{1\phi_{11}^{(1)}} = 3$ as a candidate sample. By (22), we obtain $P\left(\lambda_{1\phi_{11}^{(1)}}^{(1)} = 1|\boldsymbol{\phi}^{(1)}, \lambda_{1\phi_{11}^{(1)}}^{(0)c}, \alpha_1^{(0)}, \alpha_0^{(0)}, \mathbf{g}\right) \propto \left(\sum_j d_{j1}\right) f_1\left(g_{11}|\mathbf{g}_{11}^c\right)$. Furthermore, we have $\sum_j d_{j1} = 2$ and $f_1\left(g_{11}|\mathbf{g}_{11}^c\right) \approx 0.22971$ as calculated before.

By (23), we obtain $P\left(\lambda_{1\phi_{11}}^{(1)} = 3|\boldsymbol{\phi}^{(1)}, \lambda_{1\phi_{11}}^{(0)c}, \alpha_1^{(0)}, \alpha_0^{(0)}, \mathbf{g}\right) \propto \alpha_1 \int F(g_{11}|\theta)\mu_1(\theta)d\theta$. Moreover, we have $\alpha_1 = 1$ and $\int F(g_{11}|\theta)\mu_1(\theta)d\theta \approx 0.28208$ as calculated before. So we have $\beta = \frac{0.28208}{2*0.22971} \approx 0.614 < 1$. After the burn-in period, assume that the M–H algorithm returns a sample $\lambda_{1\phi_{11}^{(1)}} = 2$, then update $\lambda_{1\phi_{11}^{(1)}}^{(1)} = 2$ and move on to sample the remaining λ variables as well as α_0 and α_1.

After the burn-in period of the whole Gibbs sampler, we can calculate the posterior joint distribution $P(\boldsymbol{\phi}, \boldsymbol{\lambda}|\mathbf{g})$ from the samples and determine the clusters following the last two steps in the proposed Gibbs sampling algorithm.

4 Experimental results

The HDP clustering algorithm proposed in this article can be employed for gene expression analysis or as a segmentation algorithm for gene regulatory network inference. In this section, we first introduce two performance measures for clustering, the Rand Index (RI) [27] and the Silhouette Index (SI) [28]. We compare the HDP algorithm to the support vector machine (SVM) algorithm for network segmentation on synthetic data. We then conduct various experiments on both synthetic and real datasets including the AD400 datasets [29], the yeast galactose datasets [30], yeast sporulation datasets [31], human fibroblasts serum datasets [32], and yeast cell cycle data [33]. We compare the HDP algorithm to the Latent Dirichlet allocation (LDA), MCLUST, SVM, K-means, Bayesian Infinite Mixture Clustering (BIMC) the HC [4,14,34-37] based on the performance measures and the functional relationships.

4.1 Performance measures
In order to evaluate the clustering result, we utilize two measures: RI [27] and SI [28]. The first index is used when a ground truth is known in *priori* and the second index is to measure the performance without any knowledge of the ground truth.

The RI is a measure of agreement between two clustering results. It takes a value between 0 and 1. The higher is the score, the higher agreements it indicates.

Let A denote the datasets with a total number of n elements. Given two clustering results $X = \{X_1, \ldots, X_S\}$ and $Y = \{Y_1, \ldots, Y_T\}$ of A, i.e., $A = \bigcup_{i=1}^S X_i = \bigcup_{j=1}^T Y_j$ and $X_i \cap X_j = \emptyset$, $Y_i \cap Y_j = \emptyset$ for $i \neq j$. For any pair of elements (a, b) in A, we say they are in the same set under a clustering result if a and b are in the same cluster. Otherwise we say they are in different sets. Note that there are totally $\binom{n}{2}$ pairs of elements. We define the following four counting numbers: Z_1 denotes the number of pairs that are both in the same set in X and Y; Z_2 denotes the number of pairs that are both in different sets in X and Y; Z_3 denotes the number of pairs that are in the same set in X and in different sets in Y; and Z_4 denotes the number of pairs that are in different sets in X and in the same set in Y. The RI is then given by

$$\text{RI} = \frac{Z_1 + Z_2}{Z_1 + Z_2 + Z_3 + Z_4}. \qquad (30)$$

Due to the lack of the ground truth in most real applications, we utilize the SI to evaluate the clustering performance. The SI is a measure by calculating the average width of all data points, which reflects the compactness of the clustering. Let x denote the average distance between a point p in a cluster and all other points within that cluster. Let y be the minimum average distance between p and other clusters. The Silhouette distance for p is defined as

$$s(p) = \frac{y - x}{\max\{x, y\}}. \qquad (31)$$

The SI is the average Silhouette distance among all data points. The value of SI lies in $[-1, 1]$ and higher score indicates better performance.

4.2 Network segmentation on synthetic data
In regulatory network inference, due to the large size of the network, it is often useful to perform a network segmentation. The segmented sub-networks usually have much less number of nodes than the original network, leading to faster and more accurate analysis of the original network [38]. Clustering algorithms can be employed for such segmentation purpose. However, traditional clustering algorithms often provide segmentation results either too fine or too coarse, i.e., the resulting sub-networks

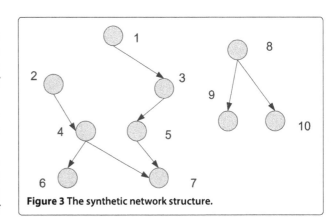

Figure 3 The synthetic network structure.

Table 1 Clustering performance of LDA, SVM, MCLUST, K-means, HC, and HDP on the AD400 data

Algorithm	RI	SI	Number of clusters
LDA	0.931	0.553	10.0
SVM	0.929	0.493	11
MCLUST	0.942	0.583	10
K-means	0.895	0.457	10
HC	0.916	0.348	9
BIMC	0.935	0.571	10.0
HDP	0.947	0.577	10.0

either contain too few genes or two many genes. In addition, the hierarchical structure of the network cannot be discovered by those algorithms. Thanks to its hierarchical model assumption, the HDP algorithm can provide better segmentation results. We demonstrate the segmentation application of HDP on a synthetic network and compare

to the SVM algorithm which is widely used for clustering and segmentation.

The network under consideration is shown in Figure 3. We assume that the distributions for all nodes are Gaussian. The directed links indicate that the parent nodes are the priors of the child nodes. Disconnected nodes are mutually independent. We generate the data in the following way. Nodes 1, 2, and 8 are generated independently by Gaussian distributions of unit variance with means 1, 2, and 3, respectively. Nodes 3, 4, 5, 6, 9, and 10 are generated independently by unit variance Gaussian distributions with means determined by their respective parent nodes. Node 7 is generated by a Gaussian distribution with mean determined by node 4 and variance determined by absolute value of node 5. The network contains two isolated segments with one segment containing nodes 1–7 and the other containing nodes 8–10. The HDP algorithm is applied to this network and segments the network into three clusters. Nodes 2, 4, 6 form one cluster; nodes 1, 3, 5, 7 form another cluster; and nodes 8, 9, 10 form the third

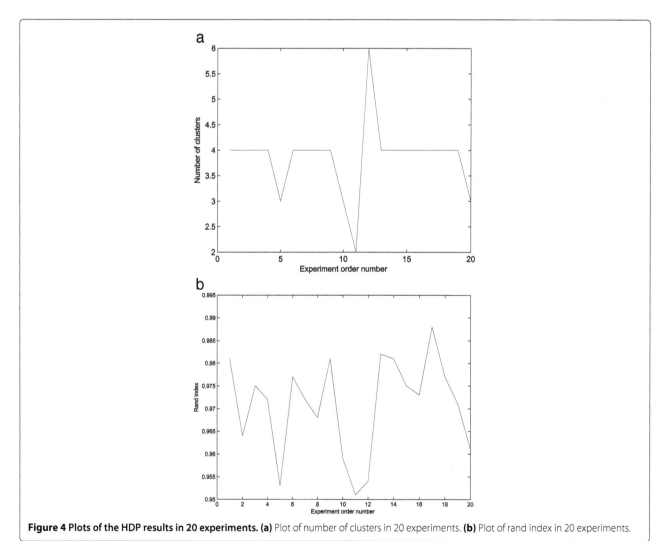

Figure 4 Plots of the HDP results in 20 experiments. (a) Plot of number of clusters in 20 experiments. **(b)** Plot of rand index in 20 experiments.

one. The SVM algorithm on the other hand produces two clusters, one containing nodes 1–7 and the other containing nodes 8–10. As one can see, the network obviously contains two hierarchies in the left segment, i.e., nodes 1–7 of the network. The SVM fails to recognize the hierarchies and provides a result coarser than that given by the HDP algorithm.

4.3 AD400 data

The AD400 is a synthetic dataset proposed in [29], which is used to evaluate the clustering algorithm performance. The dataset is constituted by 400 genes with 10 time points. As the ground truth, the AD400 dataset has 10 clusters with each one containing 40 genes.

For randomized algorithms as LDA, BIMC, HDP, we average the results over 20 runs of the algorithms. We compare the HDP algorithm to other widely used algorithms such as LDA, SVM, MCLUST, K-means, BIMC, and HC. The results are presented in Table 1. As we can see, the HDP algorithm has the similar performance of the MCLUST algorithm. While the HDP generally performs better than other widely used algorithms.

4.4 Yeast galactose data

We conduct experiment on the yeast galactose data, which consists of 205 genes. The true number of clusters based on the functional categories is 4 [39]. We calculate the RI index between different clustering results to the result in [39], which is regarded as the standard benchmark. The LDA model is a generative probabilistic model for document classifications [34], which also uses Dirichlet distribution as a prior. We adapt the LDA model to the yeast galactose data to compare the proposed HDP algorithm. Since the LDA and HDP methods are randomized algorithms, we run the algorithms 20 times and use the average for the final score. In Figure 4, we illustrate the performances of each experiments for the HDP method. The performances of the algorithms under consideration are listed in Table 2.

It is seen that the HDP algorithm performs the best among the three algorithms. Unlike the MCLUST and LDA algorithms which produce more clusters than 4, the average number of clusters given by the HDP algorithm is very closed to the "true" value 4. Compared to the SVM

Table 3 Clustering performance of LDA, MCLUST, K-means, HC, BIMC, and HDP on the yeast sporulation data

Algorithm	SI	Number of clusters
LDA	0.586	6.2
MCLUST	0.577	6
K-Means	0.324	8
HC	0.392	7
BIMC	0.592	6.1
HDP	0.673	6.0

method, the HDP algorithm produces a result that is more similar to the "ground truth", i.e., with the highest RI value.

4.5 Yeast sporulation data

The yeast sporulation dataset consists of 6,118 genes with 7 times points which were obtained during the sporulation process [31]. We pre-processed the dataset by applying a logarithmic transform and removing the data whose expression levels did not have significant changes. After the pre-process, the data have 513 genes left. In Table 3, we compare the HDP clustering result to LDA, MCLUST, K-Means, BIMC, and HC. For randomized algorithms such as LDA, BIMC, and HDP, we average the scores by running the algorithm 20 times.

From Table 3, we can see that the HDP has the highest SI score. It suggests that the clustering results provided by HDP are more compact and less separated than results from other algorithms. The K-means and HC algorithm suggest higher number of clusters. However, their SI scores indicate that their clusters are not as tight as other algorithms.

4.6 Human fibroblasts serum data

The human fibroblasts serum data consists of 8,613 genes with 12 time points [32]. Again a logarithmic transform has been applied to the data and genes without significant changes have been removed. The remaining dataset has 532 genes.

In Table 4, we show the performance of the HDP algorithm and other various algorithms. It has been shown

Table 2 Clustering performance of LDA, MCLUST, SVM, and HDP on the yeast galactose data

Algorithm	Rand index	Number of clusters
LDA	0.942	6.3
SVM	0.954	5
MCLUST	0.903	9
HDP	0.973	3.8

Table 4 Clustering performance of LDA, MCLUST, K-means, HC, BIMC, and HDP on the human fibroblasts serum data

Algorithm	SI	Number of clusters
LDA	0.298	9.4
MCLUST	0.382	6
K-Means	0.324	7
HC	0.313	5
BIMC	0.418	7.3
HDP	0.452	6.4

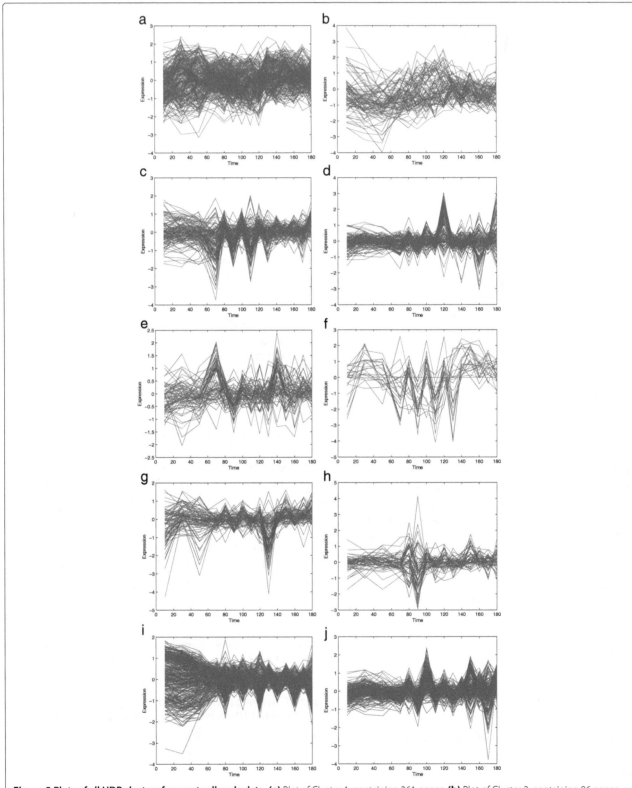

Figure 5 Plots of all HDP clusters for yeast cell cycle data. (a) Plot of Cluster 1, containing 261 genes. **(b)** Plot of Cluster 2, containing 86 genes. **(c)** Plot of Cluster 3, containing 135 genes. **(d)** Plot of Cluster 4, containing 144 genes. **(e)** Plot of Cluster 5, containing 76 genes. **(f)** Plot of Cluster 6, containing 25 genes. **(g)** Plot of Cluster 7, containing 88 genes. **(h)** Plot of Cluster 8, containing 60 genes. **(i)** Plot of Cluster 9, containing 381 genes. **(j)** Plot of Cluster 10, containing 259 genes.

Table 5 Numbers of newly discovered genes in various functional categories by the proposed HDP clustering algorithm

Function categories	Number of newly discovered genes
Cell cycle and DNA processing	20
Protein synthesis	25
Protein fate	4
Cell fate	12
Transcription	8
Unclassified protein	57

that the clustering results by the HDP algorithm are the compactest among those algorithms. The LDA algorithm suggests 9.4 clusters with the lowest SI score, which indicates that some of its clusters can be further tightened. HC provides a result consisting of five clusters. However, the SI score of the HC result is not the highest, which suggests its clustering may not be well formed.

4.7 Yeast cell cycle data

We next apply the proposed HDP clustering algorithm on the yeast cell *Saccharomyces cerevisiae* cycle dataset [2,40]. The data are obtained by synchronizing and collecting the mRNAs from cells at 10-min intervals over the course of two cell cycles. It has been used widely for testing the performances of clustering algorithm [2,14,41]. The expression data have been taken logarithmic transform and lie in the interval [−2, 2]. We pre-processed the data to remove those which did not change significantly over time. We also removed those data whose means are below a small threshold. After the pre-processing, there are 1,515 genes left. We then apply the HDP algorithm and obtain 10 clusters in total. The plots of the clusters are shown in Figure 5.

We resort to the MIPS database [42] to determine the functional categories for each cluster. The inferred functional category of a cluster is the category shared by the majority of the member elements. After applying the cell-cycle selection criterion in [2], we find that there are 126 genes identified by proposed HDP algorithm but not discovered in [2]. We list in Table 5 the numbers of newly discovered genes in various functional categories. We also observe that parts of the newly discovered unclassified genes belong to clusters with classified categories. Given the hierarchical characteristic of the HDP algorithm, it may suggest multiple descriptions of those genes that might have been overlooked before.

Note that in [14] a Bayesian model with infinite number of clusters is proposed based on the Dirichlet process. The model in [14] is a special case of the HDP model proposed in this article when there is only one hierarchy. In terms of discovering new gene functionalities, we find that

the performances of the two algorithms are similar, as the method in [14] discovered 106 new genes compared to the result in [2]. However, by taking the hierarchical structure into account, the total number of clusters found by the HDP algorithm is significantly smaller than that given in [14] which is 43 clusters. The SI score for BIMC and HDP are 0.321 and 0.392, respectively. The HDP clustering consolidates many fragmental clusters, which may provide an easier way to interpret the clustering results.

In Table 6, we list the new genes discovered by the HDP algorithm which are not found in [2].

5 Conclusions

In this article, we have proposed a new clustering approach based on the HDP. The HDP clustering explicitly models the hierarchical structure in the data that is prevalent in biological data such as gene expressions. We have developed a statistical inference algorithm for the proposed HDP model based on the Chinese restaurant metaphor and the Gibbs sampler. We have applied the proposed HDP clustering algorithm to both regulatory network segmentation and gene expression clustering. The HDP algorithm is shown to reveal more structural information of the data compared to popular algorithms such as SVM and MCLUST, by incorporating the hierarchical knowledge into the model.

Table 6 List of newly discovered genes in various functional categories

Function categories	Genes
Cell cycle and DNA processing	YBL051c YBR136w YBL016w YDR200c YBR274w YDR217c YLR314c YJL074c YJL095w YDR052c YDL126c YCL016c YDL188c YAL040c YEL019c YER122c YLR035c YLR055c YML032c YMR078c
Protein synthesis	YDR091c YGL103w YBR118w YBL057c YBR101c YBR181c YDL083c YDL184c YDR012w YDR172w YGL105w YGL129c YJL041w YJL125c YJR113c YLR185w YPL037c YPL048w YLR009w YHL001w YHL015w YHR011w YHR088w YDR450w YEL034w
Protein fate	YAL016w YBL009w YBR044c YDL040c
Cell fate	YAL040c YDL006w YDL134c YIL007c YJL187c YDL029w YDL035c YCR002c YBL105c YCR089w YER114c YEL023c
Transcription	YAL021c YBL022c YCL051w YDR146c YIL084c YJL127c YJL164c YJL006c

Appendix
Derivation of formula (19) and (21)

$$P\left(\phi_{ji} = a | \boldsymbol{\phi}_{ji}^c, \boldsymbol{\lambda}, \boldsymbol{\theta}, \alpha_1, \alpha_0, \mu_1, \mathbf{g}\right)$$

$$= \frac{P\left(g_{ji}, \phi_{ji} = a | \boldsymbol{\phi}^c(z_{ji}), \boldsymbol{\lambda}, \boldsymbol{\theta}, \alpha_1, \alpha_0, \mu_1, \mathbf{g}_{ji}^c\right)}{P\left(g_{ji} | \boldsymbol{\phi}_{ji}^c, \boldsymbol{\lambda}, \boldsymbol{\theta}, \alpha_1, \alpha_0, \mu_1, \mathbf{g}_{ji}^c\right)} \qquad (32)$$

$$\propto P\left(g_{ji}, \phi_{ji} = a | \boldsymbol{\phi}_{ji}^c, \boldsymbol{\lambda}, \boldsymbol{\theta}, \alpha_1, \alpha_0, \mu_1, \mathbf{g}_{ji}^c\right) \qquad (33)$$

$$\propto P\left(g_{ji} | \boldsymbol{\phi}, \boldsymbol{\lambda}, \boldsymbol{\theta}, \alpha_1, \alpha_0, \mu_1, \mathbf{g}_{ji}^c\right)$$
$$P\left(\phi_{ji} = a | \boldsymbol{\phi}_{ji}^c, \boldsymbol{\lambda}, \boldsymbol{\theta}, \alpha_1, \alpha_0, \mu_1, \mathbf{g}_{ji}^c\right) \qquad (34)$$

By (16), if a has appeared before, we have

$$P\left(\phi_{ji} = a | \boldsymbol{\phi}_{ji}^c, \boldsymbol{\lambda}, \boldsymbol{\theta}, \alpha_1, \alpha_0, \mu_1, \mathbf{g}_{ji}^c\right) \propto c_{ja}. \qquad (35)$$

Otherwise we have

$$P\left(\phi_{ji} = a | \boldsymbol{\phi}_{ji}^c, \boldsymbol{\lambda}, \boldsymbol{\theta}, \alpha_1, \alpha_0, \mu_1, \mathbf{g}_{ji}^c\right) \propto \alpha_0. \qquad (36)$$

If a has appeared before, by the assumption the data are conditionally independent, we also have

$$P\left(g_{ji} | \boldsymbol{\phi}, \boldsymbol{\lambda}, \boldsymbol{\theta}, \alpha_1, \alpha_0, \mu_1, \mathbf{g}_{ji}^c\right) = f_{\lambda_{ja}}\left(g_{ji} | \mathbf{g}_{ji}^c\right), \qquad (37)$$

where $f_{\lambda_{ja}}(g_{ji} | \mathbf{g}_{ji}^c)$ can be calculated by the Bayes' formula:

$$f_{\lambda_{ja}}\left(g_{ji} | \mathbf{g}_{ji}^c\right) = \frac{\int \prod_{\lambda_{j'\phi_{j'i'}} = \lambda_{ja}} F(g_{j'i'} | \theta) \mu_1(\theta) d\theta}{\int \prod_{(j',i') \neq (j,i), \lambda_{j'\phi_{j'i'}} = \lambda_{ja}} F(g_{j'i'} | \theta) \mu_1(\theta) d\theta}. \qquad (38)$$

Combining (35) and (37), we have (19).
If a has not appeared before, by (17), we have

$$P\left(g_{ji} | \boldsymbol{\phi}, \boldsymbol{\lambda}, \boldsymbol{\theta}, \alpha_1, \alpha_0, \mu_1, \mathbf{g}_{ji}^c\right)$$
$$= \sum_{k=1}^{K_{ja}} \frac{\sum_j d_{jk}}{\sum_{jk} d_{jk} + \alpha_1} f_k\left(g_{ji} | \mathbf{g}_{ji}^c\right) + \frac{\alpha_1}{\sum_{jk} d_{jk} + \alpha_1} \int F(g_{ji} | \theta) \mu_1(\theta) d\theta, \qquad (39)$$

Combining (36) and (39), we have (21).

Derivation of (22) nd (23)

$$P\left(\lambda_{j\phi_{ji}} = a | \boldsymbol{\phi}, \lambda_{j\phi_{ji}}^c, \boldsymbol{\theta}, \alpha_1, \alpha_0, \mu_1, \mathbf{g}\right)$$

$$= \frac{P\left(g_{ji}, \lambda_{j\phi_{ji}} = a | \boldsymbol{\phi}, \lambda_{j\phi_{ji}}^c, \boldsymbol{\theta}, \alpha_1, \alpha_0, \mu_1, \mathbf{g}_{ji}^c\right)}{P\left(g_{ji} | \boldsymbol{\phi}, \boldsymbol{\lambda}, \boldsymbol{\theta}, \alpha_1, \alpha_0, \mu_1, \mathbf{g}_{ji}^c\right)} \qquad (40)$$

$$\propto P\left(g_{ji}, \lambda_{j\phi_{ji}} = a | \boldsymbol{\phi}, \lambda_{j\phi_{ji}}^c, \boldsymbol{\theta}, \alpha_1, \alpha_0, \mu_1, \mathbf{g}_{ji}^c\right) \qquad (41)$$

$$\propto P\left(g_{ji} | \boldsymbol{\phi}, \boldsymbol{\lambda}, \boldsymbol{\theta}, \alpha_1, \alpha_0, \mu_1, \mathbf{g}_{ji}^c\right)$$
$$P\left(\lambda_{j\phi_{ji}} = a | \boldsymbol{\phi}, \lambda_{j\phi_{ji}}^c, \boldsymbol{\theta}, \alpha_1, \alpha_0, \mu_1, \mathbf{g}_{ji}^c\right) \qquad (42)$$

By (17), if a has appeared before, we have

$$P\left(\lambda_{j\phi_{ji}} = a | \boldsymbol{\phi}, \lambda_{j\phi_{ji}}^c, \boldsymbol{\theta}, \alpha_1, \alpha_0, \mu_1, \mathbf{g}_{ji}^c\right) \propto \sum_j d_{ja}. \qquad (43)$$

Otherwise we have

$$P\left(\lambda_{j\phi_{ji}} = a | \boldsymbol{\phi}, \lambda_{j\phi_{ji}}^c, \boldsymbol{\theta}, \alpha_1, \alpha_0, \mu_1, \mathbf{g}_{ji}^c\right) \propto \alpha_1. \qquad (44)$$

If a is used before, we have

$$P\left(g_{ji} | \boldsymbol{\phi}, \boldsymbol{\lambda}, \boldsymbol{\theta}, \alpha_1, \alpha_0, \mu_1, \mathbf{g}_{ji}^c\right) = f_a\left(g_{ji} | \mathbf{g}_{ji}^c\right). \qquad (45)$$

Otherwise, the customer chooses a new table. The data are generated from F based on a sample from μ_1. We have

$$P\left(g_{ji} | \boldsymbol{\phi}, \boldsymbol{\lambda}, \boldsymbol{\theta}, \alpha_1, \alpha_0, \mu_1, \mathbf{g}_{ji}^c\right) = \int F(g_{ji} | \theta) \mu_1(\theta) d\theta. \qquad (46)$$

Combining (43), (44), (45), and (46), we have (22) and (23).

Competing interests
The authors declare that they have no competing interests.

Author details
[1] Department of Electrical & Computer Engineering, Duke University, Durham, NC 27708, USA. [2] Department of Electrical Engineering, Columbia University, New York, NY 10027, USA.

References
1.   M Schena, D Shalon, R Davis, P Brown, Quantitative monitoring of gene expression patterns with a complementary DNA microarray. Science. **270**(5235), 467–470 (1995)

2. R Cho, M Campbell, E Winzeler, L Steinmetz, A Conway, L Wodicka, T Wolfsberg, A Gabrielian, D Landsman, D Lockhart, A genome-wide transcriptional analysis of the mitotic cell cycle. Mol. Cell. **2**, 65–73 (1998)

3. J Hughes, P Estep, S Tavazoie, G Church, Computational identification of cis-regulatory elements associated with groups of functionally related genes in Saccharomyces cerevisiae. J. Mol. Biol. **296**(5), 1205–1214 (2000)

4. M Eisen, P Spellman, P Brown, D Botstein, Cluster analysis display of genome-wide expression patterns. Proc. Natl. Acad. Sci. **95**(25), 14863–14868 (1998)

5. J MacQueen, in *Proceedings of the Fifth Berkeley Symposium on Mathematical Statistics and Probability*, vol. 1. Some methods for classification and analysis of multivariate observations (University of California Press, California, 1967), pp. 281–297

6. T Kohonen, *Self-Organization and Associative Memory*. (Springer, New York, 1988)

7. D Jiang, C Tang, A Zhang, Cluster analysis for gene expression data: a survey. IEEE Trans Knowledge Data Eng. **16**(11), 1370–1386 (2004)

8. A Dempster, N Laird, D Rubin, Maximum likelihood from incomplete data via the EM algorithm. J. R. Stat. Soc. Ser. B (Methodological). **39**, 1–38 (1977)

9. G McLachlan, D Peel, *Finite Mixture Models*. (Wiley-Interscience, New York, 2000)

10. C Fraley, A Raftery, Model-based clustering, discriminant analysis, and density estimation. Am. J. Stat. Assoc. **97**(458), 611–631 (2002)

11. K Yeung, C Fraley, A Murua, A Raftery, W Ruzzo, Model-based clustering and data transformations for gene expression data. Bioinformatics. **17**(10), 977–987 (2001)

12. G Schwarz, Estimating the dimension of a model. Ann. Stat. **6**(2), 461–464 (1978)

13. H Akaike, A new look at the statistical model identification. IEEE Trans. Autom. Control. **19**(6), 716–723 (1974)

14. M Medvedovic, S Sivaganesan, Bayesian infinite mixture model based clustering of gene expression profiles. Bioinformatics. **18**(9), 1194–1206 (2002)

15. T Ferguson, A Bayesian analysis of some nonparametric problems. Ann. Stat. **1**(2), 209–230 (1973)

16. R Neal, Markov chain sampling methods for Dirichlet process mixture models. J. Comput. Graph. Stat. **9**(2), 249–265 (2000)

17. J Pitman. Some developments of the Blackwell-MacQueen urn scheme. *Lecture Notes-Monograph Series* (1996), pp. 245–267

18. L Kaufman, P Rousseeuw, *Finding Groups in Data: An Introduction to Cluster Analysis, vol. 39*, (1990)

19. D Jiang, J Pei, A Zhang, in *Proceedings of Third IEEE Symposium on Bioinformatics and Bioengineering*. DHC: a density-based hierarchical clustering method for time series gene expression data (IEEE, Bethesda, 2003), pp. 393–400

20. J Piatigorsky, *Gene Sharing and Evolution: The Diversity of Protein Functions*. (Harvard University Press, Cambridge, 2007)

21. Y Teh, M Jordan, M Beal, D Blei, Hierarchical Dirichlet processes. J. Am. Stat. Assoc. **101**(476), 1566–1581 (2006)

22. J Sethuraman, A constructive definition of Dirichlet priors. Stat. Sinica. **4**, 639–650 (1991)

23. D Aldous. Exchangeability and related topics. *École d'Été de Probabilités de Saint-Flour XIII* (1985), pp. 1–198

24. G Casella, E George, Explaining the Gibbs sampler. Am. Stat. **46**(3), 167–174 (1992)

25. D Blackwell, J MacQueen, Ferguson distributions via Pólya urn schemes. Ann. Stat. **1**(2), 353–355 (1973)

26. S Brooks, Markov chain Monte Carlo method and its application. J. R. Stat. Soc. Ser. D (The Statistician). **47**, 69–100 (1998)

27. L Hubert, P Arabie, Comparing partitions. J. Classif. **2**, 193–218 (1985)

28. PJ Rousseeuw, Silhouettes: a graphical aid to the interpretation and validation of cluster analysis. J. Comput. Appl. Math. **20**, 53–65 (1987)

29. KY Yeung, WL Ruzzo, Principal component analysis for clustering gene expression data. Bioinformatics. **17**(9), 763–774 (2001)

30. K Yeung, M Medvedovic, R Bumgarner, Clustering gene-expression data with repeated measurements. Genome Biol. **4**(5), R34 (2003)

31. S Chu, J DeRisi, M Eisen, J Mulholland, D Botstein, PO Brown, I Herskowitz, The transcriptional program of sporulation in budding yeast. Science. **282**(5389), 699–705 (1998)

32. VR Iyer, MB Eisen, DT Ross, G Schuler, T Moore, JC Lee, JM Trent, LM Staudt, J Hudson, MS Boguski, et al., The transcriptional program in the response of human fibroblasts to serum,. Science. **283**(5398), 83–87 (1999)

33. P Spellman, G Sherlock, M Zhang, V Iyer, K Anders, M Eisen, P Brown, D Botstein, B Futcher, Comprehensive identification of cell cycle-regulated genes of the yeast Saccharomyces cerevisiae by microarray hybridization. Mol. Biol. Cell. **9**(12), 3273 (1998)

34. D Blei, A Ng, M Jordan, Latent Dirichlet allocation. J. Mach. Learn. Res. **3**, 993–1022 (2003)

35. C Fraley, A Raftery, MCLUST: software for model-based cluster analysis. J. Classif. **16**(2), 297–306 (1999)

36. T Furey, N Cristianini, N Duffy, D Bednarski, M Schummer, D Haussler, Support vector machine classification and validation of cancer tissue samples using microarray expression data. Bioinformatics. **16**(10), 906–914 (2000)

37. S Tavazoie, JD Hughes, MJ Campbell, RJ Cho, GM Church, et al., Systematic determination of genetic network architecture. Nat. Genetics. **22**, 281–285 (1999)

38. F Chung, L Lu. *Complex Graphs and Networks*. CBMS Lecture Series, vol. 107 (American Mathematical Society, Providence, 2006)

39. M Ashburner, C Ball, J Blake, D Botstein, H Butler, J Cherry, A Davis, K Dolinski, S Dwight, J Eppig, et al., Gene ontology: tool for the unification of biology. Nat. Genet. **25**, 25–29 (2000)

40. Stanford University. Yeast cell cycle datasets. http://genome-www.stanford.edu/cellcycle/data/rawdata

41. A Lukashin, R Fuchs, Analysis of temporal gene expression profiles: clustering by simulated annealing and determining the optimal number of clusters. Bioinformatics. **17**(5), 405–414 (2001)

42. H Mewes, D Frishman, U Guldener, G Mannhaupt, K Mayer, M Mokrejs, B Morgenstern, M Munsterkotter, S Rudd, B Weil, MIPS: a database for genomes and protein sequences. Nucleic Acids Res. **30**, 31–34 (2002)

7

On the dynamical properties of a model of cell differentiation

Marco Villani[1,2*] and Roberto Serra[1,2]

Abstract

One of the major challenges in complex systems biology is that of providing a general theoretical framework to describe the phenomena involved in cell differentiation, i.e., the process whereby stem cells, which can develop into different types, become progressively more specialized. The aim of this study is to briefly review a dynamical model of cell differentiation which is able to cover a broad spectrum of experimentally observed phenomena and to present some novel results.

Keywords: Cell differentiation, Dynamical model, Boolean networks, Ergodic sets

1. Introduction

Th aim of this study is to propose a dynamical model of cell differentiation, i.e., the process whereby stem cells, which can develop into different types, become more and more specialized. The model is an abstract one (it does not refer to a specific organism or cell type) and it aims at reproducing the most relevant features of the process: (i) different degrees of differentiation, that span from totipotent stem cells to fully differentiated cells; (ii) stochastic differentiation, where populations of identical multipotent cells stochastically generate different cell types; (iii) deterministic differentiation, where signals trigger the progress of multipotent cells into more differentiated types, in well-defined lineages; (iv) limited reversibility: differentiation is almost always irreversible, but there are limited exceptions under the action of appropriate signals; (v) induced pluripotency: fully differentiated cells can come back to a pluripotent state by modifying the expression of some genes; and (vi) induced change of cell type: modification of the expression of few genes can directly convert one differentiated cell type into another.

This study is a part of a series of articles [1-3] aiming to develop a single model able to describe all these phenomena, whereas till now specialized models of some specific processes have been proposed. Typically, these models make use of continuous descriptions and take into account the contributions of only few genes [4-6].

Here, we hypothesize that the differentiation process is rather an emerging property due to the interactions of very many genes: its main features therefore should be shared by a variety of different organisms. To check this hypothesis, we make use of a noisy version of a well-known model of gene networks, i.e., the random Boolean network (RBN) model. RBNs in fact, in spite of their discrete approach, have been proven to describe important experimental facts concerning gene expression [7-9], allowing at the same time simulations of large networks [9]. We find that the introduction of noise in this framework (noisy RBN, or briefly NRBN) [1,10] allows one to effectively describe all the just listed issues.

The remainder of this article is organized as follows: in Section 2 we briefly review the model (the interested readers may refer to [1-3,11] for further details) and its application to cell differentiation; in Section 3 we present new results on its scale-free version and in Section 4 we present other results that are not included in those previous papers. A brief final discussion is presented in Section 5.

2. The model of cell differentiation
2.1. NRBN

A classical RBN is a dynamical system, based on a directed graph with N nodes (genes), which can assume binary values 0 or 1 (inactive/active); time is discrete, with synchronous updating of all the node values. Each node has exactly k_{in} input connections chosen randomly with

* Correspondence: marco.villani@unimore.it
[1]Department of Physics, Informatics and Mathematics, University of Modena and Reggio Emilia, Modena, Italy
[2]European Centre for Living Technology, Venice, Italy

uniform probability among the remaining $N - 1$ nodes. To each node a Boolean function is associated, which determines its value at time t from the values of its inputs at the previous time step. The Boolean functions are chosen at random for every node, by assigning to each set of input values the outcome 1 with probability p. Within the *quenched* strategy, both the topology and the Boolean function associated to each node do not change in time. We concentrate our study on the so-called critical networks with $k_{in} = 2$ and $p = 1/2$ [12].

The network dynamics is discrete and synchronous, so fixed points and cycles are the only possible asymptotic states in finite networks; typically a single RBN has more than one attractor. Note nevertheless that attractors of RBNs are unstable with respect to noise. Noise will be modeled by random transient flips of randomly chosen nodes, therefore leading to the model of an NRBN. In fact, even if the flips last for a single time step one sometimes observes transitions from that attractor to another one. Therefore, by flipping all the states belonging to the attractors of an RBN, it is possible to create a complete map of the transitions among the RBNs' attractors (the attractors' landscape shown in Figure 1a).[a] In these conditions, and because noise is known to play a role in key cellular processes [2,13], single attractors can no longer be associated to cell types, as proposed in the past [14,15]. Ribeiro and Kauffman [10] observed that it is possible to identify subsets of attractors, which they called Ergodic sets, which entrap the system in the long time limit, so the system continues to jump between attractors which belong to the set. Unfortunately it

turns out that most NRBNs have just one such set: this observation rules out the possibility to associate them to cell types.

2.2. Threshold ergodic set

A possible solution to this problem was proposed in [1,2], where the authors observe that flips are a kind of noise fairly intense, as they amount to silencing an expressed gene or to express a gene which would otherwise be inactive: this may well be an event too rare to happen with significant probability in the cell lifetime. It is possible therefore to introduce a threshold θ, and neglect all the transitions whose occurrence probability is lower than it (Figure 1b). In such a way, the notion of Ergodic set has to be modified in that of threshold Ergodic set (briefly, TES or, when the value of the threshold is considered, TES_θ), a set of attractors linked only by jumps having a probability higher than θ, that entrap the system in the long time limit. A TES_θ is therefore a subset of attractors which are directly or indirectly θ-reachable (reachable by means of transition whose probability exceeds the threshold θ) from each other, and from which no transition can allow escaping. The threshold is related to the level of noise in the cell, and scales with the reciprocal of the frequency of flips [1].

A Ribeiro–Kauffman ergodic set is therefore a TES_θ with $\theta = 0$; this structure, by increasing the threshold, breaks into more and more TESs, till all attractors are also independent TESs (that cannot be abandoned). Statistics on the increasing of the ratio between the total number of TESs and the total number of attractors versus the increasing of the threshold are shown elsewhere [1]: in

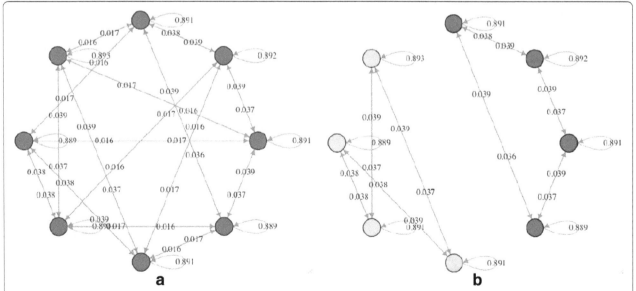

Figure 1 Attractor transition graph in an RBN. Circles represent attractors; arrows represent transitions among attractors induced by single spin flips. The numbers on each arrow are the probability that, by flipping at random the state of a node in an attractor, transition takes place. **(a)** The complete attractor transition graph; **(b)** the same graph, where links whose weight is below the threshold value $\theta = 0.02$ are removed.

any case, when θ exceeds a network-dependent value all the TESs are composed by single attractors (i.e., they are single-TESs).

In [1,2], we propose to associate cell types to TESs, that represent coherent stable ways of functioning of the same genome even in the presence of noise, and to associate *final* cell types to the single-TESs. According to this framework NRBNs can host more than one TESs, avoiding in such a way the problem that hampered the straightforward association of cell types to Ergodic sets.

2.3. Stochastic differentiation

Several authors, on theoretical and experimental bases, associate different levels of noise to different levels of differentiation [16-18]; in particular the degree of differentiation is supposed to be related to the possibility for an undifferentiated cell to wander in a portion of phase space greater than the corresponding portions covered by more differentiated cells. This fact is reflected in the presence of higher noise levels in undifferentiated cells, with respect to more differentiated forms [18-20].

In our framework, a convenient proxy for the available portion of phase space could be the number of attractors belonging to the TES. A TES_0, implying a wandering through a large number of attractors, could therefore be associated to a totipotent cell while as the threshold is increased smaller TESs appear, corresponding to more differentiated biological forms. At high enough threshold values there are only single-TESs (that describe the fully differentiated cells). The increase of the threshold would correspond to a decrease of noise level: as other authors, we hypothesize that this effect could be related to an improvement in the mechanisms whereby fluctuations are kept under control [3,21]. This association of differentiation to changes in the noise level represents the most stringent outcome of the model, and could be amenable to experimental test.

This hypothesis explains in a straightforward way the fact that there are different degrees of differentiation corresponding to different threshold values. It is then easy to describe stochastic differentiation [4,19]: in this vision the fate of a cell depends on the particular attractor where it is found when the systems' noise level changes and exceeds the threshold (and on the specific flip which occurs). The new cell type will be that corresponding to the new TES_θ to which the attractor belongs at the new threshold level.

2.4. Deterministic differentiation

There exist several processes, e.g., during the embryogenesis, in which cell differentiation is not stochastic but it is driven towards precise, repeatable types by specific chemical signals, which activate or silence some genes. In our model, we can simulate these processes by permanently fixing to 1 or 0 the state of some nodes. However, in our framework, in order to have deterministic differentiation, we need the existence of particular genes, called switch genes, whose permanent perturbation, coupled with a change in the noise level (which by itself would lead to stochastic differentiation) always leads the system through the same differentiation pathway. In other words, nodes that uniquely determine to which TES the system will evolve.

The existence of switch nodes has actually been verified to be a common property (found in about 1/3 of the nets), thereby proving the effectiveness of the model.

In [2], one can see an example of differentiation, from a multi-TES_0 to a set of single-TESs. This case represents just one possible diagram obtained from simulations; the system shows indeed a very rich and complex landscape of possible behaviors, as in biological differentiation.

Please note that the model is actually able to describe also the existence of limited exceptions to the irreversibility of cell differentiation, as well as the important phenomenon of induced pluripotency, where the overexpression of few nodes (without changing the noise level) can sometimes make the system "come back" to a less differentiated state (see [22] for an experimental counterpart), and transitions from a completely differentiated cell type to another one (see [23] for an experimental example).

3. Scale-free topology

It has been argued that genetic and metabolic networks have a different structure from the Erdos-Renyi topology [24]: in particular, these networks are characterized by the presence of some nodes (hubs) which influence a high number of other nodes. There are several ways to introduce hubs in networks: one common option is that of creating a so-called scale-free topology, where the probability $P(k)$ that one particular node belonging to the network is connected to k other nodes follows a power law:

$$P(k) = \frac{1}{Z}k^{-\gamma} \ \ with \ \ Z(k) = \sum_{k=1}^{k_{max}} k^{-\gamma}, \tag{1}$$

where k can take values from 1 to a maximum possible value $k_{max} = N - 1$ (self-coupling and multiple connections being prohibited). Z coincides with the Riemann zeta function in the limit $k_{max} \to \infty$ and guarantees the proper normalization; the parameter γ is the so-called scale-free exponent that characterizes the distribution. In this study, therefore we use a scale-free (power law) distribution of output connectivities and compare the results with those of the Erdos-Renyi topology.

In this study, we use for both classes of networks the same parameter values (a fixed in-degree $k_{in} = 2$ and the same bias $p = 0.5$). However, it should be stressed that both topologies have some nodes without outgoing links (a feature which might hold also for real genetic networks). Therefore, it is useful to consider the case where for some nodes $k = 0$. Of course, a direct extension of Equation (1) would lead to a meaningless divergence, so its simplest generalization capable to include the value $k = 0$ is [11]:

$$
\begin{cases}
P_{\text{out}}(k) = \dfrac{1}{Z'} k^{-\gamma} & \text{if } k \neq 0 \\
P_{\text{out}}(0) = P_0
\end{cases}
\quad \text{with } Z' = \dfrac{\displaystyle\sum_{k=1}^{k_{\max}} k^{-\gamma}}{1 - p_0}
$$

$$(2)$$

In order to make a correct comparison between classical and scale-free RBNs we maintain the same total number of links and use $p_0 = 0.13$ (the expected number of nodes without outgoing links for the Erdos-Renyi distribution) [11].

Applying random fluctuations (single bit flip) to simulate the noise in the scale-free model and repeating the same procedure previously described, we get results broadly similar to those of the classical model. In particular, for each analyzed scale-free networks we have only one Ergodic set.[b]

Some perhaps minor differences can be observed: analyzing the attractor transition graph's we found that the sums of the off-diagonals terms are (on average) lower than those of classical model's matrices, implying that the attractors are more stable with respect to perturbations. We also observe that in classical networks (on average) the percentage of zeros in the off-diagonal terms of the adjacency matrices of the attractor transition graph is larger than that of the scale-free nets (this percentage measures the fraction of the attractors that are not directly linked to each other). So, the result suggests that even if the scale-free networks have a stronger stability to the perturbations, the noisy events that influence the dynamic can propagate to more attractors.

These features probably reflect the peculiar organization of the scale-free nets, characterized by the presence of hubs and by the presence of a large fraction of poorly connected nodes, unlikely to significantly affect the asymptotic state of the net.

4. Dynamical properties

The general idea to describe differentiation as a process of wandering in regions of phase space which become more limited as differentiation proceeds is fairly general, and NRBNs are not the only detailed model that complies with this idea—indeed, exploring other dynamical models is one of the most interesting future directions of research. However, in this article we will focus on the dynamical characteristics of the NRBNs only.

4.1. The dynamics of TESs

We address here the analysis of the global properties of the transitions among different attractors. Starting from an attractor A, the system may jump to a new one under the action of noise. A point of rigor is in order: the proper time of the NRBN is affected by the sequence of time steps (of the RBN) when a flip is done. However, let us recall that we allow time for the system to relax back to an attractor, be it the original one or another one. So, we actually have a sequence of attractor states, and we can then define a renormalized time to be one where each time step corresponds to the interval between a flip and the next one.

Starting from an attractor A, the following one depends only on A itself and not on the previous sequence of transitions: i.e., the change from one attractor to another is a Markov process. In our system, the transition probabilities do not change in time and can be represented by a constant transition matrix $\mathbf{A}$, whose elements $\mathbf{A}_{ij}$ represent the transition probability from attractor j to attractor i.

Let $\mathbf{P}$ be a vector whose dimension equals the number of different attractors: each component is associated to an attractor and its value represents the probability that, at a random time instant, the system is in that attractor. In a way coherent with what had been said above, we neglect the transients and focus only on the time spent in attractors. Under these hypotheses, the sum of the components of P is equal to 1. We will also refer to the components of P as the occupation numbers of the attractors.

The dynamics of attractor transitions can be described, in the renormalized time, by the following difference equation (master equation)

$$P_{k=1} = A P_k \tag{3}$$

whose solution is

$$\overrightarrow{P_k} = A^k \overrightarrow{P_0} \tag{4}$$

Let us now consider the question of the dynamical behavior of the occupation numbers. We ask under which conditions they tend to a unique distribution of these components π:

$$\overrightarrow{\pi} = A \overrightarrow{\pi} \tag{5}$$

We will provide below sufficient conditions for this to happen. Indeed, since each column of A sums to one and all its elements are non-negative, $\mathbf{A}$ is a left stochastic matrix.

A remarkable theorem states that if the Markov chain is irreducible (if it is possible to get to any state from any state) and aperiodic (if the fastest return to state i can happen in only one step) there is a unique stationary distribution [25].

According to Section 2, a TES_θ is a subset of attractors which are directly or indirectly θ-reachable from each other, and from which no transition can allow escaping. Therefore, if we limit to consider those attractors that belong to a set, the condition of irreducibility is satisfied.

The second condition (aperiodicity) requires that all the diagonal terms of matrix $\mathbf{A}$ do not vanish. This condition is not required to be a TES according to our definitions, and it should be added in order to guarantee uniqueness. However, let us also observe that falling back to the original state is by far the most frequent behavior that has been observed, so this condition is easily satisfied in most networks.

Under these hypotheses, the unique final vector can equivalently be computed by solving the eigenvector problem (adding as last equation the vinculum provided by the normalization $\sum_i P_i = 1$) or by observing that for any i we have the following limit

$$\lim_{k \to \infty} \left(A_{i,j}\right)^k = \pi_i \quad \forall j \tag{6}$$

where π_i is the ith element of the vector $\boldsymbol{\pi}$ (note that in Equation 6 π_i does not depend on j). This implies that the long-term probability of being in a state is independent of the initial distribution: the systems, as a wide variety of dissipative dynamical systems, evolve over time to a stationary state. Intuitively, a stochastic matrix represents a Markov chain with no sink or source states, and the iterated application of the stochastic matrix to the probability distribution redistributes the probabilities while preserving their total initial sum (a consequence of the fact that our system cannot escape out of the TES states, each

state being reachable—directly or indirectly—from each other state). For large systems, the solution proposed by Equation (6) is more stable and computationally less expensive that the eigenvector problem: Figure 2c shows its iteration for an example of our configurations (Figure 2a) and the stable values of the occupation probability vector $\boldsymbol{\pi}$ (Figure 2b). Finally, by knowing matrix $\mathbf{A}$ and the starting configuration P_0 it is possible to estimate the number of iterations k^* needed to reach the stable configuration. In fact, if we call $\boldsymbol{P}_k$ the vector obtained by applying k times the matrix $\mathbf{A}$ to the initial vector $P_0 = \sum_{i=1}^{n} a_i \bar{u}_i$ ($\bar{u}_i$ being the n eigenvectors corresponding to the n eigenvalues of $\mathbf{A}$, ordered such $|\lambda_1| > |\lambda_2| > |\lambda_1| > \cdots |\lambda_n|$), it is possible to see that [26]

$$P_k = \lambda_1^k \left(a_1 \bar{u}_1 + a_2 \left(\frac{\lambda_2}{\lambda_1}\right)^k \bar{u}_2 + a_3 \left(\frac{\lambda_3}{\lambda_1}\right)^k \bar{u}_3 + \cdots + a_n \left(\frac{\lambda_n}{\lambda_1}\right)^k \bar{u}_n \right)$$

$$\tag{7}$$

that approaches $\boldsymbol{\pi}$ as k goes to infinity with an exponential rate equal to $|\lambda_1|/|\lambda_2|$. When we get the desired approximation we obtain also k^*, which in turn as a consequence of the fact that our typical A_{ii} elements are very close each other is roughly proportional to the time the system needs to reach its stable configuration.

Let us also remark that the above considerations lead to the conclusion that the limit distribution of occupation numbers of attractors in a TES does not oscillate (provided that all the diagonal elements of the transition matrix do not vanish).

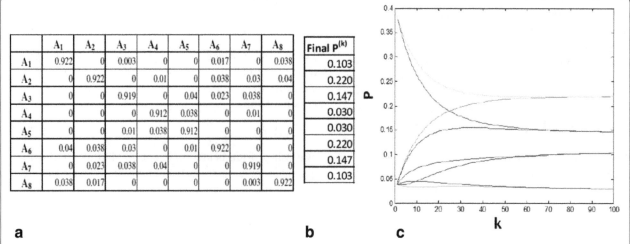

a   **b**   **c**

Figure 2 The dynamics of TESs. A transition matrix that describes our attractor landscapes (**a**), the corresponding stable distribution π (**b**), the evolution of occupation probabilities (obtained by starting from a random condition and iterating equation 6) till the reaching of the final stable situation (**c**).

Table 1 Comparison between different noise levels

N	Single flip	Double flip
10	19.2	19.1
100	10.3	11.2

4.2. Double flips

In order to test the robustness of our approach, we simulated a large noise intensity, in particular by using double transient flips, in which two different nodes are flipped at the same time; the nodes are chosen randomly with uniform probability and belong to the same attractor state.

Table 1 shows the percentage of perturbations that lead the system to a different attractor in networks of different size with different noisy intensity (single bit flip and double bit flip).[c]

As shown in Table 1, the fraction of transitions that lead the system to escape from an attractor is not strongly affected by doubling the flips, thereby indicating a robust behavior with respect to this kind of change.

4.3. Permanent perturbations

Let us now consider permanent perturbations, i.e., flips that last indefinitely (in the following we will also consider semi-permanent perturbations that last for a time long enough to allow the system to relax to an attractor). Note also that the permanent perturbation actually changes the original RBN, as it can be proved by observing that the perturbed node is now ruled by a different Boolean function, i.e., true or false. Therefore, in general the attractors of the perturbed network can be different from those of the original one (apart from the obvious difference concerning the state of the perturbed node itself).

Permanent clamping of a node is analogous to the one observed in deterministic differentiation. In that case, we concentrated on switch nodes, that always lead the system to the same attractor whatever the phase and whatever the attractor of a given TES, but of course only a fraction of the nodes have this property. It has been observed, among other behaviors, that perturbing the same node in different phases of the same attractor can lead, in a limited fraction of cases, to transitions to new attractors. It is intriguing to remark that also real cells

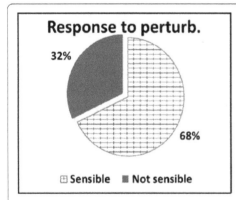
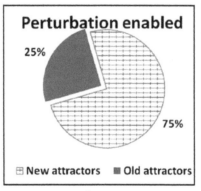
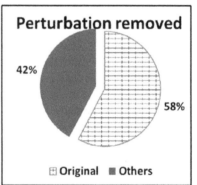

a

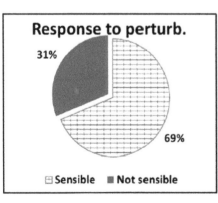
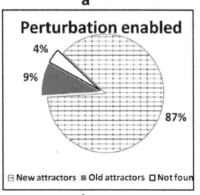
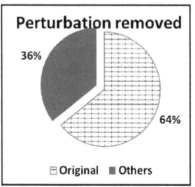

b

Figure 3 Consequences of permanent perturbation of RBNs' attractors. The first row (**a**) refers to networks having 10 nodes, whereas the second row (**b**) shows results of 100 nodes nets (100 nets for each situation). The first column shows the fraction of experiments where, under the action of a permanent perturbation, the RBN goes to a different attractor, the second column shows the fraction of cases where the new attractors are equivalent to one of the old ones, and the third column shows the fraction of cases where the original attractor is recovered after removal of the (semi-permanent) perturbation. See the text for more detailed explanations.

may have different reactions to perturbation if perturbed in different instants of their cellular cycle. And of course perturbing the same node in different attractors can lead to different attractors.

A broad discussion of permanent perturbations can be found in [7,8,11] where also experimental data referring to gene knock-out in *Saccharomyces cerevisiae* are analyzed. Let it suffice here to remark that perturbing a single node can modify the values of many others: we will refer to the number of affected genes as the size of the avalanche in gene expression.

In order to analyze these avalanches of changes in the case of differentiation processes, we considered two groups of networks with 10 and 100 nodes. To find the RBNs' attractors, we exhaustively checked all the possible initial conditions for the nets with 10 nodes, and performed a random sampling for the nets with 100 nodes. For the nets with 10 nodes, we perturbed all the nodes by starting in all the phases, whereas for the nets with 100 nodes we perturbed 20% of the total states; the main results are shown in Figure 3.

The graphs in row (a) refer to nets with 10 nodes, whereas graphs in row (b) refer to nets with 100 nodes. The first column shows the fraction of experiments where, under the action of a permanent perturbation, the RBN that is on attractor A goes to an attractor A' not equivalent to A (we define as equivalent two attractors that are equal in all the nodes, with the exception of the perturbed one). The second column shows that, among all the cases where A' is not equivalent to A, the largest part of A' attractors are also not equivalent to any attractor of the original RBN (they are new attractors). The third column refers only to the "new attractors" A', and describes what happens when the perturbation is removed and the system is allowed to relax toward the attractors of the original net. The graph shows how many times the final attractors B coincide with the original attractors A, and how many times B differs from A. Note that in a limited number of cases (with $N = 100$) it was not possible to find the attractors within the time limits of the simulations.

It is interesting to observe that the fraction of experiments that lead to new attractor (column 1 of Figure 3) seems to exhibit only a weak dependence upon network size, at least in the interval 10–100, while the fraction of cases where the new attractor is different from any of the previous ones (column 2) shrinks considerably as the network size grows. Moreover, note that permanent perturbations have significant consequences also after the perturbation has been removed (column 3).

5. Conclusions

We presented a single model that can describe all the main features of differentiation; the explanation of differentiation makes use of the global properties of a generic dynamical system, without resorting to detailed hypotheses concerning very specific control circuits. Nevertheless, the RBN framework we used is able to usefully complement the generic schema we propose, by highlighting some interesting aspect as for example the effects of the dynamical regimes and of the network size or topology, or the effects of (semi) permanent perturbations on the attractor landscape.

A possible development of the work on scale-free topology, because of the particular importance of hubs, would be the study of the influence of their assortative/ disassortative properties on the transition probabilities among attractors.

We emphasize that the picture of a cell as a dynamical system and the idea that differentiated cells are more constrained in their wandering in phase space are fairly general and can be applied also to other models of gene and cell dynamics [5].

Endnotes

[a]We assume that the noise level is small enough to allow the system to relax to an attractor before a new flip occurs. [b]For a deeply explanation of the network we used, we forward the reader to [11]. The values of γ we used is $\gamma = 2.24$ for the nets with 100 nodes, $\gamma = 2.29$ for nets with 200 nodes, and $\gamma = 2.34$ for nets with 1000 nodes. [c]For the double flip experiments in the networks with $N = 10$ we perturb 25 random couples of nodes. In the nets with $N = 100$ we perturb 250 * LA (LA = attractor's period) random couples of nodes. So, the exploration of the perturbations is not exhaustive, but sufficient robust given that in the simulations with 100 * LA random couples of nodes perturbed the result does not change.

Competing interests
The authors declare that they have no competing interests.

Acknowledgments
We greatly benefited from discussions with Stuart Kauffman, Sui Huang, Kunihiko Kaneko, Alessia Barbieri, and Andre Ribeiro.

References
1. R Serra, M Villani, A Barbieri, SA Kauffman, A Colacci, On the dynamics of random boolean networks subject to noise: attractors, ergodic sets and cell types. J. Theor. Biol. **265**, 185–193 (2010)
2. M Villani, A Barbieri, R Serra, A dynamical model of genetic networks for cell differentiation. PLoS One **6**(3), e17703 (2011). doi:10.1371/journal.pone.0017703
3. M Villani, R Serra, A Barbieri, A Roli, SA Kauffman, *Proceedings of the seventh European Conference on Complex System* (University of Lisbon, Lisbon, 2010), pp. 13–17
4. T Miyamoto, H Iwasaki, B Reizis, M Ye, T Graf, IL Weissman, K Akashi, Myeloid or lymphoid promiscuity as a critical step in hematopoietic lineage commitment. Dev. Cell **3**, 137–147 (2002)
5. K Kaneko, *Life: An Introduction to Complex System Biology* (Springer, Berlin, 2006)
6. S Huang, Y Guo, G May, T Enver, Bifurcation dynamics of cell fate decision in bipotent progenitor cells. Dev. Biol. **305**(2), 695–713 (2007)

7. R Serra, M Villani, A Semeria, Genetic network models and statistical properties of gene expression data in knock-out experiments. J. Theor. Biol. **227**, 149–157 (2004)

8. R Serra, M Villani, A Graudenzi, SA Kauffman, Why a simple model of genetic regulatory networks describes the distribution of avalanches in gene expression data. J. Theor. Biol. **249**, 449–460 (2007)

9. I Shmulevich, SA Kauffman, M Aldana, Eukaryotic cells are dynamically ordered or critical but not chaotic. PNAS **102**, 13439–13444 (2005)

10. AS Ribeiro, SA Kauffman, *Noisy attractors and ergodic sets in models of gene regulatory networks*. J. Theor. Biol. **247**, 743–755 (2007)

11. R Serra, M Villani, A Graudenzi, A Colacci, SA Kauffman, The simulation of gene knock-out in scale-free random boolean models of genetic networks. Netw. Heterogeneous Media **3**(2), 333–343 (2008)

12. M Aldana, S Coppersmith, L-P Kadanoff, Applied Mathematical Sciences Series, in *Perspectives and Problems in Nonlinear Science*, ed. by E Kaplan, JE Marsden, KR Sreenivasan (Springer, New York, 2003)

13. A Raj, A van Oudenaarden, Nature, nurture, or chance: Stochastic gene expression and its consequences. Cell **135**(2), 216–226 (2008)

14. SA Kauffman, *The Origins of Order* (Oxford University Press, New York, 1993)

15. SA Kauffman, *At Home in the Universe* (Oxford University Press, New York, 1995)

16. M Hoffmann, HH Chang, S Huang, DE Ingber, M Loeffler, J Galle, Noise-driven stem cell and progenitor population dynamics. PLoS ONE **3**(8), e2922 (2008). doi:10.1371/journal.pone.0002922

17. T Kalmar, C Lim, P Hayward, S Muñoz-Descalzo, J Nichols, J Garcia-Ojalvo, A Martinez Arias, Regulated Fluctuations in Nanog Expression Mediate Cell Fate Decisions in Embryonic Stem Cells. PLoS Biol. **7**(7), e1000149 (2009). doi:10.1371/journal.pbio. 2009

18. A Kashiwagi, I Urabe, K Kaneko, T Yomo, Adaptive response of a gene network to environmental changes by fitness-induced attractor selection. PLoS ONE **1** (2006). doi:10.1371/jour- nal.pone.0000049

19. M Hu, D Krause, M Greaves, S Sharkis, M Dexter, C Heyworth, T Enver, Multilineage gene expression precedes commitment in the hemopoietic system. Genes Dev. **11**(6), 774–785 (1997)

20. C Furusawa, K Kaneko, Chaotic expression dynamics implies pluripotency: when theory and experimentation meet. Biol. Direct **4**(17) (2009). doi:10.1186/1745-6150-4-17

21. I Lestas, J Paulsson, NE Ross, G Vinnicombe, Noise in gene regulatory networks. IEEE Trans. Autom. Control **53**, 189–200 (2008)

22. K Takahashi, K Tanabe, M Ohnuki, M Narita, T Ichisaka, K Tomoda, S Yamanaka, Induction of pluripotent stem cells from adult human fibroblasts by defined factors. Cell **131**(5), 861–872 (2007)

23. T Vierbuchen, A Ostermeier, ZP Pang, Y Kokubu, TC Sudhof, M Wernig, Direct conversion of fibroblasts to functional neurons by defined factors. Nature **463**, 1035–1041 (2010)

24. AL Barabasi, R Albert, Emergence of Scaling in Random Networks. Science **286**, 509–512 (1999)

25. E Seneta, *Non-Negative Matrices and Markov Chains* (Springer, New York, 2006)

26. GH Golub, CF Van Loan, Matrix Computations, 3rd edn. (The Johns Hopkins University Press, Baltimore, 1996)

8

Protein network-based Lasso regression model for the construction of disease-miRNA functional interactions

Ala Qabaja[1], Mohammed Alshalalfa[1,2]*, Tarek A Bismar[3] and Reda Alhajj[1]

Abstract

Background: There is a growing body of evidence associating microRNAs (miRNAs) with human diseases. MiRNAs are new key players in the disease paradigm demonstrating roles in several human diseases. The functional association between miRNAs and diseases remains largely unclear and far from complete. With the advent of high-throughput functional genomics techniques that infer genes and biological pathways dysregulted in diseases, it is now possible to infer functional association between diseases and biological molecules by integrating disparate biological information.

Results: Here, we first used Lasso regression model to identify miRNAs associated with disease signature as a proof of concept. Then we proposed an integrated approach that uses disease-gene associations from microarray experiments and text mining, and miRNA-gene association from computational predictions and protein networks to build functional associations network between miRNAs and diseases. The findings of the proposed model were validated against gold standard datasets using ROC analysis and results were promising (AUC = 0.81). Our protein network-based approach discovered 19 new functional associations between prostate cancer and miRNAs. The new 19 associations were validated using miRNA expression data and clinical profiles and showed to act as diagnostic and prognostic prostate biomarkers. The proposed integrated approach allowed us to reconstruct functional associations between miRNAs and human diseases and uncovered functional roles of newly discovered miRNAs.

Conclusions: Lasso regression was used to find associations between diseases and miRNAs using their gene signature. Defining miRNA gene signature by integrating the downstream effect of miRNAs demonstrated better performance than the miRNA signature alone. Integrating biological networks and multiple data to define miRNA and disease gene signature demonstrated high performance to uncover new functional associations between miRNAs and diseases.

Keywords: miRNA, Protein interactions, Systems biology, Disease, Regression modeling

Introduction

MicroRNAs (miRNAs) are small RNA molecules that regulate genes by binding to their 3′UTR and trigger target degradation or translational repression [1]. miRNAs play a key role in diverse biological processes including differentiation, cell cycle and apoptosis [2]. About 3% of the human genes encode for miRNAs, each miRNA is estimated to regulate hundreds of genes, and over 50% of

the human protein-coding genes are regulated by miRNAs. Computational predictions estimated that there are around 1,700 miRNAs in human genome [3]. This makes miRNAs one of the most abundant classes of regulatory genes in humans. MiRNAs are now perceived as a key layer of post-transcriptional control within the networks of gene regulation.

MicroRNAs expression is altered in several diseases including cancer and thus it is very likely that alteration in miRNA expression could lead to human diseases [4,5]. Several studies showed that miRNAs are associated with a growing list of diseases including cancer [6,7]. An increasing body of evidence suggests that miRNAs impact gene

*Correspondence: msalshal@ucalgary.ca
[1]Department of Computer Science, University of Calgary, Calgary, Alberta, Canada
[2]Biotechnology Research Center, Palestine Polytechnic University, Hebron, Palestine
Full list of author information is available at the end of the article

expression in many cancer types including prostate cancer [4,8,9]. Several studies have investigated the role of miRNAs in cancer using mRNA and miRNA expression profiling [1,10] and suggest that most diseases are attributed to more than one miRNA that affect hundreds of genes.

There are several lines of evidence suggesting functional association between miRNAs and cancer. First, miRNAs are shown to control cell proliferation and apoptosis [2,11]. Thus their dysregulation may contribute to proliferative disease. Several miRNAs showed to act as tumor suppressor or oncogenes [12]. Second, genome-wide association studies demonstrated that most human miRNAs are located at fragile sites in the genome or regions that are commonly altered or amplified in human cancer [13]. Third, miRNAs are widely deregulated in comparison to normal tissues [14]. Mutation of miRNAs, dysfunction of miRNA biogenesis and dysregulation of miRNAs and their targets may result in various diseases. The question remains how miRNA alteration might cause a disease. All these evidences support the strong necessities in understanding the functional association between miRNAs and diseases.

Currently, more than 70 diseases have been reported to be associated with miRNAs [15]. Many studies have produced large number of miRNA-disease associations and showed that the mechanisms of miRNAs involved in diseases are very complex. Uncovering disease-miRNA associations help understanding underlying mechanisms in diseases. This would give us better insights into the functional role of newly discovered miRNAs in certain diseases. Studying and analyzing the functional association between diseases and miRNAs requires large scale experiments to provide high-throughput data governing the status of diseases cells. High-throughput genomics technologies are witnessing a revolution and becoming a standard routine in many experimental laboratories. The quantity of microarray data analyzing the gene expression in diseases is exponentially increasing. As a result, disease gene signatures are delivered on a regular basis. Defining gene signature for diseases better explore the dysregulated biological pathways and cellular processes in diseases. Gene signatures bear a signature of regulatory activity of miRNAs as it is anticipated that the collective effect of miRNAs may lead to dramatic changes in the expression of their targets that may lead to diseases.

Although integrating bioinformatics approaches with miRNA expression data can predict miRNAs deregulated in certain diseases, only very few miRNAs have been functionally validated in disease context, and the underlying mechanisms of why and how miRNAs become deregulated are largely unknown. Better understanding of the regulatory role of miRNAs in cancer development and progression requires exploring their cooperative influence on target genes' protein context. Characterizing the effect of miRNA on target-context protein partners gained considerable body of attention in the past few years. Protein degree in PPI networks showed to be correlated with the number of targeting miRNAs [16]. Topological features of proteins in PPI showed to be useful to eliminate false discoveries in miRNA-target prediction algorithms [17]. These observations shed light on the influence of miRNAs on the PPI subnetwork involving the target, and highlights the importance of considering target protein partners when searching for functional miRNA-disease interactions.

To summarize the contribution of this work, we used Lasso regression to identify miRNAs whose targets' protein context are enriched in disease gene signatures. The model was applied to identify miRNAs associated with diseases by integrating disease gene signatures extracted from microarray experiments and extracted from pubmed abstracts, with miRNA-gene interactions resulting from integrating predicted miRNA-gene interactions and their influence on target protein context to predict functional association between miRNAs and diseases. The results of the model were validated against gold standard miRNA-disease interactions using ROC analysis. Finally, we focused on newly predicted prostate miRNAs from our approach and characterized their functional role in prostate cancer.

Materials and methods

In this section, we describe how the miRNA-target and disease-gene networks were constructed and preprocessed as input to the Lasso regression model proposed in this work. First, the steps to define gene-disease and miRNA-target interaction networks to define a signatures for each disease and miRNA respectively are described. The Lasso regression model used to associate miRNAs with disease is then explained. Finally, two validation steps to validate the predicted results from the proposed model were followed. First, we showed that Lasso regression model is effective and appropriate to be used to associate disease signatures with miRNAs as a proof of concept. Second, we used ROC analysis to validate the predicted disease-miRNAs against gold standard dataset.

Identification of disease-gene signatures

Gene-disease interactions were retrieved from two independent sources. We first extracted microarray data related to 23 diseases including 13 cancers from Gene Expression Omnibus (Additional file 1). 450 expression profiles including control and disease samples were extracted to define a gene signature for each disease. All microarray experiments were conducted using GPL96 platform to avoid possible platform bias. In addition

to avoid any possible bias that might result from normalization algorithms, we manually extracted raw data
and normalize them using the RMA normalization algorithm [18] implemented in bioconductor. Raw data files
related to each experiment were normalized independently. We only focused on genes related to our diseases
extracted from OMIM database. We only considered
2,414 genes that have corresponding probe set in GPL96
platform. Finally we used significant analysis of microarray (SAM) [19] in order to obtain gene signature for
each disease. For each disease, we only considered the
top 200 differentially expressed genes (top upregulated
100 and top downregulated 100) in each experiment. In
total, 1,942 genes were associated with the 23 diseases
(Additional file 2).

The second source from which we extracted gene
disease interactions is pubmed publications. We used
PolySearch [20], a web server that supports more than 50
different classes of queries against different types of scientific abstracts to extract associations between our diseases
and genes. The typical query used was given disease X,
find all Y such that Y is a gene. We used the default
keywords that PolySearch developed manually to relate
diseases with genes. The number of abstracts was set to
10,000 and thus obtained results from the most 10,000
relevant abstracts. For our experiment, we heuristically
considered all genes that have a relevance score more than
0 and citations more than ten as being a valid signature for
the query disease. 720 genes of relevance to our 23 genes
were extracted. We finally took the union of the two gene
sets (2,061 genes) across 23 diseases in a network called
DiseaseSig (Additional file 2).

Constructing miRNA-target interactions
Human miRNA target computational predictions for
miRNA with conserved 3'UTR were taken from TargetScan 5.1 [21] which showed to outperform all other
miRNA-target prediction methods [22]. These interactions are direct interactions between miRNAs and their
targets. PITA [23] miRNA-target prediction algorithm
was also used to assess how the model is sensitive to
initial input data. We also considered the non-direct interactions between miRNA and targets by considering the
effect of miRNA of protein partners of the target. We used
undirectional functional protein interactions from Reac-
tome [24], which includes proteins physically interacting,
proteins sharing biological function and regulatory interactions, and physical protein interactions from the HPRD
database [25]. Proteins that are not targeted by miRNAs
but at least five of their neighbors are targeted by miR-
NAs are considered indirectly influenced by miRNAs. In
this study, we combined both direct and indirect miRNA-
target interactions (NetmiR) and used it as input to Lasso
regression model (Additional file 3).

Lasso regression modelling to predict miRNA disease association
We used the disease-gene (DiseaseSig) and miRNA-gene
(NetmiR) interactions constructed as response and predicted variables, respectively as input to the Lasso regression model. Let DiseaseSig represent the gene signature
of particular disease, NetmiR$_j$ be the miRNA-target influence profile of miRNA (j) on all target genes. β_j is the
strength of the impact of miRNA (j) on disease gene signature which indicates how much a miRNA can explain
the genes affected in a particular disease. The proposed
regression model can be written as follows:

$$\text{DiseaseSig}(i) = \sum_{j=1}^{\text{miR}} \text{NetmiR}_j * \beta_j + \lambda P(\beta) \qquad (1)$$

where

$$P(\beta) = \sum_{j=1}^{\text{mi}} \frac{1}{2}|\beta_j| \qquad (2)$$

miR is the total number of miRNAs. $P(\beta)$ is the Lasso
penalty. This penalty is particularly useful when there are
many correlated predictor variables as in the case of miR-
NAs. β is the regression coefficient of each variable, which
indicates how each miRNA explains the gene signature.
λ is a factor that determines the sparsity of the solution;
as λ increases, the number of nonzero components of β
decreases.

To optimize λ, we tried many values of λ and used those
that minimize the mean square error. Lasso regression
was fit using ten-fold cross validation. We used glmnet
implementation in matlab from http://www-stat.stanford.
edu/tibs/glmnet-matlab/ to find miRNA coefficients. An
overall description of constructing input data and the
model to identify and validate miRNA disease associations
is given in Figure 1.

Lasso regression modeling to identify enriched miRNAs from gene lists
To demonstrate the applicability and effectiveness of using
Lasso regression modeling to identify miRNAs whose targets are enriched in gene lists, we used affymetrix gene
expression data from LNCaP cell lines treated with pre-
miR-1, pre-miR-27b and pre-miR-206 that was retrieved
from [26] under the access number GSE31620. Significant
analysis of micorarray (SAM) [19] was used to identify differentially expressed genes. 88 genes were identified to be
down regulated after pre-miR-1 treatment, 83 were downregulated after pre-miR-206 treatment, and 51 were down
regulated after pre-miR-27b treatment. NetmiR miRNA-
target interaction network is used to represent protein
targets influenced by miRNAs. The purpose of this step
was to show a proof of concept that Lasso regression could

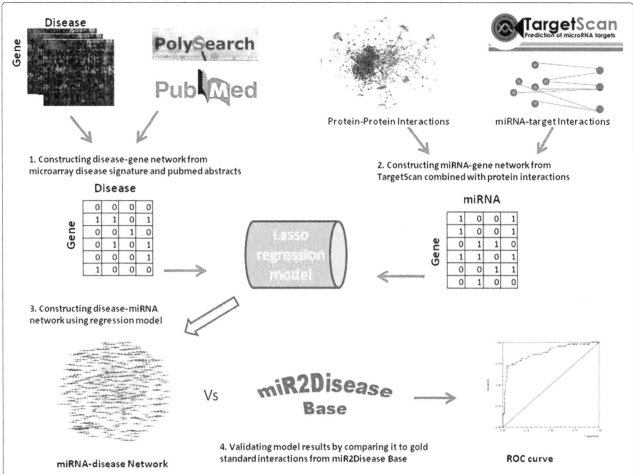

Figure 1 An overview of the framework and flow of data. Four major steps to construct functional disease-miRNA associations. First is disease-gene interactions that were constructed by integrating disease signatures from microarray gene expression data and from pubmed abstracts. Second, miRNA-gene associations was constructed by integrating computationally predicted miRNA-target interactions and protein networks. The aim of integrating protein networks is to reduce noisiness in the predicted data. Proteins that are not targeted by a miRNA but their partners are, are considered as indirect miRNA-target association. Third step is to process the two input (gene-disease and miRNA-gene) as input to the Lasso regression model. The final step is to evaluate the predicted results against gold standard miRNA-target interactions data.

be used to identify miRNAs whose targets are enriched in gene lists.

Validating Lasso regression model performance

The predicted disease-miRNA interactions of the regression model were validated against a gold standard disease miRNA associations manually extracted from miR2disease [27] and HMDD [28] databases. The gold standard network contains 743 interactions between the 23 disease and 305 miRNAs (Additional file 4). Area under curve (AUC) is used to assess the performance of the proposed model and compare it with other results. We compared the performance of the proposed integrative Lasso regression approach with Fisher test that is used to identify miRNAs enriched in disease signature. The purpose of this step was to show that integrating multiple data sources (micorarray and pubmed abstracts in our

work) to define disease gene signatures and integrating the influence of miRNAs on the target protein context is valuable to uncover disease-miRNA interactions. We further focused on miRNAs associated with prostate cancer and validated the new predictions of the model on miRNA expression data from two independent prostate miRNA profiling studies. The aim was to assess the diagnostic and prognostic value of the new predictions of the method. In here, we only focused on prostate cancer disease due to availability of miRNA data with clinical profiles.

Results

Constructing miRNA-target and disease-gene networks

We first constructed miRNA-target network and gene-disease network to be used as predicted and response variables respectively as input to the regression model. miRNA-target network was constructed by integrating results from TargetScan and protein interactions. This study only focused on genes that are targeted by a miRNA and interact with proteins at the protein level. We obtained 3,235 genes that are targeted by 305 miRNAs (Additional file 3). For the disease gene interactions, we combined disease gene signature from microarray data (1942) and pubmed abstracts (720). Taking the union of the two lists generates 2,061 genes across 23 diseases (Additional file 2). Finally we only considered genes that are directly or indirectly influenced by miRNAs and are associated with a disease. So we took the intersection of the 3235 and 2061 gene lists leading to 658 genes.

Lasso regression is able to identify miRNAs from downregulated gene sets post to pre-miRNA treatment

We first assessed the performance of the proposed regression method using several gene lists reported by recently published studies that used microarray analysis to reveal genes whose expression is affected by pre-miRNA treatment. For example, in [26] LNCaP cell lines were treated with pre-miRNA (pre-miR-1, pre-miR206, and pre-miR27b) and downregulated genes were identified using differential gene expression analysis. The downregulated gene lists that were used as DiseaseSig and NetMiR were used to evaluate the performance of Lasso regression model to identify the influential miRNAs after treatment. miRNA coefficients from the regression model were used to assess the enrichment of miRNAs' targets in the gene set. In the pre-miR-1 downregulated genes, the regression model ranked miRNA-1 first with the highest coefficient value. In the pre-miR-206 downregulated genes, the regression model showed that miR-1 and miRNA-206 have the highest coefficient that explains 25% of the downregulated genes. In the downregulated genes after miR-27b treatment, the model showed that miRNA-9 has the highest coefficient and miRNA-27b ranked second. We compared the enrichment results of the proposed model with Fisher test and hypergeometric test and two miRNA enrichment tools Geneset2miRNA [29] and Expression2Kinases [30]. The results of our method demonstrated that it is able to infer correct miRNAs from gene lists downregulated after pre-miRNA treatment and it can better infer the influential miRNAs. These findings show that integrating the influence of miRNA on the protein context of the target improves miRNA enrichment analysis and demonstrated effectiveness for using Lasso regression to predict miRNA-disease functional associations.

Reconstructing miRNA-disease functional association

After demonstrating that Lasso regression successfully identified miRNAs from downregulated gene lists post to miRNA treatment, we applied Lasso regression modeling

to identify miRNAs associated with diseases using miRNA-target and disease-gene networks. We further analyzed the resulting miRNA-disease functional associations from the regression model. In this section, we focus on the network generated using combined microarray and abstracts disease gene signature with PPI based miRNA target network. Our model generated 741 interactions between the 23 diseases and 365 miRNAs (Additional file 5). 364 interactions were common with the gold standard, 157 were in the gold standard and missed by our method, and 220 were identified by the model and not in the gold standard (Figure 2). 37 new interactions were predicted between miRNAs and prostate cancer. Further diagnostic and prognostic characterization of the 37 prostate miRNAs were conducted.

Assessing the performance of the proposed method to identify functional miRNA-disease associations

We evaluated the performance of the Lasso regression model on a gold standard miRNA-disease interactions obtained from miR2Disease database that contains experimentally verified miRNA-disease associations [27]. This gold standard data set contains experimentally validated miRNA-target interactions. We extracted 740 interactions between the 23 diseases and the miRNAs. We assessed the performance of the model using several combinations. We first used the microarray gene signature-disease network vs miRNA-target network obtained from TargetScan to predict miRNA-disease associations. We then combined disease gene signature from pubmed with the microarray gene signature vs the targetscan miRNA target network. In the third test, we used the combined microarray and text signature vs TargetScan and PPI based miRNA-target network. The goal of this step was to assess if including more disease signatures and miRNA targets would increase the performance of the model. The last combination is to use PITA miRNA-target algorithm instead of TargetScan to assess the performance of the model when changing the input data sets. The model returns miRNA-disease association values that ranged from −1 to 1. Since the model uses Lasso penalty, most of the resulted associations are zero. Here we only considered positive values and not negative values as negative values had no biological interpretations in our experiment. We performed receiver operating characteristic (ROC) curve analysis to assess the performance of the model against different network construction strategies. ROC curves for prostate cancer showed that integrating disease signature from abstracts increased the performance of the model, and integrating indirect miRNA-target association increased the performance of the model even more. We performed ROC curve analysis for six other cancer diseases and found consistent results in all

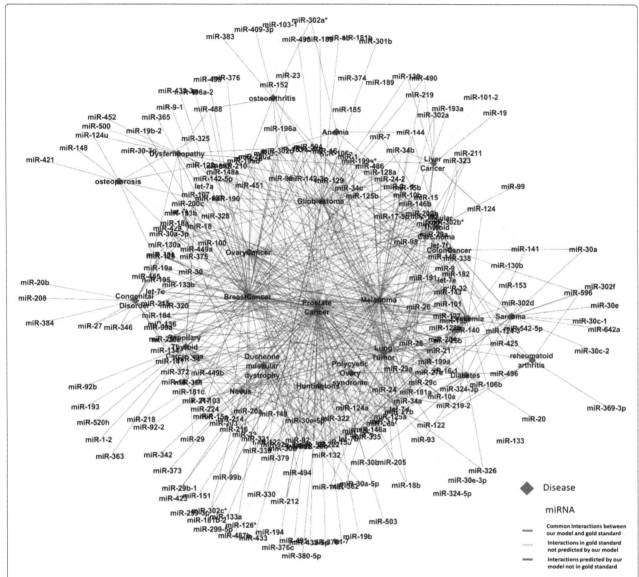

Figure 2 Predicted disease-miRNA functional association. Predicted miRNA-disease interactions using Lasso regression model. Here we used combined microarray and abstract disease gene signature as response variable and with PPI-based miRNA-target signatures predicted variable. We mapped all the common interactions between the predicted interactions and the gold standard data. We also showed the novel interaction predicted by our model and the interactions missed by our model. Results showed that results are biased to cancer diseases(prostate, breast, ovary, glioblastoma, melanoma as they have more complete gene signatures.

the diseases (Figure 3). We focused on these six cancer diseases as they have the highest number of miRNAs associated with them. We compared AUC results from the proposed Lasso regression model with results we obtained using Fisher test and found that Lasso regression performs better than Fisher test-based enrichment analysis. We also found that the model is susceptible to the initial input data sets (miRNA-target, disease-gene). This suggests that the performance of the Lasso regression model is robust and can be adapted to different networks.

Evaluating clinical implications of newly discovered associations

We used the 37 miRNAs to evaluate their association with prostate cancer. We extracted the miRNA expression from two prostate cancer data sets. The first is Taylor data [31] (GSE21032) that contains the expression of the miRNAs across 139 samples (98 primary, 12 metastatic and 29 normal). We only obtained 16 miRNAs with expression data in the Taylor data. The second data is from [32] (GSE23022) that contains expression of miRNAs across 40 samples (20 primary tumor and 20

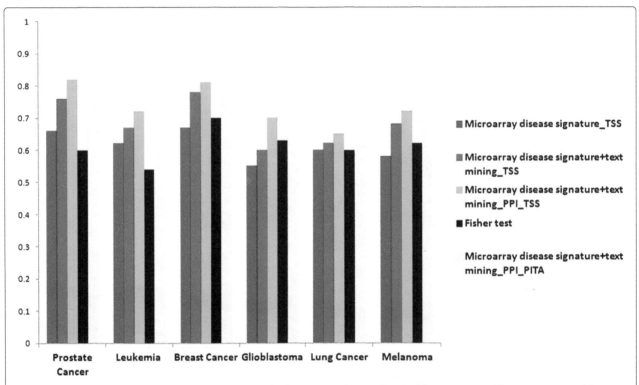

Figure 3 Comparative analysis using different integrative biology approaches. AUC using different inputs in different cancer types. We compared the ROC results from different combinations of inputs. Integrating multiple data to define disease gene signatures and including protein networks to define miRNA signature improves the accuracy of the model. Different miRNA-target interaction data leads to different results. This is due to the completeness of miRNA-target interactions.

normal). 21 miRNAs have corresponding expression in the data. We first tested the ability of these miRNAs to predict tumor samples. We used support vector machine (SVM) from LIBSVM library [33] (http://www.csie.ntu.edu.tw/cjlin/libsvm/) implemented in matlab to assess the performance. 10-fold cross validation was used to avoid overfitting problem. We compared the performance of the 16 miRNAs from Taylor data with 57 prostate miRNAs that were in common in the gold standard and our model. Results in Table 1 showed that the newly predicted prostate miRNAs are diagnostically as good as the gold standard prostate miRNAs. We then evaluated the diagnostic role of the 16 miRNAs in Taylor data with prostate cancer progression. Heatmap (Figure 4) demonstrates that the 16 miRNAs are associated with metastasis. We further conducted survival analysis to assess if the 16 miRNAs are associated with cancer recurrence. Results showed that both the 57 miRNAs in common with gold standard and the 16 miRNAs predicted are able to significantly separate high risk from low risk patients ($p = 0.00025$ and 0.007, respectively) (Figures 5 and 6).

Discussion

Over recent years, miRNAs have emerged as major players in the complex networks of gene regulation and have been

implicated in various aspects of human diseases. Deciphering functional associations between miRNAs and diseases is a major step toward understanding the underlying patterns governing miRNA disease associations. In addition, it gives better insight into the functional role of miRNAs in disease development. The accumulated data on miRNA expression levels in tumors demonstrate that miRNAs are promising diagnostic candidates to distinguish different tumors and different subtypes of tumors as well as to predict their clinical behavior [5]. The observations supported the role of miRNAs as either prognostic and/or diagnostic markers. miRNAs have therapeutic applications by which disease-causing miRNAs

Table 1 Classification evaluation of prostate miRNAs predicted by our model and common with gold standard in multiple prostate miRNA expression data sets

	Taylor data	GSE23022
miRNAs common in gold standard and our model	92.8%	77%
miRNAs predicted in our model and NOT in gold standard	90.6%	70%

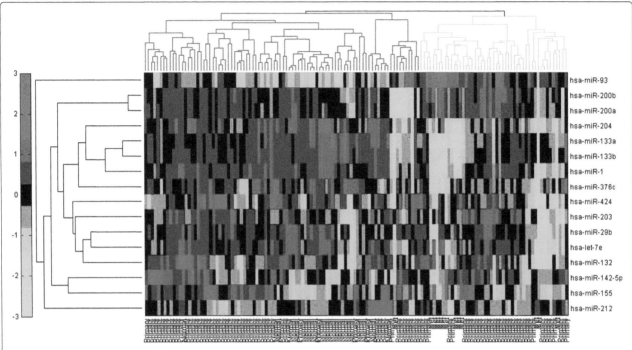

Figure 4 Heatmap of newly predicted prostate miRNAs. Novel predicted miRNAs that are not in the gold standard are associated with metastasis. Expression levels of the 16 miRNAs from Taylor prostate data reveals that there is two distinct clusters of patients. One rich with metastatic samples and the other is rich with normal prostate and non-aggressive primary cancer samples.

could be antagonized or functional miRNAs could be restored.

Lasso regression modeling demonstrated promise to to construct miRNA-target networks [34]. Motivated by this work, we used Lasso regression model to predict functional associations between miRNAs and diseases based on gene signatures of each. Since there is an explosion of disease microarray data, we used it to define gene signature for each disease. To assess the noisiness in the disease signature, we integrated disease gene signature from pubmed abstracts to generate signature that cover wider spectrum of genes. For the miRNA-gene network, we only considered genes that are interacting with other proteins or genes and are directly or indirectly influenced by the miRNAs as these genes are anticipated to have higher influence on disease progression compared to genes that are targeted by miR-NAs and not propagating their influence on the protein network.

We first evaluated the performance of Lasso regression as a miRNA enrichment analysis method as a proof of concept. Lasso regression successfully identified miR-NAs from downregulated genes after miRNA treatment. We further evaluated the performance of Lasso regression model on the disease -miRNA interaction networks. We extracted disease-miRNA association network from miR2Disease and HMDD that contain manually curated

database for microRNA deregulation in human diseases. ROC curve analysis showed that integrating microarray and text abstracts to define disease signature gives better performance compared to using the signatures separately. Similarly, integrating miRNAs' indirect influence on genes to define miRNA target signature demonstrated better performance compared to using the direct influence alone. This suggests that refining signatures is a key step for accurate regression modeling. Two key issues have big effect on the accuracy of the model. First, the completeness and noisiness in the disease and miRNA signature. The more complete and refined the signature is, the more accurate the model is. Since microarray disease gene signature might harbour many off target genes that are irrelevant to the disease, more robust disease gene signature that is based on integrating more evidences is essential for the success of the modeling process. Similarly, incomplete miRNA-target interactions showed to affect the performance of the model. Using miRNA-target interactions from PITA showed less accuracy compared with TargetScan results. This suggests that miRNa-target data plays critical role in Lasso regression modeling to predict functional associations between miRNAs and diseases.

The second issue is the gold standard data. We realized that gold standard data was biased toward certain diseases like prostate cancer, breast cancer, and glioblastoma

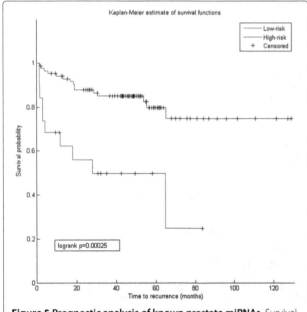

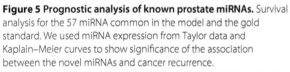

Figure 5 Prognostic analysis of known prostate miRNAs. Survival analysis for the 57 miRNA common in the model and the gold standard. We used miRNA expression from Taylor data and Kaplain–Meier curves to show significance of the association between the novel miRNAs and cancer recurrence.

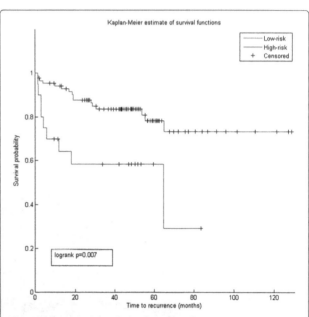

Figure 6 Prognostic analysis of predicted prostate miRNAs. Survival analysis for the 16 miRNA predicted in the model and not in the gold standard. We used miRNA expression from Taylor data and Kaplain–Meier curves to show significance of the association between the novel miRNAs and cancer recurrence. This results suggest that the 16 miRNAs are prognostic biomarkers that require further biological and clinical investigations.

that have around hundred associated miRNAs. However, other disease like sarcoma, and colon cancer are associated with very few miRNAs like let-miR-7a and miR-21, respectively. This have big impact on false discovery rates and thus AUC performance measure. A more curated miRNA-disease interactions network is required to have more accurate performance evaluation. Unfortunately, we do not have complete manually accurated miRNA-disease databases. We tried to combine miR2Disease and HMDD to reduce incompleteness in the used miRNA-target interactions.

To further validate the novel miRNA-disease associations predicted by the model, we focused on prostate cancer as a case study. The model predicted 37 miRNAs to be involved in prostate cancer development. We extracted their expression from prostate miRNA expression data (Taylor and GSE23022); 16 of which have expression in Taylor miRNA expression data. Analyzing the diagnostic potential of these new miRNAs showed that these newly discovered miRNAs are diagnostically as good as prostate miRNAs in the gold standard data. Furthermore, the 16 miRNAs showed to be prognostically significant as they are associated with cancer recurrence. When we looked deeper into the literature, we found several of the 16 miR-NAs have been validated to have a role in prostate cancer. For example, miRNA-1 showed to be a tumor suppressor miRNA that act as prognostic biomarker [26]. These

results support the the power of integrating signatures to construct functional network associations.

Finally, these results showed a promise of using regression models for integrating disease and miRNA signatures to find underlying functional associations between miRNAs and diseases. This could give us more insight on the functional role and implications of miRNAs in disease development.

Conclusion

Uncovering miRNA-disease functional association is a key step to understand disease development. Integrating disease signature from microarray data and pubmed abstract with miRNA target interactions to build miRNA-disease functional association showed promise to uncover significant associations between diseases and miRNAs. Lasso regression demonstrated effectiveness for miRNA enrichment analysis. Integrating multiple data sources and biological networks to define more accurate disease and miRNA signature is promising to uncover novel biological associations between miRNAs and disease. Newly predicted miRNAs associated with prostate cancer showed diagnostic and prognostic potential. This concludes that our model gives more insight into disease and functional role of miRNAs in disease development. Although limitations exist in the current work, the uncovered interactions are important for understanding diseases and patterns underlying miRNA-disease associations.

Additional files

Additional file 1: Gene Expression Data Titles. This file contains the gene expression data we used to find disease signature from microarray data. We provided the GEO of the 24 diseases we used in addition to the experiment title.

Additional file 2: Disease- Gene Signatures. This file represents the gene signatures for each of the 24 diseases that we extracted from microarray data and from pubmed abstracts. The file also represents the combined signature of diseases from both microarray and pubmed abstracts.

Additional file 3: PPI-based miRNA targets. This file shows the protein network-based miRNA targets. This shows the indirectly influence of miRNAs on genes to represent functional target of miRNAs.

Additional file 4: Gold standard miRNA disease. This file is the gold standard miRNA-disease associations that we extracted from miRDisease and HDMM databases to validate the performance of our approach.

Additional file 5: Predicted miRNA-disease association. This file shows the miRNA disease interactions predicted from our approach. In addition, it shows the overlap with the gold standard interactions. It shows the interactions that are common between our method and the gold standard, the interactions our method predicted that are NOT in goldstandard and the interactions that are in goldstandard and our method was unable to predict it.

Competing interests

The authors declare that they have no competing interests.

Acknowledgements

Mohammed Alshalalfa and Reda Ahajj would like to thank iCORE (Alberta Innovates) and NSERC for funding. Tarek A Bismar is supported by The Young Investigators Award of the Prostate Cancer Foundation, USA

Author details

[1]Department of Computer Science, University of Calgary, Calgary, Alberta, Canada. [2]Biotechnology Research Center, Palestine Polytechnic University, Hebron, Palestine. [3]Departments of Pathology, Oncology and Molecular Biology and Biochemistry, Faculty of Medicine, University of Calgary, Alberta, Canada.

References

1. S Sevli, A Uzumcu, M Solak, M Ittmann, M Ozen, The function of microRNAs, small but potent molecules, in human prostate cancer. Prostate Cancer Prostatic Dis. **13**, 208–217 (2010)
2. V Ambros, The function of animal miRNAs. Nature. **431**, 350–355 (2004)
3. A Gordanpour, R Nam, L Sugar, A Seth, MicroRNAs in prostate cancer: from biomarkers to molecularly-based therapeutics. Prostate Cancer Prostatic Dis. **1**, 6 (2012)
4. G Calin, C Croce, MicroRNA signatures in human cancers. Nat Rev Cancer. **6**, 857–866 (2006)
5. M Ozen, C Creighton, M Ozdemir, M Ittmann, Widespread deregulation of microRNA expression in human prostate cancer. Oncogene. **27**, 1788–1793 (2008)
6. Y Pang, C Young, H Yuan, MicroRNAs and prostate cancer. Acta Biochim Biophys Sin. **42**, 363–369 (2010)
7. A Watahiki, Y Wang, J Morris, K Dennis, H ODwyer, M Gleave, P Gout, Y Wang, MicroRNAs associated with metastatic prostate cancer. PLoS One. **6**, e24950 (2011)
8. L He, G Hannon, MicroRNAs: small RNAs with a big role in gene regulation. Nat Rev Genet. **5**, 631 (2004)
9. A Esquela-Kerscher, F Slack, Oncomirs—microRNAs with a role in cancer. Nat Rev Cancer. **6**, 259–269 (2006)
10. J Cho, R Gelinas, K Wang, A Etheridge, M Piper, K Batte, D Dakhallah, J Price, D Bornman, S Zhang, C Marsh, D Galas, Systems biology of interstitial lung diseases: integration of mRNA and microRNA expression changes. BMC Med Genome. **4**, 8 (2011)
11. G Ruvkun, Molecular biology: glimpses of a tiny RNA world. Science. **294**, 797–799 (2001)
12. B Zhang, X Pan, G Cobb, T Anderson, microRNAs as oncogenes and tumor suppressors. Dev Biol. **302**, 1–12 (2007)
13. G Calin, C Sevignani, C Dumitru, T Hyslop, E Noch, S Yendamuri, M Shimizu, S Rattan, F Bullrich, M Negrini, C Croce, Human microRNA genes are frequently located at fragile sites and genomic regions involved in cancers. Proc Natl Acad Sci. **101**, 2999–3004 (2004)
14. K Porkka, M Pfeiffer, K Waltering, R Vessella, T Tammela, T Visakorpi, MicroRNA expression profiling in prostate cancer. Cancer Res. **67**, 6130 (2007)
15. M Lu, Q Zhang, M Deng, J Miao, Y Guo, W Gao, Q Cui, An analysis of human MicroRNA and disease associations. PloS ONE. **10**, e3420 (2008)
16. S Sass, S Dietmann, U Burk, S Brabletz, D Lutter, A Kowarsch, F Klaus, F Mayer, T Brabletz, A Ruepp, F Theis, Y Wang, MicroRNAs coordinately regulate protein complexes. BMC Syst Biol. **5**, 136 (2011)
17. M Sualp, T Can, Using network context as a filter for miRNA target prediction. Biosystems. **105**, 201–209 (2011)
18. R Irizarry, B Bolstad, F Collin, L Cope, B Hobbs, T Speed, Summaries of Affymetrix GeneChip probe level data. Nucleic Acids Res. **20**, 307–315 (2003)
19. V Tusher, R Tibshirani, G Chu, Significance analysis of microarrays applied to the ionizing radiation response. Proc Natl Acad Sci. **98**, 5116–5121 (2001)
20. D Cheng, C Knox, N Young, P Stothard, S Damaraju, D Wishart, PolySearch: a web-based text mining system for extracting relationships between human diseases, genes, mutations, drugs and metabolites. Nucleic Acids Res. **36**, W399—W405 (2008)
21. A Grimson, K Farh, W Johnston, P Garrett-Engele, L Lim, D Bartel, MicroRNA targeting specificity in mammals: determinants beyond seed pairing. Mol Cel. **27**, 91–105 (2007)
22. D Yue, H Liu, Y Huang, Survey of computational algorithms for MicroRNA target prediction. Curr Genomics. **10**, 478–492 (2009)
23. M Kertesz, N Iovino, U Unnerstall, U Gaul, E Segal, The role of site accessibility in microRNA target recognition. Nat Genet. **39**, 1278–1284 (2007)
24. G Wu, X Feng, L Stein, A human functional protein interaction network and its application to cancer data analysis. Genome Biol. **11**, R53 (2010)
25. S Peri, *et al*, Human protein reference database as a discovery resource for proteomics. Nucleic Acids Res. **32**, D497—D501 (2004)
26. R Hudson, M Yi, D Esposito, S Watkins, A Hurwitz, H Yfantis, D Lee, J Borin, M Naslund, R Alexander, T Dorsey, R Stephens, C Croce, S Ambs, MicroRNA-1 is a candidate tumor suppressor and prognostic marker in human prostate cancer. Nucleic Acids Res. **40**, 3689–3703 (2011)
27. Q Jiang, Y Wang, Y Hao, L Juan, M Teng, X Zhang, M Li, G Wang, Y Liu, miR2Disease: a manually curated database for microRNA deregulation in human disease. Nucleic Acids Res. **37**, D98—D104 (2009)
28. M Lu, Q Zhang, M Deng, J Miao, Y Guo, W Gao, Q Cui, An analysis of human MicroRNA and disease associations. Plos One. **10**, e3420 (2008)
29. A Antonov, S Dietmann, P Wong, D Lutter, H Mewes, GeneSet2miRNA: finding the signature of cooperative miRNA activities in the gene lists. Nucleic Acids Res. **37**, W323—W328 (2008)
30. E Chen, H Xu, S Gordonov, M Lim, M Perkins, A Ma'ayan, Expression2Kinases: mRNA profiling linked to multiple upstream regulatory layers. Bioinformatics. **28**, 105–111 (2012)
31. B Taylor, N Schultz, H Hieronymus, A Gopalan, Y Xiao, B Carver, V Arora, P Kaushik, E Cerami, B Reva, Y Antipin, N Mitsiades, T Landers, I Dolgalev, J Major, M Wilson, N Socci, A Lash, A Heguy, J Eastham, H Scher, V Reuter, P Scardino, C Sander, W Sawyers, W Gerald, Integrative genomic profiling of human prostate cancer. Cancer Cell. **18**, 11–22 (2010)
32. S Wach, E Nolte, J Szczyrba, R Stohr, A Hartmann, I Orntoft, L Dyrskjot, E Eltze, W Wieland, B Keck, A Ekici, F Grasser, B Wullich, MicroRNA profiles of

prostate carcinoma detected by multiplatform microRNA screening. Int J
Cancer. **130**, 611–621 (2012)

33. CC Chang, CJ Lin, LIBSVM: alibrary for support vector machines. ACM
     Trans Intell Syst Technol. **2**, 27 (2011)

34. Y Lu, Y Zhou, W Qu, M Deng, C Zhang, A Lasso regression model for the
     construction of microRNA-target regulatory networks. Bioinformatics. **27**,
     2406–2413 (2011)

9

Wavelet analysis of frequency chaos game signal: a time-frequency signature of the *C. elegans* DNA

Imen Messaoudi[1*], Afef Elloumi Oueslati[1] and Zied Lachiri[1,2]

Abstract

Challenging tasks are encountered in the field of bioinformatics. The choice of the genomic sequence's mapping technique is one the most fastidious tasks. It shows that a judicious choice would serve in examining periodic patterns distribution that concord with the underlying structure of genomes. Despite that, searching for a coding technique that can highlight all the information contained in the DNA has not yet attracted the attention it deserves. In this paper, we propose a new mapping technique based on the chaos game theory that we call the frequency chaos game signal (FCGS). The particularity of the FCGS coding resides in exploiting the statistical properties of the genomic sequence itself. This may reflect important structural and organizational features of DNA. To prove the usefulness of the FCGS approach in the detection of different local periodic patterns, we use the wavelet analysis because it provides access to information that can be obscured by other time-frequency methods such as the Fourier analysis. Thus, we apply the continuous wavelet transform (CWT) with the complex Morlet wavelet as a mother wavelet function. Scalograms that relate to the organism *Caenorhabditis elegans (C. elegans)* exhibit a multitude of periodic organization of specific DNA sequences.

Keywords: *C. elegans*; Complex Morlet wavelet scalogram; Continuous wavelet transform; Frequency chaos game signal; Local signature

1 Introduction

The fundamental information for a living being resides essentially in its nucleic material—the DNA. This molecule contains all the instructions needed to produce proteins and enzymes for all of the metabolic pathways. Thus, revealing the structural and organizational features in DNA sequences is a very interesting topic. However, the search for relevant information along the genomic sequences is not an easy task. In fact, although several programs have been created which aim at detecting valuable information concerning the DNA, there is much work remaining to be done. In order to better understand the genomic sequence role and structure, several signal processing approaches have been investigated. To be able to apply such techniques, it is imperative to convert DNA characters into numerical sequences. This operation is the so-called coding technique. Thereby, various approaches for DNA character coding have been reported including the binary coding [1,2], the inter-distance signals [3], coding with the entropy measure [4], the electron-ion interaction pseudo-potential (EIIP) mapping [5], the structural bending trinucleotide coding (PNUC) [2], etc.

The choice of the most appropriate coding technique for a desired analysis represents a basic problem. It turns that coding techniques that are based on physical, chemical and structural DNA characteristics are efficient in terms of revealing specific structures as is the case with EIIP and PNUC coding approaches.

Here, we propose a new mapping technique inspired from the Chaos Game theory to which we associate the name of 'frequency chaos game signals' (FCGS). The FCGS approach relies on the frequency value of each sub-pattern assignment, which gives us the opportunity to produce several signals for the same input sequence, depending on the size of the considered sub-patterns. The

*Correspondence: imen.messaoudi@enit.rnu.tn
[1]Université de Tunis El Manar, Ecole Nationale d'Ingénieurs de Tunis, LR Signal, Images et Technologies de l'Information, BP 37, le Belvédère, 1002 Tunis, Tunisia
Full list of author information is available at the end of the article

specificity of our coding consists on exploiting the statistical properties of the genomic sequence itself, which may serve in detecting interesting structures within the DNA sequences.

The efficiency of our method in detecting different biological events is demonstrated through application of the continuous wavelet transform (CWT). The choice of such analysis method (we mean CWT) is justified by the need of a time-frequency approach that provides local frequency information which is not guaranteed by other transforms such as the Fourier transform. In fact, the classical Fourier transform does not contain local information. Thus, it appears that the short-time Fourier transform (STFT) is better suited to predict sites with biological relevance in the genomic signals. Nevertheless, this method requires a good choice of the analysis window's size that must balance the frequency and temporal resolutions. The short Fourier transform induces interferences and loss of information [6]. With the advent of the wavelet transform (WT), one can get more precise and more adequate analysis especially concerning the location of hotspots in signals with complex nature, which is the case of genomic signals [5,7-10].

In this paper, we investigate the role of the CWT in displaying the frequency-dependent structure of genomic signals by using the complex Morlet wavelet scalogram. The purpose of this analysis consists in revealing spectral features that might be of biological significance in the *Caenorhabditis elegans (C. elegans)* genome. This study is particular since it exposes a new coding technique which is efficient in terms of the DNA characterization.

This paper is divided into five sections: First, we describe the steps required to generate the frequency chaos game signals in section 2. In section 3, we deal with the complex wavelet analysis in which we give an overview on the continuous wavelet transform as well as a brief description of the complex Morlet wavelet. In section 4, we analyze the DNA sequences by the Morlet wavelet, and then we expose and discuss the results in section 5. Finally, in section 6, we conclude this paper.

2   Introduction to the frequency chaos game signals

Starting from the pioneer work of Jeffrey in 1990, representing DNA sequences by the chaos game representation (CGR) has drawn a resounding success. In fact, for more than 2 decades, the chaos game representation has been used as a platform for pattern recognition [11,12], a generalization of Markov transition tables [13], a tool for statistical characterization of genomic sequences [11,14,15], as well as a basis for alignment comparisons [16] and establishment of phylogenetic trees [17]. The CGR is an iterative algorithm that provides unique scatter picture of fractal nature. It consists on mapping a nucleotide

sequence in a unit-square, where each of its vertices is assigned to a DNA character (nucleotides: A, C, G and T). Let us consider a given DNA sequence composed of N nucleotides $S = \{S_1, S_2, \ldots, S_N\}$. Thus, an element occupying the ith position in S is represented into the square by a point x_i. The point x_i is repeatedly placed halfway between the previous plotted point x_{i-1} and the segment joining the vertex corresponding to the read letter S_i [18]. The prolific iterative function of CGR is given by

$$\text{where } y_i = \begin{cases} \begin{cases} x_0 = (0.5, 0.5) \\ x_i = x_{i-1} + \dfrac{1}{2}(y_i - x_{i-1}), i = 1, \ldots, N \end{cases} \\ \begin{cases} (0,0) & \text{if } S[i] = \text{A} \\ (0,1) & \text{if } S[i] = \text{C} \\ (1,0) & \text{if } S[i] = \text{T} \\ (1,1) & \text{if } S[i] = \text{G} \end{cases} \end{cases} \quad (1)$$

Usually, the starting point x_0 is placed at the center of the square while the choice of the corners is arbitrary and can be assigned in any other way. The figure given below (Figure 1) shows the procedure to draw the sequence 'TTAGC'.

The usefulness of the chaos game representation goes beyond the convenience of genome representation and visualization. In addition, it provides a unique image which is specific to the considered genome [19,20] and thus forms an outstanding genomic signature [21].

The CGR technique reveals several hidden patterns that arise from distinct k-tuple compositions in DNA sequences. The frequency of occurrence of these patterns can be estimated by the use of the frequency chaos game representation (FCGR) [22]. The latter approach consists on dividing the CGR image into 4^k small squares where each sub-square is associated to a sub-pattern and has a side of $1/2^k$. The number of points in each sub-square thus created is then counted. This procedure allows extraction of the frequency of k-length words occurrence by dividing the number of dots onto the correspondent sub-squares by the complete length of the DNA sequence. To visualize the frequencies of occurrence of associated patterns, a normalized colour scheme is used. The darker pixels in the FCGR images represent the most frequently used words; otherwise, the clearest ones represent the most avoided words [23]. The Figure 2 is divided into two blocks where the first block illustrates the arrangement of oligomers in the FCGR's sub-squares for $k = \{1, 2, 3\}$, and the second one is related to the frequency chaos game representations calculated for the chromosome I of the organism *C. elegans*.

Although representations based on the chaos game theory (we mean CGR and FCGR) have been successfully

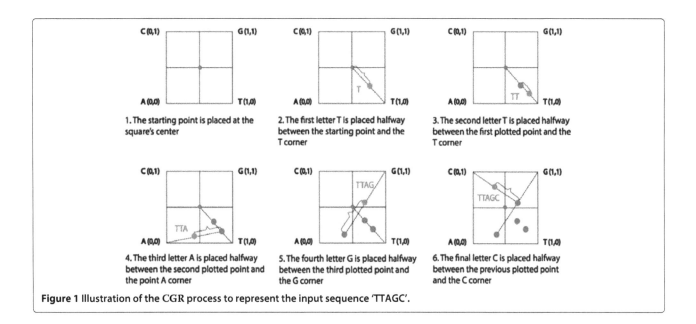

Figure 1 Illustration of the CGR process to represent the input sequence 'TTAGC'.

applied to a wide range of problems, their capacity in following the evolution of frequencies along DNA sequences remains, so far, totally unexplored. This motivates us to exploit the FCGR method in building signals in such a way that we can follow the frequency evolution of oligomers through a given sequence. We give a particular name to these signals—the FCGSs. This new mapping technique is based on assigning the frequency of occurrence of each oligomer to the same sub-pattern that exists in the sequence. For this purpose, two steps are required:

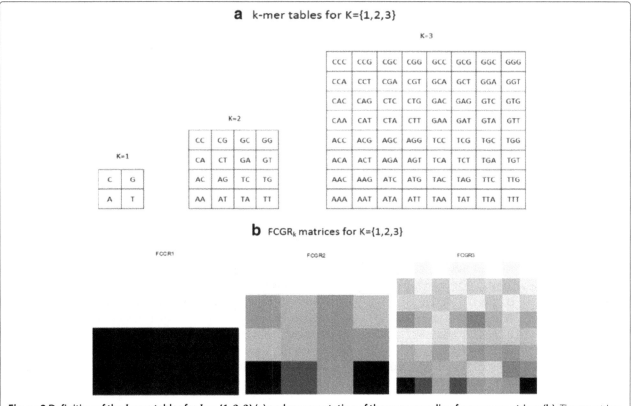

Figure 2 Definition of the *k*-mer tables for $k = \{1, 2, 3\}$ (a) and representation of the corresponding frequency matrices (b). These matrices are extracted from chaos game representation of the *C. elegans* chromosome I.

- The first step consists in the generation of the kth-order FCGR for the entire sequence. The FCGR matrix is expressed as follows:

$$\text{FCGR}_k = [f_{i,j}]_{1 \leq i \leq 2^k, \ 1 \leq j \leq 2^k} \qquad (2)$$

where $f_{i,j}$ is the frequency value of the word situated at the intersection of the ith row and the jth column in the k-mer matrix.

- The second step consists in reading the input sequence by a group of successive k-nucleotides and replacing them by the corresponding frequency already calculated in the FCGR_k matrix.

In this sense, an FCGS_k can be generated by

$$\text{FCGS}_k[n, i, j] = \sum_{n=1}^{L} \text{FCGR}_{k,i,j}[n] \cdot U_{\text{motif}_{k,i,j}}[n] \qquad (3)$$

Here, k is the frequency chaos game representation's order and $\text{FCGR}_{k,i,j}$ refers to the FCGR_k's element which is placed at the intersection of the ith row and the jth column. Regarding an illustrative example of the FCGS technique, we consider the sequence $S = \{\text{TTTTAGT GAAGCTTCTAGAT}\}$. To encode S by FCGS_1, FCGS_2 and FCGS_3, we must calculate the FCGRs matrices for orders 1, 2 and 3. Then, we extract all the oligomers of length $\{1, 2 \text{ and } 3\}$, and we attribute for each of the monomers, dimers and trimers its occurrence frequency from the convenient frequency matrix. In this case, we enumerate 20 monomers, 19 dimers and 18 trimers. For illustration, we only consider 18 oligomers which are:

- Monomers = {T, T, T, T, A, G, T, G, A, A, G, C, T, T, C, T, A and G}
- Dimers = {TT, TT, TT, TA, AG, GT, TG, GA, AA, AG, GC, CT, TT, TC, CT, TA, AG and GA}
- Trimers = {TTT, TTT, TTA, TAG, AGT, GTG, TGA, GAA, AAG, AGC, GCT, CTT, TTC, TCT, CTA, TAG, AGA and GAT}

The associated frequencies are:

- Monomer frequencies = {0.45,0.45,0.45,0.45,0.25,0.2, 0.45,0.2,0.25,0.25,0.2,0.1, 0.45,0.45,0.1,0.45,0.25,0.2}
- Dimer frequencies = {0.2632,0.2632,0.2632,0.1579, 0.2105,0.1053,0.1053,0.1579, 0.1053,0.2105,0.1053,0.1579, 0.2632,0.1053,0.1579,0.1579, 0.2105,0.1579}
- Trimer frequencies = {0.1667,0.1667,0.1111,0.1667, 0.1111,0.1111,0.1111,0.1111, 0.1111,0.1111,0.1111,0.1111, 0.1111,0.1111,0.1111,0.1667, 0.1111,0.1111}.

At the end, we obtain three different signals, which are illustrated in Figure 3.

Note that increasing the FCGS order induces a more smoothed signal which is useful in capturing the important underlying patterns [24]. The smoothing is often used in enhancing the long-term trends that can be hidden in the original signal. This makes our coding technique suitable for fine studies. To demonstrate the effectiveness and usefulness of our coding, we chose to apply the complex Morlet wavelet analysis. By such application, we will note the smoothing effect in determining the characteristic patterns of certain areas of the DNA.

3 The wavelet transform analysis

The wavelet transform (WT) was introduced by Morlet in 1983 to study seismic signals. Then, the proposed processing was well formalized in 1984 with contributions of Grossman [25]. Therefore, the wavelet theory has been the subject of diverse theoretical developments and practical applications. In this section, we focus on the application of wavelet transform on the *C. elegans* genome aiming to explore its composition.

3.1 The continuous wavelet transform

The CWT of an arbitrary signal is a linear operation that consists in projecting the signal $x(t)$ onto a wavelet basis. Mathematically, the CWT is given by Equation 4:

$$W_{a,b}[x(t)] = \frac{1}{\sqrt{a}} \int_{-\infty}^{+\infty} x(t) \psi^* \left(\frac{t-b}{a} \right) dt, a \in \mathbb{R}^{*+}, b \in \mathbb{R} \qquad (4)$$

where a ($a > 0$) and b ($b \in \mathbb{R}$) are respectively the scale and the time-shift parameters. Here, $\psi \left(\frac{t-b}{a} \right)$ is a scaled and shifted version of the so-called mother wavelet function $\psi(t)$. Mother wavelet $\psi(t)$, which is a wave-like oscillation, can be extended to its daughter wavelets in terms of the shift parameter b and the scale parameter a:

$$\psi_{a,b}(t) = \frac{1}{\sqrt{a}} \psi \left(\frac{t-b}{a} \right) \qquad (5)$$

At fixed-scale and translation parameters (a and b), the wavelet transform coefficient, denoted by $W_{(a,b)}$, represents the inner product of the daughter wavelet and the signal; this operation measures the degree of their resemblance at the concerned point. If $x(t)$ is equal to $\psi_{(a,b)}(t)$, the wavelet coefficient is set to 1. Hence, the closer to 1 the coefficient is, the stronger the similarity will be.

Mother wavelets are band-pass filters that oscillate in the time domain it expands or compresses depending on the scale value. When a is large, the mother wavelet becomes stretched and serves for the high frequencies' detection. In this case, the resolution of the time domain is low. On the contrary, when a is small, the

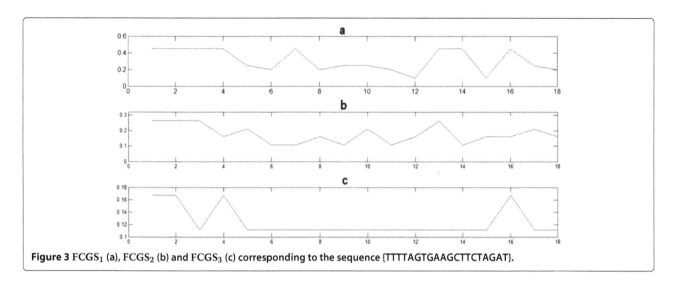

Figure 3 FCGS$_1$ (a), FCGS$_2$ (b) and FCGS$_3$ (c) corresponding to the sequence {TTTTAGTGAAGCTTCTAGAT}.

mother wavelet is compressed, i.e. the frequency domain's resolution becomes low in favor of the time domain's resolution. Mathematically, the dilated and normalized mother wavelet function $\frac{1}{\sqrt{a}}\psi\left(\frac{t}{a}\right)$ will admit $\sqrt{a}\hat{\psi}(a\omega)$ as a Fourier transform, which explains the fact that an expansion in time induces a contraction in the frequency domain and conversely. This property makes analysis with wavelets a relevant tool for characterization of signals as well as for detection and identification of special spectral features. Mother wavelet function can be real or complex like in the case of complex Morlet wavelet which will be briefly described in the following.

3.2 The complex Morlet wavelet
The effectiveness of the wavelet transform in analyzing signals with complex nature (like in the case of genomic signals) depends on the choice of the basis function. In this study, our choice went to the complex Morlet wavelet. The advantage of the proposed mother wavelet is that it admits a parametrized bandwidth. This provides extra flexibility which ensures a good time-frequency resolution. The complex Morlet wavelet is a plane wave modulated by a Gaussian envelope and presents a quick attenuation [26] whose mother wavelet function is expressed as

$$\psi(t) = \pi^{-\frac{1}{4}}\left(e^{i\omega_0 t} - e^{-\frac{1}{2}\omega_0^2}\right)e^{-\frac{1}{2}t^2} \tag{6}$$

where ω_0 corresponds to the number of oscillations of the wavelet. Strictly speaking, ω_0 must be greater than 5 to satisfy the admissibility criterion. This admissibility condition is required by all mother wavelets for the continuous wavelet transform to be invertible. Admissibility condition implies that the Fourier transform of the mother wavelet is 0 at frequency 0 [27]. This ensures the mother wavelet oscillates, which means that it acts as a band-

pass filter. The Fourier transform of the complex Morlet wavelet function is given by

$$\hat{\psi}(\omega) = \sqrt{2}\pi^{\frac{1}{4}}e^{-\frac{1}{2}(\omega-\omega_0)^2} \tag{7}$$

At a fixed scale a, the complex Morlet wavelet and its Fourier transform are given by

$$\psi_{a,b}(t) = \frac{1}{a}\pi^{\frac{-1}{4}}\left(e^{-i\omega_0\frac{t-b}{a}}e^{\frac{1}{2}\left(\frac{t-b}{a}\right)^2}\right) \tag{8}$$

$$\hat{\psi}_{a,b}(\omega) = \sqrt{2}\pi^{\frac{1}{4}}e^{-\frac{1}{2}(a\omega-\omega_0)^2} \tag{9}$$

In the frequency domain, the wavelet coefficient is a wavelet filter characterized by the constant QFactor [28]:

$$\text{QFactor} = \frac{\text{Center frequency}}{\text{Bandwidth}} \tag{10}$$

The central frequency of the mother wavelet, denoted by f_c, is the position of the global maximum of $\hat{\psi}(\omega)$ which is given by $f_c = \frac{\omega_0}{2\Pi}$. As for the bandwidth, denoted by f_b, it is centered around f_c and controls the wavelet window [29]. The complex Morlet wavelet can be expressed by the following equation:

$$\psi(t) = \frac{1}{\sqrt{\pi f_b}}e^{i2\pi f_c t}e^{-\frac{t^2}{f_b}} \tag{11}$$

To allow easy graphical interpretation, it is preferred to display the modulus of the CWT coefficients: $|W_{(a,b)}|$. This representation is called a scalogram and it represents the amplitude information of the signal at each scale a and position b. The scalogram can also be depicted in the time-frequency domain instead of the time-scale domain by converting the scales to frequencies using the formula:

$$f_c = \frac{\omega_0}{2\pi a} \tag{12}$$

Thus, a scalogram is a 2D plot where time is on the horizontal axis, frequency on the vertical axis, and amplitude of CWT coefficients are colored according to a defined

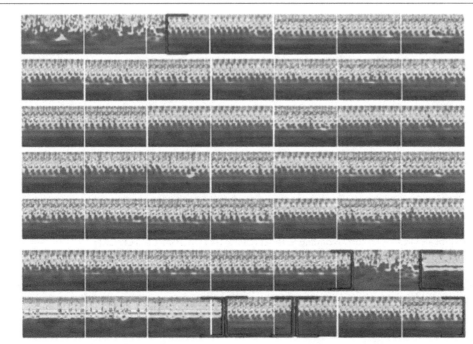

Figure 4 The scalogram representations of a sequence on the chromosome III of *C. elegans*. Coded by FCGS$_2$ (position [7403001–7452000]).

code. In the following section of this paper, we will focus on analyzing the Morlet scalogram.

4   Results and discussion

In this work, we focus our study on the analysis of DNA sequences within the *C. elegans* genome. The genomic sequences are extracted from the NCBI database [30]. As for the mapping technique, we choose the FCGS algorithm with the three first levels. Thus, the generated signals are FCGS$_1$, FCGS$_2$ and FCGS$_3$ of the whole chromosomes. Concerning the wavelet analysis, we use the complex Morlet wavelet with a support size of 1,420. Application of the continuous wavelet transform on the appropriate sequences is accomplished along 64 scales by using a mother wavelet centered on $\omega_0 = 5.4285$ (radian units).

Close inspection of the resulting scalograms shows the role played by this analysis in the characterization of different sites along the DNA sequences. In fact, we offer a standard way to represent genomes and reveal the biological hotspots, regardless of their nature or their length. Through a simple zooming of 10^3 bp, we are able to observe different features with great precision. Even the finer details are easily discerned. Several regions are visually distinguished by typical motifs which include prominent periodicities. We analyze these regions in the NCBI database [30] to ascertain their nature. Besides, it is important to note that not all revealed stretches are identified; there are some regions that we have not succeeded in understanding the related biological significance. For example, in Figure 4, we provide a series of scalograms which represent a sequence taken from the

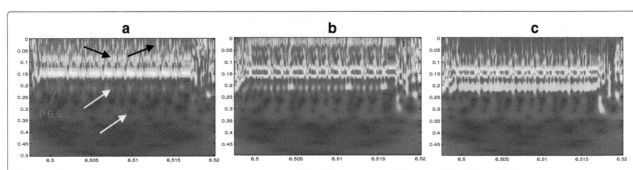

Figure 5 Scalograms of an intron found in the *C. elegans* gene Y65B4A.2. Coded with FCGS$_1$ **(a)**, FCGS$_2$ **(b)** and FCGS$_3$ **(c)**.

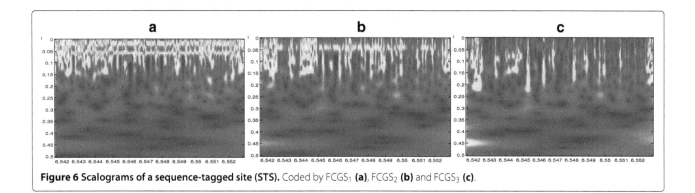

Figure 6 Scalograms of a sequence-tagged site (STS). Coded by FCGS$_1$ **(a)**, FCGS$_2$ **(b)** and FCGS$_3$ **(c)**.

chromosome III of *C. elegans*. As we can see, this example well illustrates the presence of different DNA structures which are easily observed due to their specific behaviors (the red brackets delimit the boundaries of these elements). According to the NCBI database, the prominent signatures relate to the elements CeRep59 (37,899 bp), CeRep55 (3,797 bp), CeRep59 (1,091 bp) and CeRep59 (2,844 bp).

Among the structures that possess particular signatures, we selected some elements of the *C. elegans* chromosome I to study them, namely: intron, STS and Cerp3 elements.

4.1 Intron signature

It is well-known that the genomic sequences present a strong three-base periodicity. The latter periodicity is an interesting feature of the protein-coding regions (exons). Several signal processing approaches and computational algorithms have been developed based on this periodicity for predicting exons. Most of the coding region prediction methods used the discrete Fourier transform (DFT)-based algorithms through which exons refer to the maximum of the Fourier power spectrum at the position of 1/3 frequency [31-35]. In the same context, performing the DFT on the wavelet coefficient of the correlation function at frequency 1/3 has improved the peaks that mark exons in the Fourier spectrum [36].

On the other hand, for identification of protein coding regions, the use of the CWT based on the modified Morlet wavelet has provided more accurate results [7,37]. All of these works revolve around exon prediction; whereas intron prediction has not yet drawn the attention it deserves (the intron is a non-coding region in eukaryotic gene).

The novelty in our work consists in providing an efficient way to represent main characteristics of intronic sequences. Indeed, the FCGS coding highlights motifs having different forms with a high level of energy around specific frequency values. In our work, we found that most of introns in the *C. elegans* genome present high energy around the frequency 1/6.5. Figure 5 presents an illustrative example of an intron found in the *C. elegans* chromosome I (position [649752–652010]).

This example (Figure 5a,b,c) exposes the behavior of a typical intron which is characterized by the presence of specific motifs with high energy around the frequency 1/6.5 (as shown by the red arrow; P denotes periodicity) [38,39]. Other periodic motifs are also apparent at the level of harmonics which are marked by a lower intensity line. We note that the intensity of the lower harmonics (as indicated by the yellow arrows) increases by increasing the order of the FCGS coding. Otherwise, the intensity of the upper harmonics (see the black arrows) decreases by increasing the order of the FCGS coding. From this

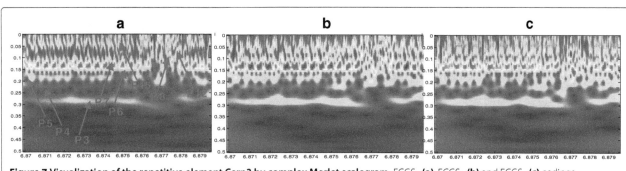

Figure 7 Visualization of the repetitive element Cerp3 by complex Morlet scalogram. FCGS$_1$ **(a)**, FCGS$_2$ **(b)** and FCGS$_3$ **(c)** codings.

Table 1 Position and frequency band of the introns, STS and Cerp3 sequences in the *C. elegans* chromosome I

| Structures | Position of the sequences in the *C. elegans* chromosome I | | | Frequency band |
	Sequence 1	Sequence 2	Sequence 3	
Introns	649752–652010	669573–671806	692688–693513	0–0.33
STS	3651199–3652332	3654158–3655291	7385764–7386961	0–0.2
Cerp3	953661–954106	593817-594993	686985–687959	0–0.28

example, we can see that this intron presents a remarkable behavior within the three levels of FCGS despite the smoothing effect of higher order FCGSs (especially noted when we code with $FCGS_3$).

4.2 STS signature

Traditional gene mapping techniques are slow and painstaking. The discovery of the sequence-tagged sites (STS) have opened a new way for geneticists to speed up the establishment of genetic and physical mapping of genes along chromosomes. An STS is a specific region of DNA which can be uniquely identified through its sequence. In addition, it is an easily PCR-amplified sequence which can contain repetitive elements as microsatellites. For the analysis of this abundant class of DNA, we choose the example of Figure 6.

By examining the $FCGS_1$ result (Figure 6a), we can note the presence of periodic patterns with high energy at the top of the scalogram (which is indicated by the red arrow). These patterns are located within a considerable frequency band. If we consider the $FCGS_2$ result, we can see that the energy level of the frequency band is weakened (Figure 6b). This is due to the smoothing property of the FCGS coding. The smoothing effect of the $FCGS_3$ is also noticed in Figure 6c.

4.3 Cerp3 signature

The last example that we are studying here is part of the Cerp3 repetitive family. The Cerp3 DNA consists of dispersed repeated elements with a length of about 1,000 bp and presents 50 to 100 copies in the *C. elegans* genome. Such a nematode segment hides specific periodicities that we are disclosing in the related scalograms (Figure 7).

All the scalograms, strikingly, display a long chain of motifs consisting of seven- and six-base periodicities. Figure 7a (related to the $FCGS_1$ coding) shows other patterns including strong periodicities on the top of the scalograms. As for the $FCGS_2$ coding (Figure 7b), it enhances periodicities of 5 bp and 3 bp and shows up other periodicities corresponding to the 15-, 12- and six-base repetitive elements. Finally, Figure 7c underlines the contribution of the $FCGS_3$ scheme in the enhancement of periodicities like 15, five and four bases.

5 FCGS and the local signatures in *C. elegans*

In this work, we have investigated the important role of color scalograms which offer an easy visual navigation through genomic sequences. Thus, we have exposed the behavior adopted by some DNA sequences in the time-frequency plan which turns out to be easily characterized by the presence of different periodic patterns within the FCGSs scalograms. These behaviors appear as strong local

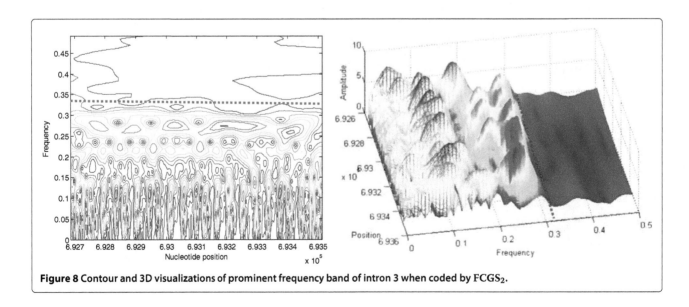

Figure 8 Contour and 3D visualizations of prominent frequency band of intron 3 when coded by $FCGS_2$.

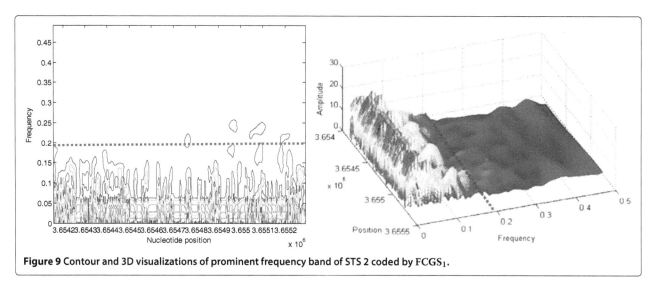

Figure 9 Contour and 3D visualizations of prominent frequency band of STS 2 coded by FCGS$_1$.

signatures within the genome. As we have seen, there are some signatures which strongly appear only when we code with FCGS$_1$ and other signatures that similarly appear within the three levels of FCGSs.

Aiming at studying the role of the FCGS order in the enhancement of the DNA signature, we consider the contribution of the percentage of the frequency band which specifies the DNA signature in terms of energy measure. This choice went to the fact that the energy of the characteristic sub-band is one of the main statistical features that can be extracted from the wavelet domain as texture descriptor [40]. The study is performed with three examples of each of the intron, STS and Cerp3 sequences (see Table 1). These sequences are coded by the frequency chaos game signal order 1, 2 and 3.

To be able to evaluate the energy contribution of the different periodic patterns in these sequences, we have to fix the frequency band limit in such a way that it includes all the periodic motifs (see Table 1).

The choice of the frequency boundaries is justified by the contour and the 3D plots given in Figures 8, 9 and 10. The dashed red lines in these figures delimit the characteristic frequency band. Figure 8 refers to the third intron when it is coded by FCGS$_2$.

In Figure 9, we provide the pattern distribution of the STS 2 sequence (coded by FCGS$_1$) through the contour and the 3D plots.

Finally, Figure 10 shows the contour and the 3D plots of the second Cerp3 sequence (coded by FCGS$_2$).

The second part of this study consists in the measurement of the strongest motifs' energy distribution for the intron, STS and Cerp3 sequences coded by the frequency chaos game signals order 1, 2 and 3. Thus, we calculate the total energy of the scalogram (which is designated by E_t) and the energy measure of the prominent frequency sub-band (which is designated by E_p). The contribution of this sub-band energy is then weighted by the percentage ratio between them.

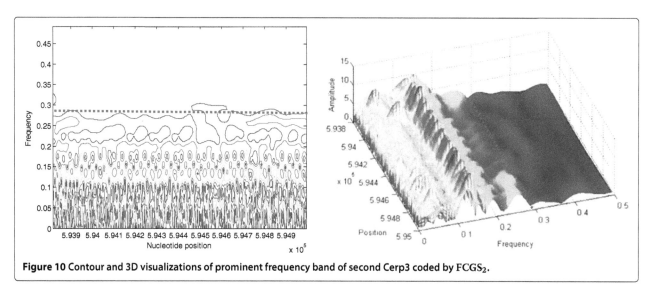

Figure 10 Contour and 3D visualizations of prominent frequency band of second Cerp3 coded by FCGS$_2$.

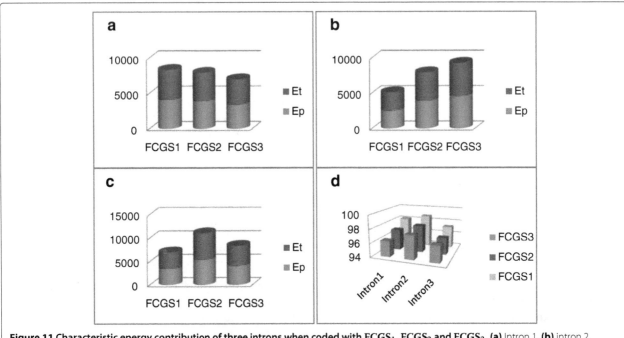

Figure 11 Characteristic energy contribution of three introns when coded with $FCGS_1$, $FCGS_2$ and $FCGS_3$. **(a)** Intron 1, **(b)** intron 2, **(c)** intron 3, **(d)** ratio.

In Figure 11, we provide the energy's values, which are calculated over a portion of 800 bp for the three introns. Based on the histogram plots, we deduce that the partial energy is so close to the total energy for all introns. In addition, $FCGS_1$, $FCGS_2$ and $FCGS_3$ yield close percentage values, which confirm the fact that they similarly characterize introns.

As for the STS sequences, the scalograms show that the $FCGS_1$ is better suited to study this DNA type. To prove this, we consider the contribution of the characteristic

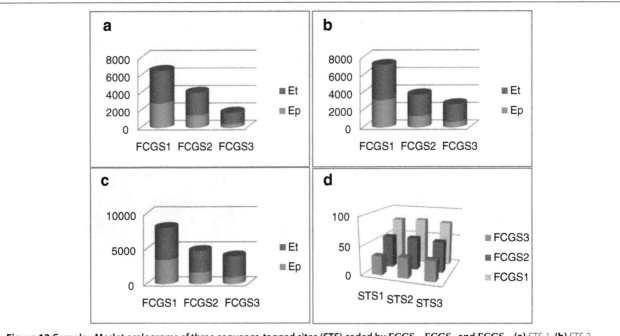

Figure 12 Complex Morlet scalograms of three sequence-tagged sites (STS) coded by $FCGS_1$, $FCGS_2$ and $FCGS_3$. **(a)** STS 1, **(b)** STS 2, **(c)** STS 3, **(d)** ratio.

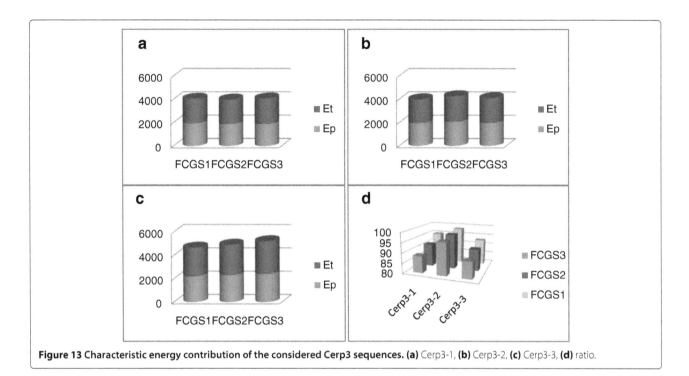

Figure 13 Characteristic energy contribution of the considered Cerp3 sequences. **(a)** Cerp3-1, **(b)** Cerp3-2, **(c)** Cerp3-3, **(d)** ratio.

patterns relating to the three first levels of FCGS. In terms of energy percentage, we provide the contribution of the characteristic patterns relating to the FCGS scalograms in Figure 12. The energy values are calculated over a portion of 1,134 bp.

Note that the energy values considerably decline when the FCGS order increases for all the STS sequences. The ratio values prove, in addition, that $FCGS_1$ is the only coding that characterizes STS sequences.

Finally, the energy values of the Cerp3 sequences (through a portion of 445 bp) are provided in Figure 13. From the latter histograms, we can deduce that the FCGS order 1, 2 and 3 allow the Cerp3 characterization, which results in close energy values.

Aside the qualification of these sequences by a specific signature, there are many DNA classes that are easily distinguished by relevant motifs in the scalograms. Therefore, based on the study of significant homology between signatures, we can establish efficient algorithms for DNA recognition and classification.

6 Conclusion

DNA coding methods play a major role in revealing information about significant biological sequences. However, the choice of such methods depends on the features that they can reflect. It appears that the available mapping techniques rely mostly on the 3-bp or 10-bp behaviors and are not well adapted to examine all periodic structures contained in the complex nature of DNA. In this context, we introduced a new mapping technique, aiming

to characterize a wealth of DNA sequences. The proposed method is based on the chaos game theory and we refer to it as FCGS. The FCGS coding consists in assigning the frequency of occurrence of each sub-pattern to the same group of nucleotides that exist in the DNA sequence. Such a mapping has the advantage of providing a multitude of signals which offer the possibility to treat the DNA sequence from different views, taking into account the statistical properties of resident oligomers.

The performance of the FCGS scheme in terms of information revelation from DNA sequences was tested by the continuous wavelet transform. The complex Morlet wavelet was employed to create color scalograms for the *C. elegans'* FCGSs (order 1 to 3).

By reviewing the resulting scalograms, we found that the selected wavelet transform readily identifies different DNA structures. Several hidden periodicities and features which cannot be revealed by classical DNA analysis methods (such as the STFT) were sharply identified. Simulation results show a pronounced 6.5 base period in intergenic residues, more specifically in intronic ones. However, there are other introns which include periodicities like 5 bp and 3 bp. These periodicities are derived from a specific organization of periodic patterns forming thus a local signature. Through this study, it is shown that the variable patterns observed in the intron DNA are all exhibited by the $FCGS_1$, $FCGS_2$ and $FCGS_3$ codings. Besides introns, we have shed the light on another type of DNA sequences: the STS. The STS are particular DNA sequences recently used in the gene mapping procedures. When we code with an FCGS order 1, we managed to find a special signature of this DNA class that derives from the microsatellite repetitive elements that it contains.

Overall, in the mapping efforts for the nematode *C. elegans*, various classes of repetitive DNA were annotated. Among them, we considered a particular class of *C. elegans* dispersed repeats: the Cerp3. The related scalograms provide clear periodical motifs of seven- and eight-base repeats. This time-frequency signature is illustrated when the coding schemes $FCGS_1$, $FCGS_2$ and $FCGS_3$ are used.

In conclusion, the results stemming from the complex Morlet wavelet analysis of the FCGSs have showed its accuracy in detection of variable DNA structures. Moreover, this could serve in discovering unknown domains with potential biological significance in genomes.

Competing interests

The authors declare that they have no competing interests

Authors' contributions

IM developed the algorithms and implemented them to characterize the DNA structures in *C. elegans* based on the NCBI datasets . IM drafted the manuscript and conceived and coordinated the study. AEO and ZL helped revise the paper. All authors read and approved the final manuscript.

Author details

[1] Université de Tunis El Manar, Ecole Nationale d'Ingénieurs de Tunis, LR Signal, Images et Technologies de l'Information, BP 37, le Belvédère, 1002 Tunis, Tunisia. [2] Département de Génie Physique et Instrumentation, INSAT, BP 676, Centre Urbain Cedex, 1080 Tunis, Tunisia.

References

1. AE Oueslati, Lachiri Z, N Ellouze, 3D spectrum analysis of DNA sequence: application to Caenorhabditis elegans genome, in *Proceedings of the 7th IEEE International Conference on Bioinformatics and Bioengineering*, (BIBE 2007), vol.2, (The Conference Center at Harvard Medical School, Boston, Massachusetts, USA, 14-17 October 2007), pp. 864–871
2. AE Oueslati, Messaoudi I, Z Lachiri, N Ellouze, ed. by SalihSalih Dr, Spectral analysis of global behaviour of C. elegans chromosomes, in *Fourier Transform Applications*, (2012), pp. 205–228. ISBN: 978-953-51-0518-3, InTech, doi:10.5772/36493
3. AS Nair, T Mahalakshmi, Visualization of genomic data using internucleotide distance signals, in *Proceedings of International Conference on Genomic Signal Processing* (GSP2005), (Bucharest, 11-1 July 2005)
4. M Riyazuddin, *Information analysis of DNA sequences*. (MS thesis, Dept of Electrical and Computer Engineering, Louisiana State University, USA, 2003)
5. E Pirogova, Q Fang, M Akay, I Cosic, Investigations of the structural and functional relationships of Oncogene Proteins. Proc. IEEE. **90**(12), 1859–1867 (2002)
6. M Sifuzzaman, MR Islam, MZ Ali, Application of wavelet transform and its advantages compared to Fourier transform. J. Phys. Sci. **13**, 121–134 (2009)
7. JP Mena-Chalco, H Carrer, Y Zana, Cesar Jr. RM, Identification of protein coding regions using the modified Gabor-wavelet transform. IEEE/ACM TCBB. **5**(2), 198–207 (2008)
8. JA Tenreiro Machado, AC Costa, M Dulce Quelhas, Wavelet analysis of human DNA. Genomics. **98**(3), 155–163 (2011). Elsevier
9. KB Murray, D Gorse, JM Thornton, Wavelet transforms for the characterization and detection of repeating motifs. J. Mol. Biol. **316**, 341–363 (2002)
10. A Rao, A clustering algorithm for gene expression data using wavelet packet decomposition, in *Conference Record of the Thirty-Sixth Asilomar Conference on Signals, Systems and Computers* (Asilomar2002), vol. 1, (Pacific Grove, CA, 3-6 November), pp. 316–319
11. JL Oliver, P Bernaola-Galvan, J Guerrero-Garcia, R Roman-Roldan, Entropic profiles of DNA sequences through chaos-game-derived images. J. Theor. Biol. **160**, 457–470 (1993)
12. ZB Wu, Metric representation of DNA sequences. Electrophoresis. **21**, 2321–2326 (2000)
13. JS Almeida, JA Carrico, A Maretzek, PA Noble, M Fletcher, Analysis of genomic sequences by chaos game representation. Bioinformatics. **17**(5), 429–437 (2001)
14. P Tino, Spacial representation of symbolic sequences through iterative function systems. IEEE Trans Syst. Man Cybern. Syst. Hum. **29**, 386–393 (1999)
15. S Vinga, J Almeida, S Renyi, Continuous entropy of DNA sequences. J. Theor. Biol. **231**, 377–388 (2004)
16. S Vinga, J Almeida, Alignment-free sequence comparison-a review. Bioinformatics. **19**, 513–523 (2003)
17. NN Li, F Shi, XH Niu, JB Xia, A novel method to reconstruct phylogeny tree based on the chaos game representation. J. Biomed. Sci. Eng. **2**, 582–586 (2009)
18. A Fiser, GE Tusnady, I Simon, Chaos game representation of protein structures. J. Mol. Graph. **12**, 295–304 (1994)
19. S Karlin, C Burge, Dinucleotide relative abundance extremes: a genomic signature. Trends Genet. **11**(7), 283–290 (1995)
20. YW Wang, K Hill, S Singh, L Kari, The spectrum of genomic signatures: from dinucleotides to chaos game representation. Gene. **346**, 173–185 (2005)
21. PJ Deschavanne, A Giron, Fagot Vilain J G, B Fertil, Genomic signature: characterization and classification of species assessed by chaos game representation of sequences. Mol. Biol. Evol. **16**(10), 1391–1399 (1999)
22. JS Almeida, JA Carrico, A Maretzek, PA Noble, M Fletcher, Analysis of genomic sequences by chaos game representation. Bioinformatics. **17**(5), 429–437 (2001)
23. P Deschavanne, A Giron, J Vilain, CH Dufraigneand, B Fertil, Genomic signature is preserved in short DNA fragment, in *Proceedings of the IEEE International Symposium on Bio-Informatics and Biomedical Engineering* (BIBE 2000), (Arlington Virginia, USA, 8-10 November 2000), pp. 161–167
24. I Messaoudi, A Elloumi, Z Lachiri, Building specific signals from frequency chaos game and revealing periodicities using a smoothed Fourier analysis. IEEE Trans. Comput. Biol. Bioinform. **11**(4), 1–15 (2014)
25. Z Grossmann, J Morlet, Decomposition of hardy functions into square integrable wavelets of constant shape: SIAM. J. Math. Anal. **15**, 723–736 (1984)
26. L Hui, Complex Morlet wavelet amplitude and phase map based bearing fault diagnosis, in *Proceedings of the 8th World Congress on Intelligent Control and Automation* (WCICA2010), (Jinan, China, 7-9 July), pp. 6923–69261
27. AH Najmi, J Sadowsky, The continuous wavelet transform and variable resolution time-frequency analysis. Johns Hopkins APL Technical Digest. **18**(1), 134–140 (1997)
28. IW Selesnick, Wavelet transform with tunable Q-factor. IEEE Transactions on Signal Processing. **59**(8), 3560–3575 (2011)
29. NCF Tse, LL Lai, Wavelet-based algorithm for signal analysis. EURASIP Journal on Advances in Signal Processing (2007). doi:10.1155/2007/38916
30. NCBI Database (National Center for Biotechnology Information, U.S. National Library of Medicine, 2013). http://mirrors.vbi.vt.edu/mirrors/ftp. ncbi.nih.gov/genomes/Caenorhabditis_elegans/. Accessed 18 Mar 2013
31. S Tiwari, S Ramachandran, A Bhattacharya, S Bhattacharya, R Ramaswamy, Prediction of probable genes by Fourier analysis of genomic sequences. Bioinformatics. **13**(3), 263–270 (1997)
32. D Kotlar, Y Lavner, Gene prediction by spectral rotation measure: a new method for identifying protein-coding regions. Genome Res. **13**, 1930–1937 (2003)
33. D Anastassiou, Frequency-domain analysis of biomolecular sequences. Bioinformatics. **16**(12), 1073–1081 (2000)
34. J Jin, Identification of protein coding regions of rice genes using alternative spectral rotation measure and linear discriminant analysis. Dev. Reprod. Biol. **2**, 167–173 (2004)

35. F Gao, CT Zhang, Comparison of various algorithms for recognizing short coding sequences of human genes. Bioinformatics. **20**(5), 673–681 (2004)

36. G Dodin, P Vandergheynst, P Levoir, C Cordier, L Marcourt, Fourier and wavelet transform analysis, a tool for visualizing regular patterns in DNA sequences. J. Theor. Biol. **206**, 323–326 (2000)

37. L Wang, Stein LD, Localizing triplet periodicity in DNA and cDNA sequences. BMC Bioinformatics. **11**(550) (2010). doi:10.1186/1471-2105-11-550

38. I Messaoudi, A Elloumi, Z Lachiri, Complex Morlet wavelet analysis of the DNA frequency chaos game signal and revealing specific motifs of introns, in *C. elegans, International Conference on Control, Engineering & Information Technology* (CEIT2013), vol. 3, (Sousse, Tunisia, 4-7 June), pp. 27–32

39. I Messaoudi, A Elloumi, Z Lachiri, Detection of the 6.5-base periodicity in the C. elegans introns based on the frequency chaos game signal and the complex Morlet wavelet analysis. International Journal of Scientific Engineering and Technology. **2**(12), 1247–1251 (2013)

40. L Dettori, L Semler, A comparison of wavelet, ridgelet, and curvelet-based texture classification algorithms in computed tomography. Comput. Biol. Med. **37**(2), 486–498 (2007)

10

Gene regulatory network inference and validation using relative change ratio analysis and time-delayed dynamic Bayesian network

Peng Li[1], Ping Gong[2*], Haoni Li[3], Edward J Perkins[4], Nan Wang[3] and Chaoyang Zhang[3*]

Abstract

The Dialogue for Reverse Engineering Assessments and Methods (DREAM) project was initiated in 2006 as a community-wide effort for the development of network inference challenges for rigorous assessment of reverse engineering methods for biological networks. We participated in the *in silico* network inference challenge of DREAM3 in 2008. Here we report the details of our approach and its performance on the synthetic challenge datasets. In our methodology, we first developed a model called relative change ratio (RCR), which took advantage of the heterozygous knockdown data and null-mutant knockout data provided by the challenge, in order to identify the potential regulators for the genes. With this information, a time-delayed dynamic Bayesian network (TDBN) approach was then used to infer gene regulatory networks from time series trajectory datasets. Our approach considerably reduced the searching space of TDBN; hence, it gained a much higher efficiency and accuracy. The networks predicted using our approach were evaluated comparatively along with 29 other submissions by two metrics (area under the ROC curve and area under the precision-recall curve). The overall performance of our approach ranked the second among all participating teams.

Keywords: Gene regulatory network (GRN); Dialogue for Reverse Engineering Assessments and Methods (DREAM); Relative change ratio (RCR); Time-delayed dynamic Bayesian network (TDBN)

Introduction

Recent development of high-throughput technologies such as DNA microarray and RNA-Seq (i.e., next-generation sequencing of RNA transcripts) has made it possible for biologists to simultaneously measure gene expression at a genome scale. High dimensional datasets generated using such technologies provide a system-wide overview of how genes interact with each other in a network context. However, reconstruction of complex networks of genetic interactions and unraveling of unknown relationships among genes based on such high-throughput datasets remain a very challenging computational problem.

Various mathematical methods and computational approaches have been proposed to infer gene regulatory networks (GRN) from DNA microarray data, including Boolean networks [1], information theory [2], differential equations [3], and Bayesian networks [4-6]. However, the relative performances among these algorithms are not well studied because computational biologists must repeatedly test them on large-scale and high-quality datasets obtained from different experimental conditions and derived from different networks. Unfortunately, experimental datasets of customized size and design are usually unavailable and most biological networks are unknown or incomplete. Since each of these methods uses different datasets and comparison strategies, it is difficult to systematically validate the interactions predicted by different computational approaches.

Due to limited knowledge of experimentally validated biological networks of gene interactions, simulated data generated artificially from *in silico* gene networks provide a 'gold' standard to systematically evaluate the performance of different genetic networks inferring algorithms [7]. *In silico* networks are composed of a known network topology that determines the structure

---

* Correspondence: ping.gong@usace.army.mil; chaoyang.zhang@usm.edu
[2]Badger Technical Services, LLC, San Antonio, TX 78216, USA
[3]School of Computing, University of Southern Mississippi, Hattiesburg, MS 39406, USA
Full list of author information is available at the end of the article

and model for each of the interactions among the genes. In such simulated data, all aspects of the networks are under full control and different types of data and levels of noise are allowed. Many methods have been proposed for creating *in silico* genetic networks, including continuous [8], probabilistic [9], and dynamic [10] approaches.

The performance of network inference algorithms has rarely been assessed and compared in terms of their strength and weakness using rigorous metrics [11,12]. As a community effort to address the deficiency in GRN reconstruction methodology, a Dialogue for Reverse Engineering Assessments and Methods (DREAM) project was initiated in 2006 [11] to catalyze the interaction between experiment and theory, specifically in the area of cellular network inference and quantitative model building (http://www.the-dream-project.org/). One of the key goals of DREAM is the development of community-wide challenges for objective assessment of reverse engineering methods for biological networks [13]. The *in silico* network inference challenge of DREAM3 was designed to explore the extent to which underlying gene networks of various sizes and connection densities can be inferred from simulated data [14]. In participation of this challenge, we developed a novel approach of combining relative change ratio (RCR) and time-delayed dynamic Bayesian network to deduce GRNs from synthetic datasets for *Escherichia coli* and *Saccharomyces cerevisiae* (budding yeast) provided by the challenge. Among 29 participating teams, the performance of our approach was second only to the best performing method in the 10-node and the 50-node network sub-challenges [14]. Here we present the details of our approach and its performance on the challenge datasets.

Materials and methods
Challenge datasets
The *in silico* network inference challenge was structured as three separate sub-challenges with networks of 10, 50, and 100 genes (nodes), respectively [13]. For each sub-challenge, five *in silico* networks (two for *E. coli* and three for *S. cerevisiae*) were created as benchmark or gold standard networks. The rationale for this design was to evaluate the consistency of inference methods in predicting the topology of five independent networks of the same type and size. These benchmark networks were generated by Daniel Marbach of Ecole Polytechnique Fédérale de Lausanne through extracting sub-networks with a topology of connections from the currently accepted *E. coli* and *S. cerevisiae* GRNs and imbuing the networks with dynamics using a thermodynamic model of gene expression [8]. The *in silico* 'measurements' were generated by continuous differential equations which were deemed reasonable approximations of gene expression

regulatory functions [8,14]. A small amount of Gaussian noise was added to these values to simulate measurement error [14].

For each sub-challenge network, three experimental gene expression datasets were simulated for both *E. coli* and *S. cerevisiae*: heterozygous knockdown, null-mutants, and time series trajectories. The heterozygous knockdown dataset contained the steady state gene expression levels for the wild-type and the heterozygous knockdown (a gene reduced by half) strains for each gene. The null-mutant dataset contained the steady state levels for the wild-type and the null-mutant (expression of a gene set to zero) strains. Time series trajectories dataset contained time courses of the network recovering from several external perturbations. All of the datasets can be downloaded at the DREAM Project website: http://wiki.c2b2.columbia.edu/dream/index.php/D3c4.

Relative change ratio
A GRN represents the interactions of all genes in the network. For a given GRN structure, the change of the expression level of one gene results in changes of the expression levels of all others genes regulated by this gene. If a gene plays an important role in the GRN, knockout or null-mutation of an important gene (key gene) leads to more significant changes of the expression levels of other genes that are directly interacted with the hub gene. Thus, the wild-type, knockout, and null-mutant datasets provide useful information (prior knowledge) that we can use for improving the accuracy of GRN inference. Here we introduce the RCR method to preprocess and analyze the given datasets to identify the key genes that can be used for further GRN inference. The RCR method can reveal the relationships between a knockout gene and the influenced genes so it can also be directly used for inference of a GRN.

For each gene in the given dataset, we took the gene expression value of the wild-type as reference and calculated the relative change ratios of gene expression levels compared to the change range of the gene, as defined in Equation 1.

$$R_{i,j} \begin{cases} \dfrac{|G_{i,j} - W_j|}{\text{Max}(G_{\cdot,j}) - \text{Min}(G_{\cdot,j})}, & i \neq j \quad i = 1, ..., n; \quad j = 1, ..., n \\ 0 & , i = j \end{cases}$$

$$(1)$$

where, $R_{i,j}$ represents the relative change ratio of gene j when gene i is knocked out. $G_{i,j}$ is the gene expression value of gene j when gene i is knocked out. W_j is the wild-type value of gene j, and $\text{Max}(G_{\cdot,j}) - \text{Min}(G_{\cdot,j})$ means the change range of gene j for all knockout genes. If $i = j$,

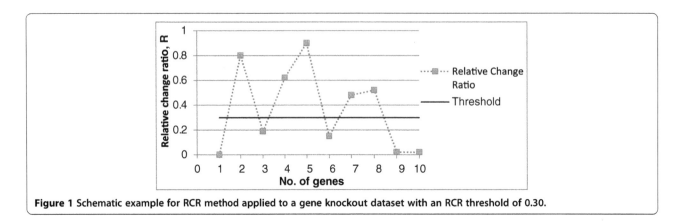

Figure 1 Schematic example for RCR method applied to a gene knockout dataset with an RCR threshold of 0.30.

$R_{i,j}$ will be set as 0 since this gene has already been knocked out.

If the change ratio is more than a chosen threshold (e.g., 0.30), we select this gene as a potential key gene and assume that it plays an important role in the network. If the change in absolute gene expression value compared to the reference is less than a threshold (e.g., 0.05) which can be defined by the user, this gene is considered as noise and ignored from the potential regulatory genes list. For example, in Figure 1, when gene 1 has been knocked out (the expression value will be set as 0), the change ratios of genes 2, 4, 5, 7, and 8 are more than 30 %, then we consider these genes as genes potentially regulated by knockout gene 1.

If the absolute change of gene expression values compared to their own reference value is less than a chosen threshold (e.g., 0.05), even though the relative change ratio is more than 0.30, we still consider these

genes as noise and remove them from the regulated genes list.

Dynamic Bayesian network

Dynamic Bayesian network (DBN) analysis is the temporal extension of Bayesian network analysis. It is a general model class that is capable of representing complex temporal stochastic processes. An example of basic DBN block is shown in Figure 2.

A DBN is defined as a pair $(B0, B1)$ representing the joint probability distribution over all possible time series of variables $X = \{X_1, X_2, \ldots X_n\}$, where $X_i (1 \leq i \leq n)$ represents the binary-valued random variables in the network. In addition, the lowercase x_i $(1 \leq i \leq n)$ denotes the values of variable X_i. It is composed of initial states of a Bayesian network $B_0 = (G_0, \Theta_0)$ and a transition Bayesian network $B_1 = (G_1, \Theta_1)$, where B_0 specifies the joint distribution of the variables in $X(0)$ and B_1 represents the transition probabilities $\Pr\{X(t + 1)|X(t)\}$ for all

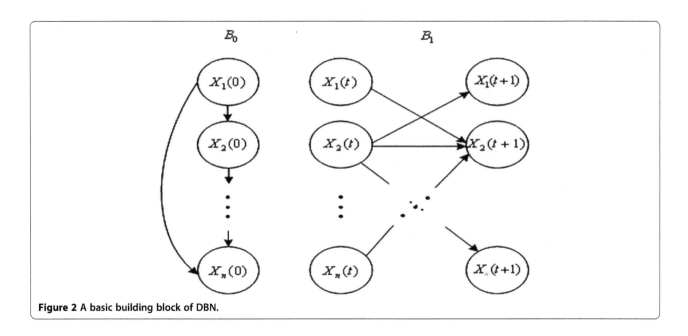

Figure 2 A basic building block of DBN.

t. In slice 0, the parents of $X_i(0)$ are assumed to be those specified in the prior network B_0, which means $\mathrm{Pa}(X_i(0)) \subseteq X(0)$ for all $1 \le i \le n$; in slice $t+1$, the parents of $X_i(t+1)$ are nodes in slices t, $\mathrm{Pa}(X_i(t+1)) \subseteq X(t)$ for all $1 \le i \le n$ and $t \ge 0$; the connections only exist between consecutive slices. The joint distribution over a finite list of random variables $X(0) \cup X(1) \cup \cdots \cup X(\mathrm{T})$ can be expressed as [15,16]

$$
\begin{aligned}
&\Pr\{x(0), x(1), \ldots, x(T)\} \\
&= \Pr\{x(0)\} \prod_{t=0}^{T-1} \Pr\{x(t+1)|x(t)\} \\
&= \prod_{i=1}^{n} \Pr\{x_i(0)|\mathrm{pa}(X_i(0))\} \times \prod_{t=0}^{T-1}\prod_{j=1}^{n} \Pr\{x_j(X_j(t+1))\}
\end{aligned}
$$

(2)

Kevin Murphy and co-workers [17,18] implemented a Bayesian network toolbox (BNT), in which the actual structure learning was performed by calling one of the BNT functions learn_struct_dbn_reveal, which used the REVEAL algorithm [4].

Time-delayed dynamic Bayesian network

In the traditional DBN proposed by [17,18], the effectiveness is not sufficient for two main reasons. The first is the extremely high computational cost. In Murphy's implementation, all the genes in the dataset are considered as parents (regulators) of a given target gene, which makes it impossible to model large-scale gene networks because of exponentially increasing computational time when the algorithm tries to find all of the subsets of parent genes given a target gene. Usually, the number of genes is restricted to less than 30, and more genes will be too much time consuming according to our testing. The second is that biologically relevant transcriptional time lags cannot be determined in Murphy's BNT, which reduces the inference accuracy of gene regulatory networks.

To address the above limitations of traditional DBN, Zou and Conzen [9] introduced a time-delayed dynamic Bayesian network (TDBN)-based analysis method, which can reconstruct GRNs from time series gene expression data. The improved method can dramatically reduce computational time and significantly increased accuracy. According to [9,10], most transcriptional regulators exhibit either an earlier or simultaneous change in the expression level when compared to their targets. In this way, one can limit the potential parents of each target gene and thus dramatically decrease the computational cost. The other improvement by Zou and Conzen [9] is to perform an estimation of the transcriptional time lag between potential regulators and their target genes. The time difference between the initial expression change of a potential regulator and its target gene represents a biologically relevant time period.

The initial expression change of a potential regulator is expected to allow a more accurate estimation of the transcriptional time lag between potential regulators and their targets, because it takes into account variable expression relationships of different regulator-target pairs. These improvements in [9] are related to transcriptional time-delayed lags between regulators and target genes, so it can also be considered as a time-delayed DBN and directly used to predict networks from time series gene expression data, such as the trajectory time series data in the DREAM3 challenge.

Inferring networks using a method that combines RCR and TDBN

In this combined method, we first used the simple RCR model to find key genes from the given heterozygous knockdown data and null-mutant knockout data. These key genes have a higher potential than other genes to play critical roles in simulated GRNs. After the data was preprocessed, we constructed a gene interaction network that indicated potential regulation among the selected key genes. The TDBN method was then used to infer another GRN from time series trajectory datasets. If gene interactions exist in both networks inferred by RCR and TDBN methods, we choose these interactions as our predicted edges in our final inferred networks. The predicted networks were assessed against the benchmark networks [13,14].

Results and discussion
Inferred networks as compared with the true networks

In this work, our approach was applied to inferring GRNs in three different ways: For *in silico* networks with 10 genes, the gene regulatory networks were inferred only by the RCR method from steady state data, in which we used mainly the gene knockout dataset; for networks with 50 genes, the networks inferred using RCR and TDBN separately were combined into the final networks; for networks with 100 genes, we used only TDBN to reconstruct gene networks from time series trajectory gene expression dataset. In doing this, we sought to determine which method had better performance in inferring gene regulatory networks.

Our approach successfully inferred networks using the synthetic datasets provided by Marbach and his colleagues [8,13,14]. For example, one of the inferred *E. coli* 10-node GRN is shown in Figure 3, where seven matching edges are correctly identified by our model, in comparison to the corresponding true network. Our model correctly identified directionality in each of the matching

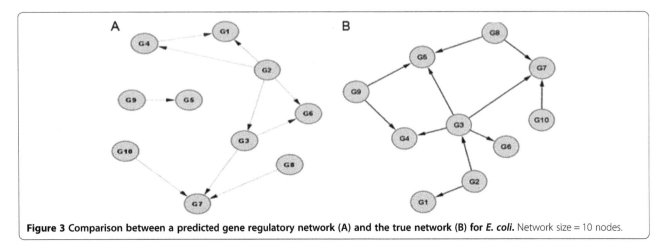

Figure 3 Comparison between a predicted gene regulatory network (A) and the true network (B) for *E. coli.* Network size = 10 nodes.

edges. One of the predicted 50-node yeast GRN is shown in Figure 4, and the matching network is shown in Figure 5. There are 52 edges correctly inferred by our method, out of a total of 77 edges in the true network.

Performance of network inference from synthetic datasets

The performance of each method was evaluated by two metrics: the area under the precision-recall (AUPR) curve and the area under the receiver operating characteristic

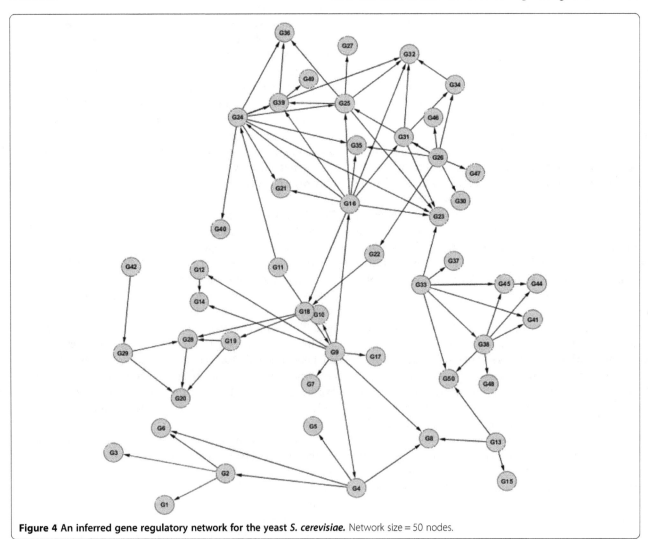

Figure 4 An inferred gene regulatory network for the yeast *S. cerevisiae.* Network size = 50 nodes.

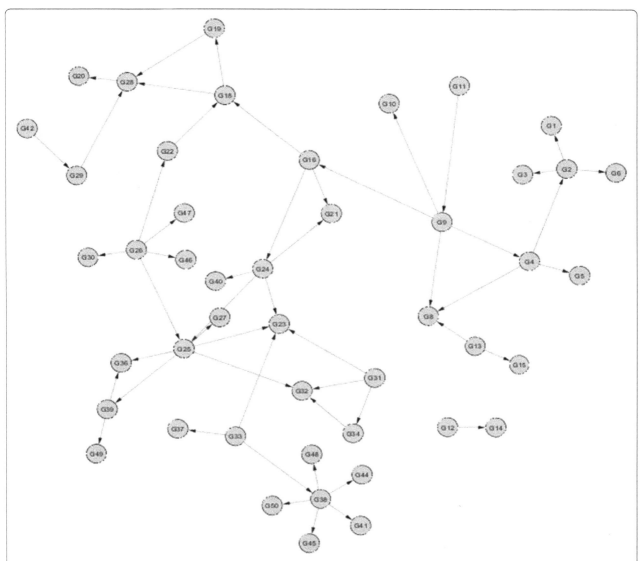

Figure 5 Matching edges between inferred and true networks. The 52 correct edges in the inferred gene regulatory network (shown in Figure 4) that matched with the true network of the yeast *S. cerevisiae* (network size = 50 nodes).

(AUROC) curve for the whole set of edge predictions for 15 networks [13,14]. Precision is a measure of fidelity, whereas recall is a measure of completeness. Recall (R) is defined as $^{Ce}/_{(Ce+Me)}$ and precision (P) as $^{Ce}/_{(Ce+Fe)}$, where Ce is the number of correct edges, Me is the total number of missed edges (missed errors), and Fe is the number of false alarm errors. A missed error is defined as the connection between genes that exists in true networks, but the inference algorithms miss or make wrong orientations. A false alarm error is the connection that the inference algorithms create but does not exist in true networks.

A P value is the probability that a given or larger area under the curve value is obtained by random ordering of the T potential network links. An overall P value is the geometric mean of the n individual P values, calculated as $\left(p_1 \times p_2 \times \ldots \times p_n\right)^{1/n}$. An overall AUROC P value represents the geometric mean of the five AUROC P values (Ecoli1, Ecoli2, Yeast1, Yeast2, and Yeast3). An overall AUPR P value is the geometric mean of the five AUPR P values.

To calculate AUPR and AUROC, each predicted network was submitted in the form of ranked lists of predicted edges. The lists were ordered according to the confidence of the predictions so that the first entry corresponded to the edge predicted with the highest confidence. In other words, the edges at the top of the list were believed to be present in the network, and the edges at the bottom of the list were believed to be absent from the network [13].

Table 1 Assessment metrics for the first set of _E. coli_ and yeast networks inferred using our approach

Metrics	Ecoli1_10	Yeast1_10	Ecoli1_50	Yeast1_50	Ecoli1_100	Yeast1_100
AUPR	5.43E − 01	7.71E − 01	6.71E − 01	4.86E − 01	1.45E − 02	1.55E − 02
AUROC	7.94E − 01	9.44E − 01	8.62E − 01	8.35E − 01	5.21E − 01	4.61E − 01
_P_AUPR_	1.34E − 04	2.09E − 06	8.57E − 55	3.91E − 39	2.27E − 01	8.91E − 01
_P_AUROC_	5.47E − 04	1.29E − 06	3.19E − 20	4.64E − 18	2.02E − 01	9.60E − 01
Overall AUPR	1.09E − 04		2.54E − 46		4.83E − 03	
Overall AUROC	2.10E − 04		8.19E − 18		2.13E − 02	

The network name consists of two parts: organism name and network set number (i.e., Ecoli1 or Yeast1) followed by network size (10, 50, or 100 genes). The two parts are separated by '_'.

The inferred GRNs of different sizes (10, 50, and 100 genes) for both _E. coli_ and yeast were evaluated by the above metrics. The larger scores of AUPR and AUROC and the smaller _P_ values of AUPR and AUROC indicate the greater statistical significance of the prediction (Table 1). The metrics of RCR and TDBN inferred networks from the 10- and 50-gene datasets were ranked second among all 29 teams participating in the DREAM3 challenge. The RCR and TDBN inferred networks from the 100-gene dataset were ranked at the 15th place. The overall performance of our methods for all three-sized networks ranked second out of all participating teams in the DREAM3 challenge.

Role of RCR and TDBN in network inference

In general, our predictions of networks with 10 and 50 genes were better than those of 100-gene networks. In most cases, predictions of _E. coli_ networks were better than those of the yeast networks, with the exception of Yeast1 (Table 2). Based on these results, RCR appears to increase the fidelity of network inference more than using TDBN alone. This might explain why the performance of inferred networks with 100 genes was not as good as with size 10 and size 50, because only TDBN was used to infer networks instead of combining prior knowledge which would be gained from preprocessing data by RCR.

To better understand the role of RCR in GRN inference, we used the networks with 10 genes as an example and

compared the performance of all three methods: RCR (using only knockout data), TDBN (using time series data without four perturbations), and the combined method (using knockout results as prior knowledge and then running TDBN with time series data). The AUPR, AUROC, and overall score ($-0.5 \times \log_{10}(P\_AUPR \times P\_AUROC)$) results obtained for the five datasets in the networks with 10 genes are shown in Figure 6A,B,C, respectively. The three metrics demonstrate that for all five tested datasets, both RCR and the combined method had better performance than TDBN. The combined method was expected to have better performance than the RCR method because the RCR results could provide prior knowledge for TDBN. For three testing datasets (Ecoli2, Yeast1, and Yeast3), the combined method performed better than RCR. But the combined method did not perform as well for the other two datasets (Ecoli1 and Yeast2). Therefore, whether RCR or the combined method has better performance depends on specific datasets. Such an observation can be explained by examining the algorithm in the TDBN method. Even though we specified 'parent regulators' as prior knowledge in TDBN to narrow down the search space of regulators, TDBN still calculated its own 'parents' based on simultaneously altered time series genes and combined two sets of parents as one group. Thus, TDBN in the combined method always inferred more connections than RCR, which might result in higher false positive rates. How to take advantage of RCR-inferred prior knowledge in the method combining RCR and TDBN to improve

Table 2 Overall performance of our approach for predicting all five sets of networks of different sizes

Size	Metrics	Ecoli1	Ecoli2	Yeast1	Yeast2	Yeast3
10	AUPR	0.544	0.748	0.771	0.352	0.493
	AUROC	0.794	0.856	0.944	0.590	0.715
50	AUPR	0.671	0.672	0.486	0.367	0.381
	AUROC	0.862	0.842	0.836	0.688	0.728
100	AUPR	0.015	0.052	0.016	0.046	0.044
	AUROC	0.521	0.544	0.461	0.576	0.428

The AUPR and AUROC metrics for the first set of networks (Ecoli1 and Yeast1) are reported in Table 1.

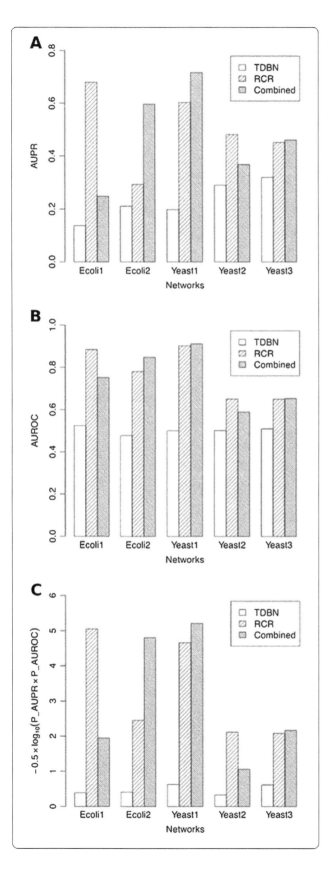

Figure 6 **Performance comparison between RCR, TDBN, and combined methods for the 10-node network inference.** As evaluated by three metrics. **(A)** AUPR, **(B)** AUROC, and **(C)** an overall score defined as $-0.5 \times \log_{10}(P\_AUPR \times P\_AUROC)$.

the performance of GRN inference remains a challenging research topic that requires further investigations.

Impact of RCR threshold on network inference accuracy

In the above analyses, we chose an empirical value of 0.30 as the RCR threshold, which implies that a gene is a potential key gene and plays an important role in the network if its change ratio is greater than 0.30. However, it is noteworthy that different RCR thresholds may affect the accuracy of network inference. To investigate the impact of a chosen RCR threshold on the prediction accuracy, we used the networks with 10 genes as an example and calculated both AUPR and AUROC P values, denoted as P-AUPR and P-AUROC, corresponding to 14 different RCR thresholds ranging from 0.05 to 0.70. As shown in Figure 7A,B, both P-AUPR and P-AUROC values were small when a RCR threshold was between 0.15 and 0.40. Furthermore, we also calculated the overall score $-0.5 \times \log_{10}(P\_AUPR \times P\_AUROC)$ to evaluate the impact of RCR values on the performance. This score was used by the DREAM3 challenges to assess the performance of all participating teams. As shown in Figure 7C, the RCR threshold of 0.25 gave the best performance and it was very close to the empirical RCR threshold we used for GRN inference for the DREAM3 challenges.

Conclusions

In this study, a novel relative change ratio method was proposed to preprocess the null-mutant steady state data in order to find the key genes and build GRNs, in which these selected key genes have a higher potential than other genes to play very critical roles. Then, TDBN was used to infer GRNs from time series trajectory data, which were combined with previous knowledge gained in the initial step. Finally, the inferred networks were evaluated by using AUPR and AUROC metrics for the whole edge predictions for a network. The overall prediction results suggest that our approach was able to infer gene regulatory networks from *in silico* DREAM challenge data very efficiently and accurately in comparison with other participating teams. We have confidence that the DREAM project will eventually lead the reverse engineering community to resolve technical problems and overcome barriers between research groups towards reliable and accurate GRN inference from high dimensional gene expression data.

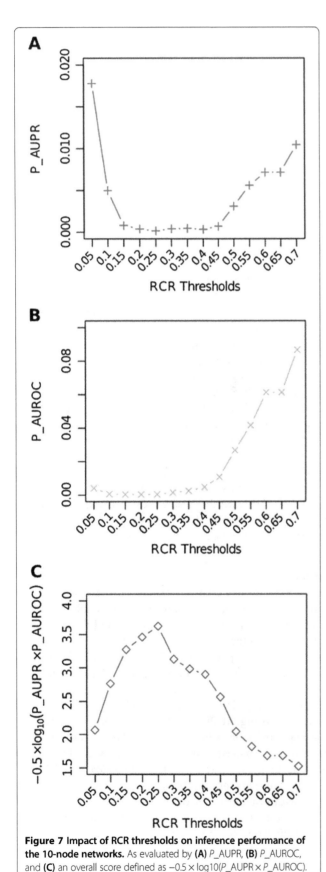

Figure 7 Impact of RCR thresholds on inference performance of the 10-node networks. As evaluated by **(A)** P_AUPR, **(B)** P_AUROC, and **(C)** an overall score defined as $-0.5 \times \log10(P\_AUPR \times P\_AUROC)$.

Abbreviations
AUPR: area under the precision-recall curve; AUROC: area under the receiver operating characteristic (ROC) curve; DREAM: Dialogue for Reverse Engineering Assessments and Methods; GRN: gene regulatory network; RCR: relative change ratio; TDBN: time-delayed dynamic Bayesian network.

Competing interests
The authors declare that they have no competing interests.

Authors' contributions
PL developed the algorithms and implemented them to infer gene regulatory networks based on the synthetic datasets provided for DREAM3 *in silico* network inference challenge. PL and CZ performed the statistical analysis. PL, PG, and CZ drafted the manuscript. HNL, EJP, and NW helped revise the paper. CZ, PG, and EJP conceived and coordinated the study. All authors read and approved the final manuscript.

Acknowledgements
We would like to thank Gustavo Stolovitzky for organizing the DREAM3 challenge and thank Daniel Marbach and his colleagues from the Laboratory of Intelligent Systems of the Swiss Federal Institute of Technology in Lausanne for providing the challenge datasets. This work was supported by the Environmental Quality and Installation Technologies Research Program of the US Army Corps of Engineers under contract #W912HZ-05-P-0145. Permission was granted by the Chief of Engineers to publish this information.

Author details
[1]Laboratory of Molecular Immunology, National Heart, Lung and Blood Institute, National Institutes of Health, Bethesda, MD 20892, USA. [2]Badger Technical Services, LLC, San Antonio, TX 78216, USA. [3]School of Computing, University of Southern Mississippi, Hattiesburg, MS 39406, USA. [4]Environmental Laboratory, U.S. Army Engineer Research and Development Center, Vicksburg, MS 39180, USA.

References
1. H Lähdesmäki, I Shmulevich, O Yli-Harja, On learning gene regulatory networks under the Boolean network model. Mach. Learn. **52**(1–2), 147–167 (2003)
2. JJ Faith, B Hayete, JT Thaden, I Mogno, J Wierzbowski, G Cottarel, S Kasif, JJ Collins, TS Gardner, Large-scale mapping and validation of *Escherichia coli* transcriptional regulation from a compendium of expression profiles. PLoS Biol **5**(1), e8 (2007)
3. I Chen, HL He, GM Church, Modeling gene expression with differential equations. Pac. Symp. Biocomput **4**, 29–40 (1999)
4. S Liang, S Fuhrman, R Somogyi, REVEAL, a general reverse engineering algorithm for inference of genetic network architectures. Pac. Symp. Biocomput. **3**, 18–29 (1998)
5. S Imoto, T Goto, S Miyano, Estimation of genetic networks and functional structures between genes by using Bayesian networks and nonparametric regression. Pac. Symp. Biocomput. **7**, 175–186 (2002)
6. G Stolovitzky, RJ Prill, A Califano, Lessons from the DREAM2 challenges. Ann. N Y Acad. Sci. **1158**(1), 159–195 (2009)
7. P Mendes, W Sha, K Ye, Artificial gene networks for objective comparison of analysis algorithms. Bioinformatics **19**(2), 122–129 (2003)
8. D Marbach, T Schaffter, C Mattiussi, D Floreano, Generating realistic in silico gene networks for performance assessment of reverse engineering methods. J. Comput. Biol. **16**(2), 229–239 (2009)
9. M Zou, SD Conzen, A new dynamic Bayesian network (DBN) approach for identifying gene regulatory networks from time course microarray data. Bioinformatics **21**(1), 71–79 (2005)
10. H Yu, NM Luscombe, J Qian, M Gerstein, Genomic analysis of gene expression relationships in transcriptional regulatory networks. Trends Genet. **19**, 422–427 (2003)
11. G Stolovitzky, D Monroe, A Califano, Dialogue on reverse-engineering assessment and methods: the dream of high-throughput pathway inference. Ann. N Y Acad. Sci. **1115**, 1–22 (2007)

12. I Cantone, L Marucci, F Iorio, MA Ricci, V Belcastro, M Bansal, S Santini, MD Bernardo, DD Bernardo, MP Cosma, A yeast synthetic network for in vivo assessment of reverse-engineering and modeling approaches. Cell **137**, 172–181 (2009)

13. D Marbach, RJ Prill, T Schaffter, C Mattiussi, D Floreano, G Stolovitzky, Revealing strengths and weaknesses of methods for gene network inference. Proc. Natl. Acad. Sci. U S A **107**(14), 6286–6291 (2010)

14. RJ Prill, D Marbach, J Saez-Rodriguez, PK Sorger, LG Alexopoulos, X Xue, ND Clarke, G Altan-Bonnet, G Stolovitzky, Towards a rigorous assessment of systems biology models: the DREAM3 challenges. PLoS One **5**(2), e9202 (2010)

15. H Lähdesmäki, S Hautaniemi, I Shmulevich, O Yli-Harja, Relationships between probabilistic Boolean networks and dynamic Bayesian networks as models of gene regulatory networks. Signal Process **86**(4), 814–834 (2006)

16. N Friedman, K Murphy, S Russell, Learning the structure of dynamic probabilistic networks, in *Proceedings of the Fourteenth Conference on Uncertainty in Artificial Intelligence (UAI)*, 1998, pp. 139–147

17. K Murphy, *Dynamic Bayesian networks: representation, inference and learning* (PhD Dissertation, University of California, Berkeley, 2002)

18. K Murphy, S Mian, *Modeling gene expression data using dynamic Bayesian networks* (Technical report (Computer Science Division, University of California, Berkeley, CA, 1999)

11

In vitro detection of adrenocorticotropic hormone levels by fluorescence correlation spectroscopy immunoassay for mathematical modeling of glucocorticoid-mediated feedback mechanisms

Martin Gerald Puchinger[1*], Clemens Alexander Zarzer[2], Philipp Kügler[2], Erwin Gaubitzer[1] and Gottfried Köhler[1]

Abstract

Performing quantitative, highly sensitive measurements at a single molecule level is often necessary to address specific issues related to complex molecular and biochemical systems. For that purpose, we present a technique exploiting both the flexibility of immunoassays as well as the low operating costs and high throughput rates of the fluorescence correlation spectroscopy (FCS) method. That way we have established a quantitative measurement technique providing accurate and flexibly time resolved data of single molecules. Nanomolar changes in adrenocorticotropic hormone (ACTH) levels have been detected in a short time-frame that are caused by fast feedback actions in AtT-20 anterior pituitary glands *in vitro*. Especially with respect to clinical diagnostic or mathematical modeling this improved FCS setup may be of high relevance in order to accurately quantify the amounts of peptide hormones—such as ACTH—as well as signaling molecules, transcription factors, etc., being involved in intra- and extracellular reaction networks.

Keywords: ACTH, FCS, AtT-20, Cortisol, CRH, Glucocorticoid membrane receptor, ODE model, Parameter identification

Introduction

Adrenocorticotropic hormone (ACTH) is a 39-amino acid long straight-chain peptide hormone (4.5 kDa) that is derived from a 266-amino acid precursor pro-opiomelanocortin. It is secreted by the anterior pituitary gland and is considered one of the major stress hormones within the hypothalamic–pituitary–adrenal (HPA)-axis system: The hypothalamus secrets corticotrophin-releasing hormone (CRH), which stimulates the release of ACTH in the corticotrophic anterior pituitary gland [1]. Consequently, ACTH causes the production of cortisol in the adrenal glands. However, beside corticotrophic feedback actions several other feedback controls on the metabolomic or genomic level provide a complex and multifaceted system. One of the most prominent and

well-studied feedback controls is the down-regulation of ACTH production by cortisol. The down-regulation is mediated via two feedback mechanisms working on a genomic and non-genomic levels (see Figure 1). Hence, we observe fast (within seconds to minutes) and slow (after several hours) negative feedback actions in response to the exposure with cortisol [2]. These feedback mechanisms are still subject of research and particularly their interplay is not fully understood. Hence, as ACTH represents the main response in regard to this glucocorticoid feedback, an accurate detection of *in vitro* extracellular ACTH concentration is of high relevance.

The fluorescence correlation spectroscopy (FCS) has proven to be a powerful tool for studying supramolecular associations [3,4], DNA hybridization reactions [5], and detecting single molecule concentrations [6,7]. Due to its high sensitivity, short analysis time and small sample volume requirements FCS have become a valuable tool in molecular biology.

* Correspondence: martin.puchinger@univie.ac.at
[1]Department of Structural and Computational Biology, Max F. Perutz Laboratories (MFPL), University of Vienna, Campus-Vienna-Biocenter 5, Vienna 1030, Austria
Full list of author information is available at the end of the article

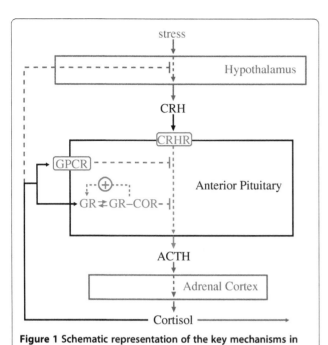

Figure 1 Schematic representation of the key mechanisms in HPA-axis glucocorticoid-mediated feedback actions. Two membrane receptors (GPCR, CRHR) mediate extracellular concentrations of cortisol and CRH, inhibiting and stimulating the secretion of ACTH, respectively. In response to a variety of external stressors, CRH is released from the hypothalamus and stimulates the anterior pituitary via CRH-receptors (CRHR) to immediately secrete ACTH, which in turn stimulates the adrenal cortex to synthesize and release cortisol. Thereby non-genomic signaling mechanisms mediate tethering and fusion of ACTH vesicles to the plasma membrane of corticotrophic cells and the fast secretion of ACTH molecules into the extracellular space within minutes after CRH administration. Whereas G-protein-coupled receptors (GPCR) are thought to mediate fast negative feedback actions of glucocorticoids (e.g., cortisol) which downregulate (CRH-induced) ACTH secretion in the anterior pituitary gland. The cytoplasmic organelles such as endoplasmic reticulum, Golgi apparatus, or vesicles are neglected for simplicity.

In this article, we present an improved FCS setup to detect nanomolar changes of peptides *in vitro* by combining the fast FCS technique [8] with the highly specific routines of an immunoassay. We exemplify this procedure by means of the *in vitro* measurement of the ACTH peptide secretion from AtT-20 mouse pituitary cells. Particularly, we use a labeled monoclonal antiACTH antibody (specific for the *N*-terminal epitope on the ACTH peptide) to capture the ACTH molecule, making it visible for the FCS. However, in order to detect low molecular weight peptides such as ACTH, the binding of a second unlabeled monoclonal antiACTH antibody to the C-terminal site of the ACTH peptide is necessary in order to cause a significant change in the diffusion time between the free labeled antibody and the mAb(*N*)-ACTH-mAb(*C*) immunocomplex. By measuring this discrepancy in the FCS, the concentration of the target peptide can accurately be determined.

Materials and methods

Cell culture

The used AtT-20 cells (ATCC no. CCL-89) were purchased from the American Type Culture Collection (ATCC, Manassas, USA) and passaged at a subcultivation ratio of 1:4 every 5 days. Cells were seeded onto polystyrene 24-well tissue culture plates (Nalge Nunc International, Japan) at a density of 1.0×10^4 cells/ml, grown in Dulbecco's Modified Eagle's Medium (Sigma-Aldrich Inc., St. Louis, USA) supplemented with 10% fetal bovine serum, 1.5 g/l sodium bicarbonate, 10 Units/ml penicillin, and 10 µg/ml streptomycin, and maintained in an incubator (HERAcell®, Thermo Scientific, USA) at 37°C, 6% CO_2 and 95% relative humidity. After 92 and 114 h of cell growing, AtT-20 cells were exposed to doses of 10 nM CRH and up to 100 nM cortisol (both from Sigma-Aldrich Inc.) for 1 min to 1 h. The supernatant was carefully removed from the cell layer and centrifuged (800 × g, 37°C, 10 min).

FCS

FCS measurements were performed on a Confocor spectrofluorimeter (Carl Zeiss-Evotec, Jena, Germany) equipped with an air-cooled 488 nm Argon-laser (LASOS Lasertechnik GmbH, Jena, Germany) and a water immersion objective (C-Apochromat 63 × /1.2 W Korr). The intensity of the laser was set to 70 µW. Intensity fluctuations were recorded by an avalanche photodiode (SPCM-CD 3017) in photon counting mode, autocorrelated with a hardware correlator (ALV 5000, ALV, Langen, Germany), and analyzed with the *FCS ACCESS* (Carl Zeiss-Evotec) software package using a multicomponent fit model (see Figure 2).

Focus control and pinhole adjustment

A drop of the organic fluorescent dye Rhodamine 6 G (diluted 1:200) was used to automatically position the chambered coverglass (Nalge Nunc International, Japan) in focus of the confocal optics of the spectrofluorimeter by a scanning procedure as well as to automatically adjust the pinhole to its correct position. The focus in *z*-direction was set 150 µm over the coverglass to record diffusions of fluorescent particles through the focal element in the drop of sample. The pinhole diameter was set to 35 µm.

Calibration of confocal volume

The confocal detection volume was determined by measuring the correlation time of a 10-nM solution of rhodamine 6 G in water with the known diffusion coefficient D of 2.8×10^{-6} cm^2/s, employing the relationship $D = r^2/(4\tau_D)$ and resulting in a confocal volume element of 0.17 µm in radian and 0.88 µm in axial dimension. In addition, DyLight488-labeled monoclonal antibody dilution series with known concentrations (ranging from 1

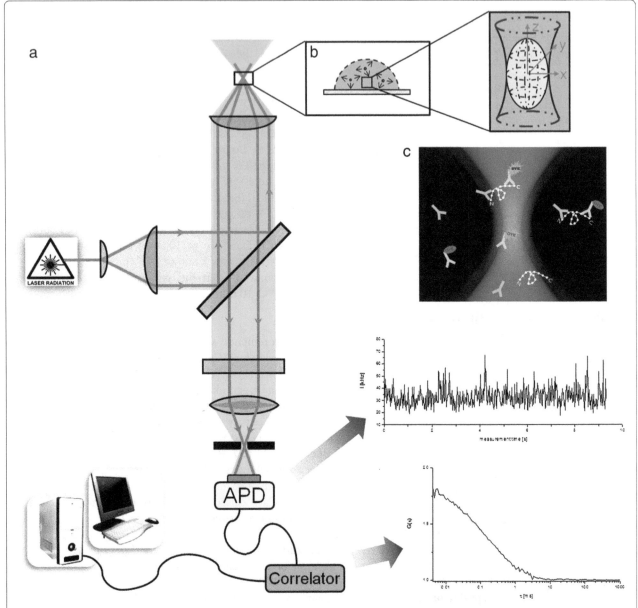

Figure 2 FCS principle and instrumentation. In the confocal setup **(a)** of a single-color FCS, the excitation Argon-laser light is directed by a dichroic mirror into a water immersion objective that focuses the light in a calibrated volume inside the sample **(a)**. Changes in diffusion behavior of fluorescent molecules entering and leaving the detection volume are monitored **(a)**. Thereby, each fluorescence signal is collected through the same objective and focused onto a pinhole, so that the laser beam waist inside the sample is imaged onto the pinhole aperture. The conjugation of the objective and the pinhole creates a spatial filter, which efficiently cuts the sampling volume to a diffraction limited size. After the pinhole, the fluorescence signal is collected directly by an Avalanche photodiode and processed into an autocorrelation function $G(\tau)$ to calculate single molecule concentrations.

to 80 nM) were measured and showed similar molarities in FCS. Confocal volume calibrations using rhodamine 6 G were carried out on each experimental day or after 3 h measurement time.

FCS immunoassay

60 nM antiACTH(N-term)-monoclonal IgG1 antibodies (Phoenix Pharmaceuticals Inc., Belmont, USA) and 60 nM-labeled antiACTH(C-term)-IgG1 antibodies (Fitzgerald Industries International, Concord, USA; labeled with DyLight488 from Pierce Biotechnology, Rockford, USA) were added in the cell-free supernatant and incubated (30°C, 15 min) to ensure a quick and absolute ACTH-capture of both monoclonal antibodies. Western blotting analysis and ELISA measurements prior to FCS showed no crossreactivity between both antibodies in absence of

ACTH. A drop (25 µl) of sample was pipetted on the chambered coverglass, excited with an 488-nm Ar-laser attenuated by an optical density filter (1.0–in. diameter), and the fluctuations in fluorescence intensity of the mAb (N)-ACTH-mAb(C) immunocomplex compared to the free labeled antibody were monitored in series of 50 measurements with identical setup (measurement time: 10 s; correlator scaling: 10 s) for each sample (see Figure 2).

Calculation

Statistical analysis of the autocorrelation function by a 2-component fitting procedure computationally distinguishes the labeled unbound antibody fraction from the desired ACTH-bound form (immunocomplex). The normalized autocorrelation function $G(\tau)$ describes the fluctuations of a signal $F(t)$ from the mean intensity at any time compared to fluctuations at any later time $F(t + \tau)$. It is given by

$$G(\tau) = \frac{\langle \delta F(t), \ \delta F(t + \tau) \rangle}{\langle F(t) \rangle^2},$$

where the angular brackets in the function represent the ensemble average, $\delta F(t)$ denotes the corresponding variance, and τ is known as the delay or correlation time interval over which the fluctuations are compared.

For a single diffusing species (a one-component model) in a Gaussian confocal volume, the autocorrelation function $G(\tau)$ is defined by [3]

$$G(\tau) = 1 + \frac{1}{N\left(1 + \frac{\tau}{\tau_D}\right)\sqrt{1 + \frac{\tau}{\left(\frac{z}{r}\right)^2 \tau_D}}},$$

where N is the particle number and τ_D the molecular diffusion time of the excited fluorophores moving in a three-dimensional confocal volume through an axial (z) to radial (r) dimension.

The molecular diffusion time for a one photon excitation is given by the following relationship to the diffusion coefficient D [cm²/s]

$$\tau_D = \frac{r^2}{4D}$$

The obtained autocorrelation functions were evaluated using a two-component model by fixing the diffusion time of the unbound labeled antibody fraction (τ_{D1}) which was achieved from one-component fitting procedure.

The analytical formula for the two-component model, which was successfully applied in a previous work [3], was used in a modified form and is given by

$$G(\tau) = 1 + \frac{1}{N'}[(1 - Y)g_{D1}(\tau) + Yg_{D2}(\tau)]$$

with $N' = N_1 + N_2$

$$g(\tau) = \left(1 + \frac{\tau}{\tau_D}\right)^{-1}\left(1 + \frac{\tau}{\left(\frac{z}{r}\right)^2 \tau_D^2}\right)^{-0.5}$$

This yields values of diffusion times (τ_{D1}, τ_{D2}) and of the related mole fractions Y and $(1 - Y)$ for the two components. Autocorrelation analysis was performed for a fixed structural parameter of 5 defining the ratio between the height and the width of the detection volume. This parameter was obtained from calibration with rhodamine 6 G in water. The fit model determines the average number of fluorescent molecules within the detection volume, and the characteristic diffusion times. Evaluations of the autocorrelation function of only labeled antibodies result in diffusion times of $\tau_1 = 220 \pm 8$ µs (mean $\pm$ t-student) through the confocal volume using a one-component fitting procedure. These results are in accordance to the diffusion time of the IgG-antibody (D of $3.7 \pm 0.2 \times 10^{-7}$ cm²/s) of 200 µs calculated by Stokes–Einstein relation. Formation of the immunocomplex results in a characteristic diffusion behavior of $\tau_2 = 483 \pm 83$ µs (mean $\pm$ t) through the confocal volume compared to freely labeled anti-ACTH IgG antibody in solution (τ_1 fixed to $\tau_1 = 220$ µs; see Figure 3).

As the amplitude of an autocorrelation function is inversely proportional to the average number of fluorescent particles within the confocal volume (V_{conf} of 5×10^{-16} l)

$$G(0) = \frac{1}{N_{D1,2}},$$

the absolute concentration of free labeled IgG antibodies (N_{D1}) and of the ACTH immune complexes (equal to number of ACTH molecules; $N_{D2} = N_{ACTH}$) can be obtained by

$$c_{ACTH} = \frac{N_{ACTH}}{6.023 \cdot 10^{23} \text{mol}^{-1} \cdot 5 \times 10^{-16} \text{l}}$$

$$= \frac{N_{ACTH}}{30.115 \times 10^7} \text{mol/l}$$

$$c_{IgG} = \frac{N_{IgG}}{30.115 \times 10^7} \text{mol/l}$$

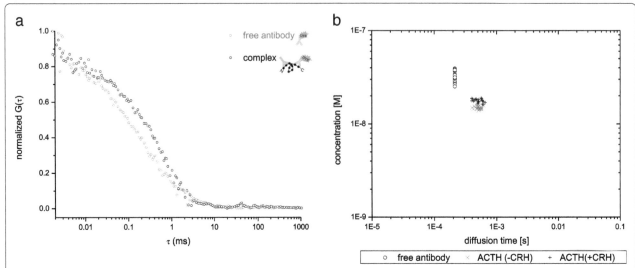

Figure 3 FCS studies of a single and two diffusion species. (a) The two autocorrelation functions were calculated from intensity fluctuations of the free antibody and that of the ACTH-bound ones. The shift of the autocorrelation curve (**a**, blue line) to the right indicates that the diffusion time of the ACTH-bound particles through the focus is higher than that of the free antibody. To eliminate the amount of unbound from the ACTH-bound forms in the sample, a two-component fit over the autocorrelated data points of the ACTH-bound form (**a**, blue line) was performed with a fixed diffusion time for the unbound antibodies (220 μs, previously calculated with a one-component fit to obtain the average diffusion time of free unbound fluorescent antibodies) and a variable one for quantifying different ACTH concentrations. (**b**) A double-logarithmic plot of calculated concentrations versus related diffusion times over 50 measurements shows the accuracy of the results obtained by FCS for different ACTH concentrations.

Results

Dose response relation of CRH and cortisol to ACTH secretion

The experimental results show a basal ACTH secretion which is not affected by extracellular CRH and cortisol signals (see Figure 4) and thus it seems not to be modulated by the main feedback controls. Moreover, our data feature a strong ACTH response (17.427 ± 0.422 nM) to an extracellular dose of 10 nM CRH over 22 h (compared to that of 5 and 36 nM), indicating an increased ACTH secretion in the AtT-20 cells *in vitro*. In addition to an extracellular dose of 10-nM CRH, an

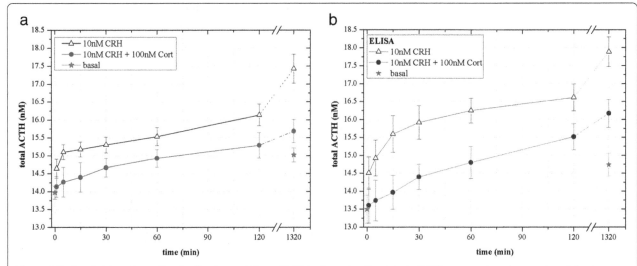

Figure 4 Fast and delayed negative feedback regulation of ACTH release *in vitro*. A typical HPA response to a strong extracellular stress signal (10-nM CRH) is simulated in AtT-20 pituitaries *in vitro* by adding 100-nM cortisol. Already minutes after cortisol incubation an inhibition and a delay of extracellular ACTH secretion is detectable (blue circular data points), which is supposed to be caused by a fast negative feedback mechanism. Long-term inhibitory effects of cortisol to ACTH secretion (interrupted line) were not analyzed. FCS datasets (**a**) are consistent with ELISA control measurements (**b**). Deviations calculated by the *t*-test distribution, α = 0.1.

administration of 50 nM cortisol partly inhibited the stimulated ACTH secretion after 22 h compared to that in absence of cortisol. A maximal inhibition of the ACTH release was achieved by adding 100-nM cortisol leading to ACTH levels close to the basal one (Table 1).

Fast feedback regulation of ACTH release

In order to demonstrate the capabilities of the method we focused on the fast negative feedback control by cortisol. Due to the fast sampling and the low sample volume we were able to detect significant differences in ACTH response within 5–15 min after CRH and/or cortisol incubation (see Figure 4).

Validation of FCS results

FCS and immunoassays (with chemiluminescent, fluorescent, or HRPO signals) are both known as quite sensitive detection techniques. Thus, a two-site ELISA (MDBioscience, Switzerland) is used to validate the data obtained by FCS. Table 2 and Figure 4 show that the ELISA results are consistent with the detected FCS datasets.

Mathematical modeling of feedback mechanisms

The improved setup for the FCS method is particularly suitable for experiments which have to be conducted repeatedly and demand a high (quantitative) accuracy of the data. A central motivation to develop such a technique comes from a mathematical modeling task initiated by the research presented in [9]. We are interested in the interplay of the genomic and non-genomic negative feedback of cortisol on the secretion of ACTH and its effect on the dynamics of the HPA-axis. This research goal demands to model both intracellular mechanisms as well as interactions of the different glands. This cannot be achieved in full detail. Consequently, we concentrated on the main feedback mechanisms related to the anterior pituitary gland and the basic controls between the hypothalamus and the adrenal

Table 2 Validation of FCS results

Time (min)	ACTH (FCS)		ACTH (ELISA)	
	% change[a]	% dev	% change to FCS	% dev
Basal				
0	0.00	±1.28	−3.39	±2.91
1320	+7.48	± 1.29	−1.86	±2.16
+10 nM CRH				
1	+4.79	±1.82	−0.91	±3.11
5	+8.08	±1.39	−1.16	±3.35
15	+8.62	±1.36	+2.77	±3.29
30	+9.51	±1.43	+4.05	±2.96
60	+11.18	±1.62	+4.61	±2.12
120	+15.50	±1.86	+2.97	±2.27
1320	+24.74	±2.32	+2.63	±2.31
+10 nM CRH + 100 nM cortisol				
1	+1.16	±2.03	−3.77	±3.58
5	+2.08	±2.88	−3.68	±4.12
15	+3.02	±2.85	−2.97	±3.38
30	+4.94	±1.75	−1.80	±2.44
60	+6.80	±1.63	−0.81	±3.01
120	+9.40	±2.31	+1.52	±2.33
1320	+12.23	±2.07	+3.10	±2.41

Validation of FCS results by ELISA measurements. The % difference in ACTH concentrations obtained from ELISA measurements refers to the FCS dataset of the same sample (in the same row in the table).
[a]The temporal % change of ACTH concentration to the basal ACTH-level of 13.9709 nM (mean value) detected by FCS. Deviations calculated by the t-test distribution, $\alpha = 0.1$.

glands. This approach of bridging several levels of complexity eventually needs validation by experimental data. In that regard the measurement of the ACTH secretion in response to CRH and cortisol serves two goals. First of all the secretion of ACTH is targeted by the main feedback controls we focus on in our model and thus allows us at least a basic assessment of the model. And secondly, we introduce no bias concerning the overall dynamics of the HPA-axis, as we consider only the anterior pituitary cells in our *in vitro* experiment and thus have no interaction with other tissues or glands.

With respect to the modeling technique we followed an approach in [10] which also focused on the anterior pituitary cells. Figure 5 provides a sketch of the considered feedback controls and the used mathematical equations in [10]. In Figure 6, we provide a graphical outline of our model and the corresponding mathematical description as set of the ordinary differential equations. Our extended model follows the approach offered in [10] but in addition considers the fast non-genomic feedback mechanism via the glucocorticoid membrane receptor in the anterior pituitary cells (red-framed pathway). Moreover, the model includes the slow genomic

Table 1 *In vitro* studies in AtT-20s within 22 h

CRH (nM)	Cort (nM)	Cell population (cells/ml)	ACTH (nM)
0	0	205164 ± 12889	15.016 ± 0.201
5	0	335938 ± 20522	16.764 ± 0.593
10	**0**	324219 ± 23935	**17.427 ± 0.422**
36	0	302084 ± 28168	16.146 ± 0.564
54	0	237500 ± 15630	15.364 ± 0.575
10	50	312500 ± 28125	16.673 ± 0.467
10	**100**	298438 ± 20625	**15.679 ± 0.337**

Cell proliferation and ACTH response to various doses of extracellular CRH and cortisol within/over 22 h of incubation (114 h total incubation time). Optimal concentrations for CRH stimulation and cortisol inhibition of ACTH secretion were used for studying feedback regulation of ACTH release (bold values). Deviations calculated by the t-test distribution, $\alpha = 0.1$.

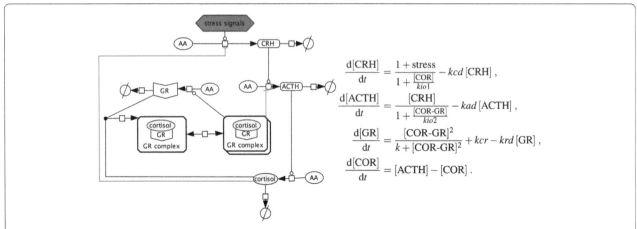

Figure 5 Parsimonious model of the HPA-axis. The figure shows a graphical outline and the corresponding mathematical equations of the parsimonious model as published in [10]. The focus of this model is the negative feedback of cortisol on the production of ACTH via an intracellular glucocorticoid receptor, which acts as a transcription factor in its dimerized form. Eventually, the model offers an intriguing explanation for the widely observed scenario of hypocortisolism.

feedback mechanism of cortisol (green-framed pathway) and CRH-mediated genomic and non-genomic effects (blue-framed pathway). To the best of the authors' knowledge the proposed model is the first one of the HPA-axis which incorporates central receptors. Consequently, it differs significantly in size and structure from most models present in literature, which focus on most prominent species cortisol, ACTH, CRH, and vasopressin (cf. [11-14]). Moreover, our model is novel in the

sense that we explicitly model an intracellular compartment and the nucleus. This allows us to take translocation processes into account and thus differ between genomic and non-genomic effects.

In a first attempt we used the model from [10] and tried to reproduce the data obtained by means of our FCS method. Figure 7 shows that if we consider only one of the conducted experiments, i.e., only a dosage of CRH or the scenario of adding CRH as well as cortisol, the model is

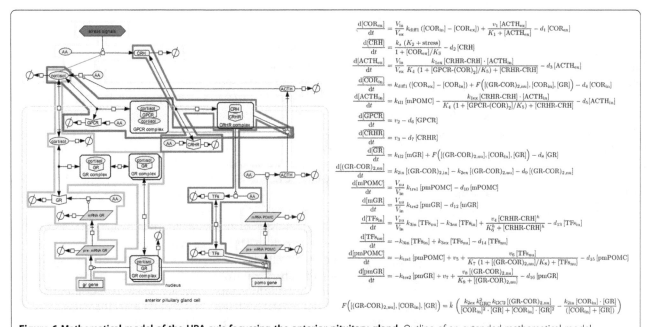

Figure 6 Mathematical model of the HPA-axis focussing the anterior pituitary gland. Outline of an extended mathematical model following the lines of the modeling approach in [10]. The image on the left-hand side provides an overview of the considered molecular mechanisms and feedback controls. In particular, it shows the three different modeled compartments, i.e., the extracellular space, the intracellular space of the pituitary gland cells, and their nucleus compartment. On the right-hand side, the equations of the ODE system are given. Based on the mathematical model from [10], these equations are deduced by introducing the different compartments and in particular two membrane receptors of the pituitary gland cells.

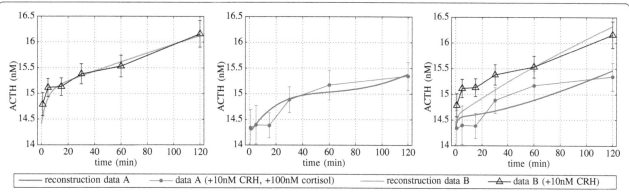

Figure 7 Fit of the experimental data by means of the parsimonious model from [10]. The figure shows the result of a numerical experiment for the obtained experimental data and the mathematical model as published in [10]. The first (left) plot shows the result of a parameter fit for the dataset without added cortisol. The second (middle) plot shows the reproduction of the ACTH response curve in the presence of CRH and cortisol. The last (right) plot presents the result when considering both experimental datasets at once. The poor quality of the obtained fit in the latter case indicates that the parsimonious model is not capable to reproduce the fast and slow dynamics related to the negative feedback via cortisol.

capable to reproduce the basic dynamics. However, we were not able to find any parameter set such that the parsimonious model is able to exhibit both scenarios. The parameter space was searched using the genetic algorithms from the MATLAB global optimization toolbox. In particular, we used different initial populations of about 10^4 to 10^5 elements. The objective functional was based on Tikhonov-type regularization functional (c.f. [9] for instance).

Figure 8 shows the data fit computed for our extended model. The parameter fit was computed by the Tikhonov regularization, where we used standard global and local optimization algorithms to minimize the objective functional. The extended model allows to correctly reproduce the observed ACTH response behavior. The fact that the model is capable to reproduce the experimental data indicates at least a feasible model and, particularly, supports

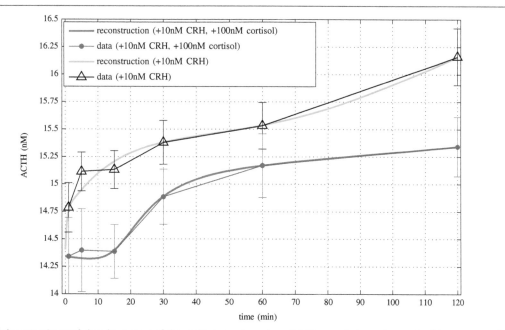

Figure 8 Fit of the experimental data by means of the multicompartment model. The graph shows the result of the parameter fitting for the extended mathematical model, including the membrane receptors for cortisol and CRH. The identified parameters allow to reproduce the observed dynamics in the two scenarios, i.e., with and without cortisol. Hence, by using different initial values for the ODE state variable both characteristic dynamics can be simulated with the same set of parameters. In particular, in the presence of cortisol the fast negative feedback can be reproduced, leading to the experimentally observed sigmoidal curve.

Table 3 FCS-immunoassay versus ELISA

Parameter	FCS-assay	ELISA
Sensitivity	μM to sub-nM	nM to sub-nM
Sample volume required	Approximately 20 μl	100 μl
Measurement time	Approximately 25 min	>2.5 h
Immunocomplex formation	In solution	On the surface
Washing steps required	No	Yes
Calibration curve required	Yes (confocal volume)	Yes
Detection mode	Size-based fluctuations in signal intensities	Changes in signal intensity

the underlying idea of distinguishing between the genomic and non-genomic feedback mechanisms. We emphasize that the present dataset is neither sufficient nor suited to identify the 'true' values of all model parameters. The conducted numerical experiment mainly serves to assess the overall behavior of the extended model, particularly in comparison with the parsimonious model as discussed in [10].

Conclusion

In 2005, Maier et al. [3] were able to provide evidence of a glucocorticoid receptor in the anterior pituitary cell membrane which may regulate fast response of anterior pituitary cells to cortisol. With our improved FCS setup it was possible to detect lowest changes in extracellular ACTH molarities (±0.3 nM) that arise from signaling of these activated G-protein coupled membrane receptors *in vitro* (see Figure 1). Even 5–15 min after cortisol administration (100 nM) we were able to monitor an inhibition of CRH-induced ACTH secretion by cortisol. Extracellular ACTH levels of 14.387 ± 0.428 nM compared to 15.131 ± 0.254 nM without addition of cortisol were measured. The fast inhibitory effects on CRH-induced ACTH secretion have become evident within at most 5 min after cortisol administration (see Figure 4). However, a detailed temporal restriction of fast and slower feedback actions on extracellular ACTH secretion was not studied with this FCS setup so far, but our results suggested that immediate ACTH secretion which has occurred within minutes after cortisol treatment can only be caused by fast non-genomic feedback actions (see Figure 1) and not by genomic-slow feedback mechanisms which have been shown to occur after several hours [15].

FCS provides a highly flexible, easy-to-use assay format with very small sample volumes (approximately 20 μl), and increased throughput, as particle numbers can be measured directly after calibrating the confocal volume once, a major disadvantage of ELISAs which need

to be calibrated quite often. In addition, FCS makes it possible to extract complex signals from high background due to the different characteristic time scales over which signal and noise occur.

In conclusion, we have demonstrated that this improved FCS setup can be used for fast and sensitive detection of a specific peptide hormone *in vitro*. By means of the mentioned model system we established this solution-based single molecule detection technique as an alternative to the commonly used approaches, such as ELISAs (with fluorescent, chemiluminescent, or HRPO signal), with respect to rapidity and sensitivity (Table 3). It was possible to even detect nanomolar changes in ACTH secretion with deviations of only 0.2–0.7 nM approximately in response to an extracellular stress signal over a short period of time. The quality of the data obtained by FCS allowed to study fast feedback mechanisms in the HPA-axis regulatory system *in vitro* and allowed to support the development of a mathematical model of that HPA-axis network. As opposed to [10] our model takes both the genomic and non-genomic feedbacks mechanisms into account. As a result it is able to feature both ACTH response curves with a single set of model parameters.

Abbreviations

ACTH: Adrenocorticotropic hormone; CRH: Corticotrophin-releasing hormone; CRHR: CRH-receptor; ELISA: Enzyme-linked immunosorbent assay; FCS: Fluorescence correlation spectroscopy; GPCR: G-protein-coupled receptor; GR: Glucocorticoid receptor; HPA: Hypothalamic–pituitary–adrenal; mAb: Monoclonal antibody; POMC: Pro-opiomelanocortin; TF: Transcription factor.

Competing interests

The authors declare that they have no competing interests.

Acknowledgments

This study was supported by the Vienna Science and Technology Fund (WWTF) Grant no. MA07-030.

Author details

[1]Department of Structural and Computational Biology, Max F. Perutz Laboratories (MFPL), University of Vienna, Campus-Vienna-Biocenter 5, Vienna 1030, Austria. [2]Johann Radon Institute for Computational and Applied Mathematics (RICAM), Austrian Academy of Sciences, Altenbergerstr. 69, Linz 4040, Austria.

References

1. JC Buckingham, HC Christian, GE Gillies, JG Philip, AD Taylor, in *The Physiology of Immunity*, ed. by M.D. Kendall, J.A. Marsh (CRC Press, USA, 1996), p. 331
2. B Hinz, R Hirschelmann, Rapid non-genomic feedback effects of glucocorticoids and CRF-induced ACTH secretion in rats. Pharm. Res. **17**, 1273–1277 (2000). doi:10.1023/A:1026499604848
3. C Maier, D Rünzler, J Schindelar, G Grabner, W Waldhäusl, G Köhler, A Luger, G-protein-coupled glucocorticoid receptors on the pituitary cell membrane. J. Cell. Sci. **118**, 3353–3361 (2005). doi:10.1242/jcs.02462
4. J Wruss, D Rünzler, C Steiger, P Chiba, G Köhler, D Blaas, Attachment of VLDL receptors to an icosahedral virus along the 5-fold symmetry axis: multiple binding modes evidenced by fluorescence correlation

spectroscopy. Biochemistry **46**(21), 6331–6339 (2007). doi:10.1021/bi700262w

5. JC Politz, ES Browne, DE Wolf, T Pederson, Intranuclear diffusion and hybridization state of oligonucleotides measured by fluorescence correlation spectroscopy in living cells. Proc. Natl Acad. Sci. USA **95**, 6043–6048 (1998). doi:10.1073/pnas.95.11.6043

6. H Glauner, IR Ruttekolk, K Hansen, B Steemers, YD Chung, F Becker, S Hannus, R Brock, Simultaneous detection of intracellular target and off-target binding of small molecule cancer drugs at nanomolar concentrations. Br. J. Pharmacol. **160**, 958–970 (2010). doi:10.1111/j.1476-5381.2010.00732.x

7. L Tang, C Dong, J Ren, Highly sensitive homogenous immunoassay of cancer biomarker using silver nanoparticles enhanced fluorescence correlation spectroscopy. Talanta **81**, 1560–1567 (2010). doi:10.1016/j.talanta.2010.03.002

8. K Bacia, P Schwille, Fluorescence correlation spectroscopy. Methods Mol. Biol. **398**, 73–84 (2007). doi:10.1007/978-1-59745-513-8_7

9. HW Engl, C Flamm, P Kügler, J Lu, S Müller, P Schuster, Inverse problems in systems biology. Inverse Problems **25**, 123014 (2009). doi:10.1088/0266-5611/25/12/123014

10. S Gupta, E Aslakson, BM Gurbaxani, SD Vernon, Inclusion of the glucocorticoid receptor in a hypothalamic pituitary adrenal axis model reveals bistability. Theor. Biol. Med. Model **4**(8) (2007). doi:10.1186/1742-4682-4-8

11. V Kyrylov, LA Severyanova, A Vieira, Modeling robust oscillatory behavior of the hypothalamic-pituitary-adrenal axis. IEEE Trans. Biomed. Eng. **52**(12), 1977–1983 (2005)

12. G Li, B Liu, Y Liu, A dynamical model of the pulsatile secretion of the hypothalamo-pituitary-thyroid axis. Biosystems **35**(1), 83–92 (1995)

13. BZ Liu, JH Peng, YC Sun, YW Liu, A comprehensive dynamical model of pulsatile secretion of the hypothalamo-pituitary-gonadal axis in man. Comput. Biol. Med. **27**(6), 507–513 (1997)

14. D Savic, S Jelic, A mathematical model of the hypothalamo-pituitary-adrenocortical system and its stability analysis. Chaos Solitons Fract. **26**, 427–436 (2005)

15. O Wang, JA Majzoub, in *The Pituitary*, ed. by M. Shlomo (Elsevier, Amsterdam, 2011), p. 68

12

40-Hz ASSR fusion classification system for observing sleep patterns

Gulzar A Khuwaja[*], Sahar Javaher Haghighi and Dimitrios Hatzinakos

Abstract

This paper presents a fusion-based neural network (NN) classification algorithm for 40-Hz auditory steady state response (ASSR) ensemble averaged signals which were recorded from eight human subjects for observing sleep patterns (wakefulness W_0 and deep sleep N_3 or slow wave sleep SWS). In SWS, sensitivity to pain is the lowest relative to other sleep stages and arousal needs stronger stimuli. 40-Hz ASSR signals were extracted by averaging over 900 sweeps on a 30-s window. Signals generated during N_3 deep sleep state show similarities to those produced when general anesthesia is given to patients during clinical surgery. Our experimental results show that the automatic classification system used identifies sleep states with an accuracy rate of 100% when the training and test signals come from the same subjects while its accuracy is reduced to 97.6%, on average, when signals are used from different training and test subjects. Our results may lead to future classification of consciousness and wakefulness of patients with 40-Hz ASSR for observing the depth and effects of general anesthesia (DGA).

Keywords: Adaptive classification; Observing sleep patterns; Features-level fusion; ASSR extraction; Depth of general anesthesia (DGA)

1 Introduction

The manual scoring of sleep patterns is a time-consuming process, consisting of the determination of sleep states using an electroencephalograph (EEG) signal. Automatic classification has been studied in sleep scoring extensively [1-3] and is considered an important tool in biomedical research. Although good results have been achieved using EEG, the classification of human EEG signals continues to be a difficult problem due to the high-dimensional and noisy nature of EEG data [4].

Auditory steady state response (ASSR) is a brain auditory evoked potential (AEP) produced with a periodic stimuli with a 40-Hz repetition rate. AEP is produced as a result of electrical changes in the ear and brain of a normally hearing person in response to acoustic stimuli. An AEP signal shows how neural information propagates from the acoustic nerves in the ear to the cortex [5]. Specifically, AEP signals are extracted from EEG [6,7]. The auditory stimuli are either the repeated clicks or tone bursts that vary in frequency and rise time. If the stimulus lasts long enough to get the response to its

steady state, then the signal is called ASSR [6]. AEP and ASSR signals are mainly used as audiology tools for predicting the hearing threshold and sensitivity of an individual.

In 1950, the first clear approach to distinguish the evoked response from background EEG was made by Dawson [8]. First AEPs were generated by averaging the EEG response by Geisler et al. [9] in 1958. Later in 1980s, the 40-Hz ASSR was described by Galambos et al. [10]. An ASSR signal is called a 40-Hz response when the stimulus has a repetition rate of around 40 Hz. The amplitude of AEP signal is much smaller than the amplitude of EEG signal, hence extracting the AEP from the background EEG is a challenging process that involves noise cancelation techniques. AEP is divided into three main parts, namely, auditory brain stem response (ABR), mid-latency AEP (MLAEP), and late latency AEP (LLAEP) [5,11-13]. Figure 1 shows an AEP signal.

The ASSR is greatly affected by the stimuli modulation rate and is phase locked and follows the modulated envelope of the stimulus [14]. Different stimulus rates result in stimulation of different portions of the auditory nerves and hence produce different ASSRs. Specifically,

* Correspondence: gulzar.khuwaja@utoronto.ca
Department of Electrical and Computer Engineering, University of Toronto, 40 St. George Street, Toronto ON M5S 2E4, Canada

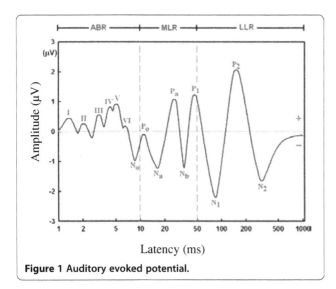

Figure 1 Auditory evoked potential.

ASSRs stimulated with stimuli of lower than 20 Hz reflect the activity of LLAEP generators. ASSRs stimulated with stimuli of 20 to 60 Hz are generated by the same generators as MLAEP generators, while those stimulated with stimuli of above 60 Hz are generated by ABR generators [14,15].

Galambos et al. [10] demonstrated that when stimuli presented at the rates of 30 to 50 Hz, the amplitude of the response was two to three times greater than the amplitude of the transient MLAEP in response to stimulus presented at 10 Hz. A 40-Hz response, like that produced by MLAEP has small inter- and intra-subjective variations [5,16], but it is strongly influenced by the subject's state of arousal [8]. Correspondingly, the amplitude in a 40-Hz response varies by the subject's level of arousal [10,14,17,18] and consciousness [19,20]. A 40-Hz response can be used as a measure of depth of general anesthesia [20-24].

Preliminary classification results of this research work have been published using linear discriminant analysis (LDA) and quadratic discriminant analysis (QDA) classifiers [25]. In this work, the average error rate for training and testing with the same subject is 1.12% with LDA and 1.66% with QDA. LDA has an acceptable error rate of 2.57% but the QDA error rate increases to 17.43% for six subjects. In other situations, the classifiers are trained with ASSRs from all subjects except for the subject whose ASSRs is to be classified. The average error rate over all subjects in this case is 5.91% with LDA and 20.69% with QDA.

Neural networks (NNs) are fundamentally analog, non-programmed data processing structures [26]. The networks are comprised of processing elements, each of which has a set of inputs, a set of weights, and one output. Inputs are multiplied by their weights and summed. The output is computed as a non-linear function of the summation. They offer fine-grained parallelism and exhibit fault tolerance. One advantage of any NN, which performs a classification task, is that it will learn its own coarse-grained features, thus does not require precise locations to form any part of an input set [27].

Classification of signal patterns is the most common NN applications. It has been demonstrated with artificial as well as natural data [28-32] that the learning vector quantization (LVQ) methods [31-34] constitute a very viable alternative to the more traditional classification approaches. LVQ classification accuracy is as good as other NN algorithms or better, whereas because of the very simple computations are applied, the learning and classification speed can be considerably higher as compared to other NN algorithms [35]. Also, LVQ methods are very easy to use.

Additionally, support vector machine (SVM) classification is incorporated. SVMs are supervised learning models with associated learning algorithms that analyze data and recognize patterns used for classification and regression analysis. Given a set of training examples, each marked as belonging to one of two categories, an SVM training algorithm builds a model that assigns new examples into one category or the other, making it a non-probabilistic binary linear classifier.

This research focuses on a fusion-based NN system classification of 40-Hz ASSR signals recorded from eight subjects used in observing sleep patterns in humans. The purpose of this work is threefold: a) to generate an automatic classification of sleep patterns (wakefulness W_0 and deep sleep N_3) based on an adaptive LVQ-NN and SVM with 40-Hz ASSR input signals, b) to develop a features-level fusion approach for combining a 40-Hz ASSR ensemble averaged sweep signals generated from two separate electrodes/channels, and c) to classify sleep patterns with the resultant ASSR sweep signals to enhance the decision confidence level.

The remainder of this paper is organized as follows: a view of previous related work is given in Section 2. Section 3 describes various stages of database acquisition from eight human subjects during sleep cycles. This is followed by a description of data extraction in the form of an ASSR ensemble of averaged sweep signals from EEG generated for classification. In Section 4, the overview of the algorithm including the proposed features-level fusion approach based on an adaptive LVQ-NN architecture is presented. The empirical results are discussed in Section 5. Finally, in Section 6, the paper is concluded.

2 Previous work

The most common physiological signal used for sleep discrimination in clinical settings is the recording of brain activity with an EEG [36]. One of the important uses of observing sleep patterns of subjects at home is early detection of sleep disorders resulting in prompt intervention and reduced health care costs [37]. In 1986, Jarger et al. [18] studied ten subjects in three stages: awake, stage 1, and stage 2 of sleep. The 40-Hz ASSR signal was generated by averaging over 128 sweeps. Amplitude and phase of the 40-Hz component of the fast Fourier transform of the signal was considered. They observed that while sleeping affects the amplitude, phase coherency remains unaffected by the level of subject arousal. A fuzzy logic approach to the classification of human sleep using EEG data is presented in [38]. In this approach, frequency and amplitude information from an epoch of the EEG signal are extracted into a vector that is then compared to previously taught vectors representing the canonical features of six stages: wakefulness, rapid eye movement (REM) sleep, and four non-REM sleep stages. For each stage, membership functions are calculated in each epoch. The stage with the maximum degree of membership is scored and classified. The system is implemented in software using the C programming language. Analysis of about 1,101 epochs of the EEG data yielded an overall agreement of 77% between the program and a human scorer.

Suzuki et al. [39] recorded 40-Hz ASSR signals from 12 subjects with normal hearing in awake and stage 2 of sleep. They compared the 40-Hz recorded SSR with synthesized SSR signals generated from superimposing the recorded ABR and middle latency response (MLR) signals. Required signal-to-noise ratio (SNR) reduction for the 40-Hz ASSR signals was achieved by averaging over 2,048 sweeps. They observed that the amplitude of the 40-Hz ASSR signal in awake state is twice as large as in sleep state and that the synthesized 40-Hz ASSR cannot predict accurately this reduction in amplitude. Lewicke et al. [40] reliably determined sleep and wake states using only the electrocardiogram (ECG) of infants. The method was tested with simultaneous 8-h ECG and polysomnogram (PSG) determined sleep scores from 190 infants enrolled in the collaborative home infant monitoring evaluation (CHIME) study. LVQ neural network, multilayer perceptron (MLP) neural network, and SVMs were tested as the classifiers. After systematic rejection of difficult-to-classify segments, the models could achieve 85% to 87% correct classification while rejecting only 30% of the data.

To overcome the limitations of inter-subject variability, Kalrken and Floreano [41] suggested a novel online adaptation technique that updates the sleep/wake classifier in real time and evaluated the performance of a newly developed adaptive classification algorithm that was embedded on a wearable sleep/wake classification system called SleePic. Their proposed algorithm processed ECG and respiratory effort signals for the classification task and applied behavioral measurements (obtained from accelerometer and press button data) for the automatic adaptation task. When trained as a subject-independent classifier algorithm, the SleePic device was only able to correctly classify $74.94 \pm 6.76\%$ of the human rated sleep/wake data. By using the automatic adaptation method, the mean classification accuracy was improved to $92.98 \pm 3.19\%$. A subject-independent classifier based on activity data only showed a comparable accuracy of $90.44 \pm 3.57\%$.

Almazaydeh et al. [42] focused on an automated classification algorithm, which processed short duration epochs of the ECG data. The classification technique was based on SVM and had been trained and tested on sleep apnea recordings from subjects with and without OSA. The results showed that an automated classification system could recognize epochs of sleep disorders with a high accuracy of 96.5% or higher. Brignol et al. [43] proposed a phase space-based algorithm for automatic classification of sleep-wake states in humans using EEG data gathered over relatively short-time periods. The effectiveness of this approach was demonstrated through a series of experiments involving EEG data from seven healthy adult female subjects and was tested on epoch lengths ranging from 3 to 30-s. The performance of the phase space approach was compared to a two-dimensional state space approach using spectral power in two selected human-specific frequency bands. These powers were calculated by dividing integrated spectral amplitudes at selected human-specific frequency bands. The comparison demonstrated that the phase space approach gave better performance for the case of short as well as standard 30-s epoch lengths.

Majdi Bsoul et al. [44] developed a low-cost, real-time sleep apnea monitoring system called 'Apnea MedAssist' which was used for recognizing obstructive sleep apnea episodes with a high degree of accuracy for both home and clinical care applications. The fully automated system uses patient's single channel nocturnal ECG to extract feature sets and uses the support vector classifier (SVC) to detect apnea episodes. 'Apnea MedAssist' uses either the general adult subject-independent SVC model or subject-dependent SVC model and achieves a classification F-measure of 90% and a sensitivity of 96% for the subject-independent SVC. A two-stage procedure based on artificial neural networks for the automatic recognition of sleep spindles in a multi-channel electroencephalographic signal was introduced in [45]. Two different networks, i.e., a backpropagation multilayer perceptron and radial basis SVM, were proposed as the post-classifier and compared in terms of their classification performances. Visual evaluation, by two electroencephalographers (EEGers), of 19 channel EEG records of six subjects showed that the best performance was obtained with a radial basis SVM providing an average sensitivity of 94.6% and an average false detection rate of 4.0%.

3 Database acquisition and preprocessing

After ethics approval was obtained from the University of Toronto Research Ethics Office, subjects having no history of hearing loss or neurological problems were recruited by the research team. Written informed consent was obtained from all the subjects, and they were rewarded $100 for their participation. The stimulus, a wideband (700 to 3,000 Hz) chirp with 40.68 Hz rate, generated by Vivosonic Inc. Integrity™ V500 (Vivisonic Inc., Toronto, ON, Canada) was presented binaurally to both right and left ears using a Vivosonic Inc. ER-3A-ABR (Etymotic Research Inc., Elk Grove Village, IL, USA) insert earphone, loud enough to generate an ASSR but not too loud to cause discomfort to the participants. The stimulus has peaks at 60 dB HL and an equivalent sound pressure level and central frequency of 500 Hz with a sampling rate of 34.8 kHz. The device records EEG signals from 11 scalp sites of the international 10-20 system (Figure 2).

For our study, we used electrode sites F_z, C_z, $C_{3,4}$, $T_{3,4}$, $A_{1,2}$, and O_z. A reference electrode was used as the common electrode of all channels. A ground electrode was used to reduce the environmental noise, and a L_oC was used for recording eye movements, in order to make sleep scoring based on raw EEG signals easier. An electrode cap by Bio-Medical Instruments Inc. (Warren, MI, USA) was custom designed with ten recording electrodes and two leads for the ear clip electrodes. A pair of 3½ inch DIN style EEG silver ear clips was used. A 10 mm in diameter gold cup electrode was used for recording eye movements. We used the Nicolet™ EEGwireless 32 (Natus Medical Incorporated, Pleasanton, CA, USA) amplifier to record the EEG amplification. Two extra electrodes were connected from the Integrity™ device stimuli generator to channel 25 of the EEG amplifier for recording the stimuli together with other EEG channels.

The sampling frequency of the amplifier was $f_s = 12$ kHz, and all electrode impedances were below 5 kΩ.

After recording, the raw mixed ASSR and EEG signals were reviewed and scored with conventional sleep scoring methods to awake W_0 and three stages of sleep namely N_1, N_2, and N_3. Signals of the W_0 and N_3 stages were transferred to MATLAB for preprocessing. Frequencies below 20 Hz and above 100 Hz were filtered out with third-order Butterworth low-pass and high-pass filters; the signals from seven recorded channels were synchronized and segmented into 295 sample sweeps. The EEG amplifier has 12 kHz sampling frequency but the Integrity stimulus was sampled with a 38.4 kHz sampling rate. Hence, the cycles for the 40-Hz response were not whole numbers. We got around this by only including cycles with 295 samples. This resulted in throwing out some of the data. However, this did not pose an issue as the required time to acquire data was not essential to the task. In almost all cases in the literature, ensemble averaging is used for extracting a 40-Hz ASSR signal from background noise [23,24]. Assuming the recorded signal as:

$$x_i[n] = s_i[n] + r_i[n] \qquad (1)$$

where $x_i[n]$ is the ASSR in response to the ith sweep of the stimuli and $r_i[n]$ is the EEG and noise from other sources. Under the assumption that $s_i[n]$ is phase locked to the stimuli, noise $r_i[n]$ is zero mean, $E(r_i[n]) = 0$, has constant variance, $var(r_i) = \sigma^2$ and is uncorrelated from one sweep to another, $E(r_i[n]r_j[n-k]) = \rho_r[k]\delta(i-j)$ ensemble average is an unbiased estimator and increases the variance of the noise. We used weighted ensemble averaging to extract the ASSR signals. The weights were calculated according to the Kalman filter coefficients. Each 40-Hz ASSR signal is extracted by averaging over a

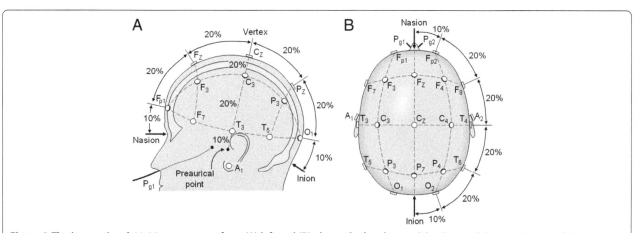

Figure 2 The international 10-20 system seen from (A) left and (B) above the head. A, ear lobe; C, central; Pg, nasopharyngeal; P, parietal; F, frontal; Fp, frontal polar; O, occipital. Source http://www.bem.fi/book/13/13.htm.

window of 900 sweeps. Each two adjacent windows have 83% overlap. After extracting 40-Hz ASSR signals, different features in time and frequency domain were compared in W_0 and N_3 stages in all seven channels. It is observed that peak-to-peak amplitude of 40-Hz ASSR decreases from W_0 to N_3. Figures 3 and 4 show five sweeps of ASSR during W_0 and N_3 for two subjects.

4 Overview of algorithm

4.1 LVQ classifier

The LVQ is a supervised classifier that was first studied by Kohonen [46]. To classify an input vector, it must be compared with all prototypes. The Euclidean distance metric is used to select the closest vector to the input vector. The input vector is classified to the same class as the nearest prototype.

The LVQ classifier (Figure 5) consists of an input layer, a hidden competitive layer, which learns to classify input vectors into subclasses and an output layer which transforms the competitive layer's classes into target classifications defined by the user. Only the winning neuron of the hidden layer has an output of one and other neurons have outputs of zero. The weight vectors of the hidden layer neurons are the prototypes, the number of which is usually fixed before training begins. The number of hidden neurons depends upon the complexity of the input-output relationship and significantly affects the results of classifier testing. Selection of the number of hidden neurons must be carefully made as it highly depends on the encompassed variability in the input patterns. Extensive experiments are performed to conduct the suitable number.

For a training set containing n input ensemble averaged sweeps of various subjects, each of these sweeps is labeled as being one of k classes which, in our case is 2, i.e., wakefulness and deep sleep states. The learning phase starts by initiating the weight vectors of neurons

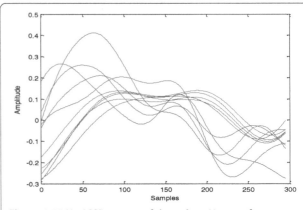

Figure 4 40-Hz ASSR sweeps of deep sleep N_3 state for subjects C (blue) and D (red) for channel Fz-A1A2.

in the hidden layer. Then, the input vectors are presented randomly to the network. For each input vector X_j, a winner neuron W_i is chosen to adjust its weight vector:

$$\left\| X_j - W_i \right\| \le \left\| X_j - W_k \right\|, \text{for all } k \ne i \tag{2}$$

The weight vector $W_i(t)$ is updated to the next step $t + 1$ as follows:

$$W_i(t + 1) = W_i(t) + \alpha\left(X_j - W_i(t)\right) \tag{3}$$

if X_j and W_i belong to the same class

$$W_i(t + 1) = W_i(t) - \alpha\left(X_j - W_i(t)\right) \tag{4}$$

if X_j and W_i belong to different classes where $0 \le \alpha \le 1$ is the learning rate, which may be kept constant during training or may be decreasing monotonically with time for better convergence [46]. Otherwise, the weights remain the same. The training algorithm is stopped after reaching a pre-specified error limit. During the test phase, the distance of an input vector to each processing element of the hidden layer is computed and again the nearest element is declared as the winner. This, in turn, fires one output neuron, signifying a particular class.

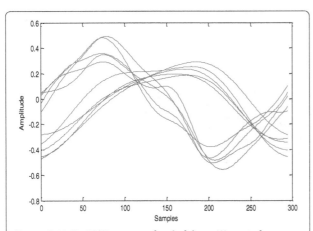

Figure 3 40-Hz ASSR sweeps of wakefulness W_0 state for subjects C (blue) and D (red) for channel Fz-A1A2.

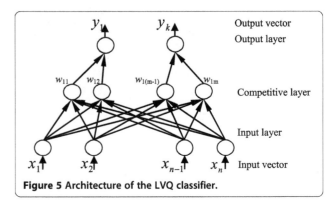

Figure 5 Architecture of the LVQ classifier.

4.2 Efficient LVQ models

Careful selection of a feature extraction method highly simplifies the design of the classifier subsystem. Extraction of appropriate features is one of the most important tasks for a classification system. As it is impractical to match a given input signal with all the signal templates stored in the system, it is necessary to find a compact set of features that can represent as much of the useful information present in the original data as possible. Selection of *good* features is a crucial step in the process since the next stage sees only these features and acts upon them [47].

A generic LVQ-NN consists of three layers. The first layer is the input layer, which consists of as many neurons as the number of input samples of the signal to be classified. The hidden layer size is problem dependent. The number of hidden layer neurons (HN) should be suitable to capture the knowledge of the problem domain. For example, when training a neural network to recognize signals which belong to a number of classes (NC), then NC hidden layer neurons are required. To capture a large range of input pattern variability, a large number of hidden layer neurons is necessary. But, the problem is calculating how large should be this required number of hidden layer neurons.

Visualizing the learned pattern of the hidden layer neurons, it is found that there are neurons with completely blurred patterns. These neurons are labeled blind neurons [48], as they do not see the signals that are clamped to the neurons of the input layer. Eliminating the blind neurons enhances the classifier performance, which is important for many biomedical applications. A classification model which considers reliability in the development of the model is very useful [40]. The compact LVQ network training algorithm for the classification system is illustrated in Figure 6. The algorithm based on efficient LVQ model parameters is as follows:

1. Select the network parameters:

   - ✓ Input layer size = Ensemble averaged sweep signal size (295 neurons)
   - ✓ Training set size = S (7 subjects) × 1,000 ensemble averaged sweeps

   - ✓ Number of classes (NC) = 2 (wakefulness = W_O and sleep = N_3)
   - ✓ Hidden layer neurons; 2(min) ≤ HN ≤ 28(max)
   - ✓ Learning rate (α) = 0.1
   - ✓ Set up the target vector which specifies the target class of each pattern in the training set
   - ✓ Display update rate = 100
   - ✓ Arrange the input patterns of the training set as one-dimensional columns in an array (P)
   - ✓ Number of training epochs (EP) = 2,500

2. Initialize an LVQ classifier: initialization of the weight matrix for competitive layer w_1 and linear layer w_2.
3. Start training of an LVQ classifier based on selected efficient model parameters.
4. Test the trained classifier on test sets and compute percentage of correct classification (pcc).
5. Get the best accuracy classification rate of wakefulness W_O and deep sleep N_3.
6. Exit.

4.3 Fusion at the features level

Multimodal classification systems help in achieving improved performance that may not be otherwise possible using a single classification system. However, an effective fusion scheme is necessary to combine the information presented by multiple domain experts. Pieces of evidence in a multi-classification system can be combined in many ways/levels and are generally divided into two categories [49], which we discuss below.

1. Before matching fusion. Fusion in this category integrates pieces of evidence before matching. This category fuses the information of multi-classification into the following levels.

   a) Sensor level. At this level, the digital input signal is the result of sensing the same characteristic with two or more sensors or electrodes. The raw data acquired from multiple sensors can be processed and integrated to generate new data from which features can be extracted. For

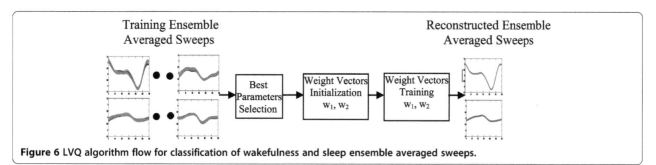

Figure 6 LVQ algorithm flow for classification of wakefulness and sleep ensemble averaged sweeps.

example, in the case of face biometrics, both 2-D texture information and 3-D depth (range) information (obtained using two different sensors) may be fused to generate a 3-D texture image of the face which could then be subjected to feature extraction and matching [50]. The combination of the input signals can provide noise cancelation, blind source separation [51], etc.

b) Feature level. The feature sets extracted from multiple data sources can be fused to create a new feature set to denote the identity. The geometric features of the hand, for example, may be augmented with the eigen coefficients of the face in order to construct a new high-dimensional feature vector [52]. A feature selection/transformation procedure may be adopted to produce a minimal feature set from the high-dimensional feature vector [53].

2. After matching fusion. Fusion in this category integrates pieces of evidence after matching. This includes the following levels.

a) Match score level. In this case, multiple classifiers output a set of match scores which are fused to generate a single scalar score [54]. As an example, the match scores generated by the face and hand modalities of a user may be combined via the simple sum rule in order to obtain a new match score which is then used to make the final decision [55].

b) Rank level. This type of fusion is relevant in identification systems where each classifier associates a rank with every enrolled identity (a higher rank indicating a good match). Thus, fusion entails consolidating the multiple ranks associated with an identity and determining a new rank that would aid in establishing the final decision.

c) Decision level. When each matcher outputs its own class label (i.e., accept or reject in a verification system, or the identity of a user in an identification system), a single class label can be obtained by employing techniques such as majority voting or behavior knowledge space [56]. In this last case, the Borda count method [57] can be used for combining the classifiers' outputs.

Integration at the feature level should provide better classification results than other levels of integration. This is because the features contain richer information about the input data than the matching score or the output decision of a classifier. However, integration at the feature level is difficult to achieve in practice due to the unknown relationship between the feature spaces of different classification systems, the concatenated feature vector with a very large dimensionality, the inaccessibility of the feature vectors of most commercial systems, and the computational cost to process the resultant vector.

In contrast, features-level fusion is easier to apply when the original characteristics are homogeneous. In this scenario, the single resultant feature vector needs to be calculated. We have adopted fusion at the features level to combine ASSR ensemble averaged sweeps of two electrode/channel vectors with the same dimensionality to concatenate into one vector which will also have the same dimensionality as the original vectors.

A fused signal is one that is created by concatenating two ASSR ensemble averaged sweeps from two channels/electrodes of one subject. Figure 7 shows a features-level fusion algorithm flow using the compact LVQ-NN algorithm discussed above. This approach is particularly suitable for this type of signal processing because the NN is able to assimilate features of both ASSR ensemble averaged sweeps during its training phase. This features combining mechanism is inherent in the algorithm of the designated LVQ network (295 input neurons, 1

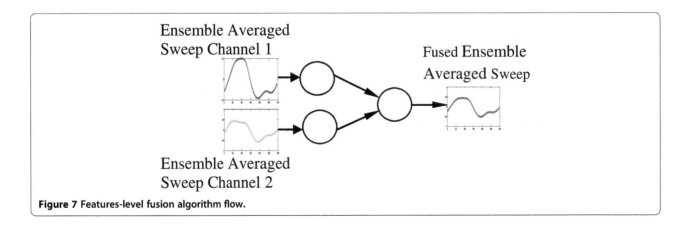

Figure 7 Features-level fusion algorithm flow.

hidden neuron, 1 output neuron, 0.01 learning rate, and 700 training epochs).

Moreover, combining of features depends on a small number of parameters. This offers the advantage that the parameters of the combining algorithm are very easy to set out, so as to produce a fused ASSR ensemble averaged sweep signal that is different enough from the original sweeps to be a new one, as well as to avoid the creation of an over noisy signal. The target for training the LVQ network on both ensemble averaged sweeps from two electrodes is set to be same, which forces the network to join the features of both signals. The resulting fused signal indicates that when one hidden layer neuron responds to two ensemble averaged sweeps, it generates a mix of these signals.

4.4 Hidden layer

Efficiency deals with the complexity of a learning machine in both space and time. The learning time must scale nicely with respect to the size of data sets. Since the size of the learning machine determines the memory required for implementation, a learning machine with a compact structure is preferred. Developing an adaptive learning system with a compact structure to achieve good performance is a challenging problem.

Experimental results [48] demonstrate that after convergence, most of the hidden layer neurons are redundant and do not evolve significantly and thus do not capture any data clusters. Typically, these neurons are initialized to points in the weight space that have relatively low overlap with the training data points. They play a little role in the pattern classification process, hence, may be eliminated without having significant effect on the detection accuracy rate.

Reducing the number of hidden layer neurons of NN to the product of subjects and classes, i.e., $S \times NC$ can help in increasing efficiency and performance of the whole system as many units not evolved properly during the training phase create confusion in the decision-making process. Thus, both the training time and the classification time are minimized.

4.5 SVM classifier

The SVM [58] is a supervised learning algorithm useful for recognizing subtle patterns in complex datasets. The algorithm performs discriminative classification, learning by example to predict the classifications of previously unseen data. The algorithm has been applied in domains as diverse as text categorization, image recognition, and hand-written digit recognition. We have used the algorithm presented in [59] available online [60].

5 Empirical results and discussion

The sleep patterns classification system is tested on 40-Hz ASSR ensemble averaged sweep signals recorded from eight human subjects [25]. A N_3 or SWS was chosen due to its similarities to the signals generated during the surgical level of anesthesia [61]. In SWS, sensitivity to pain is the lowest relative to other sleep stages and arousal needs stronger stimuli. SWS is the switching of thalamus from tonic mode in which somatosensory information is transmitted through the thalamus, to its bursting mode, in which somatosensory information are inhibited from transmitting [61].

The performance of a classification system is expressed by parameters that relate to decision accuracy. A decision made by a system is labeled as either a *true* decision or a *false* decision [62]. For each type of decision, there are two possibilities, correct and incorrect. Hence, there are a total of four possible outcomes: a true state (N_3 or W_0) is correctly classified, a true state is incorrectly classified, a false state is correctly classified, and a false state is incorrectly classified. The decisions 1 and 3 are correct while 2 and 4 are incorrect. The confidence associated with different decisions may be characterized by the true distribution and the false distribution of classifications and used to establish the following two error rates [49]:

- False accept rate (FAR). The probability that the system incorrectly matches the input pattern to a non-matching template in the database. It measures the percent of invalid inputs which are incorrectly accepted.
- False reject rate (FRR). The probability that the system fails to detect a match between the input pattern and a matching template in the database. It measures the percent of valid inputs which are incorrectly rejected.

The FAR and the FRR are dual of each other. A smaller FRR usually leads to a larger FAR, while a smaller FAR usually implies a larger FRR. Normally, the system performance requirement is specified in terms of FAR. The performance of a biometric system may also be expressed using equal error rate (EER). EER is defined as the rate at which both accept and reject errors are equal. In general, the device with the lowest EER is considered to be the most accurate device for classifying biometric signals.

Various experiments are performed to explore the best parameters for a sleep pattern classification system using a developed LVQ fusion scheme and SVM classifier. First of all, a set of 100 ASSR ensemble averaged sweeps (50 W_0 + 50 N_3) of one subject was trained and a new set of 100 ensemble averaged sweeps (50 W_0 + 50 N_3) of the same subject was tested until zero error rate classification accuracy was achieved. This was repeated

Table 1 LVQ single classifier error rate for ASSR ensemble averaged sweeps of same training and test subjects

Subject(s)	Training sweeps	Test sweeps	Error
A	$100(50\ W_0 + 50\ N_3)$	$100(50\ W_0 + 50\ N_3)$	0%
B	$100(50\ W_0 + 50\ N_3)$	$100(50\ W_0 + 50\ N_3)$	0%
C	$100(50\ W_0 + 50\ N_3)$	$100(50\ W_0 + 50\ N_3)$	0%
D	$100(50\ W_0 + 50\ N_3)$	$100(50\ W_0 + 50\ N_3)$	0%
E	$100(50\ W_0 + 50\ N_3)$	$100(50\ W_0 + 50\ N_3)$	0%
F	$100(50\ W_0 + 50\ N_3)$	$100(50\ W_0 + 50\ N_3)$	0%
G	$100(50\ W_0 + 50\ N_3)$	$100(50\ W_0 + 50\ N_3)$	0%
H	$100(50\ W_0 + 50\ N_3)$	$100(50\ W_0 + 50\ N_3)$	0%
A, B, C, D, E	$500(50\ W_0 + 50\ N_3) \times 5$	$500(50\ W_0 + 50\ N_3) \times 5$	0%

For channel Fz-A1A2.

for all seven channel/electrode signals without any mis-classification. Again, the experiments were carried out with a training of a bigger set of 500 ASSR ensemble averaged sweeps of five subjects, $5 \times (50\ W_0 + 50\ N_3)$. Another set of 500 ensemble averaged sweeps $5 \times (50\ W_0 + 50\ N_3)$ of the same subjects were tested until a zero for LVQ and very small for SVM error rate classification accuracy was secured for Fz-A1A2 channel (Tables 1 and 2).

The next phase of experiments involved training the NN classifier with ASSR ensemble averaged sweeps of five subjects and testing the ensemble averaged sweeps of the sixth subject, which was not part of the training. The sleep patterns classification system faced a real challenge in classifying the ensemble averaged sweeps of a subject, which did not form the basis of system training. Sleep patterns classification systems that rely on physiological signals suffer from inter-subject differences that make accurate classification within a single, subject-independent model difficult [41]. Although, the sleep and/or wakefulness patterns for different subjects vary slightly in shape and in amplitude levels [24], the

Table 2 SVM single classifier error rate for ASSR ensemble averaged sweeps of same training and test subjects

Subject(s)	Training sweeps	Test sweeps	Error
A	$100(50\ W_0 + 50\ N_3)$	$100(50\ W_0 + 50\ N_3)$	1%
B	$100(50\ W_0 + 50\ N_3)$	$100(50\ W_0 + 50\ N_3)$	1%
C	$100(50\ W_0 + 50\ N_3)$	$100(50\ W_0 + 50\ N_3)$	1%
D	$100(50\ W_0 + 50\ N_3)$	$100(50\ W_0 + 50\ N_3)$	2%
E	$100(50\ W_0 + 50\ N_3)$	$100(50\ W_0 + 50\ N_3)$	0%
F	$100(50\ W_0 + 50\ N_3)$	$100(50\ W_0 + 50\ N_3)$	2%
G	$100(50\ W_0 + 50\ N_3)$	$100(50\ W_0 + 50\ N_3)$	0%
H	$100(50\ W_0 + 50\ N_3)$	$100(50\ W_0 + 50\ N_3)$	1%
A, B, C, D, E	$500(50\ W_0 + 50\ N_3) \times 5$	$500(50\ W_0 + 50\ N_3) \times 5$	3%

For channel Fz-A1A2.

Table 3 LVQ single classifier error rate for ASSR ensemble averaged sweeps of different training and test subjects

Training subjects	Test subject	Training sweeps	Test sweeps	Error
A, B, C, D, E	F	$500(50\ W_0 + 50\ N_3) \times 5$	$100(50\ W_0 + 50\ N_3)$	0%
A, B, C, D, F	E	$500(50\ W_0 + 50\ N_3) \times 5$	$100(50\ W_0 + 50\ N_3)$	0%
A, B, C, E, F	D	$500(50\ W_0 + 50\ N_3) \times 5$	$100(50\ W_0 + 50\ N_3)$	0%
A, B, D, E, F	C	$500(50\ W_0 + 50\ N_3) \times 5$	$100(50\ W_0 + 50\ N_3)$	0%
A, C, D, E, F	B	$500(50\ W_0 + 50\ N_3) \times 5$	$100(50\ W_0 + 50\ N_3)$	0%
B, C, D, E, F	A	$500(50\ W_0 + 50\ N_3) \times 5$	$100(50\ W_0 + 50\ N_3)$	0%

For channel Fz-A1A2.

devised LVQ NN system is still capable of classifying the ASSR ensemble averaged sweeps with no error rate. However, SVM classification error rate jumps to significant value (Tables 3 and 4).

The reliability of the results depends heavily on the accuracy of statistical parameters involved in classifiers in general. The obtained results cannot be accurately estimated with only a small number of training samples. Therefore, it is of vital importance to include the minimum number of training samples and to ensure that the derived conclusions have a good degree of consistency. To increase the reliability of our estimations, a similar set of experiments was repeated with a higher number of subjects and/or ASSR ensemble averaged sweeps (Tables 5 and 6).

It is difficult to predict which channels/electrodes will produce noisy input data and unacceptable error rates that will challenge the performance of classification systems. These random degradations make it difficult to classify the wakefulness or deep sleep state and lower the performance of classification algorithms. Hence, in general, more channels/electrodes are used to record/monitor the sleep patterns to compensate for unexpected errors.

The final phase of experiments was carried out with input vectors of the NN sleep patterns classification system. The resultant ASSR ensemble averaged sweep signals from two channels/electrodes of one subject obtained at the features level. Tables 7 and 8 show various results of LVQ and SVM classifiers with fused ASSR ensemble averaged sweeps.

Table 4 SVM single classifier error rate for ASSR ensemble averaged sweeps

Training subjects	Test subject	Training sweeps	Test sweeps	Error
A, B, C, D, E	F	$500(50\ W_0 + 50\ N_3) \times 5$	$100(50\ W_0 + 50\ N_3)$	9%
A, B, C, D, F	E	$500(50\ W_0 + 50\ N_3) \times 5$	$100(50\ W_0 + 50\ N_3)$	28%
A, B, C, E, F	D	$500(50\ W_0 + 50\ N_3) \times 5$	$100(50\ W_0 + 50\ N_3)$	13%
A, B, D, E, F	C	$500(50\ W_0 + 50\ N_3) \times 5$	$100(50\ W_0 + 50\ N_3)$	14%
A, C, D, E, F	B	$500(50\ W_0 + 50\ N_3) \times 5$	$100(50\ W_0 + 50\ N_3)$	20%
B, C, D, E, F	A	$500(50\ W_0 + 50\ N_3) \times 5$	$100(50\ W_0 + 50\ N_3)$	23%

Of different training and test subjects for channel Fz-A1A2.

Table 5 LVQ single classifier error rate for large set of ASSR ensemble averaged sweeps

Training subjects	Test subject	Training sweeps	Test sweeps	Error
A, B, C, D, E, F, G	H	7,000(500 W_0 + 500 N_3) × 7	1,000(500 W_0 + 500 N_3)	7%
A, B, C, D, E, F, H	G	7,000(500 W_0 + 500 N_3) × 7	1,000(500 W_0 + 500 N_3)	0%
A, B, C, D, E, G, H	F	7,000(500 W_0 + 500 N_3) × 7	1,000(500 W_0 + 500 N_3)	0%
A, B, C, D, F, G, H	E	7,000(500 W_0 + 500 N_3) × 7	1,000(500 W_0 + 500 N_3)	6.6%
A, B, C, E, F, G, H	D	7,000(500 W_0 + 500 N_3) × 7	1,000(500 W_0 + 500 N_3)	0%
A, B, D, E, F, G, H	C	7,000(500 W_0 + 500 N_3) × 7	1,000(500 W_0 + 500 N_3)	0%
A, C, D, E, F, G, H	B	7,000(500 W_0 + 500 N_3) × 7	1,000(500 W_0 + 500 N_3)	0%
B, C, D, E, F, G, H	A	7,000(500 W_0 + 500 N_3) × 7	1,000(500 W_0 + 500 N_3)	5.5%

Of different training and test subjects for channel Fz-A1A2.

Table 7 LVQ multimodal classifier error rate for large set of ASSR ensemble averaged sweeps

Training subjects	Test subject	Training sweeps	Test sweeps	Error
A, B, C, D, E, F, G	H	7,000(500 W_0 + 500 N_3) × 7	1,000(500 W_0 + 500 N_3)	17.2%
A, B, C, D, E, F, H	G	7,000(500 W_0 + 500 N_3) × 7	1,000(500 W_0 + 500 N_3)	0%
A, B, C, D, E, G, H	F	7,000(500 W_0 + 500 N_3) × 7	1,000(500 W_0 + 500 N_3)	0%
A, B, C, D, F, G, H	E	7,000(500 W_0 + 500 N_3) × 7	1,000(500 W_0 + 500 N_3)	7.9%
A, B, C, E, F, G, H	D	7,000(500 W_0 + 500 N_3) × 7	1,000(500 W_0 + 500 N_3)	0%
A, B, D, E, F, G, H	C	7,000(500 W_0 + 500 N_3) × 7	1,000(500 W_0 + 500 N_3)	0%
A, C, D, E, F, G, H	B	7,000(500 W_0 + 500 N_3) × 7	1,000(500 W_0 + 500 N_3)	0%
B, C, D, E, F, G, H	A	7,000(500 W_0 + 500 N_3) × 7	1,000(500 W_0 + 500 N_3)	17.9%

Of different training and test subjects for channels C4-A1A2 and Fz-A1A2.

The efficiency of the proposed LVQ architecture is evaluated on both the time and the space scale. By setting the number of HN equal to the product of subjects and classes (S × NC), the network memory requirements for the internal representation of target signals was condensed and the processing speed was enhanced. Specifically, both the training time of the network and the test time of the ASSR ensemble averaged sweep signals were reduced. This makes it feasible for large data training and test samples in real-time application domains as the storage requirements of the sleep pattern classification system with fusion scheme are the same as a single channel/electrode classification system.

6 Conclusions

The manual scoring of sleep patterns (wakefulness W_0 and deep sleep N_3) is a time-consuming process, in which sleep states are normally determined using EEG signals of human subjects. This paper considered a LVQ-NN- and SVM-based automatic classification algorithm for 40 Hz ASSR ensemble averaged signals. 40 Hz ASSR signals were extracted by averaging over 900 sweeps on a 30-s window from EEG. EEG signals were recorded from eight human subjects. N_3 deep sleep state was selected for this task because of its resemblance to states of consciousness and wakefulness achieved by the administration of general anesthesia given to patients during clinical surgery. Future

Table 6 SVM single classifier error rate for large set of ASSR ensemble averaged sweeps

Training subjects	Test subject	Training sweeps	Test sweeps	Error
A, B, C, D, E, F, G	H	7,000(500 W_0 + 500 N_3) × 7	1,000(500 W_0 + 500 N_3)	32%
A, B, C, D, E, F, H	G	7,000(500 W_0 + 500 N_3) × 7	1,000(500 W_0 + 500 N_3)	16%
A, B, C, D, E, G, H	F	7,000(500 W_0 + 500 N_3) × 7	1,000(500 W_0 + 500 N_3)	13%
A, B, C, D, F, G, H	E	7,000(500 W_0 + 500 N_3) × 7	1,000(500 W_0 + 500 N_3)	31%
A, B, C, E, F, G, H	D	7,000(500 W_0 + 500 N_3) × 7	1,000(500 W_0 + 500 N_3)	16%
A, B, D, E, F, G, H	C	7,000(500 W_0 + 500 N_3) × 7	1,000(500 W_0 + 500 N_3)	17%
A, C, D, E, F, G, H	B	7,000(500 W_0 + 500 N_3) × 7	1,000(500 W_0 + 500 N_3)	22%
B, C, D, E, F, G, H	A	7,000(500 W_0 + 500 N_3) × 7	1,000(500 W_0 + 500 N_3)	29%

Of different training and test subjects for channel Fz-A1A2.

Table 8 SVM multimodal classifier error rate for large set of ASSR ensemble averaged sweeps

Training subjects	Test subject	Training sweeps	Test sweeps	Error
A, B, C, D, E, F, G	H	7,000(500 W_0 + 500 N_3) × 7	1,000(500 W_0 + 500 N_3)	30%
A, B, C, D, E, F, H	G	7,000(500 W_0 + 500 N_3) × 7	1,000(500 W_0 + 500 N_3)	23%
A, B, C, D, E, G, H	F	7,000(500 W_0 + 500 N_3) × 7	1,000(500 W_0 + 500 N_3)	19%
A, B, C, D, F, G, H	E	7,000(500 W_0 + 500 N_3) × 7	1,000(500 W_0 + 500 N_3)	23%
A, B, C, E, F, G, H	D	7,000(500 W_0 + 500 N_3) × 7	1,000(500 W_0 + 500 N_3)	14%
A, B, D, E, F, G, H	C	7,000(500 W_0 + 500 N_3) × 7	1,000(500 W_0 + 500 N_3)	20%
A, C, D, E, F, G, H	B	7,000(500 W_0 + 500 N_3) × 7	1,000(500 W_0 + 500 N_3)	16%
B, C, D, E, F, G, H	A	7,000(500 W_0 + 500 N_3) × 7	1,000(500 W_0 + 500 N_3)	24%

Of different training and test subjects for channels C4-A1A2 and Fz-A1A2.

studies can thus observe the depth of general anesthesia by classifying consciousness and wakefulness states of patients with 40-Hz ASSR.

A single classifier has the weakness of not providing the confidence level required in monitoring sleep patterns. As a result, a multimodal classifier using fusion scheme at the features level by combining signals from two electrodes/channels was used to enhance the classification confidence. Our three-fold objectives of a) generating an automatic classification of sleep patterns (wakefulness W_0 and deep sleep N_3) based on an adaptive LVQ-NN and SVM with 40-Hz ASSR input signals, b) developing a features-level fusion approach for combining a 40-Hz ASSR ensemble averaged sweep of signals generated from two separate electrodes/channels, and c) classifying sleep patterns with the resultant ASSR sweep signals to enhance the decision confidence level have been accomplished. LVQ-NN outperforms as compared to the SVM for 40-Hz ASSR ensemble averaged signals classification for observing sleep patterns.

Competing interests

The authors declare that they have no competing interests.

Acknowledgements

The authors would like to thank Vivosonic Inc. (Toronto) [63] for providing the Vivosonic Integrity™ System and also for their insightful suggestions on investigating the signals. Also, the authors would like to thank the Ontario Brain Institute [64] for funding this project.

References

1. R Agarwal, J Gotman, Computer-assisted sleep staging. IEEE Trans. Biomed. Eng. **48**, 1412–1423 (2001)
2. P Estevez, C Held, C Holzmann, C Perez, J Perez, J Heiss, M Garrido, P Peirano, Polysomnographic pattern recognition for automated classification of sleep-waking states in infants. Med. Bio. Eng. Comput. **40**(1), 105–113 (2002)
3. B Kim, K Park, Automatic sleep stage scoring system using genetic algorithms and neural network. Proc. 22nd IEEE. Eng. Med. Biol. Soc. (EMBS) Conf. 849–850 (2000)
4. BT Skinner, HT Nguyen, DK Liu, *Classification of EEG Signals Using a Genetic-Based Machine Learning Classifier* (Int Conf. of the IEEE EMBS Cité Internationale, Lyon, France, 2007)
5. PLL Sornmo, *Bioelectrical Signal Processing in Cardiac and Neurological Applications*. (Elsevier Academic Press, 2005)
6. T Picton, *Human Auditory Evoked Potentials*. (Plural Publishing INC., 2010)
7. A Thronton, Properties of auditory brainstem evoked responses. Rev. Laryngol. Otol. Rhinol. (Bord) **97 Suppl**, 591–601 (1976)
8. G Dawson, Cerebral responses to nerve stimulation in man. Br. Med. Bull. **6**, 326–329 (1950)
9. C Geisler, L Frishkopf, W Rosenblith, Extracranial responses to acoustic clicks in man. Science **128**, 1210–1211 (1958)
10. R Galambos, S Makeig, P Talmachoff, A 40-hz auditory potential recorded from human scalp. Proc. Natl. Acad. Sci. U. S. A. **5**, 2643–2647 (1981). USA
11. TW Picton, S Hillyard, Human auditory evoked potentials. I: evaluation of components. Electroencephalogr. Clin. Neurophysiol. **36**, 179–190 (1974)
12. C Madler, I Keller, D Schwender, E Poppel, Sensory information processing during general anaesthesia: effect of isoflorane on auditory evoked neuronal oscillations. British J. Anaesthesia. **66**, 81–87 (1991)
13. N Kraus, T Nicol, *Auditory Evoked Potential* (Encyclopedia of Neuroscience, Springer-Verlag GmbH, Berlin Heidelberg, 2009), pp. 214–218
14. S Brad, The auditory steady-state response: a premier. Hear. J. **55**(9), 10 (2002). 14,17,18
15. C Pantev, T Elbert, S Makeig, S Hampson, C Eulitz, M Hoke, Relationship of transient and steady-state auditory evoked fields. Electroencephalogr. Clin. Neurophysiol. **88**, 389–396 (1993)
16. H Vereecke, *The Use of Fast Extracted Mid-Latency Auditory Evoked Potentials Monitoring to Improve the Measurement of the Hypnotic Component Of Anesthesia*. (Ph.D. dissertation, Ghent University, Medical School, 2007)
17. KCRD Linden, KHT Picton, Human auditory steady-state evoked potential during sleep. Ear Hear. **6**, 167–174 (1985)
18. J Jarger, R Chmiel, J Frost, N Coker, Effect of sleep on auditory steady state evoked potential. Electroenceph. Tech. Audiol. Otol. **7**, 240–245 (1986)
19. C Medler, E Poppel, Auditory evoked potentials indicate the loss of neural oscillations during general anesthesia. Nature **74**, 42–43 (1987)
20. TPG Plourde, Human steady state responses during general anaesthesia. Anaesthesia Analg. **71**, 460–468 (1990)
21. V Bonhomme, G Plourde, P Meuret, P Fiset, SB Backman, Auditory steady-state response and bispectral index for accessing level of consciousness during propofol sedation and hypnosis. Anasth. Analg. **91**, 1398–1403 (2000)
22. A Yli-Hankala, H Edmonds, M Heine, T Strickland, T Tsueda, Auditory steady state response, upper facial EMG, EEG and heart rates as predictors of movement during isoflurane-nitrous oxide anaesthesia. British J. Anaesth. **73**, 174–179 (1994)
23. G Plourde, C Villemure, Comparison of the effects of enfourane/N2O on the 40-Hz auditory steady-state response versus the auditory middle latency response. Anesth. Analg. **82**, 75–83 (1996)
24. T Picton, MS John, DW Purcell, G Plourde, Human auditory steady-state responses: the effects of recording technique and state of arousal. Anasth. Analg. **97**(97), 1396–1402 (2003)
25. SJ Haghighi, D Hatzinakos, *Monitoring Sleep with 40-Hz ASSR* (22nd European Signal Processing Conference, Lisbon, Portugal, 2014)
26. MVD Chris, Neural networks for image analysis. Proc. IEEE Ultrasonic Symposium **3**, 1425–1433 (1990)
27. PA Hughes, ADP Green, The use of neural networks for fingerprint classification. Proc. 2nd Int. Conf. Neural. Networks. 79-81 (1991)
28. E McDermott, S Katagiri, *Shift-Invariant, Multi-Category Phoneme Recognition using Kohonen's LVQ2* (Proc. Int. Conf. Acoust., Speech, Signal Processing, Glasgow, U.K, 1989), pp. 81–84
29. H Iwamida, S Katagiri, E McDermott, Y Tohkura, *A Hybrid Speech Recognition System using HMMs with an LVQ-Trained Codebook* (ATR Technical Report TR-A-0061, ATR Auditory and Visual Perception Research Laboratories, Japan, 1989)
30. J Orlando, R Mann, S Haykin, *Radar Classification of Sea-Ice using Traditional and Neural Classifiers* (Proc. Int. Joint Conf. on Neural Networks, Washington, D.C., USA, 1990), pp. 263–266
31. T Kohonen, Learning vector quantization. Neural Netw. **1**(Supplement 1), 303 (1988)
32. T Kohonen, G Bama, R Chrisley, *Statistical Pattern Recognition with Neural Networks: Benchmarking Studies* (Proc. IEEE Int. Conf. on Neural Networks, San Diego, Cal., USA, 1988), pp. 61–68
33. T Kohonen, An introduction to neural computing. Neural Netw. **1**, 3–16 (1988)
34. T Kohonen, *Self-Organization and Associative Memory*, 3rd edn. (Springer-Verlag, Berlin, Heidelberg, Germany, 1989)
35. T Kohonen, *Improved Versions of Learning Vector Quantization* (Int. Joint Conf. on Neural Networks IJCNN, San Diego, CA, USA, 1990), pp. 17–21
36. R Ogilvie, The process of falling asleep. Sleep Med. Rev. **5**(3), 247–270 (2001)
37. H Colten, B Altevogt, *Sleep Disorders and Sleep Deprivation: an Unmet Public Health Problem*, eds. by HR Colten, BM Altevogt (National Academies Press, Washington, DC, 2006)
38. J Hu, B Knapp, *Electroencephalogram Pattern Recognition using Fuzzy Logic* (Conf. on Signals Systems and Computers, Pacific Grove, CA, 1991), pp. 805–807
39. T Suzuki, K Kobayashi, Y Umegaki, Effect of natural sleep on auditory steady state responses in adult subjects with normal hearing. Audiology **33**, 274–279 (1994)
40. A Lewicke, E Sazonov, MJ Corwin, M Neuman, S Schuckers, CHIME Study Group, Sleep versus wake classification from heart rate variability using computational intelligence: consideration of rejection in classification models. IEEE Trans. Biomed. Engg. **55**(1), 108–118 (2008)
41. W Karlen, D Floreano, Adaptive sleep-wake discrimination for wearable devices. IEEE Trans. Biomed. Engg. **58**, 4 (2011)

42. L Almazaydeh, K Elleithy, M Faezipour, *Obstructive Sleep Apnea Detection using SVM-Based Classification of ECG Signal Features* (Int. Conf. of IEEE EMBS, San Diego, California USA, 2012)

43. A Brignol, T Al-ani, X Drouot, *EEG-Based Automatic Sleep-Wake Classification in Humans using Short and Standard Epoch Lengths* (IEEE 12th Int. Conf Bioinformatics & Bioengg (BIBE), Larnaca, Cyprus, 2012), pp. 11–13

44. M Bsoul, H Minn, L Tamil, Apnea MedAssist: real-time sleep apnea monitor using single-lead ECG. IEEE Trans. Inf. Technol. Biomed. **15**(3), 416–427 (2011)

45. N Acır, C Güzeliş, Automatic recognition of sleep spindles in EEG by using artificial neural networks. Expert Syst. Appl. **27**(3), 451–458 (2004)

46. T Kohonen, *Self-Organizing Maps* (Springer Verlag, Berlin, Germany, 1995)

47. WF Leung, SH Leung, WH Lau, A Luk, Fingerprint recognition using neural networks, in *Proc. IEEE Workshop Neural Networks for Signal Processing*, 1991, pp. 226–235

48. GA Khuwaja, LVQ base models for recognition of human faces. Int. J. Comput. Appl. Technol. **16**(4), 181–193 (2002)

49. MM Monwar, ML Gavrilova, Multimodal biometric system using rank-level fusion approach. IEEE Trans. Syst. Man. Cybern. Part B. Cybern **39**(4), 867–878 (2009)

50. AK Jain, A Ross, *Fingerprint Mosaicking*, 4th edn. (Proc. IEEE Int. Conf. Acoust., Speech Signal Process, Orlando, FL, 2002), pp. 4064–4067

51. A Hyvarinen, I Karhunen, E Oja, *Independent Component Analysis, PA*. (John Wiley & Sons, 2001)

52. A Ross, R Govindarajan, *Feature Level Fusion using Hand and Face Biometrics* (Proc. SPIE 2nd Conf. Biometric Technol. Human Identification, Orlando, FL, 2005), pp. 196–204

53. K Chang, KW Bower, S Sarkar, B Victor, Comparison and combination of ear and face images in appearance-based biometrics. IEEE Trans. Pattern Anal. Mach. Intell. **25**(9), 1160–1165 (2003)

54. GL Marcialis, F Roli, Fingerprint verification by fusion of optical and capacitive sensors. Pattern Recogn. Lett. **25**(11), 1315–1322 (2004)

55. A Ross, AK Jain, Information fusion in biometrics. Pattern Recogn Letter **24**, 2115–2125 (2003)

56. T Kinnunen, V Hautamäki, P Fränti, *Fusion of Spectral Feature Sets for Accurate Speaker Identification* (Proc. 9th Conf. Speech Comput, St. Petersburg, Russia, 2004), pp. 361–365

57. TK Ho, JJ Hull, SN Srihari, Decision combination in multiple classifier systems. IEEE Trans Pattern Anal Mach Intell **16**(1), 66–75 (1994)

58. VN Vapnik, *Adaptive and Learning Systems for Signal Processing, Communications, and Control* (Wiley, New York, 1998)

59. P Pavlidis, I Wapinski, WS Noble, Support vector machine classification on the web. Bioinformatics **20**(4), 586–587 (2004)

60. Bioinformatics. http://bioinformatics.oxfordjournals.org/content/20/4/586.short.

61. EN Brown, R Lydic, N Schiff, General anesthesia, sleep and coma. N. Engl. J. Med. **363**(27), 2638–2650 (2010)

62. L Hong, AK Jain, Integrating faces and fingerprints for personal identification. IEEE Trans Pattern Anal Mach Intell **20**(12), 1295–1307 (1998)

63. Vivosonic Inc. (Toronto), http://www.vivosonic.com

64. Ontario Brain Institute (Toronto), http://www.braininstitute.ca/homepage

13

Optimal cancer prognosis under network uncertainty

Mohammadmahdi R Yousefi[1*] and Lori A Dalton[1,2]

Abstract

Typically, a vast amount of experience and data is needed to successfully determine cancer prognosis in the face of (1) the inherent stochasticity of cell dynamics, (2) incomplete knowledge of healthy cell regulation, and (3) the inherent uncertain and evolving nature of cancer progression. There is hope that models of cell regulation could be used to predict disease progression and successful treatment strategies, but there has been little work focusing on the third source of uncertainty above. In this work, we investigate the impact of this kind of network uncertainty in predicting cancer prognosis. In particular, we focus on a scenario in which the precise aberrant regulatory relationships between genes in a patient are unknown, but the patient gene regulatory network is contained in an uncertainty class of possible mutations of some known healthy network. We optimistically assume that the probabilities of these abnormal networks are available, along with the best treatment for each network. Then, given a snapshot of the patient gene activity profile at a single moment in time, we study what can be said regarding the patient's treatability and prognosis. Our methodology is based on recent developments on optimal control strategies for probabilistic Boolean networks and optimal Bayesian classification. We show that in some circumstances, prognosis prediction may be highly unreliable, even in this optimistic setting with perfect knowledge of healthy biological processes and ideal treatment decisions.

Introduction

NCI defines cancer prognosis as '...an estimate of the likely course and outcome of a disease. The prognosis of a patient diagnosed with cancer is often viewed as the chance that the disease will be treated successfully and that the patient will recover' [1]. A central problem in translational medicine is thus to decide, given biological knowledge and a collection of observations, whether a cancer patient will bear any chance of successful treatment.

There are a myriad of approaches to model both normal (healthy) and aberrant (cancerous) cell dynamics, including biological pathways, co-expression networks, Bayesian networks, Boolean networks (BNs), probabilistic BNs (PBNs), Petri nets, differential equation-based networks, etc. It is believed that these may be used to predict disease diagnosis, progression, and successful treatment strategies, which has led to much work on the identification and analysis of biological networks in genomics and biomedicine.

There remain two questions regarding prognosis. First, even if the underlying network of a patient were perfectly known and the best drug to use for the patient were also known, would a patient necessarily be curable? Second, suppose the precise network of a patient were unknown, but probabilities of an uncertainty class of networks, for instance all possible mutations of some healthy network, were available along with the best drug to use for each abnormal network. Then based on available measurements, say genomic or proteomic profiles of the patient, what could be said regarding a patient's treatability and prognosis? That is, might the very nature of cancer, with its uncertain progression and unique characteristics in each individual, make it impossible to predict prognosis, even given perfect knowledge of all biological processes and ideal treatment decisions? In this paper, we give quantitative answers to these questions, at least at a conceptual level in the context of optimal control strategies for PBNs, by studying intervention outcome in a framework of uncertain biology.

*Correspondence: yousefi@ece.osu.edu
[1] Department of Electrical and Computer Engineering, The Ohio State University, Columbus, OH 43210, USA
Full list of author information is available at the end of the article

PBNs are a class of dynamical models for functional gene regulatory networks (GRNs) [2]. They can capture the intrinsic uncertainty of gene interactions and measurement error, rendering GRN dynamics as Markov chains. They also provide a systematic way of modeling intervention scenarios, where the theory of discrete-time Markov decision processes can be applied to determine optimal intervention strategies. The steady-state distribution (SSD) of the model Markov chain reflects the long-term behavior (phenotypes) of the underlying network, and changes imposed on the SSD through various types of network intervention serve as a guide for developing beneficial treatment strategies. In short, given a PBN, one can optimally design an intervention strategy to alter the dynamics of the network so that the gene activity profiles (GAPs) evolve in a desired manner.

Managing uncertainty is especially important in modeling biological networks, where there is inherent uncertainty in the state of a network due to immeasurable latent variables, as well as uncertainty due to a lack of knowledge or partial knowledge of the relationships between observable variables even in a healthy network [3]. Here, we focus on a third source of model uncertainty due to the inherent unpredictability of somatic gene mutations or aberrant pathway malfunctioning that may arise in a cancer. This corresponds to listing plausible scenarios in which a healthy network may undergo a functional disruption in normal gene regulation. It is imperative to take into account this uncertainty to provide a robust decision regarding cancer prognosis.

We assume that a patient's network belongs to an uncertainty class of networks, each derived from a known healthy network that contains some structure essentially common to all networks. Each network in the uncertainty class possesses one or more 'mutations' of the healthy network, representing various possible subtypes or stages of cancer. Some networks in the uncertainty class may be very treatable (good prognosis), while others may be difficult or impossible to treat (bad prognosis). In fact, we will partition the space of networks into four classes based on the severity of disease with treatment and the benefit of treatment. We measure the severity of disease by the long-run probability that cancerous cells visit certain known undesirable states, or equivalently, the SSD mass of these undesirable states. We measure the benefit of treatment by the difference between steady-state mass in undesirable states before and after treatment, which we call the steady-state shift.

Our objective is to optimally classify patients into our four prognosis categories and to study the impact of network uncertainty on predicting prognosis. Recent work on optimal Bayesian classification (OBC) furnishes an elegant framework for designing optimal classifiers and optimally estimating their error [4,5]. In the general setting, it is assumed that the true underlying sampling distribution belongs to a parameterized uncertainty class of distributions associated with a known prior probability distribution. Closed-form solutions are available for several models with conjugate priors.

In prior work, there have been several studies developing subnetwork markers extracted from protein or gene interaction networks to improve cancer diagnosis [6-9]. While it is clear that classifier performance can be greatly improved using subnetwork markers, these works only consider groups of components known to interact and do not take full advantage of network structure itself. Furthermore, these works focus on diagnosis and do not model the effect of intervention. Work in [10] proposes a competition-based strategy using large datasets to identify the best methods to predict breast cancer prognosis. Several methods are employed using genomic or clinical information or both. While the authors demonstrate that some of the best methods for prognosis prediction incorporate molecular features selected by expert prior knowledge along with both molecular and clinical data, all methods used are based on data-driven machine learning rather than optimal prediction and error estimation and do not take full advantage of network structure to improve prediction. In [11,12], the authors present methods of constructing uncertainty classes of gene expression distributions in the OBC framework that are consistent with available pathway information to improve classification. However, the focus is on diagnosis rather than prognosis, and these works treat network uncertainty as stemming from ignorance. For instance, they assume that all data is drawn from the same sampling distribution, rather than modeling multiple subtypes of cancer that may exhibit different patterns of gene expression. While these advances improve cancer classification using various forms of prior knowledge, no work that we know of rigorously addresses optimal error rates that can be achieved in the presence of uncertain knowledge of the underlying network due to the inherent heterogeneity of cancer.

In this work, we assume a single GAP is observed from the patient, which is essentially a snapshot of the state of the patient's network at the moment the sample is drawn. The patient's sampling distribution is thus equivalent to the steady-state distribution of their network without intervention, giving a correspondence between the uncertainty class of networks and the uncertainty class of sampling distributions. We impose a prior distribution over the uncertainty class of networks, with the interpretation that certain mutation events are more or less likely with known probabilities. We can therefore cast our classification problem in a discrete Bayesian setting and directly apply closed-form optimal Bayesian classification and Bayesian error analysis. Note there is no training data *per se*, since we are modeling uncertainty in the progression of cancer itself while assuming a perfect understanding of cell regulation, as opposed to modeling uncertainty due to ignorance of biological relationships between genes, where knowledge could be enriched with training examples. Figure 1 illustrates a schematic of our procedure to study prognosis prediction.

Network model

Since PBNs fundamentally rely on the dynamics of constituent BNs, we shall define BNs first. A BN is characterized by a set of n nodes, $v_i \in \{0, 1\}$ for $i = 1, \ldots, n$, representing the expression level of genes or their products, and a collection of n Boolean *predictor functions*, $f_i : \{0, 1\}^n \rightarrow \{0, 1\}$ for $i = 1, \ldots, n$, describing the functional relationships between genes. In this setting, 0 and 1 represent down- and upregulation of genes, respectively.

The GAP is defined to be a length-n binary vector, $\mathbf{v}^k = \left[v_1^k, v_2^k, \ldots, v_n^k \right]$, describing the expression level of all n genes at time $k = 0, 1, \ldots$, where $v_i^k \in \{0, 1\}$ is the value of node i at time k. The Boolean function f_i determines the value of node i at time $k + 1$ by $v_i^{k+1} = f_i\left(\mathbf{v}^k\right)$. Although f_i takes as input the entire GAP, $\mathbf{v}^k$, in general it might depend on only $r(i)$ *predictor nodes* for gene i. We assume all genes update synchronously. Several methods for constructing transition rules have been proposed, for instance the 'majority vote' rule [3,13,14], and the 'strong inhibition' rule [15]. Here, we adopt the former method. For a BN, we define a regulatory matrix, $\mathcal{R}$, with (i, j) component

$$\mathcal{R}_{ij} = \begin{cases} 1 & \text{if gene } j \text{ activates gene } i, \\ -1 & \text{if gene } j \text{ suppresses gene } i, \\ 0 & \text{otherwise.} \end{cases} \quad (1)$$

Therefore, row i of $\mathcal{R}$ has $r(i)$ non-zero elements. The majority vote rule stipulates that a gene should become upregulated if more activating genes are ON than suppressing genes, downregulated if more suppressing genes are ON than activating genes, and stay the same otherwise. Thus, we define the regulatory functions

$$f_i\left(\mathbf{v}^k\right) = \begin{cases} 1 & \text{if } \sum_j \mathcal{R}_{ij} v_j^k > 0, \\ 0 & \text{if } \sum_j \mathcal{R}_{ij} v_j^k < 0, \\ v_i^k & \text{otherwise.} \end{cases} \quad (2)$$

There is a natural bijection between $\mathbf{v}^k$ and its integer representation $x^k \in \mathcal{S} = \{0, 1, \ldots, 2^n - 1\}$ given by $x^k = \sum_{i=1}^n 2^{n-i} v_i^k$. We call x^k the *state* of the network at time k and $\mathcal{S}$ the *state space*.

PBNs generalize BNs by introducing random switching between several *contexts*, where each context is a BN on its own. They also introduce a random gene perturbation, where the current state of each gene in the network is randomly flipped with probability p. If the PBN has only a single context, then the model becomes a BN with perturbation (BNp), which will serve as our model for GRNs in this paper.

Probabilistic transition rules of any PBN can be modeled by a homogeneous Markov chain. We denote the stochastic process of state transitions by $\{Z^k \in \mathcal{S} : k = 0, 1, \ldots\}$. Originating from state $x \in \mathcal{S}$, the successor state $y \in \mathcal{S}$ is selected according to the transition probability matrix (TPM) $\mathcal{P}$, with (x, y) element $\mathcal{P}_{xy} := P(Z^{k+1} = y \mid Z^k = x)$ for all $k = 0, 1, \ldots$ [2]. Due to random gene perturbation, the equivalent Markov chain is ergodic and has a unique invariant distribution, π, equal to the SSD of the network under no intervention. We also use π_x to denote the probability mass of π evaluated at state $x \in \mathcal{S}$.

Optimal intervention in PBNs

Treatment aims to alter the dynamics of a cell to achieve some desirable property or behavior. To formalize this for a given PBN, let $\mathcal{U}$ be a set of *undesirable* states, which may be an arbitrary subset of $\mathcal{S}$. States in $\mathcal{U}$ may correspond to pathological behavior or known cancer phenotypes. A natural measure of the performance of a treatment or control policy then becomes the long-run expected occupation of undesirable states. We now review optimal intervention, assuming the true TPM is perfectly known.

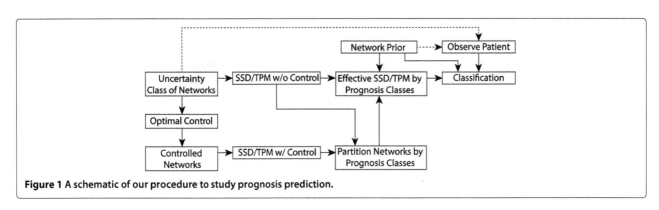

Figure 1 A schematic of our procedure to study prognosis prediction.

Two types of intervention methods for PBNs have been proposed: *structural intervention* [16] and *external control* [17,18]. The former aims to effectively change the wiring of a GRN so that long-run dynamics of the underlying Markov chain are moved toward beneficial states. Several advanced techniques, such as siRNA interference, can carry out pathway blockage [3]. The latter method involves designing a program for taking actions over time that alter the expression level of some genes (or gene products), known as *control genes*, effectively steering the long-run dynamics of the network away from undesirable states. This type of intervention corresponds to intervention using drugs to act on gene products. In this paper, we choose the latter method and assume that the PBN admits an external control input a from a set of actions, $\mathcal{A} = \{0,1\}$, where $a = 0$ indicates no-intervention and $a = 1$ indicates that the expression level of a single control gene, corresponding to a node $c \in \{1, 2, \ldots, n\}$, is flipped. Under control action $a = 1$, the transition probabilities at state x, or equivalently the row corresponding to x in the original TPM, are replaced by the row corresponding to state $\tilde{x}$ having the same binary representation as x except with node v_c flipped. Let $\{(Z^k, A^k) \in \mathcal{S} \times \mathcal{A} : k = 0, 1, \ldots\}$ denote the stochastic process of states and actions taken. The transition rules for the controlled PBN are given by a new TPM, $\mathcal{P}(a)$, with (x, y) element $\mathcal{P}_{xy}(a) = P(Z^{k+1} = y \mid Z^k = x, A^k = a)$, for $k = 0, 1, \ldots$. The ergodicity of the controlled TPM, $\mathcal{P}(a)$, for each $a \in \mathcal{A}$, is immediate from the ergodicity of the original uncontrolled TPM, $\mathcal{P}$.

Suppose we wish to optimally steer the dynamics away from undesirable states by applying a regimen of external control actions at each time $k = 0, 1, \ldots, N$. This optimization problem has been well-studied in the context of optimal Markov decision processes. We define a *control policy*, $\mu = \{\mu^0, \mu^1, \ldots, \mu^N\}$, as a sequence of instructions for taking actions that take into account the entire history of states and actions up to time k, $h^k = (z^0, a^0, z^1, a^1, \ldots, z^k, a^k)$. In particular, after observing the history, h^{k-1}, and the current state, z^k, the control policy prescribes action $a \in \mathcal{A}$ with some designated probability $\mu^k(a \mid h^{k-1}, z^k)$, satisfying $0 \leq \mu^k(a \mid h^{k-1}, z^k) \leq 1$ and $\sum_{a \in \mathcal{A}} \mu^k(a \mid h^{k-1}, z^k) = 1$.

Denote the class of all control policies by $\mathcal{M}$. Two classes of policies of particular interest are *stationary randomized* and *stationary deterministic* policies, denoted by $\mathcal{M}_{SR}$ and $\mathcal{M}_{SD}$, respectively. $\mathcal{M}_{SR}$ includes policies that are time invariant, where μ^k does not depend on k and is only conditioned on the current state. $\mathcal{M}_{SD}$ is a subset of $\mathcal{M}_{SR}$ and defined to be the set of all stationary deterministic policies such that μ^k is either 0 or 1, depending on a, for every state in $\mathcal{S}$. In this case, the control policy is a deterministic function from $\mathcal{S}$ to $\mathcal{A}$. Given the initial state $Z^0 = x$ of the Markov chain and any policy μ, one can

determine a unique probability measure P_x^μ over the space of all trajectories of states and actions, which correspondingly defines the joint stochastic processes (Z^k, A^k) of the states and actions for the controlled system [19]. Let $\mathbf{1}_A$ denote an indicator function, where $\mathbf{1}_A(x)$ is one if $x \in A$ and zero otherwise. Our goal is to minimize the long-run expected occupation of undesirable states or equivalently to minimize the objective

$$J(x, \mu) = \limsup_{N \to \infty} E_x^\mu \left[\frac{1}{N+1} \sum_{k=0}^{N} \mathbf{1}_{\mathcal{U}}\left(Z^k\right) \right], \tag{3}$$

where E_x^μ denotes the expectation relative to P_x^μ [20]. Let $J^*(x) = \inf_{\mu \in \mathcal{M}} J(x, \mu)$ for any initial state $x \in \mathcal{S}$. A policy μ^* is optimal if $J^*(x) = J(x, \mu^*)$, for every $x \in \mathcal{S}$. It can be shown that there exists an optimal control policy that belongs to $\mathcal{M}_{SD}$, and that $J^*(x)$ is independent of the initial state x [19].

While this optimization problem can be solved with dynamic programming, it may also be formulated as a classical linear program (LP) that minimizes the long-run expected frequency of undesirable states and control action pair for policies in $\mathcal{M}_{SR}$ [19,21,22]. The LP formulation, reviewed in the remainder of this section, requires that for any $\mu \in \mathcal{M}_{SD}$, the underlying Markov chain be ergodic, which holds true for PBNs. Given a family of TPMs, $\mathcal{P}(a)$ for $a \in \mathcal{A}$, and any policy $\mu \in \mathcal{M}_{SR}$, we can obtain the TPM of the controlled process, $\mathcal{Q}(\mu)$, via

$$\mathcal{Q}_{xy}(\mu) = \sum_{a \in \mathcal{A}} \mathcal{P}_{xy}(a) \mu(a|x), \tag{4}$$

where $\mathcal{Q}_{xy}(\mu)$ is the (x, y) element of $\mathcal{Q}(\mu)$, and $\mu(a|x)$ is the probability distribution on actions prescribed by μ given the current state. Let $\pi(\mu) = [\pi_0(\mu), \pi_1(\mu), \ldots, \pi_{|\mathcal{S}|-1}(\mu)]$ denote the unique invariant vector of $\mathcal{Q}(\mu)$ such that, for all $x \in \mathcal{S}$,

$$\pi(\mu) = \pi(\mu)\mathcal{Q}(\mu), \quad 0 \leq \pi_x(\mu) \leq 1, \quad \sum_{x \in \mathcal{S}} \pi_x(\mu) = 1. \tag{5}$$

The joint probability mass of any state-action pair, x and a, as a function of μ is defined by $v_{xa}(\mu) := \mu(a|x)\pi_x(\mu)$, where we have $\sum_{a \in \mathcal{A}} v_{xa}(\mu) = \pi_x(\mu)$. Then, it can be shown that for any $x \in \mathcal{S}$, $J(x, \mu) = J(\mu)$, where

$$J(\mu) = \sum_{x \in \mathcal{U}} \sum_{a \in \mathcal{A}} v_{xa}(\mu). \tag{6}$$

Hence, the original optimization problem can be reduced to the following LP:

$$\min_{\{v_{xa}\}} \sum_{x \in \mathcal{U}} \sum_{a \in \mathcal{A}} v_{xa},$$

$$\text{subject to} \begin{cases} \sum_{a \in \mathcal{A}} v_{xa} = \sum_{y \in \mathcal{S}} \sum_{a \in \mathcal{A}} v_{ya} \mathcal{P}_{yx}(a), \forall x \in \mathcal{S}, \\ \sum_{x \in \mathcal{S}} \sum_{a \in \mathcal{A}} v_{xa} = 1, v_{xa} \geq 0, \forall x \in \mathcal{S}, a \in \mathcal{A}. \end{cases}$$

Let $\{v_{xa}^*\}$ be minimizing arguments of the above problem. Then, an optimal policy $\mu^* \in \mathcal{M}_{\text{SR}}$ is given by:

$$\mu^*(a|x) = \frac{v_{xa}^*}{\sum_{a \in \mathcal{A}} v_{xa}^*}. \tag{7}$$

Although the search space for μ is $\mathcal{M}_{\text{SR}}$, it can be shown that $\mu^* \in \mathcal{M}_{\text{SD}}$ [19,21,22]. Furthermore, since the controlled Markov chain is ergodic, $\sum_{a \in \mathcal{A}} v_{xa}^* \neq 0$ for all $x \in \mathcal{S}$.

Network uncertainty class

Having established a method to model networks and optimal intervention, we next discuss a model for network uncertainty that captures variability among cancer patients due to unpredictable and compounding mutations. Essentially, we assume that the patient's network belongs to an uncertainty class of possible 'cancer' networks that are the result of one or several detrimental modifications (mutations) of a nominal 'healthy' network.

Let $\mathcal{R}^H$ denote the regulatory matrix of a nominal healthy network, which possesses a small steady-state mass in undesirable states. We denote our uncertainty set of regulatory matrices by Θ and impose two constraints: (1) regulatory matrices in Θ differ from $\mathcal{R}^H$ by only a few number of elements. For example, assuming that each mutation, or perturbation, corresponds to a random edge addition (0 is mutated to 1 or -1) or removal (1 or -1 is mutated to 0), each element in Θ might have up to some number of edges added or removed relative to $\mathcal{R}^H$. We allow different limits to the number of edges added versus removed, but assume that the total number of each type of edge mutation in any regulatory matrix of Θ is small relative to the size of the network. (2) Θ should contain only regulatory matrices for which the undesirable steady-state mass is greater than some threshold. Thus, cancers in our model have detrimental effects as mutations accumulate.

To reflect the reality that cancer cells with more mutations are more rare and that certain types of perturbations may be more or less likely, we assign prior probabilities to every network represented in Θ. To this end, we assume that the number of mutations of a network in Θ follows essentially a truncated geometric distribution, where the probability of l mutations is proportional to γ^l for some

$0 < \gamma \leq 1$ (normalization is necessary since the number of mutations of networks in Θ is bounded). We further assume that all networks with l mutations are equally likely, for example, if there are N_l regulatory matrices in Θ that have l elements mutated with respect to $\mathcal{R}^H$, then they are all equally likely with probability proportional to γ^l/N_l. Once we have calculated these values for all elements of Θ, we normalize their sum to one, guaranteeing a valid probability distribution, and denote the resulting probability distribution by Λ, i.e., we have $\sum_{\mathcal{R} \in \Theta} \Lambda(\mathcal{R}) = 1$ and $\Lambda(\mathcal{R}) > 0$ for all $\mathcal{R} \in \Theta$.

Each $\mathcal{R}$ in Θ induces a SSD under no intervention, which we denote by $\pi_{\mathcal{R}}$. Also, let $\pi_{\mathcal{R}x}$ be the SSD of $\mathcal{R}$ evaluated at point $x \in \mathcal{S}$, and let $\Pi = \{\pi_{\mathcal{R}} : \mathcal{R} \in \Theta\}$ be the multiset of all SSDs corresponding to networks in Θ. Note that SSDs in Π may not be unique.

Each $\mathcal{R}$ is also associated with an optimal control policy $\mu_{\mathcal{R}}^* \in \mathcal{M}_{\text{SD}}$ resulting in a new optimally controlled network, $\mathcal{R}^*$, with SSD $\pi_{\mathcal{R}^*}$ having minimal undesirable steady-state mass with respect to all control policies. Note that in general, every control policy $\mu \in \mathcal{M}_{\text{SR}}$ induces a controlled network, $\mathcal{R}_\mu$, for every $\mathcal{R} \in \Theta$. We can partition Θ into several sets based on intervention results. For example, one might calculate the steady-state mass of undesirable states after intervention and label the outcome with either a 'good' (low undesirable mass) or 'poor' (high undesirable mass) prognosis. One may also be interested in whether it is worth intervening in the sense that the steady-state mass of undesirable states shifts substantially with optimal control. Hence, we partition Θ into four prognosis classes:

- Class 1 (Θ^1): $\pi_{\mathcal{R}^*\mathcal{U}} < \alpha$ and $\pi_{\mathcal{R}\mathcal{U}} - \pi_{\mathcal{R}^*\mathcal{U}} < \beta_1$ (patient's condition is not critical),
- Class 2 (Θ^2): $\pi_{\mathcal{R}^*\mathcal{U}} < \alpha$ and $\pi_{\mathcal{R}\mathcal{U}} - \pi_{\mathcal{R}^*\mathcal{U}} \geq \beta_1$ (patient responds well to an effective treatment),
- Class 3 (Θ^3): $\pi_{\mathcal{R}^*\mathcal{U}} \geq \alpha$ and $\pi_{\mathcal{R}\mathcal{U}} - \pi_{\mathcal{R}^*\mathcal{U}} \geq \beta_2$ (patient's condition can be improved to some extent),
- Class 4 (Θ^4): $\pi_{\mathcal{R}^*\mathcal{U}} \geq \alpha$ and $\pi_{\mathcal{R}\mathcal{U}} - \pi_{\mathcal{R}^*\mathcal{U}} < \beta_2$ (patient's condition is poor and cannot be improved).

Here, $\pi_{\mathcal{R}\mathcal{U}} = \sum_{x \in \mathcal{U}} \pi_{\mathcal{R}x}$ and $\pi_{\mathcal{R}^*\mathcal{U}} = \sum_{x \in \mathcal{U}} \pi_{\mathcal{R}^*x}$ denote the accumulated steady-state mass of undesirable states under no intervention and optimal intervention, respectively, and $0 < \alpha, \beta_1, \beta_2 \leq 1$. Further, note the probability that a network belongs to Θ^i is given by

$$c^i = \sum_{\mathcal{R}' \in \Theta^i} \Lambda(\mathcal{R}') \tag{8}$$

and define the probability distribution Λ^i to be the conditional probability of the networks in Θ^i:

$$\Lambda^i(\mathcal{R}) = \frac{\Lambda(\mathcal{R})}{c^i} \tag{9}$$

for every $\mathcal{R} \in \Theta^i$ and $i \in \{1, 2, 3, 4\}$.

Bayesian classification

Our objective is now to study optimal classification of patients into the four prognosis classes. A classifier, ψ, is a function that takes as input observations, in our case a point $x \in S$ representing the GAP of a cancer patient at a single time epoch, and outputs a prediction of some unknown label associated with the observations, here a member of $\{1, 2, 3, 4\}$ representing one of four possible prognoses of the patient. In general, classification performance depends on the underlying sampling distribution governing observations, which in our model is precisely the steady-state distribution of the patient's network without control. Were the network of the patient perfectly known, prognosis could be determined perfectly as the class corresponding to this network, and it would not be necessary to obtain a GAP for the patient. In the case of network uncertainty, prediction is no longer perfect and observing the GAP of a patient potentially aids in making a better prognosis.

To perform optimal classification, we utilize OBC theory, which is founded on a Bayesian framework that models uncertainty in the underlying sampling distributions [4,5]. Essentially, a prior probability is assigned to all sampling distributions in an uncertainty class that may have produced the observed sample. In our application, the prior probability on the uncertainty class of networks induces a prior on the uncertainty class of steady-state distributions without control, making OBC classification very natural to implement. The main idea is to leverage minimum mean-square error (MMSE) estimation theory to obtain an optimal Bayesian error estimates for any classifier. Thanks to MMSE estimation theory, the optimal Bayesian error estimate (BEE) is precisely the expected misclassification rate with respect to the prior.

The optimal Bayesian classifier is then defined to be that classifier which minimizes the BEE.

In the usual implementation of OBC, uncertainty is interpreted as more of an issue of ignorance, where there are some true underlying class-conditional distributions, but their identity in the uncertainty class is unknown and can be revealed with training data. Here, all distributions in the uncertainty class may exist in the population, and the issue is in devising a robust classifier that can be applied generally to all distributions in the uncertainty class with minimal expected error. A consequence is that training data from different patients generally cannot be used to collapse the prior to a tighter posterior, unless care is taken to consider known connections to the patient of interest.

Given a specific network in $\mathcal{R} \in \Theta$ having label i and sampling distribution $\pi_\mathcal{R} \in \Pi$, and an arbitrary classifier ψ, let $\varepsilon_\mathcal{R}(\psi)$ denote the misclassification rate of ψ under $\pi_\mathcal{R}$:

$$\varepsilon_\mathcal{R}(\psi) = \sum_{x:\psi(x)\neq i} \pi_{\mathcal{R}x}. \tag{10}$$

Now, suppose $\mathcal{R}$ is unknown. Let $\mathcal{L} = \{1, 2, \ldots, L\}$, where L is the number of classes, each associated with a set of networks Θ^i, a multiset of sampling distributions, $\{\pi_\mathcal{R} : \mathcal{R} \in \Theta^i\}$, and priors, $\{\Lambda^i(\mathcal{R}) : \mathcal{R} \in \Theta^i\}$. A natural metric for classifier performance is the expected misclassification rate, $\hat{\varepsilon}(\psi) = \mathrm{E}_\Lambda[\varepsilon_\mathcal{R}(\psi)]$, where E_Λ denotes an expectation over $\mathcal{R}$ with respect to the distribution Λ. One can show that $\hat{\varepsilon}(\psi) = \sum_{i\in\mathcal{L}} c^i \mathrm{E}_{\Lambda^i}[\varepsilon_\mathcal{R}(\psi)]$, where E_{Λ^i} denotes an expectation over $\mathcal{R} \in \Theta^i$ with respect to conditional distribution Λ^i. This quantity is, in fact, equivalent to the BEE, where the class probabilities, c^i, are perfectly known, and $\mathrm{E}_{\Lambda^i}[\varepsilon_\mathcal{R}(\psi)]$ is the expected error contributed by class i.

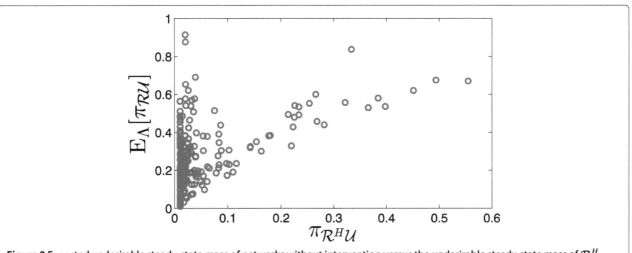

Figure 2 Expected undesirable steady-state mass of networks without intervention versus the undesirable steady-state mass of $\mathcal{R}^H$.

The OBC formalized in [4] is defined by

$$\psi_{\text{OBC}} = \arg \inf_{\psi \in \mathcal{C}} \mathrm{E}_\Lambda \left[\varepsilon_{\mathcal{R}}(\psi) \right], \tag{11}$$

where $\mathcal{C}$ is the space of all classifiers. For every $i \in \mathcal{L}$, we define the *effective density* at point $x \in \mathcal{S}$ by

$$f_x^i = \sum_{\mathcal{R} \in \Theta^i} \pi_{\mathcal{R}x} \Lambda^i(\mathcal{R}). \tag{12}$$

The following theorem shows how ψ_{OBC} can be found [4].

Theorem 1. *An optimal Bayesian classifier, ψ_{OBC}, satisfying Equation 11 exists and at point $x \in \mathcal{S}$ is given by $\psi_{\text{OBC}}(x) = i$, where $i \in \mathcal{L}$ is such that $c^i f_x^i \geq c^j f_x^j$ for all $j \in \mathcal{L}$. In the event of a tie, by convention we choose the class, i, satisfying $c^i f_x^i \geq c^j f_x^j$ for all $j \in \mathcal{L}$ with the smallest index.*

Using Equations 9 and 12, we can rewrite the above condition and assign $x \in \mathcal{S}$ to class $i \in \mathcal{L}$ if

$$\sum_{\mathcal{R} \in \Theta^i} \pi_{\mathcal{R}x} \Lambda(\mathcal{R}) \geq \sum_{\mathcal{R} \in \Theta^j} \pi_{\mathcal{R}x} \Lambda(\mathcal{R}) \tag{13}$$

for all $j \in \mathcal{L}$. The expected misclassification rate of ψ_{OBC} is

$$\hat{\varepsilon}(\psi_{\text{OBC}}) = \sum_{x \in \mathcal{S}} \sum_{\substack{j \in \mathcal{L} \\ j \neq \psi_{\text{OBC}}(x)}} \sum_{\mathcal{R} \in \Theta^j} \pi_{\mathcal{R}x} \Lambda(\mathcal{R}). \tag{14}$$

Furthermore, the probability of label i conditioned on a fixed observation $x \in \mathcal{S}$ is given by

$$\frac{c^i f_x^i}{\sum_{j \in \mathcal{L}} c^j f_x^j} = \frac{\sum_{\mathcal{R} \in \Theta^i} \pi_{\mathcal{R}x} \Lambda(\mathcal{R})}{\sum_{\mathcal{R} \in \Theta} \pi_{\mathcal{R}x} \Lambda(\mathcal{R})}, \tag{15}$$

for $i \in \mathcal{L}$. Whereas Equation 14 evaluates the overall error rate over random networks and observations, Equation 15

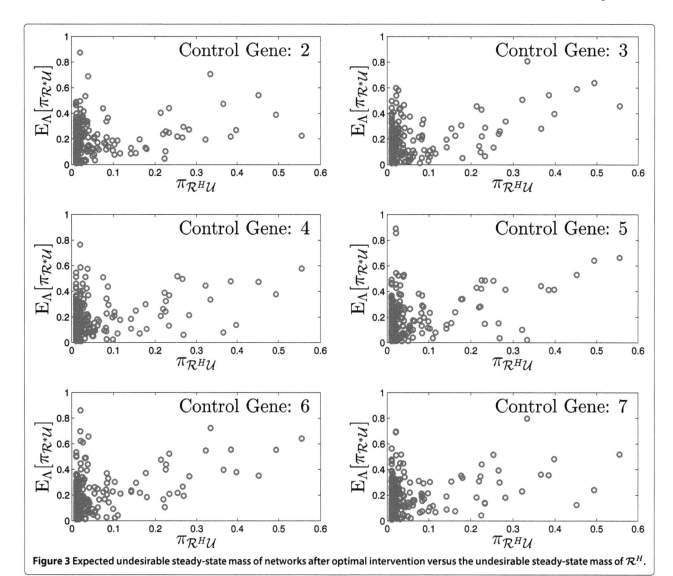

Figure 3 Expected undesirable steady-state mass of networks after optimal intervention versus the undesirable steady-state mass of $\mathcal{R}^H$.

may be used to evaluate the error rate over random networks conditioned on a particular observation, x.

Simulation results

In this section, we implement our procedure to study prognosis prediction on synthetically generated networks, as well as two real networks derived from biological processes related to cancer development. The first real network models the mammalian cell cycle, and the second emulates cell response to various stress signals such as DNA damage, oxidative stress, and activated oncogenes.

Synthetic networks

To construct synthetic uncertainty classes of networks, we begin by outlining a methodology to construct healthy networks that are calibrated to have low undesirable steady-state mass. We generate a *seed regulatory matrix*,

$\mathcal{R}^S$, by randomly filling each row of $\mathcal{R}^S$ with -1 or 1 as follows. Let $r_{\max}$ denote the maximum number of predictors for each gene. We draw the number of predictors for gene i, $r(i)$, uniformly from the set $\{1, \ldots, r_{\max}\}$. The location of the $r(i)$ non-zero elements in the ith row of $\mathcal{R}^S$, designating the predictors of gene i, are determined by drawing uniformly from the set $\{T \subset \{1, 2, \ldots, n\} : |T| = r(i)\}$. Once the predictors of each gene are determined, we assign 1 to each corresponding location in $\mathcal{R}^S$ with probability $\beta \in [0, 1]$ and -1 with probability $1 - \beta$. β reflects a bias toward what type of regulatory relationship (activation or suppression) is more likely to occur. Given the perturbation probability p, we calculate a TPM and its SSD for the network corresponding to the seed regulatory matrix [23]. We then select a nominal healthy network, $\mathcal{R}^H$, as the network with minimum undesirable steady-state mass among all possible networks with a single mutation relative to $\mathcal{R}^S$.

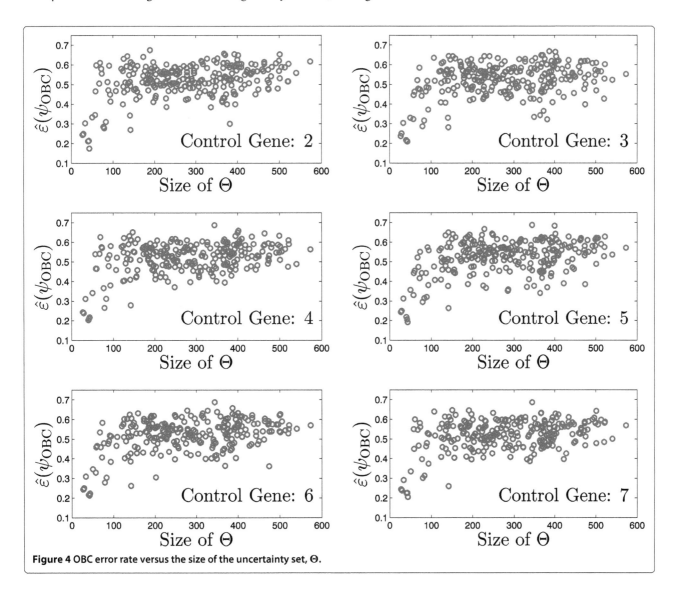

Figure 4 OBC error rate versus the size of the uncertainty set, Θ.

Let REM and ADD be two non-negative integers. We enumerate all regulatory matrices such that no greater than REM and ADD edges are removed from or added to $\mathcal{R}^H$, respectively. We then exclude networks that have lower undesirable steady-state mass than the healthy network, as well as networks with undesirable steady-state mass less than the average undesirable mass of all networks with single mutations. This guarantees that the set Θ contains only networks with unfavorable steady-state distributions. Given γ, we then calculate the probability distribution Λ for elements of Θ.

We generate 250 random seed networks with seven genes ($n = 7$). For each network, we select at most three predictors for each gene ($r_{max} = 3$), with both types of edges being equally likely ($\beta = 0.5$) and set the BNp random gene perturbation probability p to 0.01. We define the set of undesirable states, $\mathcal{U}$, to be the set of all states in which the gene corresponding to the most significant bit (ν_1) in the binary representation of

the state is downregulated. This results in half of the states being undesirable. We also set the number of edge removals to REM $= 1$, the number of edge additions to ADD $= 1$, and the mutation probability γ to 0.5. Each seed network corresponds to an uncertainty set Θ.

In the next stage of our procedure, given a control gene, we design the optimal intervention policy for each $\mathcal{R} \in \Theta$, which results in a controlled SSD $\pi_{\mathcal{R}*}$. In our classification settings, $L = 4$ and we partition Θ into four subsets by choosing α, β_1, and β_2 such that these subsets have (almost) equal sizes. Given Λ, the prior probability of networks in Θ, we use Equation 13 to find the OBC for the uncertainty set Θ and probability distribution Λ. We also estimate the error of this classifier using Equation 14. Changing the control gene does not affect Θ, however it will change the partitioning of Θ and classification results. Thus, we set the control gene, in turn, to every gene in the network excluding the target gene.

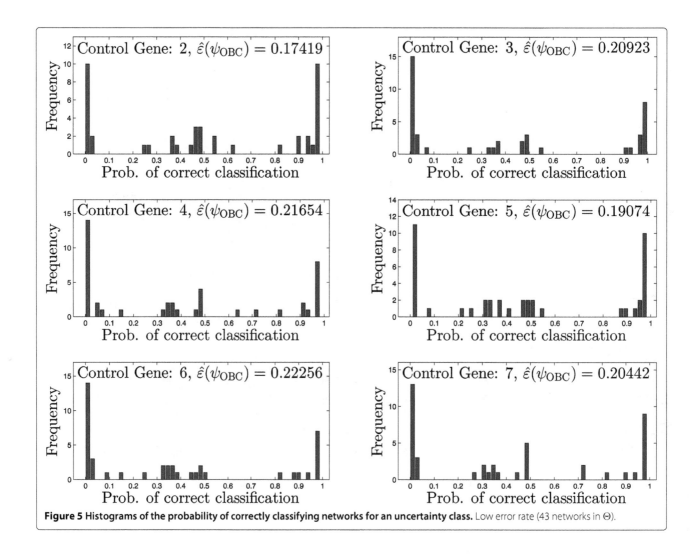

Figure 5 Histograms of the probability of correctly classifying networks for an uncertainty class. Low error rate (43 networks in Θ).

Figures 2 and 3 show the relationship between the undesirable steady-state mass in the healthy network and the expected (relative to Λ) undesirable mass of networks before and after optimal intervention, respectively. In each scatter plot, each point represents a specific seed network and its corresponding uncertainty class. In general, we observe smaller undesirable mass after control, which is not unexpected since, by definition of the objective function, the undesirable mass after applying the optimal control cannot exceed that of the uncontrolled network.

Since the seed networks are randomly generated, they differ in the total number of edges and thus produce different sized uncertainty sets, Θ. Furthermore, the size of Θ is affected by the steady-state criteria for including mutated networks in the set. We expect that as uncertainty regarding the underlying mechanism of cancer increases, i.e., as the size of Θ increases, classification becomes a harder task. This effect is observed in Figure 4, where we show

scatter plots with respect to the OBC classifier error rate (vertical axis) and the size of uncertainty set Θ (horizontal axis). As uncertainty sets grow in size, we observe a trend of increasing error rates.

For a fixed network having label i, consider the probability of correct classification with respect to random observed states:

$$\sum_{x \in \mathcal{S}: \psi_{\text{OBC}}(x)=i} \pi_{\mathcal{R}x}. \tag{16}$$

Figures 5, 6, 7 and 8 provide histograms of this probability across all networks in a given uncertainty class. Each figure corresponds to a different uncertainty class (each generated from different seed regulatory matrix) with classification errors at different ranges from low to high, and results under all possible control genes are shown. In almost all cases, the probability of correct classification depends highly on the specific network, for example, in

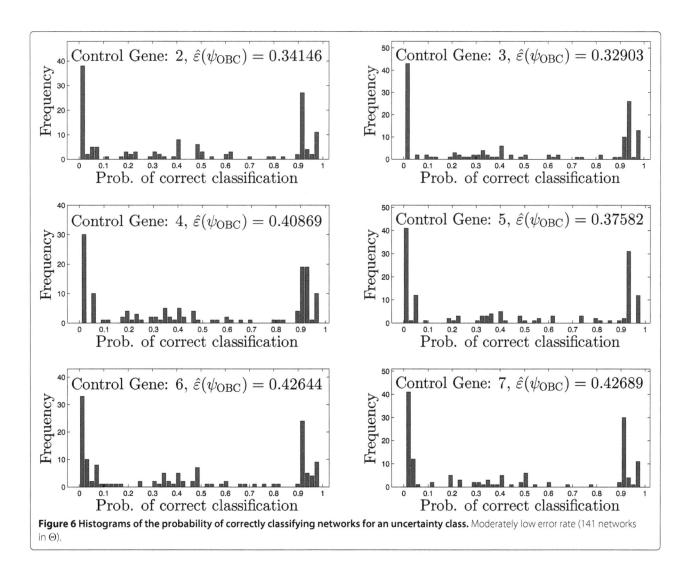

Figure 6 Histograms of the probability of correctly classifying networks for an uncertainty class. Moderately low error rate (141 networks in Θ).

Figure 5, control gene 2, we observe 10 networks out of 43 with nearly zero probability of correct classification, along with 10 networks with nearly perfect classification.

For each uncertainty set, class probabilities conditioned on each state may be found across all networks via Equation 15. Figure 9 illustrates the average of these probabilities over all 250 uncertainty sets under control gene 7. By convention, undesirable states are on the left (states 0 through 63). If we observe an undesirable state from the patient, we will most likely classify the patient as class 3 (improvement to some extent), otherwise the classification outcome is most likely class 1, which implies that the patient's condition is not that critical. However, this figure reflects only an average trend, and results vary considerably for a particular state and uncertainty set.

See the supplementary materials for analogous results on 54 different settings, varying $\beta \in \{0.1, 0.5, 0.9\}$, $p \in \{0.1, 0.5, 0.9\}$, $\gamma \in \{0.005, 0.01, 0.1\}$, and $r_{max} \in \{2, 3\}$, and a discussion on the effect of these parameters.

Real networks

Mammalian cell-cycle network

We now apply our methodology to a dynamical network modeling the behavior of normal mammalian cells during the cell cycle [24]. The network has ten genes, CycD, Rb, p27, E2F, CycE, CycA, Cdc20, Cdh1, UbcH10, and CycB. Regulatory relationships between genes in this network are shown in Table 1. Three key genes are cyclin D (CycD), retinoblastoma (Rb), and p27. Under normal conditions, extracellular signals, which control the activation of CycD, coordinate cell division with overall growth. The tumor-suppressor gene Rb is expressed in the absence of the cyclins. When present, however, cyclins inhibit Rb by phosphorylation. The gene p27 is also active in the absence of the cyclins. An active p27 blocks the action of CycE or CycA and, hence, Rb can also be expressed even if CycE or CycA are present. This results in a mechanism that stops uncontrolled cell division. However, undesirable cell proliferation in the absence of any growth

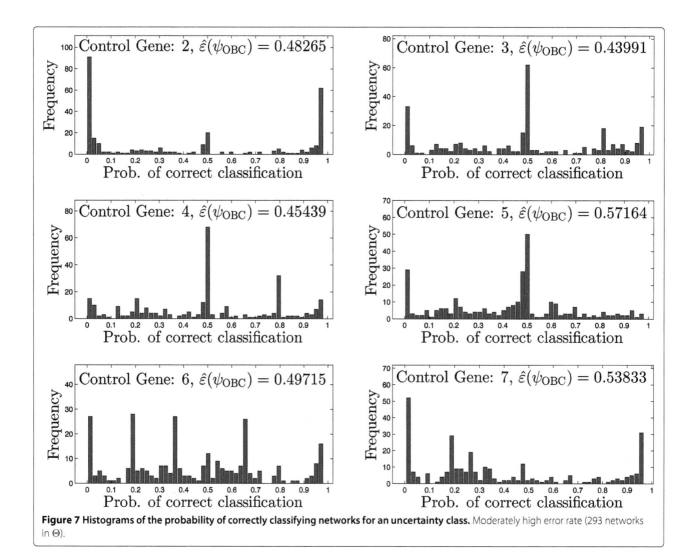

Figure 7 Histograms of the probability of correctly classifying networks for an uncertainty class. Moderately high error rate (293 networks in Θ).

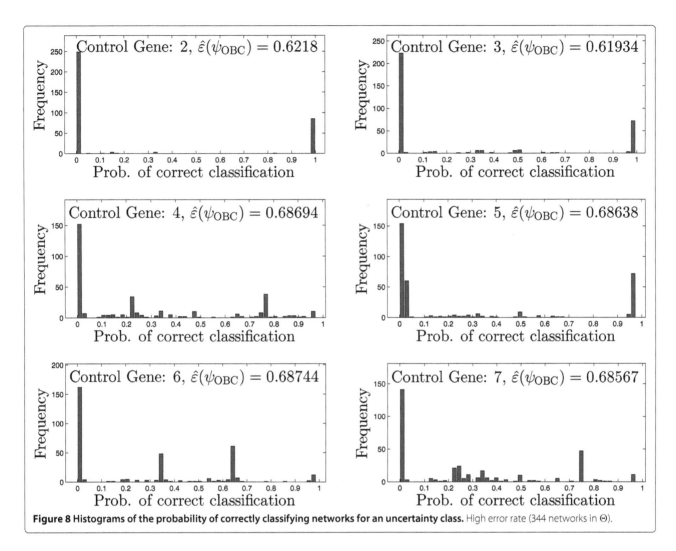

Figure 8 Histograms of the probability of correctly classifying networks for an uncertainty class. High error rate (344 networks in Θ).

factor might arise if CycD, Rd, and p27 are all simultaneously downregulated. Therefore, we define the states corresponding to this condition as undesirable states.

We construct a BNp following the majority-voting updating rule for this network and set $p = 0.01$. This

network will serve as the nominal healthy network in our analysis. Due to computational constraints, we only consider regulatory networks for which no more than one edge is removed from $\mathcal{R}^H$ and also exclude those having lower undesirable steady-state mass than the healthy

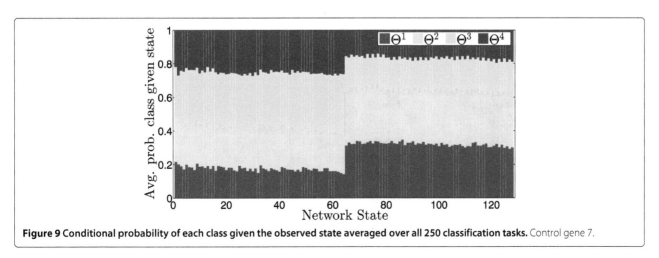

Figure 9 Conditional probability of each class given the observed state averaged over all 250 classification tasks. Control gene 7.

Table 1 Regulatory relationships of the mammalian cell cycle network

Gene	Predictors: regulatory type (+/−)
CycD	CycD: +
Rb	CycD: −, p27: +, CycE: −, CycA: −, CycB: −
p27	CycD: −, p27: +, CycE: −, CycA: −, CycB: −
E2F	Rb: −, p27: +, CycA: −, CycB: −
CycE	Rb: −, p27: +, E2F: +, CycE: −, CycA: −
CycA	Rb: −, E2F: +, CycA: +, Cdc20: −, Cdh1: −, UbcH10: −
Cdc20	Cdh1: −, CycB: +
Cdh1	p27: +, CycA: −, Cdc20: +, CycB: −
UbcH10	CycA: +, Cdc20: +, Cdh1: −, UbcH10: +, CycB: +
CycB	Cdc20: −, Cdh1: −

network or the average undesirable mass of all networks with a single edge mutation. The set of mutated networks constitutes Θ, and since we only allow one mutation, the distribution Λ will be uniform. For every network in Θ, we take each gene in the network, excluding CycD, Rb, and p27 as control genes in turn, and find the optimal intervention, which maximally shifts the SSD away from undesirable states. Given Λ, Θ, a control gene and the controlled networks, we follow a similar procedure for partitioning Θ as used for the synthetic networks and design an OBC. The results are presented in Table 2 for each control gene, where $\pi_{\mathcal{R}\mathcal{H}\mathcal{U}} = 0.3405$, $E_\Lambda[\pi_{\mathcal{R}\mathcal{U}}] = 0.3541$ and Θ contains 21 mutated networks. Although the average improvement in the SSD of undesirable states is significant, the classification error rates are poor, which indicates that prognosis classification is difficult for this network. The best classification performance in achieved when E2F is the control gene, which is slightly better than random guessing.

Table 2 The expected undesirable mass after intervention and the OBC error rate for the mammalian cell cycle network

Control gene	$E_\Lambda[\pi_{\mathcal{R}*\mathcal{U}}]$	$\hat{\varepsilon}(\psi_{\mathrm{OBC}})$
E2F	0.2889	0.6572
CycE	0.2334	0.6733
CycA	0.2872	0.6650
Cdc20	0.3386	0.6799
Cdh1	0.3371	0.6704
UbcH10	0.3497	0.6705
CycB	0.2941	0.6631

Stress response network

We next consider a p53 signaling pathway derived from the KEGG database [25]. p53 is the tumor suppressor protein encoded by the TP53 gene in humans. p53 activation plays a crucial role in cellular responses to various stress signals that might cause genome instability. These responses include a transient cell cycle arrest, senescence, and apoptosis. The original p53 network involves many genes or proteins, which makes it impossible for us to analyze. Therefore, we only focus on the genes upstream of p53 in its regulatory pathway and construct a BNp based on the relationships listed in Table 3. The network has nine nodes: DNAdamage, p53, p14ARF, ATR, ATM, CHEK1, CHEK2, MDM2, and MDMX. We assume that the states for which DNAdamage and p53 are active and inactive, respectively, are undesirable.

We construct a BNp following the majority-voting updating rule with $p = 0.01$. We then enumerate all the networks that have no greater than one edge removed from or added to the nominal p53 network and use the same criterion as in the mammalian cell cycle example to select networks for inclusion in the uncertainty set of mutated networks. We also calculate the distribution Λ assuming a mutation probability of $\gamma = 0.5$. Each node in the network, except DNAdamage and p53, is allowed as a control gene. Given Λ, Θ, a control gene, and the controlled networks, we partition Θ and design an OBC. For this network, $\pi_{\mathcal{R}\mathcal{H}\mathcal{U}} = 0.0057$, $E_\Lambda[\pi_{\mathcal{R}\mathcal{U}}] = 0.0183$, and Θ consists of 829 mutated networks. The classification results are shown in Table 4 for each control gene. Although the uncertainty set is much larger, classification error rates are better than observed for the cell cycle network. The best classification performance is achieved when ATR is the control gene.

Conclusion

We have outlined a framework in which it is possible to utilize prior knowledge regarding cell regulation, for

Table 3 Regulatory relationships of a p53 signaling network

Gene/protein/signal	Predictors: regulatory type (+/−)
DNAdamage	DNAdamage: +
p53	ATR: +, CHEK1: +, CHEK2: +, MDM2: −, MDMX: −
p14ARF	p14ARF: +
ATR	DNAdamage: +
ATM	DNAdamage: +
CHEK1	ATR: +
CHEK2	ATM: +
MDM2	p14ARF: −, MDMX: +
MDMX	MDM2: −

Table 4 The expected undesirable mass after intervention and the OBC error rate for the stress response network

Control gene	$E_\Lambda[\pi_{\mathcal{R}^*\mathcal{U}}]$	$\hat{e}(\psi_{OBC})$
p14ARF	0.0095	0.5175
ATR	0.0104	0.4789
ATM	0.0150	0.5935
CHEK1	0.0110	0.5218
CHEK2	0.0134	0.5561
MDM2	0.00666	0.5376
MDMX	0.0084	0.5220

instance pathway information in healthy and aberrant networks, to optimally predict prognosis. That being said, there are several important generalizations of our model that merit further study: (1) integrating partial ignorance of the healthy network itself into our uncertainty class of networks, (2) allowing the network to change over time, thereby taking into account the progressive deterioration of cancer as mutations accumulate, (3) modeling uncertainty in the ideal drug regimen for each network, (4) integrating different types of observations into the analysis, and (5) combining optimal prognosis prediction with optimal treatment recommendations under network uncertainty.

While ψ_{OBC} makes optimal prognosis predictions under network uncertainty, obtaining the GAP or any other relevant information from a patient has the effect of reducing uncertainty. A key point in this work is that we study performance with respect to prognosis only. Although one must overcome network uncertainty, it is not necessary to be able to actually infer the network or any mutations, rather, for our purposes one only needs enough relevant data to make good predictions regarding prognosis. Thus, a second major question we address is whether it is possible to successfully predict prognosis with a relatively small amount of data and available biological knowledge.

The larger the uncertainty class, generally the more difficult prognosis becomes. This is an intuitive result: more uncertainty requires more information to draw accurate conclusions. Furthermore, prognosis performance depends on many factors, including the type of cancer (the original healthy network and its associated uncertainty class), the individual patient's network, and the particular sample drawn from the patient. Very often, prognosis prediction from a single GAP is highly unreliable, even in this optimistic setting with perfect knowledge of healthy biological processes and ideal treatment decisions. In this case, the remedy is to collect more data, for instance time-series GAP measurements, to help identify the patient's network or at least ensure reliable prognosis prediction. One may be lucky and find that their condition is quite clear from a single measurement, but, at least in our examples, it is typical to find that very little is revealed about one's condition, necessitating additional lab tests.

Competing interests
The authors declare that they have no competing interests.

Authors' contributions
MRY and LAD contributed to the main idea, designed and implemented the algorithms, designed and carried out the simulation, analyzed the results, and drafted the manuscript. Both authors read and approved the final manuscript.

Acknowledgements
The authors would like to thank Edward R. Dougherty for his fruitful discussions.

Author details
[1]Department of Electrical and Computer Engineering, The Ohio State University, Columbus, OH 43210, USA. [2]Department of Biomedical Informatics, The Ohio State University, Columbus, OH 43210, USA.

References
1. Understanding Cancer Prognosis. (www.cancer.gov/cancertopics/factsheet/Support/prognosis-stats)
2. I Shmulevich, ER Dougherty, S Kim, W Zhang, Probabilistic Boolean networks: A rule-based uncertainty model for gene regulatory networks. Bioinformatics **18**(2), 261–274 (2002)
3. BJ Yoon, X Qian, ER Dougherty, Quantifying the objective cost of uncertainty in complex dynamical systems. IEEE Trans. Signal Process. **61**(9), 2256–2266 (2013)
4. LA Dalton, ER Dougherty, Optimal classifiers with minimum expected error within a Bayesian framework – Part I: Discrete and Gaussian models. Pattern Recognit. **46**(5), 1301–1314 (2013)
5. LA Dalton, ER Dougherty, Optimal classifiers with minimum expected error within a Bayesian framework – Part II: Properties and performance analysis. Pattern Recognit. **46**(5), 1288–1300 (2013)
6. HY Chuang, E Lee, YT Liu, D Lee, T Ideker, Network-based classification of breast cancer metastasis. Mol. Syst. Biol. **3**(140) (2007)
7. E Lee, HY Chuang, JW Kim, T Ideker, D Lee, Inferring pathway activity toward precise disease classification. PLoS Comput. Biol. **4**(11), e1000217 (2008)
8. J Su, BJ Yoon, ER Dougherty, Accurate and reliable cancer classification based on probabilistic inference of pathway activity. PLoS One **4**(12), e8161 (2009)
9. J Su, BJ Yoon, ER Dougherty, Identification of diagnostic subnetwork markers for cancer in human protein-protein interaction network. BMC Bioinf **11**(Suppl 6), S8 (2010)
10. E Bilal, J Dutkowski, J Guinney, IS Jang, BA Logsdon, G Pandey, Sauerwine B A, Y Shimoni, HK Moen Vollan, BH Mecham, OM Rueda, J Tost, C Curtis, MJ Alvarez, VN Kristensen, S Aparicio, AL Børresen-Dale, C Caldas, A Califano, SH Friend, T Ideker, EE Schadt, GA Stolovitzky, AA Margolin, Improving breast cancer survival analysis through competition-based multidimensional modeling. PLoS Comput. Biol. **9**(5), e1003047 (2013)
11. M Shahrokh Esfahani, J Knight, A Zollanvari, BJ Yoon, ER Dougherty, Classifier design given an uncertainty class of feature distributions via regularized maximum likelihood and the incorporation of biological pathway knowledge in steady-state phenotype classification. Pattern Recognit. **46**(10), 2783–2797 (2013)
12. M Shahrokh Esfahani, Dougherty E R, Incorporation of biological pathway knowledge in the construction of priors for optimal Bayesian classification. IEEE/ACM Trans. Comput. Biol. Bioinf. **11**, 202–218 (2014)
13. F Li, T Long, Y Lu, Q Ouyang, C Tang, The yeast cell-cycle network is robustly designed. Proc. Nat. Acad. Sci. USA. **101**(14), 4781–4786 (2004)
14. Y Wu, X Zhang, J Yu, Q Ouyang, Identification of a topological characteristic responsible for the biological robustness of regulatory networks. PLoS Comput Biol **5**(7), e1000442 (2009)

15. A Garg, AD Cara, I Xenarios, L Mendoza, GD Micheli, Synchronous versus asynchronous modeling of gene regulatory networks. Bioinformatics **24**(17), 1917–1925 (2008)

16. X Qian, ER Dougherty, Effect of function perturbation on the steady-state distribution of genetic regulatory networks: Optimal structural intervention. IEEE Trans. Signal Process **56**(10), 4966–76 (2008)

17. A Datta, A Choudhary, ML Bittner, ER Dougherty, External control in Markovian genetic regulatory networks. Machine Learning. **52**(1-2), 169–191 (2003)

18. MR Yousefi, A Datta, ER Dougherty, Optimal intervention in Markovian gene regulatory networks with random-length therapeutic response to antitumor drug. IEEE Trans. Biomed. Eng. **60**(12), 3542–3552 (2013)

19. C Derman, *Finite State Markovian Decision Processes* (Academic Press, New York, 1970)

20. MR Yousefi, ER Dougherty, Intervention in gene regulatory networks with maximal phenotype alteration. Bioinformatics **29**(14), 1758–1767 (2013)

21. LCM Kallenberg, *Linear Programming and Finite Markovian Control Problems*. (Mathematisch Centrum, Amsterdam, 1983)

22. E Altman, *Constrained Markov Decision Processes* (Boca Raton, Chapman Hall/CRC, 1999)

23. I Ivanov, P Simeonov, N Ghaffari, X Qian, ER Dougherty, Selection policy-induced reduction mappings for Boolean networks. IEEE Trans. Signal Process. **58**(9), 4871–4882 (2010)

24. Fauré A, A Naldi, C Chaouiya, D Thieffry, Dynamical analysis of a generic Boolean model for the control of the mammalian cell cycle. Bioinformatics **22**(14), e124–e131 (2006)

25. M Kanehisa, S Goto, KEGG: Kyoto encyclopedia of genes and genomes. Nucleic Acids Res. **28**, 27–30 (2000)

14

Modeling and systematic analysis of biomarker validation using selected reaction monitoring

Esmaeil Atashpaz-Gargari[1], Ulisses M Braga-Neto[1,2]* and Edward R Dougherty[1,2]

Abstract

Background: Discovery and validation of protein biomarkers with high specificity is the main challenge of current proteomics studies. Different mass spectrometry models are used as shotgun tools for the discovery of biomarkers. Validation of a set of selected biomarkers from a list of candidates is an important stage in the biomarker identification pipeline. Validation is typically done by triple quadrupole (QQQ) mass spectrometry (MS) running in selected reaction monitoring (SRM) mode. Although the individual modules of this pipeline have been studied, there is little work on integrating the components from a systematic point of view.

Results: This paper analyzes the SRM experiment pipeline in a systematic fashion, by modeling the main stages of the biomarker validation process. The proposed models for SRM and protein mixture are then used to study the effect of different parameters on the final performance of biomarker validation. Sample complexity, purification, peptide ionization, and peptide specificity are among the parameters of the SRM experiment that are studied. We focus on the sensitivity of the SRM pipeline to the working parameters, in order to identify the bottlenecks where time and energy should be spent in designing the experiment.

Conclusions: The model presented in this paper can be utilized to observe the effect of different instrument and experimental settings on biomarker validation by SRM. On the other hand, the model would be beneficial for optimization of the work flow as well as identification of the bottlenecks of the pipeline. Also, it creates the required infrastructure for predicting the performance of the SRM pipeline for a specific setting of the parameters.

Keywords: Proteomics; Biomarker validation; Mass spectrometry (MS); Selected reaction monitoring (SRM); Triple quadrupole (QQQ) systems

Introduction

Proteomics and mass spectrometry

Proteomics deals with the study of gene and cellular function at the protein level. Microarrays, 2D gel electrophoresis, and mass spectrometry (MS) are the most widely used technologies for high-throughput proteomics. Among these technologies, MS has increasingly become the method of the choice for analysis of complex protein samples [1]. Among its unique advantages are unsurpassed molecular specificity and very high detection sensitivity [2]. MS analysis is composed of thee major steps: 1) *ionization*: conversion of the analyte molecules or atoms into gas-phase ionic species, 2) *mass analysis*: separation and mass analysis of ions on the basis of their mass-to-charge (m/z) ratio, and 3) *detection*: detection and measurement of the mass-separated ions.

Time of flight (TOF), linear quadrupole/3D-quadrupole ion trap, Fourier transform ion cyclotron resonance (FT-ICR), and orbitrap are some of the main mass analyzers used in MS instruments. Application of two or more stages of mass analysis leads to tandem mass spectrometry (MS/MS) which enables us to examine selectively the fragmentation of particular ions in a mixture of ions [3]. Selected reaction monitoring (SRM) is a specific mode of tandem mass spectrometry, which is widely used for quantitative measurement of analytes present in complex mixture and for validation of low-abundance biomarkers.

*Correspondence: ulisses@ece.tamu.edu
[1]Department of Electrical and Computer Engineering, Texas A&M University, 3128 TAMU, College Station, TX 77843-3128, USA
[2]Center for Bionformatics and Genomic Systems Engineering, Texas A&M University, 101 Gateway Blvd College Station, TX 77845, USA

Biomarker discovery and validation

The identification of biomarkers is a major goal of biomedicine in this century [4], and proteomics using different mass spectrometry tools has played a key role in this area. One well-known example of peptide biomarker is prostate-specific antigen (PSA), which is a marker for early diagnosis of prostate cancer in men. The PSA test is an FDA-approved serum or plasma-based population screening tool but has very low specificity, resulting in $750 million annual cost for unnecessary medical follow-up. The lack of biomarkers with high specificity shows how challenging the problem of proteomic biomarker identification is and the need for sensitive and accurate instruments, powerful techniques, and careful analysis of proteomics data.

One of the important challenges of biomarker discovery is identification of low-abundance biomarkers. Abundant biomarkers are easy to detect and quantify, but these have already been identified for the most part. The current emphasis is therefore on the discovery of low-abundance biomarkers [4]. Figure 1 displays the biomarker identification pipeline and the two main stages in this process, the *discovery* and *validation/qualification* phases. The global discovery phase is done on a small number of samples, and then a larger number of samples is used for the validation of potential biomarkers, before going to clinical application [4].

Selected reaction monitoring

For over 30 years, SRM has been the method of choice for doing mass spectrometry on small molecules in order to study drug metabolism. However, its application to protein identification and quantification was limited by the low mass range of the instruments used for metabolite identification. The introduction of the quadrupole

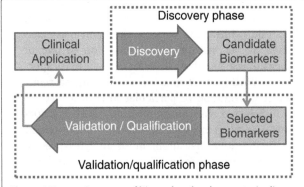

Figure 1 Two main stages of biomarker development pipeline. The discovery phase requires MS experiments with high resolution and short duty cycles and typically involves small number of samples. Selected biomarkers from the discovery step are validated in the next stage before moving on to further analysis in clinical studies [4].

instrument with extended mass range removed this restriction in the application of SRM for studying proteins and peptides [4-6]. Although SRM can be done on some of the other tandem MS instruments (e.g., EB- and BE-magnetic sector tandem MS), it is preferably implemented on triple-quadrupole, due to low cost, linear mass scale, operational simplicity, and straightforward scan laws. The first and third quadrupoles in the triple quadrupole (QQQ) systems act as mass filters to specifically select a predefined m/z values, controlled by direct current (dc) and radio frequency (rf) potentials. The second quadrupole in SRM operates as rf-only quadrupole passing all ions. In fact, this quadrupole acts as the collision-induced dissociation (CID) unit. This is done in two steps: *collision activation* and *collisionally activated dissociation* and is performed in the *high-* and *low-energy* regimes. The later is the mode that is preferably implemented in quadrupole. One of the main disadvantages of CID over other ion activation and dissociation methods is that ion-dissociation efficiency gradually falls off as the precursor ion's weight increases.

Figure 2 displays the idealized schematics of SRM analysis on QQQ MS. The co-eluting analytes that enter the first quadrupole are filtered based on predefined m/z values and enter the second quadrupole for collision-induced dissociation. The resulting fragment ions are then filtered by the third quadrupole passing the preset m/z values for the desired fragment ions. The two stages of mass filtering in SRM and its targeted nature lead to an increased sensitivity by one or two orders of magnitude compared with usual full scan methods. It is worthy mentioning that the term 'multiple reaction monitoring' (MRM) has been used to describe parallel acquisition of SRM for measurement of several target ions. However, to avoid ambiguity between the number of transitions monitored and number of stages used in the mass spectrometry analysis (MS^n), its use is deprecated by IUPAC [7].

A prototypical SRM experiment consists of three major steps. First, a list of candidate proteins is determined. The list of proteins of interest is determined based on previous knowledge from discovery studies and the scientific literature. The available information about the potentially relevant proteins (e.g., Human Protein Atlas) can also be employed in this step. In the next stage, for each candidate protein, a set of proteotypic peptides (PTPs) should be identified and targeted to determine the presence of the protein and to quantify it. PTPs of a specific protein should be able to uniquely identify that protein or one of its isoforms as well as have a good ionization efficiency. Moreover, their mass-to-charge ratio should be in the mass range of the MS instrument. Besides these general characteristics, in a quantitative experimental workflow, PTPs should be fully recovered in the sample preparation and also present good chromatographic behavior to

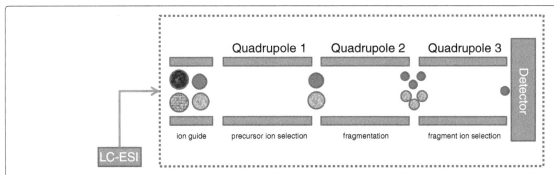

Figure 2 Idealized schematics of QQQ MS used in SRM analysis. The first quadruple (Q1) filters out most co-eluting ions from the chromatographic system. However, interfering ions may pass Q1 and enter the second quadruple (Q2). Ions in Q2 are fragmented and form the input of the third quadruple (Q3). Ideally, the specific m/z selection in Q3 passes only fragments of the desired ion and eliminates interfering ions.

reduce the chemical background [8]. Furthermore, post-translational and chemically induced modifications of the peptides should be taken into account. These types of peptide modifications are described in more detail in the next section, where they form a part of the model for the SRM process. Along with experimental methods, computational tools are also used to select MS-observable peptides for proteins. In the third step, for each selected peptide, the fragment ions that can unambiguously represent the targeted peptide from others should be identified. Based upon the experiments on the QQQ instrument or data from previously done shotgun experiments, two to four fragment ions are selected for each PTP. For example, being integrated with PeptideAtlas [9], TIQAM [10] can be used in this step [11].

Determination of the pairs of m/z values for the first and third quadrupoles is referred to as the selection of a *transition* [12]. The selection of transitions are of high importance for reaching high quantification accuracy and different factors such as ionization and fragmentation conditions should be taken into account. Fragmentation conditions and specially the distribution of fragment ion intensities depends on the type of instrument and the operating parameters. In the QQQ system, singly charged y-type ions are the predominant type of fragments generated by CID in a linear collision cell, as b-type ions and doubly charged fragments are significantly less stable than their y-type N-terminal counterparts [12,13]. On the other hand, tryptic peptide ions are predominantly doubly or triply charged with one charge at each terminus. Therefore, the single-charge fragments will generally have a larger m/z value than the precursor value. On the other hand, single-charged chemical background will produce fragments with smaller m/z than the precursor. Therefore, the selection of transitions for which fragments have larger m/z than the precursor is essential for transition selectivity and high signal-to-noise ratios [12].

In spite of the two narrow filtering stages in SRM, the selected transitions may not be specific for the peptide of interest in a complex sample. This lack of specificity can result in false quantification values for the targeted peptide. Several methods are used to validate selected transitions before using them in SRM. Spiking heavy isotope-labeled peptides to the sample, which match the sequence of the target peptide, can help in distinguishing the effect of unspecific signals. However, the cost of using heavy labeled peptides is high for quantification of large number of proteins, and usually other methods (e.g., SRM-triggered MS/MS scanning) are used, but those are unable to validate the transitions for low-abundance proteins in the detection limit of SRM [12]. Figure 3 summarizes the main steps in an SRM experiment.

Methods

In spite of the widespread application of SRM in the protein biomarker validation process, there is little work on the integration of the different modules in SRM workflow,

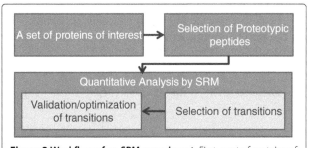

Figure 3 Workflow of an SRM experiment. First, a set of proteins of interest are determined for a specific study. Then, for each protein, some proteotypic peptides are found. In the next step, for each PTP, those fragments that are able to discriminate the peptide from others are found. The transitions (pairs of m/z values for precursor/fragment ions) are then validated to decrease the effect of unspecific signals.

and their systematic study to assess the impact of different parameters on the overall biomarker validation pipeline. A model-based approach toward the SRM experiment will help us to have a better understanding of the characteristics of the different modules of the SRM-based biomarker validation process. Here, the SRM pipeline is modeled as a noisy channel affecting the underlying protein abundance signal; a model for the noise channel is proposed and used to analyze the effect of different parameters and experimental settings on the final performance of the SRM-based biomarker validation pipeline and the ability of SRM to detect true biomarkers among a set of candidate ones. Although the aim of the SRM model proposed here is not to determine the exact value of each parameter, it will be useful in providing a systematic view towards studying the individual components of the SRM experiment.

Protein mixture model

The first major component of the model is the *protein mixture model*. This part models the abundance of the proteins in the actual SRM experiment. *Marker* and *non-marker* proteins, as well as low-abundance and high-abundance proteins, are modeled in this part. The list of candidate biomarkers in the biomarker validation stage enters the SRM pipeline as described in the previous section. As mentioned previously, there are different sources of error in the SRM workflow that result in false quantification values for the protein abundance. The situation is exacerbated when dealing with low-abundance protein biomarkers. Background high-abundance proteins, inefficiency of peptide ionization, chemically induced modification, and transition noise are the most widely quoted sources of error in SRM experiments [4,8,12].

In a typical experiment, the total set of samples are divided into two sample classes (e.g., *control* vs. *treatment*). There are a total number of N_a^{pr} proteins in the mixture, among which there are N_c^{pr} candidate proteins going through the validation stage $\left(N_a^{pr} > N_c^{pr}\right)$. Based on the observations reported in [14], the protein concentration in the pooled sample can be modeled by a Gamma distribution [15].

$$\eta_i \sim \text{Gamma}(t, \theta), \qquad i \in \left\{1, 2, \ldots, N_a^{pr}\right\} \qquad (1)$$

where t and θ are shape and scale parameters, and as an example, $t = 2$ and $\theta = 1,000$ present a realistic model with dynamic range of approximately 4 orders of magnitude.

As mentioned in the 'Introduction' section, many of the high-abundance protein bio-markers are already found by shotgun experiments and the focus of the SRM

experiment is on validation of low-abundance candidate biomarkers. In order to model the concept of low-abundance and high-abundance proteins, we use two different Gamma distributed concentration models. For all the N_a^{pr} proteins, and $i \in \left\{1, 2, \ldots, N_a^{pr}\right\}$,

$$\eta_i \sim \begin{cases} \text{Gamma}(t_c, \theta_c), & i \in \left\{1, 2, \ldots, N_c^{pr}\right\} \\ \text{Gamma}(t_a, \theta_a), & i \in \left\{(N_c^{pr}+1), (N_c^{pr}+2), \ldots, N_a^{pr}\right\} \end{cases}$$
$$(2)$$

where t_c, θ_c, t_a, and θ_a are the shape and scale parameters for the candidate list and background proteins, respectively. This reflects the nature of a real SRM experiment where the goal is to validate a set of low-abundance biomarkers among a complex set of high-abundance ones. We denote the number of true biomarkers in the set of N_c^{pr} candidate list and N_a^{pr} all proteins in the list by N_c^m and N_a^m, respectively. The values of t_c, θ_c, t_a, and θ_a are given in Table 1.

Biomarkers are proteins in the sample for which the expression level in the treatment and control sample differ significantly. The difference between markers and non-markers in the expression level can be modeled by fold change [15]:

$$f_i = \begin{cases} a_i, & \text{if protein } i \text{ is over-expressed} \\ \frac{1}{a_i}, & \text{if protein } i \text{ is under-expressed} \\ 1, & \text{otherwise} \end{cases} \qquad (3)$$

where the fold change parameter, a_i, is uniformly distributed in $[1, h]$, $h > 1$. This results in a distribution that is approximately log-normal for the fold change itself [16,17]. The value of h used in the simulations is specified in Table 1.

The sample variation of proteins in the mixture is modeled by a Gaussian distribution as proposed in [18], where a block model is used for the covariance matrix. The

Table 1 Parameter settings in simulation of biomarker validation model

Parameter	Defaults value
Number of classes	2
Sample size	$n = 80$
Block size	$b = 5$
Block correlation	$\rho = 0.8$
Fold change	$h = 2, a_l \sim Unif(1, 2)$
Modification noise	$\alpha_{pm} = 0.03, \beta_{pm} = 3.6$
Peptide efficiency factor	$\alpha_{pe} = 0.5, e_i \sim U(0.5, 1)$
Gamma parameters	$t_c = 2, \theta_c = 100, t_a = 5, \theta_a = 10e6$
Purification	$\beta_\gamma = 10e - 6$
Protein mixture	$N_a^{pr} = 250, N_c^{pr} = 40$
Ranking power	$d = 2, r = 0.01$

following multivariate Gaussian is used to model the concentration of the protein $i \in \{1, 2, \ldots, N_a^{\mathrm{pr}}\}$ in class $j \in \{0, 1\}$ and the interaction among all the proteins in the sample:

$$
C_{ij}^{\mathrm{pr}} \sim \begin{cases} \mathcal{N}\left(\left[\eta_1, \eta_2, \ldots, \eta_{N_a^{\mathrm{pr}}}\right], \Sigma\right), & j \in \text{class } 0 \\ \mathcal{N}\left(\left[f_1 \eta_1, f_2 \eta_2, \ldots, f_{N_a^{\mathrm{pr}}} \eta_{N_a^{\mathrm{pr}}}\right], \Sigma\right), & j \in \text{class } 1 \end{cases}
$$
(4)

The covariance matrix Σ has a block structure, such that

$$
\begin{aligned}
\Sigma &= \left[\sigma_{ij}^2\right]_{N_a^{\mathrm{pr}} \times N_a^{\mathrm{pr}}} \\
\sigma_{ij}^2 &= \sigma_{ii} \sigma_{jj} \lambda_{ij} \\
\sigma_{ii} &= \phi_i \times \eta_i
\end{aligned}
$$
(5)

where the constant ϕ is the coefficient of variation and the correlation matrix Λ is defined as follows:

$$
\Lambda = [\lambda_{ij}] = \begin{bmatrix} R_\rho & 0 & \cdots & 0 \\ 0 & R_\rho & \cdots & 0 \\ \vdots & \vdots & \ddots & \vdots \\ 0 & 0 & \cdots & R_\rho \end{bmatrix},
$$
(6)

where R_ρ is a $b \times b$ matrix with 1's on the diagonal and ρ's elsewhere. The block-based structure of the covariance matrix represents the real interaction among the proteins. The proteins in each block (e.g., proteins within a pathway) are correlated, while there is no interaction among the proteins of different blocks [18]. The correlation ρ and block size b control the level of interaction among the proteins and their corresponding value used in simulations are specified in Table 1.

Sample complexity and purification

Many of the biomarkers with high abundance have already been found, and the main interest in SRM-based biomarker validation process is in the quantification of low-abundance proteins. In biological samples, there is a wide dynamic range in protein abundance ($> 10^{10}$), which is much larger than the dynamic range of many MS instruments. For example, while interleukin has very low abundance, albumin makes up more than 50% (about 60%) of human plasma protein (30 to 50 g/L for albumin compared to below 100 pg/L for interleukin) [19].

Presence of high-abundance proteins interfering with the low-abundance ones biases the detection and quantification of biomarkers in complex samples. For example, due to the suppression of their ionization by high-abundance proteins, low-abundance proteins escape detection. This makes purification and removal of high abundant proteins an important stage of biomarker validation workflow. Purification removes background noise in the data, i.e., the nonspecific contributions of proteins not being evaluated as candidate markers [2,20]. There are different commercial and noncommercial options for the

enrichment of samples for low-abundance proteins, and the amount of energy that is put in this step greatly affects the overall performance of biomarker identification in the SRM process. For example, albumin precipitation, size exclusion, and immuno-depletion are strategies that have been developed to eliminate some of the most abundant proteins from blood serum. As an specific example, Seppro® IgY12 (Sigma-Aldrich, St. Louis, Missouri 63103, USA) removes 12 high-abundance proteins from human biological fluids such as serum, plasma, and cerebral spinal fluid (CSF) [21].

In this paper, we model purification by removing a set of high-abundance proteins from the protein mixture model. The parameter p_{p} controls the purification in the model by indicating the percentage of high-abundance proteins that are successfully removed. Denoting the set of proteins selected for purification by $\mathcal{G}_{\mathrm{p}}$, we have the following:

$$
\hat{C}_{ij}^{\mathrm{pr}} = \begin{cases} \gamma_i C_{ij}^{\mathrm{pr}}, & \text{if protein } i \in \mathcal{G}_{\mathrm{p}} \\ C_{ij}^{\mathrm{pr}}, & \text{otherwise} \end{cases}
$$
(7)

where $\gamma_i \sim U(0, \beta_\gamma)$. The value used for β_γ ($0 < \beta_\gamma << 1$) in the simulations is given in Table 1.

Peptide mixture model

As mentioned in the 'Introduction' section, for each protein in the list of candidate biomarkers, a set of PTPs is identified and targeted to determine the presence of the protein and to quantify it. PTPs should uniquely identify the proteins, have good ionization efficiency, be fully recovered during sample preparation, and also present good chromatographic behavior to reduce the chemical background [8].

The molar concentration of C_i^{pp} of peptide i in each sample, in class j, is given by

$$
C_{ij}^{\mathrm{pp}} = \sum_{k \in \Omega_i} \hat{C}_{kj}^{\mathrm{pr}}, \quad i \in \left\{1, 2, \ldots, N_c^{\mathrm{pp}}\right\}, j \in \{0, 1\}
$$
(8)

where Ω_i is the set of all proteins sharing peptide species i and N_c^{pp} is the number of peptides. In an usual SRM experiment, for each protein, 1 to 2 PTPs are used. Denoting the number of peptides per protein by N_{pp}, then N_c^{pp} is equal to $N_{\mathrm{pp}} \times N_a^{\mathrm{pr}}$. In the results reported in this paper, we set $N_{\mathrm{pp}} = 2$. In the ideal case, the cardinality of the set Ω_i is 1, that is C_i^{pp}, the concentration of peptide i, is related to only one protein. Equation (8) can be rewritten as following:

$$
C_{ij}^{\mathrm{pp}} = \sum_{k=1}^{N_a^{\mathrm{pr}}} \xi_{ik} \hat{C}_{kj}^{\mathrm{pr}}, \quad i \in \left\{1, 2, \ldots, N_c^{\mathrm{pp}}\right\}, j \in \{0, 1\}
$$
(9)

where for $i \in \{1, 2, \ldots, N_c^{\mathrm{pp}}\}$ and $k \in \{1, 2, \ldots, N_a^{\mathrm{pr}}\}$, ξ_{ik} is as follows:

$$\xi_{ik} = \begin{cases} 1, & \text{protein } k \text{ has peptide } j \\ 0, & \text{otherwise} \end{cases} . \tag{10}$$

In an ideal SRM experiment, each peptide is specific to one protein and then the peptide-protein relation matrix $\Xi = [\xi_{ik}]_{N_c^{\mathrm{pp}} \times N_a^{\mathrm{pr}}}$ has only one element equal to 1 in each row. In real SRM experiments, the complexity of the sample increases the possibility of having target peptides as a part of other proteins. To model this fact, we define s_i, the specificity of the ith PTP, as

$$s_i = 1 - P\big(|\Xi_i^1| \neq 1\big) \tag{11}$$

where $|S|$ shows the cardinality (the number of elements) of the set S and Ξ_i^1 is the set of nonzero elements of the ith row of PTP-protein relation matrix Ξ. A peptide among the list of PTPs is called *specific* if its share in the sample is created by only its parent target protein. The specificity s_i of a specific PTP is then equal to 1. However, in real SRM experiments, this idealized situation does not occur and for some of the proteotypic peptides, the specificity will be less than 1.

There are many factors that should be considered in choosing the PTPs for each protein. For example, for each PTP, MS properties, uniqueness, and chemical behavior should be taken into account [12]. Increasing the number of proteins exacerbates the problem of finding PTPs that are specific to the target proteins and comply with other PTP selection criteria. On the other hand, we are not interested in the exact specificity value of each PTP but rather want to observe the general effect of PTP specificity on the overall performance of biomarker validation process by SRM experiment. We thus define s as the average specificity over all peptides and study its effect on the identification of low-abundance protein biomarkers.

Peptide ionization efficiency

The abundance of a peptide is represented by the ion abundance in MS data. The abundance of a peptide i in class j is modeled by

$$\mu_{ij} = \kappa \, e_i \, C_{ij}^{\mathrm{pp}}, \tag{12}$$

where e_i is the peptide efficiency factor, similar to [22], and κ represents the instrument response factor, being the ratio between the ion current signal and the original analyte concentration.

The efficiency of different peptides in passing through the liquid chromatography column is mainly controlled by their hydrophobicity [2], followed by ionization efficiency, which is affected by sample complexity, peptide

concentration, and characteristics such as polarity of side chains, molecular bulkiness, and so on [15,23]. Efficiency is also affected by the destabilizing effect of some amino acids at the N-terminal end of peptides. Some methods have been proposed for the prediction of e_i for different peptides. However, these methods fail to address the complexity issue and dependence of the efficiency on not only the underlying peptide but also on the other peptides present [15].

This makes the prediction of e_i for all the peptides problematic. Here, instead of the exact value of e_i, we are more interested in its effect on the overall performance of the SRM experiment. In the ideal case, e_i is 1 for all peptides. A model based on the uniform distribution $U(\alpha_{\mathrm{pe}}, 1)$ models the variation of the peptide efficiency. The parameter α_{pe} controls the dispersion of the ionization efficiency and in the 'Results and discussion' section, we analyze the model over a wide range to observe the effect of this parameter on the performance of the biomarker validation process.

Transition

In a complex sample, a particular precursor/fragment combination may not be specific to a targeted peptide, and other peptides with precursor/fragment ion pairs of similar masses might create unspecific signals. In the case that SRM is used to target low-abundant peptides, such unspecific signals, might still be well above the detection limit and might be easily mistaken as being derived from the targeted peptide and thus lead to misquantifications [12]. Validation methods are used to ensure that the origin of the quantified signal is the targeted peptide. SRM-triggered MS/MS scanning is the method of choice in different studies. However, this method is challenging when used for the most low-abundance peptides [24]. Spiking heavy-isotope-labeled peptides into the sample is an alternative for the use of SRM-triggered MS/MS. But the costs of such method can be very high for projects targeting a large number of proteins. In addition, the application of stable isotopes is limited by the resolution of the quadrupole as isotope labeling should introduce a sufficiently large mass difference between precursor and fragment ions [12]. Using smaller mass differences in isotope-labeling requires a higher resolution for the quadrupole, which in turn decreases the sensitivity. Low resolution has been reported in many papers as a source of error for SRM experiments using triple quadrupole mass spectrometers in complex samples [4].

The effect of transitions from background high-abundance peptides is considered as a significant source of error in quantification of the low-abundant peptides. Unspecific signals are created from other peptides with ion pairs of similar masses with the targeted peptide.

By increasing the measured abundance of the targeted peptide, the unspecific signals create misquantification. Therefore, the noise is always positive. The exponential distribution is a simple and adequate choice to model this kind of unipolar additive noise

$$\zeta_{ij} = \mu_{ij} + \epsilon_{ij}^{t}, \tag{13}$$

where

$$\epsilon_{ij}^{t} \sim \exp(\mu_{\text{tran}}\mu_{ij}). \tag{14}$$

Peptide modification

Standard sources of error, including variation in experimental conditions, instrument variance, and thermal noise, can affect the accuracy of quantitative MS experiments. Besides these general factors, peptide modification is reported as one of the important causes of misquantification in SRM experiments [12].

Some peptides contain amino acids with high propensity to chemical modifications and can bias the quantification. Cysteine alkylation, methionine oxidation, asparagine deamidation, and N-terminal cyclization of glutamic are some of the chemically induced modification of peptides [8]. Oxidation, for example, is reported to inversely affect the performance of MS experiments for quantification of peptides [25]. Since a part of the targeted peptide is converted into the modified form during the process, chemically induced modification is reported to be a potential source of error in quantitative MS experiments [8,12].

The Gaussian distribution is the standard model for the cumulative effect of independent additive disturbances (distinct noise sources). In [26], a Gaussian noise model with quadratic dependence of the variance on the expected abundance of peptide is used to model the overall effect of different noise sources affecting the actual abundance of a peptide in LC-MS. Likewise, we propose to use the Gaussian noise to model the effect of peptide modification as well as the other sources of error with significant impact on modifying the actual abundance of the peptide in SRM (LC-MS-MS). We have

$$\nu_{ij} = \zeta_{ij} + \epsilon_{ij}^{m}, \tag{15}$$

where

$$\epsilon_{ij}^{m} \sim \mathcal{N}\left(0, \alpha_{\text{pm}}\nu_{ij}^{2} + \beta_{\text{pm}}\nu_{ij}\right). \tag{16}$$

The two parameters α_{pm} and β_{pm} control the severity of the noise. In [26], a replication analysis is proposed to estimate the values of these two parameters. The values of α_{pm} and β_{pm} used in simulations are specified in Table 1. Having fixed β_{pm}, we will investigate the effect of α_{pm} on the performance of the biomarker validation in the next section.

Results and discussion

The previous modeling strategy is used to analyze the performance of biomarker validation workflow using SRM experiments, using different model parameter settings. Figure 4 displays the simulation process. The list of candidate biomarkers generated based on the protein mixture model is the input of the SRM pipeline. In different stages of this process, the protein mixture data is affected by different noise sources depending on the experiment setting. Then, the output of the SRM process enters the validation block. Ranking power [27] and percentage of true biomarkers are used as the metrics to assess the performance of the biomarker identification process. The model parameters are changed during the simulation and for each parameter setting the average performance is found. The ranking power is described in the next section.

Experimental setup

We perform a total of 5,000 Monte Carlo runs in this experimental study, using the parameter settings given in Table 1, and compute average performance metrics over all the runs.

The performance metrics used to evaluate SRM performance are the percentage of peptides correctly identified and the *ranking power* [27]. The former is computed by applying the *t*-test as a feature selection method to find the best discriminant set of features, and computing the ratio of true biomarkers detected in that list. The latter defines a measure of goodness based on how close the estimate-based feature sets are to optimality. Let A_{best} be the best feature set relative to the feature-label distribution, ε_0 be the true error of the classifier for A_{best} designed on the sample, and $A_{(1)}, A_{(2)}, \ldots, A_{(m)}$ be a list of feature sets ordered by the classification errors $\epsilon_1, \epsilon_2, \ldots, \epsilon_m$,

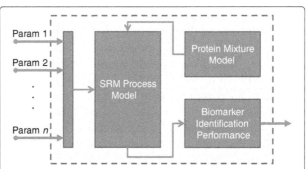

Figure 4 The entire simulation process. The protein abundance mixture data enters the SRM process and is affected by different noise sources in different levels of the process. The noisy data enters the biomarker validation block, where the ranking power and true positive rate are used to measure the performance of the overall biomarker validation process.

sorted from lowest to highest. The ranking power of the list is defined by

$$\Delta_{D,d}^{n,r} = P(\epsilon_1 - \epsilon_0 < r), \qquad (17)$$

for $r > 0$. The ranking power gives the probability that at least one feature set in the list has error within r of the best feature set. The closer $\Delta_{D,d}^{n,r}$ is to 1, the better the performance is (as long as m is small; here, $m = 10$ is used).

The pseudocode for computing the power rank is described in Algorithm 1.

Algorithm 1 Power rank computation algorithm

Set up data model M and determine A_{best}.
for $i = 1$ **to** N **do**
    1) Generate n-point sample T for M.
    2) Compute the true error, ϵ_0, for A_{best} using the samples from M.
    3) For every feature set of size d, design a classifier from T.
    4) Compute the true and estimated errors for the classifiers from step (3).
    5) Rank all the feature sets by their estimated errors to get the top m estimated-error list.
    6) Select the feature set in the list with the lowest true error, ϵ_1.
    if $\epsilon_1 - \epsilon_0 \leq r$ **then**
        count $\Leftarrow$ count $+ 1$
    end if
end for
$\Delta_{D,d}^{n,r} \Leftarrow$ count$/N$
return $\Delta_{D,d}^{n,r}$;

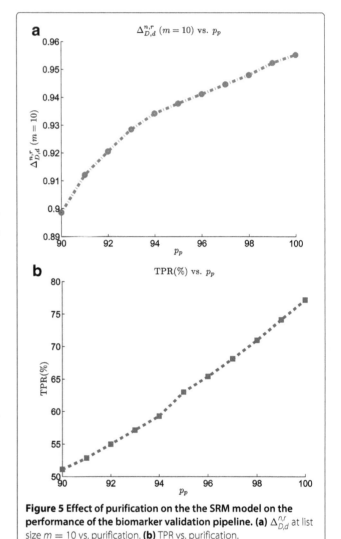

Figure 5 Effect of purification on the the SRM model on the performance of the biomarker validation pipeline. **(a)** $\Delta_{D,d}^{n,r}$ at list size $m = 10$ vs. purification. **(b)** TPR vs. purification.

Effect of purification

Figure 5 displays the effect of purification on the performance of the SRM biomarker validation process. We can see that increasing the purification factor from 90% to 99% increases the ranking power by 7%. Increasing the purity from 90% to 99% translates into the increase of TPR from 50% to 80%. Although our purpose is not to focus on the exact value of each parameter in the model, the results show how purification is an important step in the SRM experiment. This confirms the fact that purification strategies, such as albumin precipitation, size exclusion, and immuno-depletion, directly control the accuracy of the SRM-based biomarker validation.

Effect of peptide specificity

Figure 6 shows the effect of peptide specificity on the performance of SRM biomarker validation process. The results show that a very small amount of decrease in the specificity factor can bias the quantification of the low-abundance proteins to a great extent. For example, decreasing the specificity from 1 to 0.95 decreases the TPR by about 75%. These results indicate the importance of the selection of proper set of proteotypic peptides emphasizing on the fact that PTPs of a specific protein should be able to uniquely identify the protein (being specific peptides).

Effect of peptide efficiency

Although the exact distribution of the peptide efficiency is not known, observing its effect on the overall performance of the biomarker validation process provides us with a good insight into the effect of this parameter on the SRM experiment. This effect can be seen in Figure 7. The variation of peptide efficiency factor, α_{pe} (the lower bound of e_i), in the interval $[0, 1]$ changes

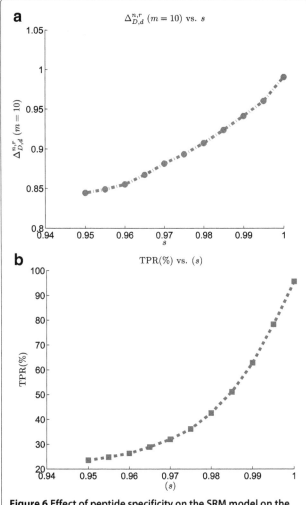

Figure 6 Effect of peptide specificity on the SRM model on the performance of the biomarker validation pipeline. **(a)** $\Delta_{D,d}^{n,r}$ at list size $m = 10$ vs. peptide specificity. **(b)** TPR vs. peptide specificity.

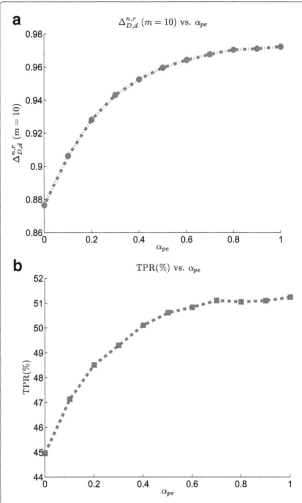

Figure 7 Effect of peptide efficiency on the SRM model on the performance of the biomarker validation pipeline. **(a)** $\Delta_{D,d}^{n,r}$ at list size $m = 10$ vs. peptide efficiency. **(b)** TPR vs. peptide efficiency.

the TPR by 6%, increasing it from 45% at $\alpha_{pe} = 0$ to 51% at $\alpha_{pe} = 1$. Based on the ranking power plot, we observe a similar trend: $\Delta_{D,d}^{n,r}$ increases from 0.88 to 0.97 by increasing the peptide efficiency factor from 0 to 1. These results agree with our expectations as the increase of the peptide efficiency reduces the transmission loss.

Effect of transition noise

Figure 8 shows the effect of transition noise on the performance of SRM biomarker validation process. Both the ranking power and TPR curves show that an increase of the transition noise decreases the overall performance of the biomarker validation. For example, the ranking power is 0.96 when the effect of this noise is set to zero. However, by increasing the noise factor to 2, $\Delta_{D,d}^{n,r}$ reduces to 0.91. We observe a similar behavior, looking at TPR curve, where the rate decreases

by 7% as the transition noise increases. This emphasizes the importance of applying the proper methods for validation of the transitions to increase the confidence on the origin of the quantified signal. Based on the experiment constraints, methods such as SRM-triggered MS/MS scanning and spiking of heavy-isotope-labeled peptides should be used to prevent the contribution of unspecific signals in the quantification of the proteins of interest.

Effect of modification

Figure 9 displays the effect of modification noise on the performance of the SRM biomarker validation process. Increasing the modification noise factor α_{pm} from 0 to 0.5 reduces the TPR value by 17%. On the other hand, the ranking power plot behaves the same by decreasing α_{pm} from 0.96 to 0.8. Decreasing the modification noise from 0.2 to 0 dramatically increases the ranking

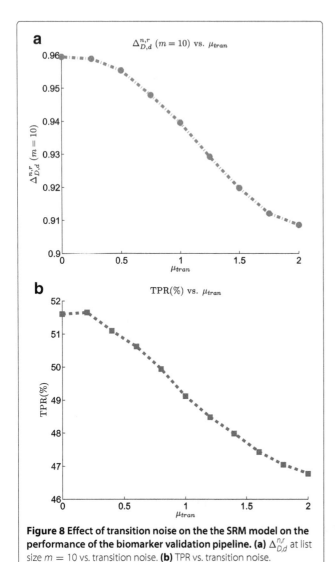

Figure 8 Effect of transition noise on the the SRM model on the performance of the biomarker validation pipeline. **(a)** $\Delta_{D,d}^{n,r}$ at list size $m = 10$ vs. transition noise. **(b)** TPR vs. transition noise.

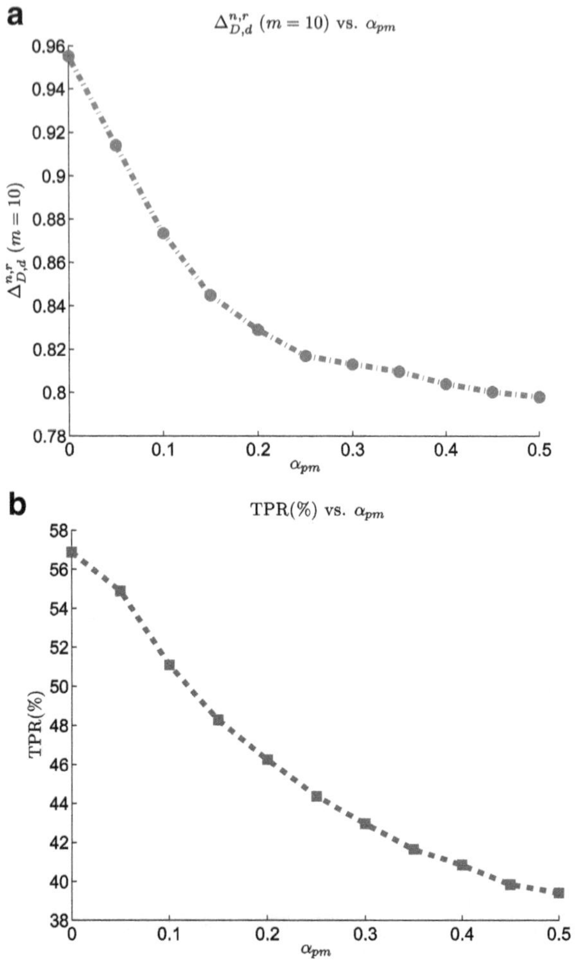

Figure 9 Effect of modification noise on the the SRM model on the performance of the biomarker validation pipeline. **(a)** $\Delta_{D,d}^{n,r}$ at list size $m = 10$ vs. modification noise. **(b)** TPR vs. modification noise.

power value, emphasizing the fact that reduction of this source of error in quantification of the low-abundance biomarkers is crucial for a successful SRM experiment. This also shows that one should avoid using peptides with high tendency for chemical modifications in the list of PTPs.

Effect of sample size

Compared to the discovery stage of biomarker development, where thousands of analytes are measured, a validation experiment deals with the quantification of a limited list of analytes, meaning that the sample size requirement is less demanding. However, the time and cost of the experiment as well as the challenges of finding patients with correct demographics for the disease of interest, with proper medical history and lifestyle, still restricts the number of samples in a biomarker validation

experiment to the 'small-sample' region [28]. Observing the effect of the number of samples on the performance of the biomarker validation process will be beneficial to the selection of the right amount of replicates considering the limitations on the time and cost of the experiment. Figure 10 shows the effect of sample size on the performance of SRM biomarker validation process. Both TPR and ranking power plots show that these two performance indices are greatly affected by the increase of the sample size. Increase of the sample size from 40 to 100 results in 10% increase in the TPR value. The similar change in the sample size translates into the increase of ranking power value by 0.07.

Summary

General facts can be gleaned from the results reported above in the paper on the relative importance of each

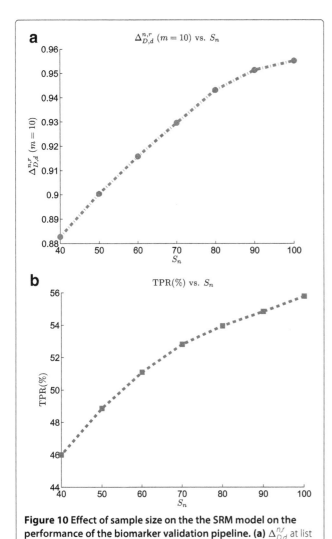

Figure 10 Effect of sample size on the the SRM model on the performance of the biomarker validation pipeline. **(a)** $\Delta_{D,d}^{n,r}$ at list size $m = 10$ vs. sample size. **(b)** TPR vs. sample size.

parameter to the sensitivity of biomarker validation performance using the QQQ-based SRM system.

- Purification critically increases the efficiency of the whole pipeline by reducing the background high-abundance proteins.
- On the other hand, peptide ionization efficiency also plays an important role in the success of biomarker validation experiment.
- A high value of modification noise can greatly compromise the performance of the system, as measured by the decreases of the TPR and ranking power value.
- Likewise, a decrease of peptide specificity reduces the TPR and ranking power to a great extent.

The results emphasize the importance of the correct selection of peptides in an SRM experiment. If the selected peptides are not unique to the targeted protein, it is hard to have high-precision quantification of the abundance of the targeted peptides, which will show itself in the unsuccessful protein validation results. An additional factor is of course sample size, which not surprisingly showed a clear effect on the performance of the biomarker discovery pipeline.

Conclusions

In this paper, the key components of the typical SRM-based biomarker validation workflow were reviewed, modeled, and analyzed. Based on the synthetic data, the process was simulated and the effect of different parameter setting on the performance was studied. Ranking power and the TPR were used as two different metrics to assess the performance of the biomarker validation process as a function of the parameters of the model. The goal of this study was not the determination of the exact value of each parameter for reaching a given performance value but rather to investigate the effect of the different parameters, namely, sample purification, peptide ionization efficiency, peptide specificity, modification noise, and sample size, on the overall performance of the SRM experiment utilized for biomarker validation.

The model presented here can not only be utilized to observe the effect of different instrument and experimental settings on biomarker validation by SRM but also could be useful for experimental design, providing an insight on the working range of the important parameters of the SRM pipeline. It creates the required infrastructure for studying the inverse problem, where one can use the model to set the parameters of the entire experiment to reach the highest performance considering technical, experimental and financial constraints. Also, the model has the advantage of being flexible to future possible extension in order to include more detailed modules of the SRM pipeline.

Abbreviations
QQQ, triple quadrupole; MS, mass spectrometry; SRM, selected reaction monitoring; PSA, prostate-specific antigen; CID, collision-induced dissociation; PTP, proteotypic peptides; TPR, true positive rate.

Competing interests
The authors declare that they have no competing interests.

Authors' contributions
EAG developed and implemented the pipeline model, conducted all simulations, and wrote the initial draft of the paper. UBN proposed the use of the pipeline model, advised EAG on the simulations, and revised the paper. ERD advised EAG on the simulations and revised the paper. All authors read and approved the final manuscript.

Acknowledgements
The authors thank the support of the Partnership for Personalized Medicine (PPM) project, through the Translational Genomics (TGen), contract C08-00904.

References

1.   R Aebersold, M Mann, Mass spectrometry-based proteomics. Nature **422**(6928), 198–207 (2003)

2.   C Dass, *Fundamentals of Contemporary Mass Spectrometry*. (John Wiley & Sons, New York, 2007)

3.   E de Hoffmann, Tandem mass spectrometry: a primer. J. Mass. Spectrom. **31**(2), 129–137 (1996)

4.   NR Kitteringham, RE Jenkins, CS Lane, VL Elliott, BK Park, Multiple reaction monitoring for quantitative biomarker analysis in proteomics and metabolomics. J. Chromatogr. B **877**(13), 1229–1239 (2009)

5.   D Zakett, R Flynn, R Cooks, Chlorine isotope effects in mass spectrometry by multiple reaction monitoring. J. Phys. Chem. **82**(22), 2359–2362 (1978)

6.   J Baty, P Robinson, Single and multiple ion recording techniques for the analysis of diphenylhydantoin and its major metabolite in plasma. Biol. Mass Spectrom. **4**(1), 36–41 (1977)

7.   KK Murray, RK Boyd, MN Eberlin, GJ Langley, L Li, Y Naito, Standard definitions of terms relating to mass spectrometry (IUPAC recommendations 2013), Analytical Chemistry Division. Pure Appl. Chem. **85**, 1515–1609 (2013). doi.org/10.1351/PAC-REC-06-04-06

8.   S Gallien, E Duriez, B Domon, Selected reaction monitoring applied to proteomics. J. Mass Spectrom. **46**(3), 298–312 (2011)

9.   EW Deutsch, H Lam, R Aebersold, PeptideAtlas: a resource for target selection for emerging targeted proteomics workflows. EMBO Rep. **9**(5), 429–434 (2008)

10. V Lange, JA Malmström, J Didion, NL King, BP Johansson, J Schäfer, J Rameseder, CH Wong, EW Deutsch, MY Brusniak, P Bühlmann, L Björck, B Domon, R Aebersold, Targeted quantitative analysis of streptococcus pyogenes virulence factors by multiple reaction monitoring. Mol. Cell. Proteomics **7**(8), 1489–1500 (2008)

11. L Malmström, J Malmström, N Selevsek, G Rosenberger, R Aebersold, Automated workflow for large-scale selected reaction monitoring experiments. J. Proteome Res. **11**, 1644–1653 (2012). doi:10.1021/pr200844d

12. V Lange, P Picotti, B Domon, R Aebersold, Selected reaction monitoring for quantitative proteomics: a tutorial. Mol. Syst. Biol. **4**(1), 222 (2008). doi:10.1038/msb.2008.61

13. KW Lau, SR Hart, JA Lynch, SC Wong, SJ Hubbard, SJ Gaskell, Observations on the detection of b-and y-type ions in the collisionally activated decomposition spectra of protonated peptides. Rapid Commun. Mass. Spectrom. **23**(10), 1508–1514 (2009)

14. Y Taniguchi, PJ Choi, GW Li, H Chen, M Babu, J Hearn, A Emili, XS Xie, Quantifying *E. coli* proteome and transcriptome with single-molecule sensitivity in single cells. Science **329**(5991), 533–538 (2010)

15. Y Sun, Braga-U Neto, ER Dougherty, A systematic model of the LC-MS proteomics pipeline. BMC Genomics **13**(Suppl 6), 2 (2012)

16. C Furusawa, T Suzuki, A Kashiwagi, T Yomo, K Kaneko, Ubiquity of log-normal distributions in intra-cellular reaction dynamics. Biophysics **1**, 25–31 (2005). doi:10.2142/biophysics.1.25

17. C Furusawa, K Kaneko, Universal statistics for chemical abundances in a reproducing cell. J. Korean Phys. Soc. **50**(1), 142 (2007)

18. J Hua, WD Tembe, ER Dougherty, Performance of feature-selection methods in the classification of high-dimension data. Pattern Recognit. **42**(3), 409–424 (2009)

19. NL Anderson, NG Anderson, The human plasma proteome history, character, and diagnostic prospects. Mol. Cell. Proteomics **1**(11), 845–867 (2002)

20. X Xu, TD Veenstra, Analysis of biofluids for biomarker research. Proteomics-Clinical Appl. **2**(10-11), 1403–1412 (2008)

21. JE Bandow, Comparison of protein enrichment strategies for proteome analysis of plasma. Proteomics **10**(7), 1416–1425 (2010)

22. W Timm, A Scherbart, S Böcker, O Kohlbacher, TW Nattkemper, Peak intensity prediction in MALDI-TOF mass spectrometry: a machine learning study to support quantitative proteomics. BMC Bioinf. **9**(1), 443 (2008)

23. NB Cech, CG Enke, Practical implications of some recent studies in electrospray ionization fundamentals. Mass Spectrom. Rev. **20**(6), 362–387 (2002)

24. P Picotti, O Rinner, R Stallmach, F Dautel, T Farrah, B Domon, H Wenschuh, R Aebersold, High-throughput generation of selected reaction-monitoring assays for proteins and proteomes. Nat. Methods **7**(1), 43–46 (2009)

25. JM Froelich, GE Reid, The origin and control of ex vivo oxidative peptide modifications prior to mass spectrometry analysis. Proteomics **8**(7), 1334–1345 (2008)

26. M Anderle, S Roy, H Lin, C Becker, K Joho, Quantifying reproducibility for differential proteomics: noise analysis for protein liquid chromatography-mass spectrometry of human serum. Bioinformatics **20**(18), 3575–3582 (2004)

27. C Zhao, ML Bittner, RS Chapkin, ER Dougherty, Characterization of the effectiveness of reporting lists of small feature sets relative to the accuracy of the prior biological knowledge. Cancer Inf. **9**, 49 (2010)

28. X Ye, J Blonder, TD Veenstra, Targeted proteomics for validation of biomarkers in clinical samples. Brief. Funct. Genomics Proteomics **8**(2), 126–135 (2009)

Permissions

The contributors of this book come from diverse backgrounds, making this book a truly international effort. This book will bring forth new frontiers with its revolutionizing research information and detailed analysis of the nascent developments around the world.

We would like to thank all the contributing authors for lending their expertise to make the book truly unique. They have played a crucial role in the development of this book. Without their invaluable contributions this book wouldn't have been possible. They have made vital efforts to compile up to date information on the varied aspects of this subject to make this book a valuable addition to the collection of many professionals and students.

This book was conceptualized with the vision of imparting up-to-date information and advanced data in this field. To ensure the same, a matchless editorial board was set up. Every individual on the board went through rigorous rounds of assessment to prove their worth. After which they invested a large part of their time researching and compiling the most relevant data for our readers.

The editorial board has been involved in producing this book since its inception. They have spent rigorous hours researching and exploring the diverse topics which have resulted in the successful publishing of this book. They have passed on their knowledge of decades through this book. To expedite this challenging task, the publisher supported the team at every step. A small team of assistant editors was also appointed to further simplify the editing procedure and attain best results for the readers.

Apart from the editorial board, the designing team has also invested a significant amount of their time in understanding the subject and creating the most relevant covers. They scrutinized every image to scout for the most suitable representation of the subject and create an appropriate cover for the book.

The publishing team has been an ardent support to the editorial, designing and production team. Their endless efforts to recruit the best for this project, has resulted in the accomplishment of this book. They are a veteran in the field of academics and their pool of knowledge is as vast as their experience in printing. Their expertise and guidance has proved useful at every step. Their uncompromising quality standards have made this book an exceptional effort. Their encouragement from time to time has been an inspiration for everyone.

The publisher and the editorial board hope that this book will prove to be a valuable piece of knowledge for researchers, students, practitioners and scholars across the globe.

List of Contributors

David Murrugarra
Department of Mathematics, Virginia Tech, Blacksburg, VA 24061-0123, USA
Virginia Bioinformatics Institute, Virginia Tech, Blacksburg, VA 24061-0477, USA

Alan Veliz-Cuba
Department of Mathematics, University of Nebraska-Lincoln, Lincoln, NE 68588, USA

Boris Aguilar
Department of Computer Science, Virginia Tech, Blacksburg, VA 24061-0123, USA

Seda Arat
Department of Mathematics, Virginia Tech, Blacksburg, VA 24061-0123, USA
Virginia Bioinformatics Institute, Virginia Tech, Blacksburg, VA 24061-0477, USA

Reinhard Laubenbacher
Department of Mathematics, Virginia Tech, Blacksburg, VA 24061-0123, USA
Virginia Bioinformatics Institute, Virginia Tech, Blacksburg, VA 24061-0477, USA

Ronny Feuer
Institute for System Dynamics, University of Stuttgart, Pfaffenwaldring 9, 70569 Stuttgart, Germany

Katrin Gottlieb
Institute of Microbiology, University of Stuttgart, Stuttgart, Germany

Gero Viertel
Institute of Communications Engineering, University of Ulm, Ulm, Germany

Johannes Klotz
Institute of Communications Engineering, University of Ulm, Ulm, Germany

Steffen Schober
Institute of Communications Engineering, University of Ulm, Ulm, Germany

Martin Bossert
Institute of Communications Engineering, University of Ulm, Ulm, Germany

Oliver Sawodny
Institute for System Dynamics, University of Stuttgart, Pfaffenwaldring 9, 70569 Stuttgart, Germany

Georg Sprenger
Institute of Microbiology, University of Stuttgart, Stuttgart, Germany

Michael Ederer
Institute for System Dynamics, University of Stuttgart, Pfaffenwaldring 9, 70569 Stuttgart, Germany

Xiangfang Li
Department of Electrical and Computer Engineering, Texas A&M University, College Station, TX 77843, USA

LijunQian
Department of Electrical and ComputerEngineering, Prairie View A&M University, Prairie View, TX 77446, USA

Edward R Dougherty
Department of Electrical and Computer Engineering, Texas A&M University, College Station, TX 77843, USA
Computational Biology Division, Translational Genomics Research Institution, Phoenix, AZ 85004, USA
Department of Bioinformatics and Computational Biology, University of Texas M.D. Anderson Cancer Center, Houston, TX 77030, USA

Kirk K Durston
School of Computer Science, University of Guelph, 50 Stone Road East, Guelph, ON N1G 2W1, Canada

David KY Chiu
School of Computer Science, University of Guelph, 50 Stone Road East, Guelph, ON N1G 2W1, Canada

Andrew KC Wong
Department of System Design Engineering, University of Waterloo, 200 University Ave. W, Waterloo, ON N2L 3G1, Canada

Gary CL Li
Department of System Design Engineering, University of Waterloo, 200 University Ave. W, Waterloo, ON N2L 3G1, Canada

Noah Berlow
Department of Electrical and Computer Engineering, Texas Tech University, Lubbock, TX 79409, USA

Lara Davis
Department of Pediatrics, Oregon Health & Science University, Portland, OR 97239, USA

Charles Keller
Department of Pediatrics, Oregon Health & Science University, Portland, OR 97239, USA

Ranadip Pal
Department of Electrical and Computer Engineering, Texas Tech University, Lubbock, TX 79409, USA

Liming Wang
Department of Electrical & Computer Engineering, Duke University, Durham, NC 27708, USA

Xiaodong Wang
Department of Electrical Engineering, Columbia University, New York, NY 10027, USA

Marco Villani
Department of Physics, Informatics and Mathematics, University of Modena and Reggio Emilia, Modena, Italy
European Centre for Living Technology, Venice, Italy

Roberto Serra
Department of Physics, Informatics and Mathematics, University of Modena and Reggio Emilia, Modena, Italy
European Centre for Living Technology, Venice, Italy

Ala Qabaja
Department of Computer Science, University of Calgary, Calgary, Alberta, Canada

Mohammed Alshalalfa
Department of Computer Science, University of Calgary, Calgary, Alberta, Canada
Departmentof Computer Science, University of Calgary, Calgary, Alberta, Canada Biotechnology Research Center, Palestine Polytechnic University, Hebron, Palestine

Tarek A Bismar
Departments of Pathology, Oncology and Molecular Biology and Biochemistry, Faculty of Medicine, University of Calgary, Alberta, Canada

Reda Alhajj
Department of Computer Science, University of Calgary, Calgary, Alberta, Canada

Imen Messaoudi
Université de Tunis El Manar, Ecole Nationale d'Ingénieurs de Tunis, LR Signal, Images et Technologies de l'Information, BP 37, le Belvédère, 1002 Tunis, Tunisia

Afef Elloumi Oueslati
Université de Tunis El Manar, Ecole Nationale d'Ingénieurs de Tunis, LR Signal, Images et Technologies de l'Information, BP 37, le Belvédère, 1002 Tunis, Tunisia

Zied Lachiri
Université de Tunis El Manar, Ecole Nationale d'Ingénieurs de Tunis, LR Signal, Images et Technologies de l'Information, BP 37, le Belvédère, 1002 Tunis, Tunisia
Département de Génie Physique et Instrumentation, INSAT, BP 676, Centre Urbain Cedex, 1080 Tunis, Tunisia

Peng Li
Laboratory of Molecular Immunology, National Heart, Lung and Blood Institute, National Institutes of Health, Bethesda, MD 20892, USA

Ping Gong
Badger Technical Services, LLC, San Antonio, TX 78216, USA

Haoni Li
School of Computing, University of Southern Mississippi, Hattiesburg, MS 39406, USA

Edward J Perkins
Environmental Laboratory, U.S. Army Engineer Research and Development Center, Vicksburg, MS 39180, USA

Nan Wang
School of Computing, University of Southern Mississippi, Hattiesburg, MS 39406, USA

Chaoyang Zhang
School of Computing, University of Southern Mississippi, Hattiesburg, MS 39406, USA

Martin Gerald Puchinger
Department of Structural and Computational Biology, Max F. Perutz Laboratories (MFPL), University of Vienna, Campus-Vienna-Biocenter 5, Vienna 1030, Austria

Clemens Alexander Zarzer
Johann Radon Institute for Computational and Applied Mathematics (RICAM), Austrian Academy of Sciences, Altenbergerstr. 69, Linz 4040, Austria

Philipp Kügler
Johann Radon Institute for Computational and Applied Mathematics (RICAM), Austrian Academy of Sciences, Altenbergerstr. 69, Linz 4040, Austria

Erwin Gaubitzer
Department of Structural and Computational Biology, Max F. Perutz Laboratories (MFPL), University of Vienna, Campus-Vienna-Biocenter 5, Vienna 1030, Austria

Gottfried Köhler
Department of Structural and Computational Biology, Max F. Perutz Laboratories (MFPL), University of Vienna, Campus-Vienna-Biocenter 5, Vienna 1030, Austria

Gulzar A Khuwaja
Department of Electrical and Computer Engineering, University of Toronto, 40 St. George Street, Toronto ON M5S 2E4, Canada

Sahar Javaher Haghighi
Department of Electrical and Computer Engineering, University of Toronto, 40 St. George Street, Toronto ON M5S 2E4, Canada

Dimitrios Hatzinakos
Department of Electrical and Computer Engineering, University of Toronto, 40 St. George Street, Toronto ON M5S 2E4, Canada

Mohammadmahdi R Yousefi
Department of Electrical and Computer Engineering, The Ohio State University, Columbus, OH 43210, USA

Lori A Dalton
Department of Electrical and Computer Engineering, The Ohio State University, Columbus, OH 43210, USA
Department of Biomedical Informatics, The Ohio State University, Columbus, OH 43210, USA

Esmaeil Atashpaz-Gargari
Department of Electrical and Computer Engineering, Texas A&M University, 3128 TAMU, College Station, TX 77843-3128, USA

Ulisses M Braga-Neto
Department of Electrical and Computer Engineering, Texas A&M University, 3128 TAMU, College Station, TX 77843-3128, USA
Center for Bionformatics and Genomic Systems Engineering, Texas A&M University, 101 Gateway Blvd College Station, TX 77845, USA

Printed in the USA
CPSIA information can be obtained
at www.ICGtesting.com
JSHW051445221024
72173JS00006B/1582

9 781682 860243